OUT OF THE PAST:
ULSTER VOICES SPEAK

OUT OF THE PAST:
ULSTER VOICES SPEAK

Compilation and Historical Background
by
M. K. LYLE

VANTAGE PRESS
New York / Washington / Atlanta
Los Angeles / Chicago

FIRST EDITION

Published by Vantage Press, Inc.
516 West 34th Street, New York, New York 10001

Manufactured in the United States of America
Standard Book Number 533-04292-5

Library of Congress Catalog Card No.: 79-63923

Kathleen Annette Lyle

To the memory of
Kathleen Annette Lyle,
Preserver of the letters and diaries
that prompted this book

Contents

Part II

Part III

Foreword

Here are vivid glimpses of the past, given by Ulster men and women in letters or to the privacy of their diaries with no thought of publication. Thus, one receives living pictures of events known to history as well as some record of ordinary life in the period from 1778 to 1905.

Some of the writers were well known. The earl of Antrim writes to a prospective Volunteer in 1778, and a future ambassador confides to his private diary something of his life and work, first as a junior attaché in Paris and then in Dresden and Copenhagen.

Others mention anecdotes of well-known people, including Queen Victoria, George V when Prince of Wales, and the Duke of Wellington, or write with firsthand knowledge of events such as the potato famine in Ulster, the Indian Mutiny, and the Chinese Rebellion of 1853. There is a letter from a former resident of Cuba voicing criticism of the American "liberation" of that island in 1898. Among the most moving letters is one from a trooper in the horse artillery, written after the Battle of Waterloo.

All events have their roots in the past, and in Ulster's turbulent past lies the key to the character of the Ulster people and to the history of the province.

Irish history is controversial, and this book does not evade some of the existing conflicts of interpretation and of facts.

Historical events, of course, do not occur in a vacuum and are frequently influenced by events in other parts of the world.

A historical background clarifies the statements made by these numerous voices, scattered in time, which speak from a vanished age.

Acknowledgments

The author acknowledges, with thanks, permission to quote material in this book as follows:

1. The late Earl of Antrim K.B.E. (Letters dated 1778 and 1779)
2. The Rt. Hon. the Lord Dunleath TD DL (Letter dated 1867 from Frances Mulholland, later Lady Dunleath)
3. Major Warre M.C. (Private Diary of Charles Stewart Scott)
4. Mr. William Rathbone (Letters of William Rathbone 1813)
5. The Honourable the Irish Society (Extracts from Leaflet on its origin, constitution, etc.)
6. The Public Record Office of Northern Ireland (No. T2609 Irish Elections and Facsimile No. 32)
7. Deputy Keeper, Public Record Office of Ireland (Extracts from Relief Commission Records 1845/47)
8. Historical Society of Pennsylvania (Extracts from Mrs. Abigail Adams's writings)
9. Northern Constitution, Ltd. (Extracts from John Galt's diary, etc.)

Thanks are also due to Professor McCracken (New University of Ulster) and Mrs. Ruby Godfrey, both of whom read the manuscript, and to Mr. F.J.E. Hurst (New University of Ulster) and the Public Record Office of Northern Ireland for supplying helpful information.

xiii

Part I

1 / Signposts to Reality in Ulster

Ulster's history does not, of course, fill this book. Inevitably, however, much of it does gradually emerge in the following pages. The terrible controversies of Ireland, their roots deep in the distant past, are thus highlighted and sometimes illuminated.

Ulster, in the North of Ireland, was once an independent kingdom. During the period 1778–1905, it was already a province, at first governed by an Irish Parliament in Dublin, under the control of Westminster, and later directly by Westminster. It then formed part of the United Kingdom of Great Britain and Ireland.

Since prehistoric times, Ulster has always been "different" from the rest of Ireland.

Even the folklore of the two areas is startlingly different. Ulster (and also Scottish) folklore tells of towering giants as well as of human heroes larger than life and possessed of magical powers. The rest of Ireland with more shadowy giants is famed for its "Little People," traditionally the shrunken descendants of the Dedannans, prehistoric human colonists from Greece who settled in the South. Today, they are not only tiny but invisible to all but those possessed of psychic sight.

Controversy surrounds the question of the racial origin of Ulster's first human inhabitants, whose archaeological remains have been found near Cushendon in County Antrim, along the banks of the Lower Bann, and near Toomebridge. One theory, the most convincing, holds that these early settlers came from Pictland, Scotland being only thirteen miles distant from Ulster by sea at the nearest point, which is in County Antrim. There is proof of the matrilinear system in Ulster under which inheritance passed not from father to son but through the female line, from father to sister's son. This was the custom in Pictland, but no trace of it has been found in any other part of Ireland.

A legendary tale claims that Ireland was once ruled by three Milesian kings, brothers, one of whom ruled Ulster, but their connection with Ulster appears to be myth. In folklore, it is, of course, impossible to disentangle fact from fiction.

3

Unfortunately, even since history supplanted folklore, many well-publicised misunderstandings and distortions of history have for centuries embittered all Ireland's political life. This chapter seeks to put the record straight on a few of the best-known historical fantasies.

About 400 B.C., at the end of their victorious progress on the Continent, Celts landed in the South of Ireland. They overran the country, making the existing inhabitants their slaves. The Celts also attempted the conquest of Ulster. There they encountered ferocious resistance and failed to cross the kingdom's Southern border. Tradition tells of a great earthen wall and a ditch thirty feet wide and fifteen feet deep. Running from the River Shannon on the east coast to the River Boyne in the west, this formidable obstacle is said to have been constructed for the defensive battle against the Celtic invaders. Traces of this boundary still survive in Armagh. In consequence of their defeat, these Celts made no racial impact on Ulster.

Celts also settled in Scotland, and from there some Celtic blood will have entered Ulster. That, however, would not be similar to the entry of Celts from the South of Ireland because of the immense difference between the native inhabitants of Scotland and those enslaved native inhabitants of Ireland. Even if one discounts the psychological theory that the subconscious of the conquered invades the subconscious of the victors, it is clear that the assimilation of Celts in Scotland would result in a people very different from those resulting from the assimilation of the Celts into the population of the oft-invaded inhabitants of Southern Ireland in whose veins already ran so many different racial strains.

Later, a Danish king ruled in Dublin for 500 years. Viking ships also appeared in Lough Neagh. Their object was the conquest of Ulster. However, the Danes, successful in naval warfare, proved no match for the Ulstermen in land battles. They failed to conquer, and once more Ulster was saved from foreign invasion, unlike their neighbors in the rest of Ireland. The Danes failed to establish any towns in Ulster, as they did in other parts of Ireland.

The first arrival of the British in Ireland—very generally described by historians and others as "The Anglo Norman Invasion of Ireland"—has engendered much lasting bitterness in Ireland and a very general guilt complex in Great Britain. This is perhaps the most poisonous of the many Irish historical myths that have for centuries helped to disturb the peace of the whole island and reduce its standard of living.

The facts of this so-called invasion are well documented and can be found clearly set out in most histories, generally preceded by the above misleading description. In reality, the invasion is a non-event. The British never invaded Ireland. The British presence in Ireland is wholly due to the initiative of a native Irish king.

4

In 1155, the Pope granted the Lordship of Ireland to Henry II so that he might reform and extend Christianity in Ireland. The king, then fighting in France, took no action.

In 1166, Ireland was divided into five kingdoms, Ulster, Munster, Leinster, Connaught, and Meath. Ostensibly, these kingdoms were united under a High King. In reality, the normal state of Ireland was one of incessant war, one or more of the kings, including the High King, at war with another or others. Periods of unity were fleeting.

In 1166, Dermot McMurry, hated King of Leinster, was defeated in war by High King Rory O'Connor and his allies.

The kingdom of Leinster was awarded to two other contenders. Dermot McMurry then traveled to France to see Henry II. He sought Henry's help in recovering his kingdom. In return, he offered his unsought allegiance. Henry gave no direct help, only a letter giving McMurry permission to raise an army in Britain if he could. The English were not interested. Eventually, Dermot McMurry, with great difficulty, succeeded in raising an army in Wales, mainly consisting of Anglo Normans with previous war experience. In order to recruit these mercenaries, it was necessary to offer both money and grants of Leinster land. To secure an experienced commander—the Earl of Pembroke (Strongbow)—McMurry gave his lovely daughter Eva, his heiress, in marriage to Strongbow and also promised him succession to the throne of Leinster at his own death. Not until 1170 was the King of Leinster's mercenary army ready to land in Ireland. Mercenary armies were very usual in those days. This one was victorious. The king of Leinster regained his kingdom. The following year he died. Strongbow then became King of Leinster. He was immediately attacked by a Viking army of mercenaries supported by the forces of the High King. The Earl of Pembroke, King of Leinster, defeated both his attackers. Some of his barons, jubilant at this second success, then suggested to Strongbow a plan for the conquest of all Ireland and the setting up of an independent Irish state. This would have meant breaking their vows of allegiance to Henry II and would also have been a potential danger to England's security.

At this juncture, Henry, hearing of this scheme, at last decided to visit Ireland. He was received with the greatest enthusiasm by the native Irish, his journey through Ireland having been described as "a triumphal progress."

The Irish bishops were happy to accept the overlord appointed by the Pope. All the Irish chiefs, including the High King, most willingly paid homage to him. The High King agreed to collect and remit to England the annual tributes from all the Irish chiefs. All chiefs paid homage in person except two detained in the North by trouble in their own territory. There were no objections and no resistance. It is impossible to imagine

5

the quarrelsome and warlike Irish behaving in this way if they had regarded Henry as a foreigner who had invaded Ireland. Strongbow and his no doubt reluctant barons also renewed their allegiance.

The subsequent history of Ireland contains many faults on both the Irish and the British side. However, the period in which any particular event occurred must be taken into consideration when forming a critical judgment. For centuries after 1170, fighting was natural, conquest glorious, and also meritorious.

As time passed, the Anglo-Norman barons made themselves thoroughly at home in Ireland, joined with zest in incessant wars, and frequently married Irish princesses.

Ulster, however, was not an easy prey, and they were less successful there than elsewhere in Ireland. De Courcy, sometimes regarded as the conqueror of Ulster, in reality only made himself complete master of a narrow coastal strip. It was not by conquest that Ulster eventually came under complete British control.

Modern visitors to Ireland, some of whom have afterwards written books after a brief tour, have remarked on the Mediterranean character of the Irish in the South. No one, however, could imagine that the Ulsterman had a Mediterranean character.

Another spectacular difference between Ulster and the rest of Ireland is to be found in their literature. Irish plays are a good example. It is inconceivable that any Ulsterman could have written such plays as *The Playboy of the Western World*, or *The Drums of Father Ned*.

In Ireland, questions of history and politics arouse passionate emotions. This is understandable when it is realized that the questions are not academic ones but literally matters of life and death.

No one is expected blindly to accept the statements in this chapter. Treat them as signposts. With the other relevant information that will be found among the varied contents of the rest of this book, readers will find themselves in a position to draw their own conclusions at its end.

2 / 1778—The Irish Volunteers

In 1778, England had been at war with her American colonists for three years when France, followed by Spain, declared war on her, and this at a time when she was short of armed forces due to the demands of her American campaign.

Ireland, denuded of troops by England's needs, was practically defenseless when she faced the risk of invasion from France. The imminence of this danger was swiftly brought home to the population by two incidents. French privateers were sighted off the coast of Southern Ireland, and the intrepid Paul Jones, famous Scottish captain of a privateer then flying the American flag, entered Belfast Lough and captured a British warship off Donaghadee. Privateers, vessels privately owned, armed, and for hire, were then frequently used in war.

Despite the facts that the American War of Independence had widespread sympathy in Ulster, Ulstermen then forming one-sixth of the American population and being in the forefront of the struggle, and that all Ireland had suffered severely from England's restrictive trade policies, the whole island, North and South, remained generally loyal, while France was disliked and feared.

After the Paul Jones episode, Ulster felt particularly at risk, and Robert Joy[1] in Belfast suggested that new volunteer companies should be raised to strengthen the existing negligible force. Two such companies were immediately formed there, and the volunteer movement quickly spread over the whole of Ireland, with a final membership of 100,000, although it always remained strongest where it originated—in Ulster.

The Volunteers were a Protestant body, though with a few Catholic members, and received universal support. Self-disciplined, paying for their own uniforms, and appointing their own officers, the Volunteers placed themselves voluntarily under the command of the governor of their own county.

In the county of Antrim, John Cromie of Cromore, in Portstewart (then in that county), wrote to the earl of Antrim, its governor.

Copy undated

To the Right Hon[ble] the Earl of Antrim
The Petition of the United Volunteers of the Parishes of Ballywillan and Ballyachron.
Humbly Sheweth that your Petitioners the principal Inhabitants of the said Parishes, in these times of Publick alarm & danger, have formed themselves

7

into an Independent Company for his Majesty's Service, for the defence & protection of the Sea coast, and for the preservation of the Peace of said Parishes in particular; That your Petitioners have chosen John Cromie Esq., for their Captain, and are now Exercising and learning Discipline, and they humbly beg that as the said Parishes are Part of the Manor of Dunluce, & almost all your Lordship's Estate, that your Lordship will be so good as to Grant them Fifty Stand of arms for the above mentioned loyal purposes, upon receiving good security for the Re-delivery of them, whenever your Lordship shall think proper to call them in, and your Petitioners will immediately cloath themselves in Uniform and will hope to be considered as one of the Companies under your Lordship's Patronage, and your Petitioners will for Ever Remain Your Lordship's most obliged & most obedient humble Ser[ts]

Glenarm Castle Octo[br 21st 1778]

Gentlemen

I shall ever be happy in attending to the Wishes of any part of this County that does me the Honour of calling on me for Advice, Assistance, or Direction, as Governor of the County at any time of Disturbance & Alarm like the present.

Tho the application is not as early as it might have been, (or in the Form by Letter from Mr. Cromie, that it ought to have been) I shall Comply with your Wishes. Being sensible of Your attention to Me & to the Service of your King & Country at this Critical Time.

If You do me the Honor of Declaring Yourselves entirely Under My Command as Governor of this County, You Will Signify It by a list of Your Names, And I shall then Arrange every thing for your Proper Appearance.

I am, Gentlemen
Your very Obedient Hum[ble] Servant
ANTRIM

Glenarm Castle Oct[br] 28th,1778

Sir

I am just now Favord with Your Letter inclosing a list of the Volunteers, Under Your Command.

I return You My Best thanks for this Proof of Your attention to Me.

The Command that You have offer'd Me I accept with a Due Sense of the Compliment paid Me by You & the Volunteers that Compose Your Company.

I shall have the Honor of presenting You with a Standard of Colors, as a testimony of the Sensibility I have of Your putting Yourselves Under My Direction.

The pattern of the Uniform M[r] William Dunker of Clogher can furnish

8

you with & I shall write to Order That Quantity of Arms which you apply
for, May be Delivered immediately to You.

I am Sir
Your most Obe^t
Humb^{le} Servant
ANTRIM

I shall be happy
in hearing of
your progress

Dublin Octr 15th 1779

Sir,

It is with infinite satisfaction to myself that I have the Honor of being
directed by the House of Peers to communicate to You the Underwritten
Resolutions which your Spirited conduct so Justly merits. You are therefore
with all convenient speed to parade the Company under your Command and
read this to them at the Head of the Line I am Sir

Your most obed^t Ser^t

ANTRIM

RESOLUTION OF HOUSE OF LORDS

Die Jovis 14th Octobris 1779

Resolved by the Lords Spiritual and Temporal in Parliament assembled
that the Thanks of this House be given to the different Volunteer Corps in
this Kingdom, for their spirited and (at this time) necessary Exertions in its
Defence.

Ordered that the said Resolution be sent by the Clerk of the Parliaments
to the Governor of the different Counties.

W. Watts GAYER
Edwd GAYER

CLERKS
PARLIAMENT

After the danger of invasion passed when the war ended, the Volunteers did not immediately disband but turned their attention to politics.

At this time, Ireland had its own all-Ireland Parliament, under the
control of Westminster. In the interests of English traders, policies had
been imposed by Westminster that almost ruined Ireland's export trade,
with consequent great increase in poverty and suffering.

Although the political activities of the Volunteers were wholly peaceful, they pressed for numerous reforms, and there was obvious danger in the existence of so large a body of armed and disciplined men in no way under the control of the government. It was largely owing to the Volunteers that the British government became convinced of the absolute necessity of granting reforms, and, in England, exhausted by a war against four adversaries, Holland having joined the colonists, France, and Spain in 1780, there was no opposition.

In 1782, the Volunteers held a convention in Dungannon, presided over by Lord Charlemont, their Commander in Chief, at which the delegates from Antrim and Down made a notable contribution to the proceedings. Gratton, one of Ireland's greatest statesmen, proposed, and the convention passed, the following resolution-motion:

As Irishmen, Christians, and Protestants, we rejoice at the relaxation of the penal laws against our Roman Catholic fellow subjects.

In 1783, the war ended in victory for the American colonists, who won complete independence.

There had already been various reforms improving conditions for Roman Catholics and reducing the legal disabilities under which they had so long suffered as well as measures that reduced the most damaging of the restraints on Irish trade. Now, a bill was passed in January 1783 giving to Ireland its greatest desire—legislative independence under the crown. The relevant wording was as follows:

Be it enacted that the right claimed by the people of Ireland to be bound only by laws enacted by His Majesty and the Parliament of that Kingdom, in all cases whatever shall be and is hereby declared to be established and ascertained for ever and shall at no time hereafter be questioned or questionable

Ireland had achieved virtual legal independence; the steady evolution of democracy in England should, with satisfactory progress in Ireland, have resulted in real independence and a mutually beneficial relationship between the Irish and their English neighbors.

The Irish Volunteers, who had achieved so much in so short a time, now peacefully disbanded, and the memory of them passed into history.

The earl of Antrim, Governor of the county of Antrim in 1778 and 1779, was a MacDonnell, a family prominent in Ulster history. A MacDonnell of Ulster married Somerled, sister of the Danish ruler of the Isle of Man. The head of this Ulster family, descended from the MacDonnells of Scotland, was created Earl of Antrim by Charles I.

3 / 1778—Dr. McBride Writes to John Cromie

Dublin 19th May, 1778

Dear Sir

I have most carefully considered your little Daughter's case, as drawn up by Dr. Thompson, to whom please to present my Compliments, and tell Him, that now (since we may believe any sharpness which might have been in her blood is pretty well corrected) a strengthening course of Diet, and Medecine, aided by Bathing in the Sea, will bid fairest to remove these swellings, and restore the Child to perfect Health.

What I therefore propose, if he does not see any thing to contraindicate, is an Infusion of the Bark, according to the inclosed prescription. I do not think that keeping Her on a low diet will be of any use, but rather the Contrary. Every day let her have a bit of fowl, beef or mutton, for Dinner, and a Glass of Claret afterwards.

While she is using the Sea bathing, I should wish her to drink as much of the Water twice a week as will purge her two or three times.

Washing her Throat (Morning and Evening) with an Astringent Gargle, made of Equal parts Tincture of Roses and Claret, with Ten grains of Alum, to eight ounces of Gargle, I should expect will help to brace up these relaxed Tonsils.

It will give me very sincere pleasure to hear that what I have proposed shall be found to answer expectation.

Mrs. McBride desires her best Compliments to you and joins me in the same to Mrs. Cromie.

I am, Dear Sir,

Your Most Obedient and Very Humble Servant

David McBride

As soon as you can conveniently get rid of the Flannels about her throat, let them be laid aside; and neither muffle her, nor rub anything to the parts.

John Cromie, of Cromore in Portstewart, then in the county of Antrim, who took his daughter Eleanor to Dr. McBride, was of Huguenot descent, an ancestor having settled in Dublin, a refugee from the persecution of Protestants in France. John Cromie was the son of Michael

Cromie and his wife Ursula, daughter of Sir John Blackwood. Portstewart was owned by the Cromie family, having been bought for casks of wine and a peppercorn rent.

Eleanor Cromie, who does not appear again in this book, grew up to marry Sir John Godfrey. Her father is the John Cromie who wrote to the earl of Antrim.

4 / 1783—Sam Thompson Writes to His Brother-in-Law John Cromie

St. Croix 25th May 1783

Dear Sir,

It is so long since we corresponded that we are almost worn out of acquaintance in that way, however the recollection of our past society, and what is far more valuable to me the happines my worthy sister enjoys under your kind auspices fills me with affection to the author of it. Yours and Nancy's tender care of our little ones has laid their Mother and me under the greatest obligations and we only wish for an opportunity of shewing our gratitude—the plan that was laying out for the children's living in Dublin was a good one, and I have only to request your kind acquiescence in suffering your daughter Elinor to be educated in the same manner as my own without any charge coming against you—it will be a satisfaction to me to have it so, and I most sincerely wish our children to grow up in Love and Unity together.

If it pleases God to spare my Son and he discovers a proper Genius I think to breed him up to the Law; if he should have occasion his inclination would lead him to practice he can do it—if not he has the prospect of £1,000 a year clear Estate in Ireland besides what I may be able to leave him in this country, which will make a handsome provision—and with merit on his side he will sett out with tolerable advantage in Life—thus we Fathers flatter ourselves with prospects which God alone knows if ever they'l be fulfilled, however they serve a valuable End in exciting our Industry and discharging the Duty that is incombent in us towards them—I brought out the Deed of Settlement with me that my Father made of Mount Stafford and Ballybunion, and as it can be of no manner of use here I return it by Bob and request your care and preservation thereof—further if you think it necessary for my Mother to do anything in confirmation thereof, that you will prevail on her to do it—I do not understand anything of law or settlements, but recollect it was optional in her to accept of the Settlement made on her therein or abide by her Thirds—now I have no reason to doubt my Mother, however what is right ought to be done, and if you join in opinion with me & think it wd not be giving offence (although it certainly ought not) to ask her, I beg you

12

would—but if otherwise let it alone & I'll be content.

I long to know how the value of Lands is affected in Ireland by the rise of a New Empire in the American World, and whether many are Emigrating to it—also if by the extensive liberty granted our Native Country of late; many New Manufactures are Established—or if any quantity of Genevans are gone over—further if the old Linen Trade which my heart always warms to flourishes—your kind information about these things or anything else that concerns & is of advantage to Ireland by late regulations will be very pleasing to me—I also would be very glad to know if you have any Leases dropped how you are Letting in the New—whether higher or lower—for my part I have requested my Father to let his Tenants sit easy & by no means to dispossess the old ones if they can possibly renew—& not to screw them up to dishearten them and break their spirits—neither would I wish the Roman Catholic Tenants to be turned out on account of Protestants whereby to strengthen our Interest at the County Elections—as all that is vanity and folly in comparison of the happiness and justice we owe our fellow Creatures—I know medium price for Lands is much the best, for if lett too low the People become slothful—& if too high they are dejected & oppressed—therefore the proper course ought to be steered & as far as I have any Concern wd wish them happy & more than a three lives & 31 years Lease I never wd grant, neither ought the appointment of Lives to be left to the Tenants, as I wd have the Lives Publick ones that when they drop one knows at once—whereas private ones are not so easily discovered—therefore not so Eligible—31 years for Catholics is enough, and they ought to be bound up to make certain improvements—indeed was I a Landlord and settled among them I wd keep a Nursery of all kinds of trees wch should be given them gratis for an encouragement—& upon my word I cannot conceive a happier Life existing than that of an Independent Country Gentleman—happy in seeing his Tenants thrive about him, looked up to as a Father among them—distributing impartial Justice—& esteemed as an Honest skilful Grand Jurer in his County—Free of ambition and cares he enjoys the rational pleasures of Life & by proper Exercise and Temperance, the greatest of all blessings—good Health.

The War is now ended & my prospect of getting to Europe diminishes—12 months ago I thought it pretty near, but various are the disappointments of this kind of Life I am engaged in particularly I have lost considerably in many ways & only made 170 14 hds of Sugar this Crop wch is poor indeed, so that I must stick to it a few years longer & work on with patience & resignation—My Wife is contented to assist me — our Children being young dont require our immediate care & attention over them—happily indeed we have such friends to assist us in that Duty—for without that we wd be obliged to Sacrifice our Interest for their good—now they are doing well & we are working to give them the proper outfit in Life.

I have lately sold my Estate in St. Kitts for £10,000 ster.—one half to be paid this year & the other Half in 7 years with 6% interest—my Loss is very great but it cant be helped—now I know the end of it & can better regulate my affairs—indeed I am striving all that lyes in my power to bring them within a narrow Compass & hope in a little time to succeed—a moderate Fortune will satisfie me & I am sure that the best way of obtaining it is to pursue one object without grasping at more—so long as Betty's Hope is in Debt I wd not wish to quit it, & without making use of other Funds which can be employed in Europe, my intention is to let it clear itself.

Bob goes Home to make some Arrangements with my Father & you'l have pleasure in his Company—he is a worthy young Man & deserves encouragement—I shall long for his return as my State of Health becomes more & more precarious—thank God the Gout is my only complaint, but the last fit alarmed me—& confinement in any place wd be dreadful to a Man of my turn—but more particularly in this Country. It will make me particularly happy to hear now and then from you & by Bob I shall expect a long detail—Ever believe me to be.

> My Dear Sir
> Your Affte friend & Brother
> Sam Thompson

St. Croix, where this letter was written, is an island of the West Indies that was discovered by Christopher Columbus in 1493. Since then, it has changed hands many times, having first been owned by Spain, Great Britain, and Holland. In 1651, it was taken by France and later presented by France to the Knights of Malta. In 1733, it was bought by Denmark and in 1783 was part of the Danish West Indies.

St. Kitts, mentioned in the letter, is an island of the British West Indies.

Sugar was the West Indies main product, many of the planters then being Europeans. Some were British and wealthy, as in the case of Sam Thompson.

The Thompson home in Ulster was "Greenmount"[1] Muckamore. The other estates mentioned—Mount Stafford and Ballybunion—are in the South of Ireland.

In 1783 and later, it was usual for Ulster leases to be based on lives.

Ulster had far fewer absentee landlords than Southern Ireland, where numbers seldom visited their Irish estates, were rapacious and heartless, and have given Irish landlords a shameful reputation. Many Ulster landlords lived on their estates and took a humane interest in their tenants.

Tenants in Ulster were, in another way, more fortunate than those in the South in having the protection of "Ulster Custom," under which they received compensation for any improvements made to the property during their tenancy at its termination. Ulster Custom was not legally enforceable but was normally honored. In the South, there was no such mitigation of the cruel legal position of tenants.

It was quite usual for landlords to keep a nursery of trees, and many of them planted extensively. Various acts were passed from time to time governing tree planting. In 1783, the position was that provided the tenant registered any trees he planted with the clerk of the peace of the county, he was entitled to all such trees on the expiration of his lease, and during its currency he could cut any timber he required for his own use.

Ulster was always the most prosperous area of Ireland. English and foreign travelers, when entering Ulster from the South, have frequently commented on the contrast between the poverty-stricken aspect of the Southern countryside and the cheerful and thriving impression received in Ulster.

With this letter, Sam Thompson makes his sole contribution to this book. No reference to him is made in later letters or diaries in this collection, although a brief, undated, unsigned note refers to other members of the Thompson family and to John Cromie—"Three old Miss Thompsons, very rich, used to go to London and entertain Royalty" and "Old John Cromie who married Ann Thompson Father remembers as an old man at Roe Park with his old butler "Clinton" who attended to him dressed in knee breeches and buckles."

Notes

1. Now a government agricultural college.

5 / 1783—William Richardson Invites John Cromie to a Scrape

21st June '83

Dear Sir,
I find the young Ladies in the course of their Expedition this Day have picked up a Fidler for Monday Evening next, if you Mrs. Cromie and the Ladies will dine with us at 3 o'clock and take share of the scrape we will be glad of your Company.
I am Sir
Your very humble Ser^t
Wm. Richardson
Portrush Saterday

15

Dr Sir,

I received your fav^r, requesting this Family to dine with you next monday; Mrs. Cromie & I would wait on you with great pleasure, but for one reason, which recurs to our recollection, & which I will very candidly tell you.

The last time that we were your Guests, We thought ourselves ill treated, & as we have never been informed whether it was by mistake or intention, we cannot consistently accept your kind invitation, until that point be ascertained.

Miss Cromie & Miss Thompson will do themselves the fav^r of waiting on you etc.

I am Sir
Your etc
J.C.

6 / John O'Neill Stands in the County Antrim Election

TO THE
ELECTORS
OF THE
COUNTY OF ANTRIM

Gentlemen,

When at the County of Antrim Meeting, I stated my objection to that part of the Declaration which required, that, "at all times the Representative should obey the Instructions of his Constituents regularly assembled," I omitted one distinction on the subject; which is, That in every case in which the Constituents shall at any time conceive that the Constitution or Commerce of Ireland is in the most remote degree affected or concerned, in my opinion Representatives should implicitly obey the Instructions of Constitutents—a Jury which I solemnly acknowledge myself bound by, and amenable to, if I shall have the honor of receiving those of the County of Antrim.

I have only to add, that the mode of collecting the sense of County Constituents, to which I will be amenable, is by a Call of the Sheriff, or of Sixty Freeholders, a previous notice of Fourteen Days being given. —A substantial reform of Parliament, and faithful attendance of my Duty, I have formerly in the Fullest manner declared.

JOHN O'NEILL

BELFAST
21st JULY, 1783.

John O'Neill had represented Randalstown since 1761 in the old Irish Parliament. In 1783, he stood for County Antrim for the new, independent Irish Parliament and was successful. He was a progressive M.P. and a strong supporter of Catholic emancipation.

In the later election of 1790, he and the Hon. Hercules Rowley stood as independent candidates sponsored by the merchants and freeholders against the nominees[1] of powerful landlords,[2] who, as other great families, were accustomed to select the candidate and have him elected.

In this election, the victory in Down of Robert Stewart (afterward Lord Castlereagh), then under 21 years of age, who won the seat, although opposed by the nominee of the influential Downshire family, was also momentous.

The success of O'Neill, Rowley, and Stewart was a victory for democracy and a further step for Ireland on the road to becoming a democratic modern state.

In 1793, the Hon. John O'Neill became Baron O'Neill of Shane's Castle, and, in 1795, he was created a viscount.

Another young man, Arthur Wellesley also stood for the first time in this election and was elected by a constituency in the South of Ireland. Later, he became well known as the duke of Wellington.

Notes

1. James Leslie and Edmund McNaghten.
2. Marquis of Antrim, Lord Donegall, Lord Hertford, Lord Mountcashell, Lord Dungannon, Lord McCartney.

7 / After 1783—James Lyle Emigrates

James Lyle, third son of Hugh Lyle and Eleanor Hyde, emigrated to America as a very young man, soon after the end of the American War of Independence.

It may be assumed that he sailed from the tiny harbor of Portrush, for Portrush was one of the five Ulster ports that handled the emigrant traffic to America and the nearest one to his home in Coleraine. Although Portrush was the smallest port of the five, it handled the largest proportion of this traffic.

When James Lyle left Ulster, emigration to America was no longer so heavy as between 1720 and 1770, when 50 percent of the Presbyterians of Ulster had emigrated to start life afresh in the American Colonies[1] in order to escape from the religious discrimination and penal legislation that crippled their activities in Ulster.

It must be realised that it was not only Roman Catholics who suffered from religious discrimination and restrictive legislation in Ireland. In Europe, also, religious discrimination was the general rule and tolerance the exception. The flight of 400,000 Protestants from France from Roman Catholic persecution between the years 1683 and 1686 is only one of many examples proving that no one sect of the Christian church had the monopoly of suffering or inflicting religious discrimination.

James Lyle went to Philadelphia, in the state of Pennsylvania, where the great city of Philadelphia was then at the pinnacle of its prosperity and power.

The War of Independence, in which Ulstermen, who then formed one sixth of the American population, had played a prominent part, had ended in American victory. It was in Philadelphia that the Declaration of Independence had been signed. This historic document, drafted by Thomas Jefferson, was first read in public by an Ulsterman, printed by an Ulsterman, and eight Ulstermen were among its signatories.

When James Lyle arrived in Philadelphia, it was the seat of government, which was then the Continental Congress, for it was not until 1789 that the United States was first governed under its new Constitution.

Lafayette, from the new French Republic, Wolfe Tone and other United Irishmen, Talleyrand, and many other well-known characters of those days came to Philadelphia, some staying permanently and others only temporarily. It was planned that Marie Antoinette should take refuge there, and a house was built for her, but she did not succeed in escaping from the French bloodbath and was executed by the guillotine.

In Ulster, the Lyles were linen merchants, and their father, Hugh Lyle, having died in 1778, Hugh Lyle, James Lyle's eldest brother, continued the family linen business. Coleraine was then the center of the fine linen trade. Flax seed was imported into Ulster from America, one of the ports from which it was shipped being Philadelphia, so that any member of the Lyle family arriving in this city would be unlikely to find himself entirely among strangers when the population contained so many Ulstermen and so much business activity.

James Lyle became a merchant in Philadelphia and, in partnership with John Beauclerc Newman, established the firm of Lyle and Newman, dealing in a very wide variety of goods, including Irish linen. Of his business correspondence, one letter to an insurance company survives and is in the possession of the Historical Society of Pennsylvania. The

James Lyle (Philadelphia)

business prospered, and, by 1792, at the age of twenty-seven, he was one of Philadelphia's leading merchants.

In 1792, he married Ann Hamilton, daughter of Andrew and Abigail Hamilton and great niece of James Hamilton, the last colonial governor of Pennsylvania under George III.

In 1785, only two years after the end of the war, the United States appointed their first minister to the court of St. James's, John Adams, later to become the second president of the United States. John Adams's wife, Abigail Adams, was a prolific letter writer, and because of her ability, her correspondence has been published and is regarded as of historical importance. All her comments were not on weighty matters, of course, and in two of her letters she happened to mention Ann Hamilton, before her marriage to James Lyle. When her husband was minister in London, she writes "Notwithstanding the English boast so much of their beauties I do not think they have really so much of it as you will find amongst the same proportion of people in America . . . . I have not seen a lady in England who can bear a comparison with Mrs. Bingham, Mrs. Platt, or a Miss Hamilton who is a Philadelphia young lady " . . . and, again, writing on November 21, 1700, "Our Nancy Hamilton is the same unaffected affable girl we formerly knew her. She made many kind enquiries after you."

Ann Hamilton's claim to beauty can still be judged today, for there is a full-length portrait of her and her uncle entitled *William Hamilton of the "Woodlands" and his niece Mrs. James Lyle.*[2] The artist was Benjamin West, and in the lower left-hand corner is a note: "This picture was began in 1785 and finished in London in 1812." When finished, the painting was sent by ship from London to James Lyle in Philadelphia.

Benjamin West has been described as the father of American painting. In 1756, he was a portrait painter in Philadelphia, moving to New York in 1762. The subscriptions of leading Pennsylvania merchants then helped him to go to Europe. He studied in Italy for three years before going to London, where he became the favorite painter of George III. He was one of the four artists who suggested to the king in 1768 a plan for the Royal Academy, of which he became president in 1792, succeeding Sir Joshua Reynolds.

Ann Lyle died in 1798, leaving two young daughters, Mary, born in 1796, and Ellen, born in 1797. James Lyle never remarried.

In 1817, James Hamilton died unmarried and intestate in New York. Letters of administration were granted to James Lyle, his brother-in-law. Among the items listed as part of the estate were twelve Negroes, valued at 4,400 dollars, a sharp reminder that full freedom had not come to all the American states, some of which had not yet joined the Union. In

Pennsylvania, slavery was already prohibited, but it was not abolished in all the American states of the Union until the end of the Civil War, 1864–1865, which was fought on this issue.

In 1818, both James Lyle's daughters were married, Mary to Henry Beckett, a merchant of Philadelphia, son of Sir John Beckett, and Ellen to Hartman Kuhn, son of the well-known Philadelphia surgeon.

James Lyle died in 1826. He was survived by both his daughters and five grandchildren: Marianne and Hamilton Beckett and Mary, Charles, and Cornelius Hartman Kuhn.

It seems clear that James Lyle did not lose touch with his Ulster home, for a Coleraine Lyle family record gives his marriage, those of his daughters, and the names of their children, the last entries being the marriage of Hamilton Beckett's daughter, Constance Mary, in 1880 to Henry, Second Lord Aberdare, and the death of Hamilton Beckett in 1883. It was also noted that James Lyle had been very successful in business.

James Lyle lived in one of the most important and exciting periods of American history, and, in 1823, three years before he died, there occurred an event that changed the history of the world and the future of the British and American people. It would seem, therefore, to have its place in the historical background of this book.

After the end of the American War of Independence, America's relationship with Great Britain did not always remain amicable, and, in 1812, after a period of stormy disagreements, America declared war on Great Britain, a war that lasted until 1815.

In 1823, Thomas Jefferson, third president of the United States, who had drafted the Declaration of Independence, had retired from public life. He was living at "Monticello," the house built to his own design, when he received a letter from the president of the United States, then James Monroe. His historic reply is given below.

Monticello

To James Monroe
October 24, 1823
Dear Sir,
The question presented by the letter you have sent me, is the most momentous which has ever been offered to my contemplation since that of independence. That made us a nation, this sets our compass and points the course which we are to steer through the ocean of time opening on us. And never could we embark on it under circumstances more auspicious. Our first and fundamental maxim should be, never to entangle ourselves in the broils of Europe. Our second, never to suffer Europe to intermeddle with cis-Atlantic affairs. America, North and South, has a set of interests distinct from those

21

of Europe and peculiarly her own. She should therefore have a system of her own, separate and apart from that of Europe. While the last is laboring to become the domicile of despotism, our endeavour should surely be to make our hemisphere that of freedom. One nation, most of all, could disturb us in this pursuit; she now offers to lead, aid and accompany us in it. By acceding to her proposition, we detach her from their hands, bring her mighty weight into the scale of free government, and emancipate a continent at one stroke, which might otherwise linger long in doubt and difficulty. Great Britain is the nation which can do us the most harm, of anyone, or all on earth; with her on our side, we should most sedulously cherish a cordial friendship, and nothing would tend more to knit our affections than to be fighting once more, side by side in the same cause. Not that I would purchase even her amity at the price of taking part in her wars. But the war in which the present proposition might engage us, should that be its consequence, is not her war but ours. Its object is to introduce and establish the American system, of keeping out of our land all foreign powers, of never permitting those of Europe to intermeddle in the affairs of our nation. It is to maintain our own principle, not to depart from it. And if to facilitate this, we can effect a division in the body of the European powers, and draw over to our side its most powerful member, surely we should do it. But I am clearly of Mr. Cannings opinion, that it will prevent instead of provoking war. With Great Britain withdrawn from their scale, and shifted into that of our two continents, all Europe combined would not undertake such a war. For how would they propose to get at either enemy without superior Fleets. Nor is the occasion to be slighted which this proposition offers of declaring our protest against the atrocious violations of the rights of nations, by the interference of anyone in the internal affairs of another so flagitiously begun by Bonaparte, and now continued by the equally lawless alliance, calling itself, holy.

But we have first to ask ourselves a question. Do we wish to acquire to our confederacy one or more of the Spanish Provinces? I candidly confess that I have ever looked on Cuba as the most interesting addition which could ever be made to our system of states. The control which, with Florida point, this island would give us over the Gulf of Mexico, and the countries and isthmus bordering on it, as well as all those whose waters flow into it, would fill up the measure of our political well-being. Yet, as I am sensible that this can never be obtained, even with her own consent, but by war, and its independence which is our second interest, (and especially its independence of England) can be secured without it I have no hesitation in abandoning my first wish to future chances, and accepting its independence with peace and the friendship of England, rather than its association at the expense of war and her enmity.

I could honestly therefore join in the declaration proposed, that we aim not at the acquisition of any of those possessions, that we will not stand in the way of any amicable arrangement between them and the mother country, but that we will oppose, with all our means, the forcible interposition of any other power as auxiliary, stipendiary, or under any other form or pretext, and most especially their transfer to any other power by conquest, cession or acquisition in any other way. I should think it therefore advisable that the Executive should encourage the British government to a continuance in the disposition expressed in their letter, by an assurance of his concurrence with them as far as his authority goes; and that as it may lead to war, the declaration of which requires an Act of Congress, the case shall be laid before them for consideration at their first meeting, and under the reasonable aspect in which it is seen by himself.

I have been so long weaned from political subjects, and have so long ceased to take any interest in them, that I am sensible I am not qualified to offer an opinion on them worthy of any attention. But the question now proposed involves consequences so lasting, and effects so decisive of our future destinies, as to rekindle all the interest I have heretofore felt on such occasions, and to induce me to the hazard of opinions, which will prove only my wish to contribute still my mite towards anything which may be useful to our country. And praying you to accept it at only what it is worth, I add the assurance of my constant and affectionate friendship and respect.

Th. Jefferson

The Holy Alliance referred to in Thomas Jefferson's letter was the project of the tsar of Russia, proposed by him in 1815. His dream was a confederation of European nations. The Alliance was not a treaty but a declaration, very piously worded and expressing impeccable principles. Russia signed first, followed with some reluctance by Austria and Prussia. Eventually, all the European rulers signed except the Pope and the Ottoman Sultan, who were not invited to do so, and Great Britain's Prince Regent (during the insanity of the King), who refused to sign in a most tactfully worded letter, influenced by Castlereagh[3], who, with robust realism, declared the Holy Alliance to be "a piece of sublime mysticism and nonsense."

In theory, interpretation of the declaration could have led to idealistic and progressive action. Unfortunately, Castlereagh's view was quickly justified, as, in practice, the Holy Alliance became a reactionary body, firmly opposed to Europe's growing demand for civil liberties. Finally, the Holy Alliance decided, despite the strong protests of Great Britain, that France, so recently a danger to all Europe, should invade Spain in order to help the Spanish monarchy in its constitutional difficulties at home, while abroad its American colonies, the empire of Brazil, and the republics of Mexico and Colombia, had revolted.

The possibility that a French invasion of Spain might lead to the French also attempting reconquest of the Spanish colonies in America disturbed George Canning, the British Prime Minister, who had agreed with Castlereagh's original estimate of the Holy Alliance. Accordingly, he made the proposition to the United States, which was referred to Thomas Jefferson for his opinion. Jefferson's advice, which reversed his policy of a lifetime toward England, was followed, thus changing the course of history.

Great Britain recognized the independence of the revolting Spanish colonies and warned the French government that Great Britain would not tolerate reconquest of these colonies by a foreign force. At the same time, President Monroe laid the veto of America on any interference of Europe in the affairs of the American continent. The immediate danger of war was averted, the Monroe Doctrine, which guided American policy for so long, was established, and there commenced the enduring special relationship between Great Britain and the United States the consequences of which were to affect the history of the world.

Notes

1. This emigration from Ulster must not be confused with the Great Famine emigration to America 150 years later when starving peasants from Southern Ireland fled from death.

2. The painting was deposited with the Historical Society of Philadelphia by Charles Kuhn in 1873.

3. Lord Castlereagh, 2nd Marquess of Londonderry, the Robert Stewart, who won his first election in 1790.

8 / 1798—Insurrection in Ireland

After 1782, the first results of Ireland's legislative independence under the crown were satisfactory.

Acts of reform were passed by the Irish Parliament, abolishing some of the severe legal disabilities of Roman Catholics, although many remained. Presbyterians also suffered from less well publicized grievances; for example, they were effectively excluded from public life by the legal requirement that those holding public office must take communion in the Episcopal Church.

Westminster removed some of their most damaging restraints on Irish trade, while the Irish Parliament pursued protectionist policies, the results being rapidly increasing prosperity.

At that time, linen was one of Ireland's most important industries.

The Coleraine Linen Market was held weekly in the Diamond and was one of the best linen markets in Ireland, where webs of the finest linen were sold.

Hugh Lyle, brother of James Lyle of Philadelphia, was born in 1756 and married to Sarah Greg in 1786. He was a magistrate, a post then unpaid, and also a member of the Grand Jury of the City and County of Londonderry.

In London, the King and Westminster were sympathetic to further Catholic reform, and so were many Irish Protestants, but progress was hampered by differences between the members of the Irish Parliament, all of whom were Protestants, including leading statesmen. Gratton supported full emancipation, while Flood opposed it. Opposition to Catholic reform was rooted in sectarian fears, not without justification in the light of Ireland's bloodstained history, the horrors of the rising of 1641, and the Rebellion of 1688 when the Protestants of Ulster were in danger of annihilation. The constitutional "Protestant Ascendancy," established after William of Orange's victory at the Battle of the Boyne, was a defensive measure, and many Protestants feared any relaxation of it.

Further difficulties arose because in spite of the Irish Parliament's nominal independence of Westminster, that Parliament could still exercise strong influence in various ways; by influencing the King, by its right to appoint and dismiss the Viceroy, by the use of bribery, then normally used in political life both in England and Ireland, and by the fact that a few families privately owned many Parliamentary seats. (Gratton estimated over two-thirds in 1790.) Of course, not only in England and Ireland but also in all Europe, democracy, where it existed at all, was still at a very early stage.

Nevertheless, much had been achieved, and greater changes for the better were on the way. Democratic ideas were gaining increasing support not only among the poor and obscure, who would benefit most, but also among those richer and more powerful, who were in a better position to influence events.

Tragically, an event in Europe sparked off repercussions in Ireland that resulted in a temporary reversal of the trend toward reform.

In 1789, France, suffering severely from incompetent government under Louis XV, a weak, amiable responsibility-shirking King who habitually gave pleasure precedence over state duties, however urgent, broke into revolution under the slogan "Liberty, Equality and Fraternity." Idealists led France at first, and with them and their successors the King weakly and amiably cooperated. Before the end of the year, France had a new constitution, all privileges had been legally abolished, and the new French National Assembly had issued a Declaration of the Rights of Man.

In England, the French Revolution was at first widely welcomed, many people there regarding it as the herald of a new and perfect era.

In Ireland, the well-educated, prosperous Whig element tended to feel the same way, while the hopes and impatience of the Catholics of the South and the Presbyterians of Ulster, then the most radical and, as always, the most determined of Ireland's five provinces, were raised to fever pitch.

Amidst the general enthusiasm for the new French republic, the first note of warning was struck by the storming of the Bastille, a bloodthirsty incident when the garrison of men who surrendered on a promise of safe conduct were immediately massacred, their heads on pikes being paraded through the streets of Paris by a blood-crazed mob, an episode having a more sinister and prophetic background than the widely publicized version of its being merely a case of a Paris mob getting out of hand.

Then, in November 1790, Edmund Burke, Irish, Whig M.P. for an English constituency, widely known as a writer on political matters, who had supported the English colonists during the American war, wrote a hostile pamphlet "Reflections on the Revolution in France," prophesying that the result of the revolution would not be democracy but anarchy, ending in rule by an oligarchy.

This attack did not go unanswered. In 1791, a biting reply was published, written by Thomas Paine, English ex-staymaster, ex-exciseman, Secretary for Foreign Affairs to Congress during the American war, who was already well known for his writings in support of the colonists.

Paine's famous pamphlet "The Rights of Man" was dedicated to George Washington. In 1791, Paine was a French citizen, a respected member of the French National Assembly, so he could be regarded as having inside knowledge of his subject. His defense of the French Revolution was eloquent, and he demolished Burke's arguments far more convincingly than Burke expressed them. He was also a greater man than Burke, for modern democracies are based on Paine's theories, and most of his practical recommendations of state education, state pensions, etc., have already been widely implemented.

Nevertheless, Paine had serious blind spots; for example, he cherished the naive fallacy that all evil emanated from the aristocracy and the church, so that were these removed, the common man would always act with perfect justice and kindness.

In 1791, in England and Ireland, public opinion became polarized as a result of the Burke/Paine controversy into the two extremes of blind opposition and blind support. Wolfe Tone, just then coming into prominence, described the opposing groups, misleadingly, as aristocrats and democrats, declaring himself to be a democrat.

In 1791, the Society of United Irishmen, destined to make a serious impact on Irish history, was formed in Belfast with the assistance of Wolfe Tone, then the paid Protestant secretary of the Catholic Association of Dublin, which was pledged to work for Catholic emancipation. The new society was the idea of William Drennan, a nonconformist and a native of Belfast, and at its inception was a perfectly legal body. As time went on, William Drennan ceased to take any active part, and Wolfe Tone was, from the first, a dominating influence. After their formation, the United Irishmen issued a Declaration and Resolution as follows:

DECLARATION AND RESOLUTION OF THE SOCIETY OF UNITED IRISHMEN OF BELFAST

In the present great era of reform, when unjust Governments are falling in every quarter of Europe; when religious persecution is compelled to abjure her tyranny over conscience; when the rights of men are ascertained in theory, and that theory substantiated by practice; when antiquity can no longer defend absurd and oppressive forms, against the common sense and common interests of mankind; when all Government is acknowledged to originate from the people, and to be so far only obligatory as it protects their rights and promotes their welfare: We think it our duty as Irishmen to come forward, and state what we feel to be our heavy grievance and what we know to be its effectual remedy.

WE HAVE NO NATIONAL GOVERNMENT; we are ruled by Englishmen and the servants of Englishmen, whose object is the interest of another country, whose instrument is corruption, and whose strength is the weakness of Ireland; and these men have the whole power and patronage of the country, as means to seduce and subdue the honesty, and the spirit of her representatives in the legislature. Such an extrinsic power, acting with uniform force in a direction too frequently opposite to the true line of our obvious interests, can be resisted with effect solely by *unanimity, decision, and spirit in the people*; qualities which may be exerted most legally, constitutionally and efficaciously, by that great measure essential to the prosperity and freedom of Ireland. AN EQUAL REPRESENTATION OF ALL THE PEOPLE IN PARLIAMENT.

We do not here mention as grievances the rejection of a place-bill, of a pension bill, of a responsibility-bill, the sale of peerages in one House, the corruption publicly arrowed in another, nor the notorious infamy of borough traffic between both; not that we are insensible of their enormity, but that we consider them as but symptoms of that mortal disease which corrodes the vitals of our Constitution, and leaves to the people, in their own Government, but the shadow of a name.

Impressed with these sentiments, we have agreed to form an association to be called THE SOCIETY OF UNITED IRISHMEN: And we do pledge ourselves to our country and mutually to each other, that we will steadily support, and endeavour, by all due means, to carry into effect, the following resolutions:

First Resolved That the weight of English influence in the Government of this country is so great, as to require a cordial union among ALL THE PEOPLE OF IRELAND to maintain that balance which is essential to the preservation of our liberties and the extension of our commerce.

Second That the sole constitutional mode by which this influence can be opposed, is by a complete and radical reform of the representation of the people in Parliament. *Third* That no reform is practicable, efficacious or just which shall not include *Irishmen* of every religious persuasion.

Satisfied, as we are, that the intestine divisions among Irishmen have too often given encouragement and impunity to profligate, audacious, and corrupt administrations in measures which, but for these divisions they durst not have attempted: we submit our resolutions to the nation, as the basis of our political faith.

We have gone to what we conceive to be the root of the evil: we have stated what we conceive to be the remedy. With a Parliament thus reformed, everything is easy; without it, nothing can be done: and we do call on and most earnestly exhort our countrymen in general to follow our example, and to form similar societies in every quarter of the kingdom for the promotion of constitutional knowledge, the abolition of bigotry in religion and politics, and the equal distribution of the rights of man through all sects and denominations of Irishmen.

The people, when thus collected, will feel their own might, and secure that power which theory has already admitted as their portion, and to which, if they be not roused by their present provocation to vindicate it, they deserve to forfeit their pretensions *FOR EVER* Signed by order of the Society of United Irishmen of Belfast

Robert Simms, Secretary
October 1791

By 1792, the situation in Ireland, particularly in Ulster, was a source of anxiety to responsible people, as serious disturbances appeared to be a possibility.

At the Summer Assizes of 1792, the Grand Jury of the City and County of Londonderry, in an attempt to contribute to greater stability, issued a declaration and resolution, of which Hugh Lyle was one of the signatories:

City and County of Londonderry
Summer Assizes 1792

Whereas a paper has been circulated through this county signed "Edward Byrne" purporting to come from a body of men styling themselves "The Sub-Committee of the Catholics of Ireland."

We, the Grand Jury of the city and county of Londonderry, assembled at an assizes held at Londonderry, on the 30th day of July 1792, feel it our indispensable duty to express our most decided disapprobation of such a proceeding, and to declare our sentiments thereof by the following resolutions

Resolved That in our apprehension, the constitution of this Kingdom is unacquainted with any such body of men as "The Sub-Committee of the Catholics of Ireland"

Resolved That the meetings and delegations recommended by such Sub-Committee, in the above mentioned paper, if adopted, would tend to produce discontent and disorder, more especially as they presume to say that, by a general union of the Catholics of Ireland, the objects they are looking for MUST BE ACCOMPLISHED, as expressed in their letter "WE SHALL RECEIVE IT" and further that "We have the first authority for asserting, this application will have infinite weight with our gracious Sovereign, and with Parliament, if our friends are qualified to declare, That it is the universal wish of every Catholic in the nation.

Resolved That the system of union between the clergy and laity, recommended to the people of the Catholic persuasion in the above mentioned paper, insidiously conveys the idea of an hierarchy which would eventually destroy the Protestant ascendancy, the freedom of elective franchise, and the established constitution of the country. And that we are determined to support, with our lives and fortunes, that happy constitution as established at the Revolution of 1688, and to maintain the Protestant ascendancy in this Kingdom, against every attempt made to lessen or interfere with it by any body of men, let their union or number be what they may.

Resolved That we love and highly respect our Catholic brethren of the Kingdom, and recommend, that if they mean to look forward for further favours, it may not be through the medium of committees or such publications, but from a continuance of the same well-regulated conduct which has already excited the legislature in their behalf.

Hugh Hill, Foreman

John Miller	Marcus Gage
Hugh Lyle	Daniel Patterson
William Alexander	David Ross
John Darcus	James Patterson
John Spotswood	William Lecky
Robert Galt	J.C. Beresford
Samuel Curry	John Ferguson
John Stirling	George Ash
William Ross	C.L. Cunningham
Andrew Knox	Alexander Young
John Hart	Dom. McCausland

Edward Byrne, who signed the letter referred to by the grand jury, was a leading Southern Irish member of the Dublin Catholic Committee, which had recently expelled its aristocratic members in order to embark on more positive action.

29

Grand juries, which were not abolished in Ulster until the twentieth century, originated in Anglo-Saxon times and consisted of not less than twelve members of local good standing. It was not their duty to try the accused but, meeting in private, to decide whether bills of indictment laid before them should go forward for trial or be rejected. Treason, with its severe penalties of flogging, transportation, or hanging, was one of the crimes normally first considered by a grand jury.

In 1792, the Catholic Committee sent a deputation to London, which included their secretary Wolfe Tone. There they were kindly received by King George III, who later sent a message to the Irish Parliament that it was his wish that Parliament should consider the situation of his Catholic subjects. The result was the Catholic Relief Act of 1793, which gave very substantial relief to Catholics, although they still could not be members of Parliament or hold high command in the army or navy.

In the meantime, in France, events had proved Burke's forecast to be correct. The situation there had swiftly deteriorated into anarchy, the idealistic aims of liberty, equality, and fraternity were forgotten, common men, deified by Paine, seized power and proved themselves human by being even less just and kind than aristocrats and priests. A reign of terror ensued during which innocent and guilty, revolutionary leaders, aristocrats and common men, were executed in an endless stream before the approving eyes of bloodthirsty spectators whose pleasure it was to watch the severed heads roll from the guillotine's knife.

The weak French King, who had made no effort to save from the slaughter many of his most loyal subjects, at last took fright and tried to escape with his wife and children. Recaptured, tried for treason and found guilty, he was sent to the guillotine early in 1793. His execution was opposed by Thomas Paine, who soon fell from favor on account of this. He eventually left France and spent the rest of his life in America. Later, in 1793, Queen Marie Antoinette, accused and convicted of the same crime as the King, bravely met the same fate. Among thousands of other victims was the royal duc d'Orleans, a personal friend of the Prince of Wales, later George IV, who had been converted to democratic ideas in England. He was a member of the French Convention under the Republican title of Citoyen Egalite, and his Palais Royal was thrown open to the people. However, it became the ruling view ''There is no need for evidence against royal conspirators,'' and he was sent to the guillotine. He met his death with smiling calm.

In 1793, France declared war on England. The Irish Parliament gave their full support for the war, voting large sums of money for it with the support of such reforming statesmen as Gratton. In the country, also, there was general support.

At Westminster, the Tory government formed a coalition with the

Whig opposition with the result that Irish administration came under Whig control.

With reforming zeal, the Whigs immediately appointed Lord Fitzwilliam, an Irish peer and supporter of reform, the Lord Lieutenant. The appointment was most popular in Ireland, and hopes rose high for immediate and widespread reforms. Lord Fitzwilliam's intention was to fulfill all these hopes. Unfortunately, he decided that the first necessity was to break the power of the great families that held a monopoly of it and from whom he anticipated opposition to his plans. As he did not receive an immediate reply to a letter of his to London, he rashly assumed that silence denoted consent to his having a free hand. He immediately dismissed Sir John Beresford, one of the most powerful men in Ireland with a very large and influential family connection. Fitzwilliam also planned to dismiss other leading Irish statesmen, including Fitzgibbon in order to remove all hindrances to Whig reforms. The reaction was swift, and with Pitt and also the King opposed, Lord Fitzwilliam was soon abruptly recalled, and in his place Lord Camden was appointed with instructions to oppose both Catholic emancipation and the reform of Parliament, a policy in keeping with his own natural inclinations.

In Ireland, these events produced bitter disappointment and revolutionary ferment on the one hand and intensified fears and loyalty on the other.

Admirers of the French Revolution remained blind to all its horrors and were in no way influenced by the significant action of France's Irish Brigade, known as "The Wild Geese."

The Wild Geese originated among those Irish soldiers who had fought for James II in Ireland against William of Orange. When James was finally defeated at the Battle of the Boyne, the subsequent treaty allowed them to leave Ireland, and, like James II, many of them took refuge in France, where they formed the Irish Brigade. Kept up to strength by their descendants and later Irish refugees, this famous force had fought for France for over 100 years, taking part in important battles in many parts of Europe. Enemies of England by heredity and training, the Wild Geese, in the War of 1793 pledged their allegiance to King George III and fought for England against France, the adopted country of their ancestors, the refuge of generations of Irish rebels, which the Wild Geese now stigmatised as a "godless republic."

In 1793, the United Irishmen became a revolutionary body, with a secret oath, and began to organize their members on a military basis.

In the same year, Jackson, an English clergyman living in France, came to England as a French agent to investigate the prospects for a French invasion of England or Ireland.

On arrival in Ireland, accompanied by Cockayne, an old friend,

31

Jackson met several United Irishmen, including Wolfe Tone, who unwisely gave him a written memorandum that he had prepared on the rosy prospects for an invasion of Ireland. Cockayne, who, unknown to Jackson, was a government informer, sent the memorandum to the British government. Jackson was arrested, and at his trial in 1795, its result being certain, Jackson committed suicide, dying in the dock after taking poison. Some of the United Irishmen implicated fled from Ireland. Wolfe Tone, whose name had been frequently mentioned during the trial, was particularly at risk, with his probable end the gallows. With the help of influential friends, he came to terms with the government, supplying them with a written confession and undertaking to leave the country. Accordingly, accompanied by his wife and children, Tone sailed from Belfast in 1795 after an emotional farewell to his friends and supporters there. Soon after their arrival in Wilmington, North Carolina, Wolfe Tone moved to Philadelphia and later in the same year sailed alone for France as representative of the United Irishmen, a mission hardly compatible with his release agreement with the British government. On their side, the government undertook that Wolfe Tone's confession would not be used against any of the people mentioned in it except to prevent any treasonable practices and that he would not be brought to trial or called as a witness.

In 1795, Henry Joy McCracken, good-looking, young, enthusiastic, and idealistic, already a member of the United Irishmen, joined one of its recently formed extremist Belfast branches. He was a cousin of Henry Joy, the widely respected, moderate proprietor of the Belfast *Newsletter*.

Also, in 1795, there occurred another event, momentous in Ulster's history. After one of the frequent sectarian clashes, the "Battle of the Diamond," between the Protestant Peep o' Day Boys and the Catholic Defenders, the latter being defeated, there was formed the first Orange Society (later known as the Orange Order) in Ireland. Originating in Holland in the reign of William of Orange (William III of England), Orange Societies in due course spread to other parts of the world. In "The Loyal Orange Institution," published in Australia in 1898, it is stated, "Orangism is a union of Protestants without regard to denomination, and while pledged to observe the principles of toleration, is determined to resist by all lawful means, papal encroachments on the glorious civil and religious liberty now enjoyed by all." In Ulster, the Orange Order eventually became a political factor of overwhelming strength and, its principles of toleration too often forgotten, of deplorable religious bigotry.

In 1796, the war with France was not going well for England, and plots and disorders increased in Ireland.

The government passed an Insurrection Act, which meant that Ireland was governed by martial law with free quarters and house burning and an Indemnity Act to protect magistrates if they exceeded their legal duty. Yeomanry were raised, generally consisting of tenants, mainly Protestants, under the command of their landlord and commissioned under the crown.

The existing militia, recruited mainly by conscription and containing many Catholics, was enlarged.

In France, Wolfe Tone worked hard to convince the French government that the Irish would welcome a French invasion and that large numbers would revolt in their support. In this task, he was assisted by several other United Irish leaders, including Lord Edward Fitzgerald, son of the duke of Leinster, who had served in the British army in the American war as A.D.C. to Lord Rawdon (later Lord Moira). Lord Edward Fitzgerald's wife was the adopted daughter of the duc d'Orleans (Citoyen Egalite) who died in the holocaust of the French Revolution.

Carnot was much impressed by Wolfe Tone; so also was General Hoche, one of the republic's most brilliant generals, second in importance to Napoleon.

Napoleon also met the Irish leaders but was not impressed by them or by the success prospects for an invasion of Ireland. However, in December 1796, a French fleet sailed from Brest bound for Ireland, carrying 15,000 men under the command of General Hoche. Wolfe Tone accompanied them.

In Coleraine, John Galt, a leading Methodist of that town, wrote in his diary:

December 20th 1796—This morning despatches to the officer in command here are to have a sharp look-out for 40 vessels of war with 24,000 troops have set sail from France for the invasion of Ireland.
December 25th At the usual hour of meeting 6 o'clock—it being Christmas morning—we could hardly hear the preacher. Some were lamenting the severity of the morn, when Stephen Douthitt, the father of our society, remarked "Well, friends, we do not know what good this storm may be doing us"
January 14, 1797 The Lord God Omnipotent reigneth! He had only to command the storm to rise and the French fleet has been dispersed—one ship cast a wreck on the shores of Ireland, several sunk, and the rest driven back or otherwise disabled to their disappointed Government. Allowing for the time it would take the news to travel, it is almost certain that the storm that caused their destruction was the one we had on Christmas morning.

On Christmas Eve, on board the *Indomitable*, Wolfe Tone had looked forward to landing in Ireland on Christmas day, but at two o'clock next morning, he was awakened by the rising wind of the storm.

In Southern Ireland, there was little sign of enthusiasm for invasion, but the situation was very different in Ulster, and the mainly Presbyterian members of the United Irishmen there were fiercely disloyal.

The French expedition from Brest was a clear danger signal to the government, which decided that Ulster must be disarmed. This unpleasant task was assigned to General Lake, who carried it out with ruthless efficiency. Large quantities of arms were seized, many arrests were made, and severe punishments inflicted, including executions by hanging.

In all parts of Ireland, the well educated and well informed were, in general, fully aware of the terrible consequences should civil war or anarchy ensue, while the French republic's treatment of the European countries that they had ostensibly "liberated" served as a grim warning of Ireland's fate if England should lose the war. Much evidence of loyalty also came from the general population, both Protestant and Catholic, the majority of whom feared France. A loyal address was presented to the lord lieutenant by the whole Catholic hierarchy.

In June 1797, a Franco-Dutch fleet of the Batavian republic assembled at Texel for a second attempt to invade Ireland, this time with a force of 14,000 men. The moment was well chosen, with the weather propitious and England in severe difficulties as mutinies at Portsmouth, Plymouth, and the Nore practically immobilized her fleet for eight weeks. But all was not ready at Texel; time dragged slowly on, with Tone, in a state of increasing impatience and alarm, fretting impotently on shore. In August, the French decided against the original plan, but, finally, when the mutinies were over, and Wolfe Tone was absent in Paris, the Dutch fleet sailed, only to meet and be defeated by the British under Admiral Duncan at Camperdown. After this misfortune, it was known that there was no hope of any further substantial help from France.

Irresponsibly undeterred, the United Irishmen decided to go on alone and fixed the date of their rising as May 23, 1798.

Lord Edward Fitzgerald was appointed commander in chief.

In Ulster, Robert Simms was chosen as general for County Antrim, and (according to two informers) the Rev. Steele Dickson, a clergyman deeply involved with the United Irishmen, was to command in County Down.

The government was kept adequately informed on all developments, as they were well served by innumerable spies and informers.

In March 1798, the lord lieutenant, by proclamation, declared the whole of Ireland to be in a state of rebellion.

In 1797, Thomas Reynolds, whose wife was a sister of Mrs. Tone, joined the Leinster Directory of the United Irishmen, and, in March 1798, being already a government informer, he betrayed the members of the Leinster Directory. In consequence, fifteen of their members were arrested at one of their meetings. Lord Edward Fitzgerald was not present and went into hiding, but another informer, for money, disclosed his whereabouts to the authorities, and he was fatally wounded while resisting arrest.

In Ulster, the Rev. Steele Dickson was arrested, and at the last moment, Robert Simms, who had been foremost in advocating violent action, resigned for reasons which he never revealed.

These shattering blows delayed but did not halt the plans of the brave but foolhardy remnant of the leadership.

In the South, there was not wide general support for the Insurrection, although there was a serious rising in Wexford, with early, and dangerous, successes.

In Coleraine, John Galt's diary gives some information about the position in Ulster:

June 6th 1798—The rebels are in possession of Ballymoney and we are every hour waiting for an attack. Self-preservation is lawful, and I and my companions in grace are ready to say "Here we are prepared to stand up for our lives and families, our King and country, when called upon".

June 14th—We feared our chapel was going to be made a temporary barrack for new troops, but he who is worshipped in it directed the authorities to the Town Hall. Today we heard of the "Battle of Antrim" where 200 men were killed, and of the death of Lord O'Neill, who was piked by his own tenants while attempting to dissuade them from their mad enterprise, as well as the occupation of Ballymena by the insurgents.

June 25—This has been an awful day in Coleraine. The first execution here has taken place. Some years ago the deluded individual was a member of our society in Ballymoney, but the way was too narrow and the society too strict. He forsook both, and found society more congenial. But alas! he has this day atoned with his life to the injured laws of his country.

July 1—Another unhappy rebel was executed today. These are the first executions in Coleraine since it was the county town some 200 years ago.

July 9—Two more were hanged yesterday. Although strangers my soul was deeply concerned for their salvation. All access to the prison having been cut off, I was going up to my room when the keeper of the prison came and said "Lieut. Colonel Small has given orders to admit you". I received the message with joy, and went to the dungeon at 8 o'clock, and remained till 9 o'clock next morning, and he was in the enjoyment of pardoning love six hours before he died. The other appeared truly penitent, and I have hope also in his death. While I was with the prisoners on one occasion one of the officers came in to read the sentence of the court-martial on some of them who had been tried—to some flogging, to some transportation, and to one he said "And you are to be hanged" We had a solemn time when we got the prison to ourselves.

July 19—I am just returned from a last inverview with one who is being taken off to Ballymoney to be hanged. The idea of being hung up as a spectacle to his family and connections, and in the town of his birth, is worse to him than death itself.

Lord O'Neill, killed by his own tenants, was the John O'Neill who had won in the County Antrim election of 1783 and whose silk election badges had borne the words "Independent Interest. O'Neill and Liberty." He had always supported reforms.

In Coleraine, which escaped attack, the Somersetshire Regiment and the Manx Fencibles were stationed, as well as local yeomanry such as the Coleraine Cavalry and the Macosquin Infantry. Hugh Lyle served in the yeomanry. After the death of Lord O'Neill, County Antrim Yeomanry were also quartered in Coleraine.

New commanders had been hastily appointed to replace Dickson and Simms, Henry Monroe taking over in County Down and Henry Joy McCracken in County Antrim, the latter dating his proclamation "The First Year of Liberty 6th June 1798." The capture of Ballymena and Ballymoney, both towns in County Antrim, were initial successes for McCracken, but an informer disclosed his plans to Colonel Nugent, whose arrival in command of regular troops soon reversed the position.

Henry Joy McCracken was captured, tried, and sentenced to be hanged but was offered his life in exchange for the name of the commander he had replaced. He refused. At the foot of the scaffold, the offer was repeated. Again he refused and was immediately hanged, his honorable conduct serving as a reproach to too many United Irishmen who either enriched themselves or saved their lives by betraying fellow members of their society.

In the same year, other United Irishmen were also hanged, but sixty-four of those imprisoned and likely to be executed, led by Samuel Neilson, son of a Presbyterian minister in County Down and one of the original members of the United Irishmen in Belfast, saved their lives by giving the government full details of the United Irishmen's revolutionary plans and of their negotiations with France, accepting the government's condition that they should also emigrate to some country not at war with England. Among the sixty-four were Thomas Addis, Emmet and O'Connor, who was so skilled in dissimulation that his Irish and English Whig friends were certain he was loyal until the insurrection broke out. Samuel Neilson, the ringleader, in his betrayal is said to have told a government official, "I hold in my hand every muscle, sinew, nay, fibre of the internal organisation—of every ramification—of the United Irishmen, and I will make it as plain as the palm of my hand if our terms are complied with.''

In all Ireland the poorly armed rebels under uncoordinated command were soon suppressed, it being impossible for them, however brave, to succeed against regular troops, sometimes mounted.

By the end of June 1798, the insurrection was over, and Westminster appointed Lord Cornwallis Commander in Chief and Lord Lieutenant. An experienced soldier and a humane man, he issued a general pardon as soon as conditions in the country made this possible.

Napoleon had left for Egypt a few days before the insurrection broke out, taking with him 50,000 men.

However, in August and September, the French belatedly dispatched two small expeditions, which at that stage could achieve nothing but fruitless bloodshed.

The first, under Humbert, landed at Killala and with some local support scored successes against yeomanry and militia before being defeated by regular soldiers under the command of Lord Cornwallis. Matthew Tone, who had been doing well in India until he became enmeshed in his brother's ambitious schemes, was captured, court-martialed, and hanged.

The second, with Wolfe Tone on board, wearing the uniform of a French officer and calling himself General Smith, aimed at a landing in Ulster, but a British squadron met them not far from Lough Swilly, and most of the French ships were captured. Wolfe Tone was recognized, arrested, tried, and condemned to be hanged, drawn, and quartered. This horrible fate he escaped by committing suicide the night before his execution. He cut his throat with a penknife.

The following year, 1799, in France, a bloodless coup, brilliantly engineered by Talleyrand, made Napoleon its first consul, with a sovereign's powers and dictatorial control over France's foreign policy. This change, which received popular support, was a step away from the tenets of the revolution and brought France an unrealized step nearer to the eventual restoration of the monarchy.

At Westminster, with the insurrection over, England was faced once again with the problem that had plagued her down the centuries, ever since the king of Leinster had followed Henry II to France to pressurise him into accepting his unsought allegiance. What was to be done about Ireland?

In 1703, when the union with Scotland was under consideration, the Irish Parliament had asked Westminster for a similar union but had been refused.

Now Pitt, the prime minister, came to the conclusion that union was essential in the interests of both countries.

The insurrection had highlighted the fact that Ireland, if independent, might endanger England's existence, while the Irish Parliament had proved itself an obstacle to reforms that Pitt considered both desirable and necessary.

In Ireland, the union had some supporters, but there was also bitter opposition to it. However, even among those leading statesmen most opposed to union, there was no desire for a complete separation from England. As early as 1789, the year of the French Revolution, Fitzgibbon had warned the Irish House of Commons, "The only security of your liberty is your connection with Great Britain, and gentlemen who risk breaking the connection must make up their minds to a Union. God forbid I should ever see that day, but if ever a day on which a separation may come, I shall not hesitate to embrace a Union rather than a separation." Gratton also, heartbroken at the prospect of union, still considered that the interests of Ireland and England were inseparable.

In order to force union through the divided Irish Parliament, the usual weapons of bribery by money, titles, and lucrative posts were freely used.

In 1800, the Act of Union was passed and received royal assent.

The Irish Parliament ceased to exist, and henceforward, for more than 100 years, all Ireland was governed from London.

9 / 1801—First Year of the Union

As a result of the insurrection, Ireland had lost her bright prospects of increasing prosperity, reforms, and greater independence under her own Parliament.

Ulster, the center of the revolt, suffered from many scars.

In addition to the mourning for those executed or killed in the fighting, transportations and flights accounted for many more men lost to their families, with the practical certainty in many cases of no return, thus increasing the sorrows and anxieties in many Ulster homes.

The army's punitive destruction had also brought much hardship; for example, the thriving town of Ballymoney had been totally destroyed, all that remained of it being uninhabitable ruins. An exception to the general business depression was Coleraine, which had suffered no damage in the insurrection. Its enterprising business community continued to prosper.

Nor were there at that stage any of the later benefits of Westminster rule that transformed the industrial situation, removed all the legal disabilities of both Presbyterians and Catholics, and transformed the province from the most disaffected to the most loyal in Ireland.

Mr. Pitt had planned that the Act of Union should be immediately followed by reforms, but when he approached the King, royal assent being necessary for all legislation, he found him obdurately convinced that his agreement to further reforms would be an infringement of his coronation oath.

Fitzgibbon, influential member of the Irish Parliament who was opposed to reforms, has been blamed for suggesting this idea to the King, but may it not have also been that Fitzgibbon's suggestion was reinforced by the old king's recollection of how he had ensured the passing of the Catholic Relief Act of 1793, the most substantial measure of Catholic emancipation ever yet enacted, and of the persuasive eloquence of Wolfe Tone, with his convincing protestations of loyalty, at a time when he was already plotting treason.

However it may have been, King George III, recently recovered after a period of insanity, clung obstinately to his belief, and Mr. Pitt, with the knowledge that too strong opposition might endanger the King's mental health, reluctantly had to accept defeat and abandon his reform plans during the King's lifetime. Nevertheless, Pitt, one of Britain's great prime ministers, considered these reforms essential and himself morally bound by the hopes he had raised in talks with Catholic representatives held earlier when he had not anticipated any particular difficulty over Catholic emancipation. Since he could not carry the reforms he took the honorable course of resigning in spite of many appeals not to do so. Some other members of his Cabinet resigned also, including the Ulsterman Lord Castlereagh, who, as young Robert Stewart, had won his first election to Parliament in 1790.

It is fair to recall also that the French Revolution and the Irish insurrection had produced a violent widespread reaction against reforms among the general population of both England and Ireland, so that the continuing efforts of the Whigs and other reformers met with little support. It has been estimated that these two events and, in particular, the revolution in France delayed reforms, which had previously been making promising progress, by forty years.

The view was held then by many people, and is still held now, that had reforms been granted more readily, the insurrection would never have occurred, as gratitude and loyalty would have replaced resentment and desperation. This may well be so, but there is no certainty. Unfortunately, history also supplies instances of sudden liberty leading to excesses, like suddenly acquired wealth (which is a form of liberty), sudden liberty producing insatiable demands accompanied by violence and sudden wealth, instead of benefiting its recipient, resulting in ruin through crazy spending and foolish speculation.

These facts should not be regarded as support for injustice or the failure to remedy it but as a necessary recognition of the very real difficulties that face a government in a divisive situation of controversy and danger such as that which confronted the British government in 1800.

10 / 1802—The Rev. C. Vaughan Sampson Surveys the County of Londonderry

This statistical survey "with observations on the means of Improvement" was published in 1802 by the Dublin Society. It certainly bears testimony to the energy, thoroughness, and hard work of its author. The statistics are innumerable, the information most varied, and the views and recommendations of Mr. Vaughan Sampson illuminating. Some of the closely packed material is of general interest, and, therefore, some brief extracts are given here.

The book opens with a fulsome dedication to a General Vallancey, followed by thanks to some of those who helped with information, several of whom have been, or will be, mentioned elsewhere in this book.

> To my most judicious and well informed friend James Acheson Esq., I am indebted for communications on the subject of bleaching and for the pains he took in reducing and embellishing the map of the county.
> To several other gentlemen I am under obligation, and in particular John Crombie, Esq., James Scott Esq., Hugh Lyle Esq., ...

Then follows some information about some of the houses and properties in the county, which emphasizes the continuing importance of tree planting.

> Jackson Hall demesne contains some well grown timber. The situation is not without scenery. The mansion is of brick in a peculiar style, somewhat Chinese as to windows and railings. It is, in the absence of the proprietor, tenanted by one of our worthiest and most hospitable country gentlemen and farmers, Mr. Hugh Lyle.

Mr. Samuel Lyle had done something considerable in the planting of trees before he disposed of his place at Greenfield to Mr. Bennet. This gentleman[1] has lately made several additions to his property, particularly in the mountainous district of Sluggady (Thief's mountain). His exertions in lime burning and reclaiming are suitable to the spirit and activity which characterizes all his pursuits.

The improvement of Willsboro' brings this comfort to its present possessor, that whatever rude outlines had been sketched by his ancester, the whole of the decoration is a creation of his own. As a planter, Mr. Scott stands nearly in the same eminent point of view as he ranks among our farmers. According to my information from the gentleman, trees can be had from Scotland at 5s per thousand equal to any from Derry or Portglenone, which sell at 6s to 8s per thousand. . . . . . What an addition if through all this tract we had resident and enterprising landlords. In this respect Mr. Scott has shown that not only the gentleman, but the cottager can ornament the country.

Oaks, the neat lodge of Mr. James Acheson, is a spot of singular beauty. The woods of Lord Blanquiere have partly been saved from the hatchet by the good taste of Mr. Acheson. The windings and alternate rapids and levels of the Fahan, the jutting rocks, green banks, fringes of trees, natural and planted, the near scenery of a well ordered garden, immediately contrasted by bold rocks and rugged outlines—all this is calculated to make the external of this mansion as captivating, as the inmates are estimable

Mr. Cunningham of Spring-hill has an excellent demesne; it produces almost all manner of crops. I remarked to Mr. Cunningham that I saw no flax; his reply was that management would be very troublesome at home, and if the crop was auctioned on foot, the Buyers would only be of the poorest classes, and such as he could not bring himself to press for payment, without which no payment would be had. I hope that Mr. Cunningham will find some expedient to reconcile his interests with humanity; there is surely no better crop in a country where rents are paid by the wheel and the loom, rather than by the plough.

I have heard lately of a most benevolent action done by one of His Lordship's[2] principal tenants, Mr. McCausland of Fruit-hill having advanced money to his labourers in the late distressing times, found that it was more in the wish, than in the power, of these poor men to repay. Mr. McCausland, pitying their situation, drew his pen over their accounts, and ordered them to begin again. What a noble contrast to some other transactions!

. . . . . Lord Bristol remitted half a year's rent to his poorer tenants in the late dearth.

Mr. Stapleton lets his land extremely reasonable. I have seen some excellent grounds let by him at one guinea, when those of the same quality on the opposite bank of the river are let at two guineas.

On Mr. Ponsonby's estate the leases are some for 21 years some for 71 and three lives; the size of farms varies from 10 to 200 acres. The tenantry on this property are in the first class of farmers, and might justly be called a yeomanry. . . . . At Cross 200 acres are let for £57.

Some information is also given regarding the Houses of Small Farmers and Cottiers.

The best are divided into two apartments, the inner of which is without a fireplace, and serves for the sleeping and storing room . . . In countries where stone is convenient, it is used in building them; in general the cement is only mud. These are cold in their nature, and not the less so, when, according to the usual plan the back door is exactly opposite to the front door.

There is remarkable distinction in the plan of the houses on the Antrim side of the Bann. The fireplace is advanced some feet from the gable wall, so that the persons of the family can nearly sit round it. It seems to mark a difference in the time or colonists of the two counties. I did not perceive any inconvenience as to smoak in these last mentioned houses; at least not so great as in the common chimnies on the Derry side. Very many of these are without any brace, and consequently the house is in such a state that the eye is galled and the looks and apparel of the inhabitants greatly sullied; besides this every article of food, especially butter, is nauseous except to those who, from long habit, have had their palates habituated to such flavour.

There is nothing worthier of the beneficient attention of proprietors, than the erection of such cottages, as would reconcile cheapness and comfort. These would serve as models; and without example, what signifies preaching? A few deals cut into four leaves, and then sawn into laths, with brown paper pasted over the vacant places; these connected by four pieces of wood, two of which should be against the wall, the other two joined at an angle, and projected beyond the current of the smoak about four feet; this is all the contrivance necessary to keep a cottage from smoak.

Some comments are also made on the habits, maxims, customs, and character of the people.

The people of the county of Derry, like those of Down and Antrim, afford a striking contrast to those of the more southern counties
Much of this superiority is to be attributed, among other inestimable benefits, to the staple manufacture; particularly so with regard to females.
Employments exercised indoors, however they may take away from the robust structure of the man, conduce greatly to the good appearance of women.
As to the courtesy of both sexes, it is remarkably in their favour. When you enter the house, though the family be seated on low stools, someone is instantly desired *"to fetch down a chair"* from the inner apartment. This apartment, in other instances, is so far considered the place of reception, that even in cold weather, the visitant is desired to *"walk up"* to the room, though perhaps without fire or fireplace. The terms ''Up'' and ''down'' have no reference to stairs, for all the houses are but of one story.
There is a remarkable vein of piety pervading all their phrases for ex-

ample, no orderly person says positively *"I will do this or that"* but qualifies this intention by adding "With the help of God" "If I be spared" "If it be the Lord's Will" or some such expression.

There is a strong turn towards predestination . . . In many cases however they seem to give little faith to human sagacity; and for this reason, rather than for want of affection, they sometimes leave each other superstitiously to the will of God, instead of obeying the true dictates of religion in applying for medicine or advice. . . . . it is very certain, when anyone ails nothing can be sick but the heart . . . . The specific is whiskey, either to keep it *off the heart*, or *strike it from the heart* . .

Tobacco is also reckoned as so essential to health that many a poor and hungry labourer prefers a *quid* or a *smoke* without a dinner, to a dinner without a *quid* or a *smoke*. The beggars also, with starving children, relying on your sympathy in this respect, think it advisable to ask for "a penny to buy tobacco" rather than to buy bread.

At the Scotch weddings, the groom and his party vie with the other youngsters, who shall gallop first to the house of the bride; nor is this feat of gallantry always without danger, for in every village through which they are expected, they are received with shots of pistols and guns: these discharges, intended to honour the parties, sometimes promote their disgrace, if to be tumbled in the dirt on such an occasion, can be called a dishonour. At the bride's house is prepared a bowl of broth to be the reward for the victor in the race, which race is therefore called the running for the *brose*.

The Irish wedding is somewhat different, especially in the mountainous districts. However suitable the match, it is but a lame exploit, and even an affront, if the groom does not first run away with the bride. After a few days carousal among the groom's friends, the *weddingers* move towards the bride's country, on which occasion, not only every relative, but every poor fellow who aspires to be the *well wisher* of either party, doth bring with him *a bottle of whiskey,* or the price of a bottle, to the rendez-vous. After this second edition of matrimonial hilarity, the bride and groom proceed quietly to their designed home, and forgetting all at once their romantic frolic, settle quietly down to the ordinary occupations of life.

Such are the difficulties for providing for offspring that mothers in the poorer, and even in the better, conditions of life, endeavour to suckle their children for three or four years. In the yarn market of Coleraine, I once heard a boy four years old call out to his mother to sit down and give him a suck.

The Synthian custom of feeding on blood has something like a revival in the mountains of this country. I actually surprised the wretched inmates of a poor herdman's house, on one of my rambles through unfrequented parts: five children, with the father and mother, were eating blood, thickened by boiling, but without any addition. It was in the year 1800, when the people were nearly starving. God grant I may never again behold so overcoming a spectacle.

I have observed also that the character of my good countrymen is not without its share of superstition: for instance, in certain circumstances the cow is said to be elf-shot, in which case salt and water on three half pence, and a fairy's bullet (that is a petrified sea urchin found common in limestone) are an infallible remedy.

Bees must not be given away, but sold: otherwise neither giver nor taker will have *luck*.

Between the end of March and the beginning of April there are certain days, called borrowing days. The meaning is that March, when he fails in doing sufficient damage, borrows from April for that purpose: the old style continues still to be observed in all our rural calculations.

Virgil's husbandmen prayed for moist summers and dry winters. Our farmers most particularly desire a dry May and a *leaky* June. On this subject there is a rhyming proverb, and I love to record these verdicts of rural experience

> The farmer in May,
> Comes weeping away,
> He goes back in June
> And changes his tune

The meaning of which is that May is generally a cold month and the corn only lying down to *stool*; but in June, being refreshed by warm showers, it begins to rise off the stool or, in other words, to push forth its shoots; after which it appears more promising.

Tokens of weather observed by farmers:

When geese fly violently about, a storm of wind is expected.
When the ducks wash and dive in the ponds it is a sign of rain
When the dog eats couch grass (avenor elatior) or when his bowels
  give a guggling noise, wet weather is expected
When the gulls fly inland it is a sign of hard weather
When the barnacle flies from Lough Foyle to Lough Neagh it is a
  sign of an alteration in the weather.

Calves are liable to a disorder called the *strings*; it is a contraction of the muscular part of the abdomen, proceeding from acrid quality of the gastric juice, acting on the empty stomach. Nature intended that all young animals should take nourishment at frequent returns. Persons who heedlessly disregard this allow the calf food but twice in the day. This long interval of fasting, I found to be the cause of the disease: I lost many calves before I thought of this, but since I had my calves fed three or four times in the day, I have not had a single one attacked. The ignorant people drag with great force the hind and fore legs of the wretched little animal as soon as dropt to *prevent* the strings: they also say, the longer it remains without food at first, the more certain will be its exemption from all future disease; and to complete the misery of the young sufferer, they stuff its month with the dung of the mother, instead of allowing it her milk.

Unfortunately, space does not permit any further extracts from this interesting and informative survey of an area where, in past times, pearls were to be found in the rivers and when there was also Irish gold.

Notes

1. Samuel Lyle.
2. Lord Bristol.

11 / 1803—The Last Flicker of the Insurrection

In March 1802, the Treaty of Amiens ended England's war with France.

In Ireland, few leaders of the United Irishmen were still in the country, most of them having fled, been executed, transported, or required to emigrate as a condition of their lifesaving compact with the government.

In the summer of 1803, the war with France broke out again.

The resumed hostilities roused, among the remaining United Irishmen, fresh hopes of help from France, and Robert Emmett, a younger brother of one of the leaders of 1798, tried to rally the remnant of their organisation for a fresh rising.

Robert Emmett was an idealist, a brave and honorable man, but he was not a realist.

Ireland was still being governed under the Insurrection Act, and there was an amply supply of troops there.

Ulster was no longer interested, and the rest of the country had no stomach for revolt.

Napoleon, now in full control in France, had never believed that an invasion of Ireland had any hope of success. He was planning to invade England, so that the idea of help from France was simply a pipe dream.

The prospects of success for Robert Emmett were hopeless, and the attempt could only result in suffering and death for those who joined his

45

conspiracy. However, blind to this reality, he struggled on.

It was planned that on July 23 armed insurgents should meet in Dublin and seize Dublin Castle. To the dismay and horror of Emmett, his followers did not attack the castle but on their way there ran amok in the streets. The Chief Justice, Lord Kilwarden, driving with his daughter and a nephew, was dragged from his carriage and murdered in front of his daughter. His nephew was also murdered, and there were other killings. The revolt was of no practical importance and was easily suppressed.

In September, Robert Emmett was hanged, his pathetic, unnecessary, and really suicidal death resulting in his being revered as a martyr by Irish rebels of the future.

After this sad incident, Ireland embarked on a long period of political peace, such disorders as did occur being criminal acts or clashes of a sectarian nature, which were not in any sense political revolts.

12 / 1806—The County Londonderry General Election

By the union, Coleraine lost its separate representation and, in 1806, as part of the constituency of the county of Londonderry sent two members to Westminster. There were four candidates. Lord George Beresford and General Stewart stood as Tories against the Whig candidates The Hon. Colonel William Ponsonby and Samuel Lyle.

The Ponsonbys were a leading Whig family, supporting Catholic emancipation and other reforms. Colonel William Ponsonby's father, William Brabason Ponsonby, the first Baron Ponsonby, had been a member of the Irish Parliament. His better known uncle, George Ponsonby, was in 1806 Chancellor of Ireland and, from 1808 until his death in 1817, was the official leader of the Whig opposition at Westminster. The Ponsonby family owned property in County Londonderry, and Colonel William Ponsonby's brother, Richard, became Bishop of Londonderry.

Samuel Lyle, born in 1761, would appear to be the second son of Hugh Lyle and Eleanor Hyde, who lived at Greenfield near Coleraine until he sold his property. In 1806, he was High Sheriff of Fermanagh.

The Rev. Vaughan Sampson, author of the Londonderry Survey and Rector of Ahanloo in the county of Londonderry, was a Whig and an enthusiastic canvasser for Ponsonby and Lyle. During the election, an anonymous poem, set out below, casting ridicule on the Rev. Vaughan

46

Sampson, was circulated in the constituency. Beneath its amusing quips and insults lie the fears roused by the recent Insurrection, and the French attempts at invasion, which no doubt played some part in influencing voters:

Tune "Derry Down"

Many wonderful Tales in the Scriptures we're told
Of the Valorous Deeds of great SAMPSON of old,
How he minded a Lion no more than a Mouse,
And pull'd down the Philistines' Parliament House.

Derry Down &c.

But a Rival we've found for this Hero transcendant,
In Efforts and Wish his Superiors depend on't,
For of both our great Houses he wishes the fall,
The Lords and the Commons, KING, Council and All!

Derry Down &c.

Old SAMPSON when robb'd of his Wig and his Vision,
Was brought out for Philistine Mirth and Derision,
But so roughly he handled two lusty Stone Pillars,
That they reel'd like a Pig coming from the Distillers.

Derry Down &c.

But our modern SAMPSON, far higher his Aim,
Tho' blinded by Frenzy, more daring's his game,
Who, unaw'd by the Horrors of French Revolution,
Would shake the firm Pillars of our CONSTITUTION!!

Derry Down &c.

As a Donkey's Jawbone his great Ancestor us'd,
When his enemies sorely he batter'd and bruis'd,
So this mimicking Modern, with Visage of Brass,
Still wags 'gainst his Foes the Jawbones of an Ass.

Derry Down &c.

So far there exists Similarities rare,

Yet a diff'rence we'll shew 'twixt this wonderful Pair,
In their Diet, at least, there's a difference small,
For that liv'd on Honey, and this upon Gall.

Derry Down &c.

In vain thro' old Chronicles all we may look,
To find the old SAMPSON indited a Book,
A County's Affairs he ne'er turn'd topsy turvy,
By scribbling of Gath a "Statistical Survey".

Derry Down &c.

47

While our Modern, most LEARN'DLY, gives us to know,
That mountains are HIGH, and that Vallies are LOW,
That Meadows are GREEN, and oh, Wonderful fellow!
That Fields of ripe Oats, for the most part are YELLOW.

Derry Down &c.

How Ganders will cackle when Rain is at hand,
How (gooselike) the Farmers the Note understand,
How the Poor dine at One, when Rich are at Lunch,
How the Rectors drink Port, and the Curates drink Punch.

Derry Down &c.

And a thousand queer things, which would make you quite wise,
Could Wisdom be gain'd from a Budget of Lies,
There's the price of Estates, and of Salmon, and Eels,
of Brooms by the Dozen, and Turf per the Creels.

Derry Down &c.

His Ancestors once dealt in Firebrands, we hear,
And burnt all the Country around far and near,
So this modern mimicking Dealer in Fibs,
Would kindle a Blaze in old DERRY with Squibbs.

Derry Down &c.

But vain his endeavour to kindle the Fire,
They blaze to be hooted, explode to expire,
Extort from young PONSY a simpering Smile,
But for Wit will not pass, no, not e'en with SAM LYLE

Derry Down &c.

Ye curious in Monsters who wish to behold,
This wonder of wonderful Wights, new or old,
The journey is short, and you quickly may view,
The foul-venom'd Snake in his Den—AHANLOO

Derry Down &c.
Coleraine, November 21, 1806

To the Gentlemen, Clergy and Freeholders of the City and County of Londonderry:
Gentlemen,
      That the present situation of this County calls for the exertion of every elector who wishes to see it rescued from the condition of a close borough, is a fact, and you know it. To rescue it from this degradation, it is indispensable that every individual on the present occasion should stand forth with the utmost energy of his character, and the fullest extent of his means—I feel

this in common with a great proportion of the Independent Interest of your County, and at their suggestion have offered myself a Candidate for the honour representing you in Parliament. I must likewise frankly inform you, that I have been led to this step, by the particular request of Colonel Ponsonby and his friends, by whom I shall be supported with all their influence.

Should you elect me I shall endeavour to do my duty. If you do not my consolation shall be that I have aimed at rendering you an important service, and satisfied with this, I shall resume my normal occupation, convinced that I shall not have forfeited the esteem of any respectable Man, by having come forward in defence of your independence.

> I have the honour to be
> Gentlemen
> Your most faithful and devoted servant,
> Samuel Lyle
> Londonderry Nov. 1st, 1806

Samuel Lyle's letter, as well as those of the other candidates, were published in the Belfast *Newsletter*.

Lord George Beresford's relied mainly on his family's 200-year connection with the county and their past services to it. On actual policy for the future, he was silent, merely saying "With reference to our general policies I know them to be congenial, particularly congenial to the distinguished loyalty of the County of Londonderry."

After a close contest, the Tory candidates won the election.

After the election, William Ponsonby, thanking the voters, declared he intended to petition the House of Commons, as he believed that he had not lost through lack of support, but should have come second, and believed that a number of the votes against him were from people not legally entitled to vote, a situation that would not have been unusual in an election in those days. Whether he did petition the House of Commons is not known.

13 / 1809—From Jackson Hall, Coleraine, Mrs. Hannah Greg
Writes to Mrs. Hannah Rathbone on the Seventeenth of July

Dear Hannah,

It is in vain my dear friend, for Bessie to wish every day to write to you, there is so much for the young ones to be shown, and they are in such constant requisition amongst their multitude of cousins, that they have little time for retirement, and now Bessie is in her Aunt Warre's native scenery and surrounded by her family, she feels she has many claims on her pen, where every word is truly interesting, for though Mrs. Warre has lived much in separation she has a faithful and affectionate heart. Alas! separation only serves to increase attachment and to be perpetually ascertaining its strength, and no wonder she is attached to her own family, for in the world in which she has mixed so much she can seldom have met their superiors, generally speaking. Mrs. Batt is a lovely woman, Mrs. Lyle very amiable and engaging, with seven strikingly handsome children grown up almost, and Mr. Lyle is one of the best of men, has exemplified that honour, integrity and good sense will stand any ground, for during the rebellion and various bad times few could have stood so firm and high, a loyal officer and impartial magistrate, the protection of the oppressed, especially the catholics. He has been allowed at all times to keep his middle course, and is still like a demi-god in the country, which an accident which nearly proved fatal to him last year evinced. But I must not begin to describe; we will hope to tell you all at Quarry Bank, and you will kindly wish to hear something of ourselves. I can indeed describe little of the country of the journey, for I sit still while the rest indulge a curiosity which I have so amply possessed that it requires something more than prudence to repress and deny, it requires inability. I rather think I told your Mother at Glasgow that we then heard all Mrs. Greg's family, gay people from the South (a more distinct race from the Northern Irish than any two kingdoms), were come here. This appeared so formidable and so different from becoming weary and sick among old friends, that we instantly decided to dash into the Highlands and sail from Campbeltown down to Ballycastle. It is well we did not, for I hear it is here considered a dangerous passage, but we rested at a lovely cottage of our sister Batt's a few days, and then proceeded on the scene of peace and goodness, where I am at home and petted and nursed by all the family, who have always been particularly attached to me, and I hope to obtain strength for the formidable visit to Ballymenoch, Mrs. C. Greg's. I should have considered all my trouble and anxiety were compensated on seeing Mr. S.G.[1] such a different being to what he left home; he looks years younger, and in such delight that it enforces gaiety even in me and we insensibly talk and laugh like 15 years ago, the grown up children only helping us to remember the lapse. The pleasure and affection testified at seeing us and our children is very engaging and gratifying and I am pleased to see Mr. Greg proud of his own children, even among

those he has been accustomed to consider as standards. I sometimes almost wonder at him having foregone a country so delightful for one where his attachments were so few and small, but in many respects it is more alluring to visit than to live in it. I think I should prefer Scotland for a country to any one. I have dreaded the state of my health in impairing his enjoyment but in persevering sitting when not standing I creep on tolerably but in travelling has so terribly disagreed with me, as the weather so cold. It has been beautiful for views and exercise, but an east or north wind has been a constant enemy to me in an open carriage, and I have not yet left off fires in my room. Tomorrow ten or twelve young ones go off to the Giant's Causeway and I suppose they will afterwards go to Derry. All which time I will rest with two or three sisters. I find I have seized on a letter Bessie has begun to her Aunt Warre which I am very vexed at, as the writing will be a loss to her, as the room is to me. I write what first comes into my head and at what times I can, so fear the different piecings will scarce be intelligible, but I know you will excuse me. I looked so pale and tired that my friends have sent me up to lie down, and there is my rest to think of and to speak to dear Green Bank, that scene of peace and love and virtue. This is also a peaceful scene, but Irish scenes though so striking and alluring to the young especially, are not so sound and do not bear probing, for I believe the intercourse with lower ranks of housekeeping with regard to principle, still more with regard to cleanliness, is full of mortification, and in all ranks that very openess of heart and warm kindness of manners, so delightful to strangers and always so agreeable certainly lead to living too much in common, and to inevitable dissipation. I am afraid of my young people admiring Ireland too much, for all its agreements and delights are prominent and laid out before them, and they will not have time to discover or penetrate its disadvantages, yet even the conversation of these most engaging young people is so mingled with prejudice that I depend upon well educated young people remarking them rather than adopting them, at least if they can be pointed out to them without fostering a critic spirit, of which I have a great dread in young people. My letter will be all shapes. Give my best love to all. If you are so good as to write instantly, please to direct to Hugh Lyle, Coleraine, where we will be ten or twelve days longer.
Hannah Greg
of Quarry Bank,
Cheshire

1809—Bessie Greg's unfinished undated letter to her aunt, Mrs. Warre.

My dearest Aunt Warre,
    I intended to have written to Ellen, but as she never was in Ireland, she cannot enter into the delights of it, and a letter from me when I have grown a little soberer may be more welcome. We left Glasgow of Thursday, got to Girvan, slept there, got to Port Patrick at one the next day, had a delightful passage of three hours and a half. We sat on deck and were not the least

sick. We had a specimen of Irish posting, not the most favourable, from Donghadee, for they galloped us down the hills as if they would break our necks, and the harness had to be mended three times in the first mile. We overtook my Uncle and Aunt C. and Aunt Mary on the road just at Bally-menoch, and my Uncle and Aunt Batt a little further. I cannot tell how delighted I am to get to Ireland, and with everyone and everything in it. I was determined to be the first one who landed, if possible, and I was. This is the sweetest spot I was ever in

Hannah Greg (née Lightbody) was the wife of Samuel Greg, son of Thomas Greg and Elizabeth Hyde. The Gregs were a Scottish family, one of whose members settled in Belfast in 1693.

Samuel Greg of Quarrybank in Cheshire was a merchant, and in religion the family were Unitarians.

Mrs. Warre, Mrs. Batt, and Mrs. Lyle were all sisters of Samuel Greg and aunts of his daughter Bessie.

Samuel and Hannah Greg and their daughter Bessie were staying at Jackson Hall with Hugh Lyle and his wife Sarah Greg.

Jackson Hall was built in 1668 by the Jackson family, which came to Ireland in the reign of Charles I and exercised great power and influence in the county of Londonderry for a long period. Later on, Jackson Hall was known as the Manor House and became the home of H. T. Barrie, M.P., and later still that of Mr. D. Hall Christie, C.B.E., D.L., a mayor of Coleraine. Toward the end of the twentieth century, Jackson Hall was demolished, and Coleraine County Hall was built on the site.

Hannah Rathbone (née Hannah Mary Reynolds) was the wife of William Rathbone of Greenbank, Liverpool.

14 / 1813—William Rathbone Writes to his Wife, Bessie (née Greg), From "Oaks" near Londonderry

July 30th 1813
Oaks

My Dearest Bessie,

The family are all gone to bed, but I must devote a short space and reply to your letter of the 23rd inst. brought me from Coleraine by Mr. Lyle. It does indeed give me pain to see your letter written with such constant feelings of disappointment and self-reproach, not because I do not wish your whole heart laid before me, it will be my great pleasure to try and wait to possess your heart and thoughts, so that even in a letter you can open them to me. I wish you, however, to feel cheerful, to acknowledge to your own heart that you are my beloved invaluable friend, that none other could be the true wife you are. You are not perfection, it is not the lot of humanity to be so, but in the eyes of your husband you approach nearer it than anyone he knows, except his mother. You have not gone through the severe but effectual school of sorrow that she has, I hope you never will, but that her experience and example will render it unnecessary. Do not dwell too much on what you consider your deficiencies. This weakens the mind. I cannot do better than repeat my mother's advice to you 'do not let us mistake constitutional melancholy or timidity for contrition, the past is gone and can only be useful to us as regulating our future conduct'. I wish few had as little reason to regret the past as you have, and if during your marriage, your husband has rendered the right path difficult to you, upon whose shoulders does the burden rest? But I must not go on with the subject. In three weeks more I hope to see my Bessie again, my heart, I might also say my eyes fill with the thought. I am thankful that the future time of our stay will not be on my ccount. We are now among your relations, they are all kind and excellent, but they are not my Bessie. I am urging your father to stay four days instead of two at Coleraine. My motive is perfectly pure. At another time I should have enjoyed the visit very much, I know I shall enjoy it greatly, but my heart bounds back with increasing impetuosity to be at home, yet I do wish your father to appear at ease, and to be devoted to your aunts at Coleraine, and it will be soothing relief to the widowed heart of Mrs. Lyle who is leaving Jackson Hall in three weeks. Although Mrs. Mary Greg is wonderfully recovered, yet I think it is very possible that different circumstances may prevent your father being in Ireland during her life, so that something renders it very desirable that the visit should not be cut short so as to give anybody pain. At Belfast I have no motive for delay, whenever your father can leave his relatives I shall feel thankful to feel myself on the way home. Let me just add that a considerable deal of the delay through the journey has arisen from your fathers desire that Robert and myself should not miss seeing any curiosity in the country. The journey was taken on our account. I hope I shall ever retain a grateful recollection, but let me not be thought to have been wholly the cause of the extension of the time. We are just setting out on an excursion, so that I have only time to beg you will say how much I feel obliged to my mother for her letter.

Mr. Greg and Robert are gone on an excursion to meet us at Coleraine, and tomorrow I take Elizabeth Lyle and her cousin home. By the way I think there is some danger of her not continuing E. Lyle, Mr. Hunter seems very attentive to her. I am sorry to have been detained here, as I should have liked to have spent the Sunday at Jackson Hall. Everything here is tranquil and beautiful. Mr. & Mrs. Acheson are most pleasing and excellent. The trees before my window, the sound of the water, the situation of the Oaks altogether carry me strongly to Quarry Bank, but my Bessie is not here, not one of the family, and I feel glad to have retreated to my room to let my thoughts wander to you, to breathe my wish as a prayer for your happiness. I received your welcome letter of the 26th just as we were setting forth to Buncrana, the place that formerly belonged to your grandfather. We had a pleasant day and a fine view of the extensive Lough and surrounding hills. I thought you knew your father better than to expect me to mention any time for our return. I said in one of my letters that by the 20th of this month I trusted we might be at home. I see no reason at all to alter the day. Your father's present idea is to be in Belfast by the end of the week. He calculated on five days being sufficient there, or four days hard travelling, adding one for getting over the water may, without any delay on the road, bring us home.

Most affectionately yours,
William Rathbone

"Oaks" where William Rathbone was staying with Mr. and Mrs. Acheson when he wrote this letter, was originally the property of the Acheson family.

In 1787, Samuel Lyle, born in 1761, second son of Hugh Lyle and Eleanor Hyde, married Esther Acheson. They had three sons and two daughters.

Esther Acheson's brother James Acheson married Sarah Lyle, sister of Samuel. At her brother's death, Esther Lyle inherited the "Oaks" property, and, thus, it passed to the Lyle family, its next owner being Acheson Lyle, second son of Samuel and Esther. Samuel Lyle died in 1815.

Since 1809, when Mrs. Hannah Greg had written from Jackson Hall to Mrs. Hannah Rathbone, Bessie Greg had married William Rathbone, becoming Mrs. Hannah Rathbone's daughter-in-law.

Four days after writing to his wife from "Oaks," William Rathbone wrote to her again, this time from Jackson Hall.

Jackson Hall.
August 3rd 1813.

My Dearest Bessie,

From the place of which I have heard more almost than any other I am enabled to write to you, having seen all the cousins of whom every tongue speaks praise, yet I am unable to say I know your cousins. Many circumstances will make me glad to leave the place. They are all feeling that in a few weeks they will be deprived of their house, and I am not justified in intruding on feelings which are sacred to all but their most intimate friends. It makes me feel in the way, but I have seen enough to make me look forward with pleasure to making their acquaintance at a future day under different circumstances. Your Aunt Mary is wonderfully better. Mrs. Lyle is very low,

54

though I believe her health is pretty good. Elizabeth is the weather glass to her mother, but if I am not mistaken has many causes for anxiety. Ellen has a bad cold but that does not prevent her exerting herself for the amusement of her friends. Mary has been ill for some time, but is better, though still languid, and not in good spirits. Sally is in good health and spirits and constantly alive and seems to think of everybody but herself. Hugh fell out of curricle and sprained his ankle, which has confined him to the house for the last fortnight. He still can only walk short distances and, having caught cold has been today a good deal on the bed. Thomas and Samuel are both well with all the glee of health and youth. Your father is very well and Robert. This finishes the bill of health and of the house. Aug. 4th. We shall leave this place on Friday and hope to reach Belfast on Monday next, probably to stay all the week. I shall write very shortly from here, for I should really inflict you with melancholy if I were to indulge in thought. This is a beautiful spot, and it feels like the breaking up of the family, leaving the house. All are probably entering on the chequered scene of life without a head to guide them. Everything recalls our heavy loss. They are ignorant how truly I sympathise in their present feelings. Hugh's heart and disposition are excellent, but although much that a mother could feel thankful for, yet not everything that the arduous post a head of a family requires. The loss of a parent, of a father particularly, at this time of life is incalculable. None but a person who has experienced it and not had resolution to look to himself to supply the loss, can properly estimate it. Indeed my love, I do feel very uncomfortable about myself. I am like a sieve, much good, much information has been poured into me, but none of it remains. I fear it is the unalterable formation of my mind, the heavy burden will rest upon you. When I return home, I intend, if I can have resolution to act upon it, to make an effort to try whether any change is to be made, in which I trust to look to you for support, and in place of giving way to ideal deficiences you must exert yourself for me. You know that nature has been bountiful to you, and till your husband clogged your powers you had to acknowledge that you had properly cultivated your advantages. He hopes not to be so great a bar to your advancement if he should be convinced of his own capacity, and our children, yet unborn, will thank you for the effort. At no place in Ireland have I been so pleased as at the Oaks. Mr. Acheson was in pretty good health, and is a scholar and a gentleman. Mrs. Acheson is very pleasing, and they have with them a Miss Long, also very pleasing and intelligent. Mrs. Acheson begs her love to you. I think if you were to send them an invitation that they could come and spend a short time with you in Liverpool. If you think well of it, I wish you would write Mrs. Acheson, asking them and Miss Long to spend a short time with you, if at the music meeting it would be more pleasant, as there will be a leisure time and Mr. A. is very fond of music. Mary Lyle has been singing every evening. I hear nothing of your practicing. When I come home I shall seriously ask you whether you consider keeping up your music as incompatible with your other duties. If it is, I shall not have a word to say, and will make up my mind to the loss, but if you should decide otherwise, I shall be glad and trust that it will be not necessary to say more about your practising singing and playing, as you should really decide and act upon it. I think it has a bad effect on your mind. I am sure it had on mine. I must finish this letter. Ellen has a necklace and cross of bog oak for you which you will value.

Your most affectionate husband,
William Rathbone.

Hugh Lyle had died on March 20, 1812, and, in consequence, the family had to leave Jackson Hall.

The eldest son, Hugh, was twenty-one in 1812 and, in 1813, married Harriet Cromie, daughter of John Cromie and Anne Thompson.

William Rathbone had been twenty-two when his own father died in 1809.

Elizabeth Lyle did not marry Mr. Hunter but T. Ovens in 1815. Her sisters also married in due course: Ellen, Major Martin; Mary, Colonel Graydon; Sarah, Ross T. Smith.

After leaving Jackson Hall, the Lyles moved about for some time, leasing houses in the area. Eventually, Hugh Lyle built Knocktarna about 1827 near Coleraine, which became the family's permanent home.

After 1813—William and Bessie Rathbone.

The Rathbones of Liverpool were a prominent family, originally Quakers but later becoming Unitarians, wealthy merchants of independent character and liberal view.

William Rathbone, who died in 1789, lived at a time of worldwide controversy over the question of slavery, when persistent efforts were being made by numerous humane people to have this vile trade prohibited. The Quakers were the first body to combine to work for its abolition, and in his business William Rathbone allowed nothing to be sold for use in a slave ship.

William Rathbone's son, born in 1757, also William and the father of Bessie's husband, was an enterprising merchant, the first to import American cotton into England as well as a supporter of worthy causes. He married Hannah Mary Reynolds, daughter of Richard Reynolds, known in his home city of Bristol as "The Philanthropist." Hannah Reynolds was a remarkable woman, and her son's comments on her in his letter to his wife merely echoed a general opinion. She is mentioned in glowing terms in the *Autobiography of Henry Chorley*. "She had been throughout her life the admired friend and counsellor of many distin-

Knocktarna, Coleraine, built by Hugh Lyle

guished men, all belonging to the liberal school of ideas and philosophies."

William Rathbone, husband of Hannah Rathbone, died in 1809.

William Rathbone, the husband of Bessie, brought up in this tradition, was no less distinguished than his father and grandfather for his progressive ideas and active benevolence.

Bessie, with boundless energy and great intelligence was the strongest of Samuel Greg's twelve children, only two of whom died before the age of seventy. Accustomed from childhood to participate in a wide range of charitable and cultural activities, she was an ideal partner for William Rathbone. He consulted her about everything, and they worked together in the closest collaboration, some of his projects being due to her initiative, although she remained in the background, as was the custom for women in Victorian times.

William Rathbone was fearless and outspoken in supporting what he thought right and has been described as having a caustic tongue, never a particularly popular attribute. In fact, these traits brought William Rathbone much unpopularity in his early life, together with suspicion and, at times, threats of violence. He was a Whig in politics, took a deep, permanent interest in the troubles of Ireland, supported complete Catholic emancipation there, and at the time of the great Irish Famine of 1845–1848 when the potato crop, staple food of the Irish peasants, failed completely in all parts of Ireland, he took an active part in relief operations to reduce the misery and deaths of the starving population. He also outraged public opinion by taking the chair at a dinner in Liverpool for Daniel O'Connell, lawyer and Irish reformer loyal to the Crown, who did not believe in violence and had declared that Irish freedom was not worth the shedding of a single drop of blood. Nevertheless, the early professed loyalty of Wolfe Tone, so swiftly to turn to revolutionary fervor, was too recent to be forgotten by the British public, and O'Connell, adored by the poor of Southern Ireland, was hated and feared in England.

As a member of the Reform Party, William Rathbone's name was included in a list of "Suspects" prepared for the information of an Irish member of the government, Lord Castlereagh, against it being noted "Dangerous, but has done nothing yet."

William Rathbone and his wife did valuable work for education in Liverpool. Until the Whigs gained a majority on the Corporation, Liverpool's two elementary schools were run "on the principles of the Church of England," thus effectively depriving of education children of other denominations, the majority of whom were Catholics.

The Whigs disagreed with this sectarian discrimination, and when they became a majority on the Corporation, of which William Rathbone was an influential member, the system was changed to the Irish National

System, under which children of all denominations were taught together in all subjects except religion, for which they were segregated in different rooms, each sect being taught by a minister or priest of their own faith. The change, beneficial to the children who worked happily and amicably together, did not have the support of the Low Church Party, and when the Whigs lost the election of 1841, in which William Rathbone lost his seat, they were defeated on the question of education in the Corporation.

After this misfortune for Liverpool's children, William and Bessie turned their attention to the city's Hibernian schools, which became noted for their success and the high standard of teaching as a result of their efforts, and the Irish National System, which worked equally happily in these schools.

In 1838, a letter from Heidelburg University gives an indication of the Rathbones' wide acquaintance and continuing links with Ulster. "We then went to call on Muncke, who received us most warmly, inquired after Dr. Trail and his family most particularly." Dr. Trail was the well-known Provost of Trinity College, Dublin, and head of the Trail (later spelt Traill) family of Ballylough, near Bushmills in the county of Antrim.

At home in Liverpool, William and Bessie Rathbone were very hospitable, and innumerable well-known and unknown people of a wide variety of views and aims stayed with them at Greenbank, including Dorothea Dix, reformer of U.S. lunatic asylums, Father Matthew, the Irish temperance reformer, and Blanco White, former Spanish priest. Should the visitor be obscure, unsuccessful, eccentric, or derided by the rest of the world, the warmer and kinder would be their welcome at Greenbank.

William Rathbone died in 1867, aged eighty, soon after an operation that offered the only hope of prolonging his life. All his affairs were left in meticulous order, and he refused to express any wishes or give any advice regarding them to his sons, saying, "While in the world I have done what I thought right; when I am gone the responsibility will be theirs and I will not fetter their freedom."

During William Rathbone's long life, the hostility and criticism he had roused earlier had given place to general appreciation of his great qualities of mind and heart and his immense services to the community. He had been mayor of Liverpool, and after his death, his portrait was hung in the council chamber, and a statue of him in Sefton Park, erected by public subscription, bore testimony to the appreciation of Liverpool's citizens.

After his father's death, the eldest son, William, born 1819, who strongly resembled his mother in all respects, and his wife went to live at Greenbank at Bessie's suggestion.

William was an M.P. at Westminster when in 1870 Mr. Foster's education bill was being prepared. His mother, then eighty, retained her intense and intelligent interest in education and sent him various memoranda, dealing in particular with the practical aspects and the problems that would arise, drawn from her own long practical experience as a school manager. These were shown to Mr. Foster, who told William Rathbone that his mother's comments had been the most useful to him of all those he had received while the bill was under consideration.

Bessie Rathbone died at the age of ninety-three in 1873.

William Rathbone's first wife had died young, and this sad event aroused in him a special interest in nursing. He consulted Florence Nightingale continuously on this subject and on her advice built a training school for nurses, which he presented to the infirmary on the condition that they gave it a fair trial. If it was not a success, they would be entitled to use the building for any other purpose. In 1863, the building was handed over to the nurses.

In 1862, William Rathbone married again, and this time his wife came from "Oaks," where his father had written to his mother so many years before. He married a second cousin, Emily Lyle, daughter of Acheson Lyle, related to him through Bessie's family, the Gregs.

Notes

1. Her husband.

15 / 1815—After the Battle of Waterloo, Gunner William Henning Writes to John Cromie, Eldest Son of John Cromie and Ann Thompson

In January 1814, Napoleon Bonaparte, the Corsican corporal, was Emperor of France and the conqueror of a great part of Europe. As a result of his success, the Bonaparte family had risen high in the world. Joseph Bonaparte ruled Naples, Louis was King of Holland, Jerome became son-in-law to the King of Wurtenberg, Eugene de Beauharnais son-in-law to the King of Bavaria, and Stephanie de Beauharnais married the Duke of Baden. It had become clear that Napoleon's insatiable ambition aimed at the conquest of all Europe. England, partially blockaded, once more lived with the threat of invasion. For years, naughty English children had been threatened "Boney will get you if you are bad."

All over Europe and in England, Napoleon's many enemies planned to overthrow him and entered into alliance toward this end. In 1814, military defeat, treachery, and internal dissension in France brought success to their efforts. The Allies entered Paris. Napoleon was forced to abdicate and was banished to the Island of Elba. The Bourbon monarchy was restored. Sir Arthur Wellesley, now Duke of Wellington after his success in Spain, was appointed British Ambassador in Paris.

In 1815, Napoleon escaped from Elba, returned to France, swiftly regained power, took command of the French army, and marched at the head of 124,000 men toward Belgium where British, Dutch, German, and Belgium troops under the command of the duke of Wellington awaited him. Louis XVIII fled.

On the June 18, 1815 the two great armies met in decisive battle at Waterloo. The Allies victory broke the power of Napoleon immediately and finally. The rest of his life was spent on the island of St. Helena. France was occupied by an allied army commanded by Wellington. In July 1815, Louis XVIII stayed at St. Denis on his way back to Paris where he appointed Talleyrand, renowned throughout Europe for his diplomatic skill, President of the Council (Prime Minister).

In England, news of the victory was received with great joy and celebrations. When the first jubilation was over, there came the reckoning as news came slowly from the battlefield into countless soldiers' homes, bringing, too often, tidings of disablement and death—that heaviest and irreplaceable portion of the cost of victory—human suffering and bereavement.

In the British army at Waterloo were many Ulstermen, among them Thomas Cromie, second son of John Cromie and Ann Thompson. Thomas Cromie was a regular, Lieutenant in the Horse Artillery. He was wounded at the battle of Waterloo, and from St. Denis, where the battery camped afterwards, his soldier servant wrote to his elder brother.

There is much of interest in this letter, written before the days of state education, when general literacy mainly depended on the efforts of the churches and of many private individuals.

Some people may be interested to learn that horses were sold at Tattersalls before 1815, others may shudder at the glimpse of the medical treatment and attention before the discovery of anesthetics, while those concerned with such matters will note the reference to sectarian religion.

This moving letter may be ill spelled and not punctuated, but it is vividly written. It illuminates the characters of Thomas Cromie and of William Henning, who made such a great effort to tell John Cromie all he would wish to know. To some people, it may seem that, as they read, they are in the camp, present at all the scenes described in the letter:

Letter from Gunner William Henning to Mr. John Cromie. Letter folded sealed and addressed "For Mr. John Cromie Esq, Cromore near Colrain, Irland" (Postmark "St Denis")

Stain Agust 2 1815

Dear Sir I resceved Both your kind Lettrs on the 31st July one dated the 4 and one the 6 and I let mr bruce see your Letter and he told me that Captian Millar was gon away from this place but he wold take it upon himself to see my master things exposed off as for my masters soard and watch I have got them and the Morning that his Leg was cut off the surgon cut off his pantlawns and drawers and boots I stod by him and the surgon toke his watch out of his pocket and give it to me and my master said to me you Will keep that watch henning and give it to my brother john and likeways tell him from me that he is to have every thing belonging to me dear sir you wished to know how my master bore his suffirings he bore it with great pations according to his satition that he was in and all ways lived in good behops of Recoviring untill the Last minits when his Leg was cut off he scarsly said oh only asked for a drink onse or twise and the first time his Legs was opned the surgon asked him how he fealt himself and he said with a smile very well considring and that morning that he died he said to me dont you think i look better this morning i wish you wold get the razor and soap box and give me a shave which i did but had littel thoughts it to be the Last time then he wished to have his legs dresed and sent me for the surgon to dress them and the staff surgon wold not com to dress him to one came not a purticlar frend of my masters how was aquented with my master at sandgate castel he belongs to the staff Corps how laid at Hythe Brarracks at the same time and he was dressed betwen one and tow oclock and he died beafor 4 and i wold have stude it better to see my master go off and Leave me had Mr. Curk Cubbage not came up into the Room about ten minits beafor my master died and seed him i was siting by him and he came to me and claped me on the Back and said com to me my man and i will tell you what to do and he brusted out into teers and went out of the room and left me puting his pocket handkirtchef on his face And when he went out and left me with my master alone my heart filed like to brust to think i must part from him how had bean so good to me even if he had but one glas of spirits and thought i wanted he wold give me the half of it he went off quit easy being quit Exastued with Loss of Blood and for want of somthing in his insid to suport him for he never eat anything that wold ly on his stomack only what he drank and wine wold not stay on his stomack it is self you wished to know if he spoke of his famly But he never menchened one belonging to him but you he was quite sensable till within 20⅔ minits before he died But he reaved a littel in corse of his suffiring and for my Master funerl it was very neatly pirformed he had a good

62

oak coffin stained black with his name and age as ner as I cold gess it was 26 years we put on it and major jones Company of the artillery came in clean dress and one officer and capian welver and staff surgon mr cavenor atended His funeral an the caried on thire shoulders and Marshed to slow time to his grave which was made in the outside of the town ramparts and the officer of the fot artillirey pirformed the funral sermon The reason why my master was not bireed in the grave yard was beacois if he had ben bired in it he wold had ben taken up again by the roman cathlicks Dear sir as for the old brown horse and the young horse that My master bought at tatsils yard in London the ware Both sold when i resceved your Letter cap welvr sold them to major winets in paris and he will give you back the old brown again dear sir if you can obteain me Leave to com hom to england i will bring you home the horse watch and sord saife to any place you apoint for me to come to

Direct to gunner william Henning of Troop R.H.A.

neair Stain

i hop sir you will exques my writing and speling i remean your humbel servent

W. Henning

16 / 1816–1830—Political Change in England and Ireland

When the Battle of Waterloo finally ended the Napoleonic War, a prolonged period of extreme danger for the British people, they were left at the war's end with its legacies of economic distress, political fears, and a depleted treasury.

The French Revolution had been precipitated mainly by idealists seeking liberty, equality, and fraternity for all men. Its achievement was a blood bath, followed by the dictatorship of Napoleon Bonaparte, a megalomaniac who had plunged all Europe into the war so recently ended, which had resulted in the restoration of the monarchy in France.

As sufferers of the aftermath of the revolution, it was not surprising that in England and Ireland there was, after 1815, widespread distrust of reforming idealists, particularly of the British Whig Party, whose members had so enthusiastically supported the French Revolution, some of them continuing to do so even after its worst excesses became known. In consequence, reforms in England and in Ireland suffered a setback, as the electors consistently returned the Tories to power at Westminster.

In Ireland, increased economic distress, which existed in England, also, was intensified in 1817 and again in 1822 by partial failure of the potato crop, staple food of the people, and this was inevitably accompanied by increased violence and crime, for there was then no poor law to provide relief for the starving, and the people were dependent almost entirely on local efforts and private charity from farther afield. Some thousands of pounds were subscribed by the government to the relief committees, and, in 1816, three-quarters of a million pounds were subscribed in England and elsewhere from private sources, an immense sum when the very high purchasing power of the pound in those days is taken into consideration. But these efforts could only mitigate the suffering, for private resources were inadequate to deal with repeated disaster.

The king, George III, originally sympathetic to Catholic emancipation but hostile to it since the 1798 insurrection, died in 1820. During the last nine years of his reign, his ill health necessitated government by his eldest son as Prince Regent but with strictly limited powers, for despite his ability and charm, the Prince Regent was distrusted by his ministers. From 1815 to 1820, the question of Catholic emancipation remained at a standstill.

On the death of George III, the Prince Regent became George IV. Born in 1762, George IV was very handsome, generous and well educated, a good linguist, fluent in French, German and Italian, besides taking a discriminating interest in music and the arts. However he was also dissipated, and from an early age led a most profligate life of which his father had strongly disapproved. In 1785 he secretly married Mrs. Fitzherbert[1] in a church ceremony, and when, in 1795, he married his cousin, Princess Caroline of Brunswick, it was only for the sake of the succession. The only child of the marriage, Princess Charlotte, heiress presumptive to the English throne, married, in 1816, Prince Leopold of Saxe-Coburg-Gotha, later King of the Belgians, but died in childbirth within twelve months.

In 1821, George IV visited Southern Ireland, the first English monarch to visit Ireland since William of Orange led his international army to victory over the French and Southern Irish troops of James II at the Battle of the Boyne. The novelty of seeing their King was much appreciated by his volatile Irish subjects, and the enthusiasm of the cheering crowds that lined his route turned his journey into a triumphal progress. With attractive tact, the King declared that "rank, station and honours, were to him nothing compared to the exalted happiness of living in the hearts of his Irish subjects," so the visit was an outstanding success, although the fervent loyalty soon passed away, as is usual with volatile emotions.

Some Irish historians have commented critically on the lack of any further royal visits until the reign of Queen Victoria and also on the lack of any royal personal interest in Irish problems. However, the British government has a responsibility for the safety of their sovereign, and a study of the history of Ireland should make it quite understandable that there might be hesitation regarding royal visits to that turbulent land. The strong personal loyalty to the English crown, which had lasted for centuries in all parts of Ireland, had been fatally eroded in the South by the activities of Wolfe Tone and his associates at the end of the eighteenth century, although, in unvisited Ulster, the Act of Union gradually won majority support, adding one more vital difference between Ulster and the rest of Ireland.

It should not be forgotten also that George III had taken a most personal interest in Irish problems and had intervened to improve the legal situation of Roman Catholics. In addition, Ireland had achieved independence of Westminster under the crown, thus opening up the possibility of eventual equal partnership between England and Ireland. Unfortunately, these favorable developments were swiftly followed by the insurrection of 1798, with French troops being landed in Southern Ireland at the urgent request of Irishmen for use against England, at a time when England was engaged in a war with France. From then onward, George III was unalterably opposed to Catholic emancipation. Can it be wondered at if later British sovereigns felt it best to refrain from meddling in the affairs of so irrational a people.

George IV was a Whig in his younger days, a supporter of reform, and a close friend of the duc d'Orleans (Citoyen Egalite) who was sent to the guillotine by his revolutionary comrades. Under the pressure of harsh realities and the heavy responsibilities of government, however, George IV, when King, lost most of his reforming zeal. Nevertheless, as time passed, some progress in reform was made by successive Tory governments, for the Tories, throughout their history, while often not the instigators, have frequently been the perpetrators of important measures of reform.

In 1821, Plunket, an Irish M.P., proposed a resolution granting Catholic emancipation that was passed by the House of Commons. This resolution was violently opposed by Daniel O'Connell, who, though not a member of Parliament, was the most influential political leader in Southern Ireland because he disagreed with the veto[2] included in the resolution, although this had been agreed to by the Pope and the Irish Roman Catholic bishops.

Daniel O'Connell, whose political aims were Catholic emancipation and the repeal of the Union, had been active in politics since the turn of the century. In theory, he was opposed to violence for political ends, having been an eyewitness of some of the worst excesses of the French Revolution, an experience that left him with an abiding horror of anarchy. Illogically, however, his speeches increasingly tended to rouse violence, always near the surface in the South of Ireland, because of his intemperate language, although, for a time, his immense personal control over his followers maintained discipline.

On this occasion, he helped to delay a most desirable reform, which would inevitably have led to others in spite of the fact that the proposed veto was not unreasonable in the prevailing circumstances and could be regarded as a necessary safeguard against the breakdown of law and order, a development from which the poor, as always, would have suffered most. Priests of the Roman Catholic Church had then an awakening interest in politics. This grew to alarming proportions in the next few years. Many priests were provincial in outlook, embued with local prejudices. They received their clerical training at Maynooth in Ireland instead of, as in the eighteenth century, on the Continent and accepted the distorted and inaccurate historical fantasies that have caused so much bloodshed in their unhappy land. The promotion of such men to high office in their church in Ireland would naturally have been most welcome to Daniel O'Connell, for they had great influence over their parishioners, but it would have boded ill for the peace of the country, a consideration that no doubt influenced the Pope and the Irish Roman Catholic bishops in their decision to agree to the veto.

The failure of Plunket's resolution fostered an increasing sense of grievance in Southern Ireland. When, in 1823, Daniel O'Connell formed a "Catholic Association of Ireland," with a subscription of one penny a month, known as "the Catholic rent," with Roman Catholic priests as ex officio members, its numbers grew rapidly, greatly increasing O'Connell's strength and alarming the government.

In 1825, a Suppression Act made the Catholic Association illegal, but O'Connell, a lawyer, skillfully evaded the terms of the act by transforming the Catholic Association into a legal Constitutional Society with the admirable aim of "promoting concord among all classes of Irishmen."

In 1826, the growing power of O'Connell and his Constitutional Society was put to the test in the Waterford election, where Lord George Beresford, owner of most of the county, a popular Protestant landlord, supporter of reform, whose election was regarded as a certainty, was opposed by another Protestant, Villiers Stewart, related to the Duke of Devonshire and an ardent follower of Daniel O'Connell. The election was won by Villiers Stewart.

In 1828, the Duke of Wellington, victor of Waterloo, became Conservative Prime Minister. He was an Irishman who, as Arthur Wellesley, had won his first election to the Irish Parliament in 1790. The King, George IV, stipulated that Catholic emancipation should not be included in the government's program.

Wellington appointed Sir Robert Peel Home Secretary and Vesey Fitzgerald, an Irishman, president of the Board of Trade. The second appointment necessitated Fitzgerald standing for reelection in Clare. He was so popular in the constituency that no Protestant could be found willing to stand against him, so O'Connell himself opposed him, winning such overwhelming support that Vesey Fitzgerald withdrew from the contest.

Although the legally elected representative of the electors, O'Connell was unable to take his seat at Westminster because he would not take the compulsory oath of supremacy, anathema to Roman Catholics because its wording denied authority to the pope, spiritual or temporal, within the kingdom. O'Connell's constituents were therefore effectively disenfranchised, a most inflammable situation in a most inflammable country.

The Duke of Wellington was a strong and decisive Prime Minister, with the advantage that he understood Ireland. Despite the reluctance of the King, which was only overcome with great difficulty, Wellington acted immediately to defuse a most explosive situation.

In 1828, the year in which Wellington took office, Lord John Russell proposed that the tests for office (Test and Corporation Acts) should be repealed insofar as they affected Protestant dissenters, thus removing the legal disabilities under which Protestant dissenters (mainly Ulster Presbyterians) had suffered for so long, for the new oath of allegiance did not contain the sacramental test that had been unacceptable to Presbyterians. This was swiftly followed by a Relief Act in 1829 for the benefit of Roman Catholics, which the Duke of Wellington, in spite of powerful opposition, steamrollered through Parliament by making it quite clear that if his act was not passed, the result in Ireland would be civil war. This act threw open all the offices of state to Roman Catholics, with the exception only of Regent, Lord Lieutenant, and Lord Chancellor. It was no longer compulsory for Roman Catholic members of the Commons or the Lords to take the oath of supremacy.

Lord George John Beresford, Protestant Archbishop of Armagh, member of the powerful Beresford family, opposed the Relief Act in a long speech containing the following words: "Emancipation involves in its consequences, not so much a sharing of power as a transfer of power, the Catholics not being satisfied until they had overthrown the Protestant Ascendancy." The speech has been described as bigoted and intolerant, but later events proved it to be merely a factual statement by a man who knew his own country, for, in the twentieth century, all that the Archbishop prophesied came true. Southern Ireland became a Roman Catholic state and, later, a republic opting out of the Commonwealth. Ulster remained in the United Kingdom of her own choice, once more demonstrating her difference from the South, surviving down the centuries.

In 1830, George IV died. The old roue, womanizer of many infidelities, had always worn a miniature of Mrs. Fitzherbert, and, at his request, this miniature was buried with him.

The Duke of Clarence, born in 1765, brother of George IV, then became King William IV. At twelve years of age, he joined the navy and in due course was given command of a ship. Discipline resistant, he first flouted it by sailing home from the West Indies without orders, only to be sent back by his father as soon as his ship was made ready to return. In 1827, having become heir to the throne on the death of his brother, the Duke of York, he was appointed Lord High Admiral. He ignored the terms of his patent under which he could act only with the advice of his council. However, he was determined to exercise independent control, so that his brother George, then the Prince Regent, had no option but to require his resignation. His request then to be sent on active service in the war with France not being granted, he followed the example of his brothers and embarked on a life of dissipation. Socially, he was pleasant and attractive, but in command he was so brutally strict a disciplinarian that his men were kept on the verge of mutiny, and the savagery of his punishments, sometimes for trivial offenses, eventually resulted in his being given no further commands. In politics, he claimed to be a Whig, yet he supported slavery. His mistress, Mrs. Jordan, was an actress. He lived with her for twenty years, only leaving her to marry Adelaide of Meningen for the sake of the succession. Political marriage for this reason was accepted by all the sons of George III as a compulsory royal duty, reluctantly performed by George IV, William IV, and the Duke of Kent, all of whom had mistresses of long standing of whom they were very fond.

As King, William IV meant well and did his best, but, unfortunately, he was incapable of prompt or firm decision, a weakness that made it impossible for his Cabinet to govern satisfactorily, so that even England, normally law-abiding, was threatened finally by revolution. In 1830, it enviously observed from a distance France's "Three Glorious Days," during which France replaced their unpopular and reactionary King Charles X by Louis Philippe, Duc d'Orleans, who was the son of Citoyen Egalite.

In 1830, the long eclipse of the Whigs at last came to an end when they won that year's Westminster election, an event that was probably influenced by the success of democracy in America, for it is open to question whether France's contribution to the growth of democracy has not been overrated and that of America understated. It was in America that the first viable democracy was established, which, under capable and honorable leaders, brought great and immediate benefits to its citizens.

After the Whig election victory, the Tory government at Westminster resigned, and the Whigs returned to power, after fifty years out of office, full of reforming plans. Their first Reform Bill was introduced in March 1831. This passed its second reading but only by one vote, and after this it was defeated in Committee. The Whig government offered to resign, but the King could not make up his mind. He would neither accept the resignation nor dissolve Parliament, one or other action being essential in the circumstances.

The Tories, with their immense political experience, saved the country from the impending dangerous crisis by moving an address against dissolution. The wavering king regarded this as an impertinence and an attack on his royal prerogative. He immediately dissolved Parliament.

The election that followed dissolution was won by the Whigs with a satisfactory majority, and their Reform Bill passed the House of Commons in October 1831, but the Lords rejected it. This precipitated another crisis, and once more the King could not decide what to do; eventually, he agreed to create new peers so that the bill would be passed in the Lords. This alarming prospect proved effective, and the Lords passed the bill for parliamentary reform without the necessity for such drastic action.

Repercussions of these events were felt in all parts of the United Kingdom, including Coleraine.

Notes

1. The marriage was illegal; under the Royal Marriages Act, marriage without the king's consent was null and void.
2. The power to veto episcopal appointments on the grounds of political unsuitability.

17 / 1830/1832—Coleraine Wins a Victory for Democracy

The ancient town of Coleraine is believed by some to have been founded by St. Patrick, while others maintain that it was an important town much earlier. Coleraine has a most interesting history, having been involved in many events of historical importance. Among these, its participation in the political ferment, which reached culmination in 1832, has particular interest at the present time when democracy, for which our ancestors fought so hard, is under challenge.

In the great struggle for democratic rights, the town of Coleraine played a sturdy part and one of interest, showing the part that could be played by the ordinary citizen in the stormy battles in which the great political figures of the day were then engaged.

Local participation in this epic victory was recalled in the Northern Constitution in the issue of the December 29, 1928, from which the following extracts are quoted:

> The Act of legislative Union between England and Ireland was passed in 1800. At that time the Right Honourable John Beresford and Walter Jones, who had been elected in 1798 as the town's representatives in the Irish Parliament, were the sitting members for Coleraine. The Borough was, however, by this Act, deprived of one member, and a new election ensued. At this period, the Mayor and Corporation, with some "Freemen" associates had the exclusive right of election to this position and it was established that Jackson and Beresford could always secure the return of their nominee. Eventually, the Beresfords purchased the Jacksons interests in the Corporation for £7,000 and in the nomination of aldermen, burgesses and everything else connected with that body, acted as if the Borough was their own property.
>
> Colonel Walter Jones, of Cook Abbey, County Wicklow, was elected as the first member for Coleraine to the Imperial Parliament. He held the seat until 1806 when Sir George Fitzgerald Hill, Londonderry, was returned, but regained the position in 1807. Lord George Beresford was appointed in 1812, Rear-Admiral Sir John Beresford in 1818, and Sir William Head Brydges, an Englishman, who was connected by marriage with the Beresford family, in 1826.
>
> About the time of the Rebellion in 1797 the Corporation had, at the instigation of the Marquis of Waterford, recognised the loyalty and services of the corps of yeomanry enrolled in the town by conferring on its members the "freedom" of the Borough. They had never, however, up to this time exercised the privilege thus afforded them by voting for any parliamentary candidate.
>
> In 1830 several leaders of public opinion urged upon such of them as survived, and others whom they thought entitled to the same right, the im-

portance of its assertion, and on 12th August of that year "being the day fixed upon for the election of a special burgess to serve in the ensuing Parliament for the Borough" the first active public step was taken towards reform.

The Court of Common Council assembled in the Market House, when the Mayor, Dr. Boyd, took the chair. Among other members present were: Aldermen Rev. Thomas Richardson, John Knox, Richard Hunter, John Cromie, Hugh Lyle, Sir James Bruce: Burgesses Barre Beresford, Rev. Spencer Knox, Marcus McCausland, James Stirling, J.C. Beresford, W.H. Ash and Thomas Scott.

A number of the inhabitants of the town attended to present petitions, and claim their freedom. They were assured by the Mayor and Barre Beresford the Chamberlain, that their petitions would be taken into consideration at the next Common Council. The Mayor then proceeded to read the writ directing him to return a burgess to represent the Borough in the ensuing Parliament, and the Rev. Thomas Richardson moved and Mr. John Cromie seconded, that Sir John Brydges be appointed.

The Mayor was about to proclaim Sir John elected, and before doing so, said "Let all who are for Sir John's return say "Aye", and all who are against it say "No." The greater part of the Common Council were heard to say "Aye", but "No No" burst from the freemen and others.

Mr. James Gribbon, addressing the Mayor on behalf of those who said "No" said they had not come there for the factious purpose of opposing the return of Sir John Brydges because he was the nominee of the Corporation, but because the inhabitants were excluded from all participation in the privilege of electing a Parliamentary representative. Before they would consent to the election of Sir John they wished to ask him a question—"Did he or would he consider himself bound in case of his return to represent the interests of the freemen and inhabitants generally of the Borough, or merely the Corporation?" Sir John replied that he considered himself only bound in case of his return to represent those who had the elective franchise, whoever they might be.

Mr. Gribbon then exclaimed "According to this we have nothing to do with Sir John; he has said he will not represent us in Parliament". Mr. Gribbon added that it had been suggested to him that Alderman Thorpe, one of the Governors of the Irish Society, would be a proper person to represent the Borough in Parliament. He called upon the freemen to come forward, assert their rights, and return Alderman Thorpe as their member.

Mr. George McLoughlin, one of the freemen, then proposed and Mr. Thomas Lundy seconded Alderman Thorpe's nomination.

The Alderman and Burgesses were about to be polled when Mr. James Gribbon objected to Sir James Bruce's competence to vote, not being a resident burgess in the Borough, and said he would likewise object to all other non-residents.

The Mayor, however, did not consider these objections valid, and closed

71

the election declaring that Sir John Brydges was duly elected, against which the freemen protested. Amid some disturbance the meeting broke up, and in the evening tar barrels were burnt, while the people turned out en masse, many bearing placards with the words "Thorpe and the freedom of the people".

The agitation to secure their rights had now been well begun by the people, and under the able leadership of several men of ability in the town a contest for popular privileges was waged, which enlisted the interest of the whole country. A few months after the election of Sir John Brydges a petition against his return was lodged on behalf of Alderman Thorpe and the 4th January, 1831 was appointed for its hearing before the Committee of the House of Commons.

The petition was never brought to an issue, and Sir John Brydges remained the sitting member until May, 1831. At that time the Irish Society, who had manifested much interest in endeavouring to obtain for the people their municipal and electoral rights, nominated Alderman Copeland, one of the London Corporation, and also a member of their own body, as a candidate in the election to take place in that month. Alderman Copeland received strenuous support from the old freemen of 1798, and from any others who claimed a right to record votes in his favour, but had their claims refused by the Corporation.

Sir John Brydges was again declared elected by the Mayor, Mr. Hugh Lyle, in spite of protests. Alderman Copeland petitioned and succeeded in establishing the legal rights of the freemen and some other inhabitants of the Borough to the electoral franchise, and thereby ousted Sir John Brydges from the seat, and was himself declared the member for Coleraine.

In the year 1832 the political struggle was renewed in Coleraine, but under much more favourable circumstances for the party of reform. The verdict of the House of Commons had established the claims to the franchise of the old freeman as well as of many other inhabitants who had sought the "Freedom of the Borough." The Reform Bill, too, had reached an advanced stage, and considerably improved their position.

The number of electors for the borough now amounted to about 200, and on the dissolution of Parliament in December 1832, Alderman Copeland, on the one side, and Vice-Admiral Sir John Poer Beresford on the other, sought their suffrages. After two days' polling the number of accepted votes stood equally balanced—97 each side. Over and above these were thirteen votes tendered in favour of Alderman Copeland by persons claiming their right (in virtue of possessing the freedom of the town) to do so, but were disallowed by the Mayor, who acted as Returning Officer.

Mr. Richard Hunter, in this capacity, conducted the election and recorded his own as a casting vote in favour of Sir John Beresford, but did so in rather a bungling fashion, thus: "I now declare the poll closed, and I give my casting vote in favour of Sir John Beresford" "Mark that," cried a sharp legal gentleman, he closed the poll first, and then gave his casting vote which therefore cannot count". Notwithstanding numerous protests, Mr. Hunter persisted in declaring Sir John Beresford returned.

When the Mayor appeared at the door of the Market House to announce the result there were about 2,000 people in the Diamond, and in the disorder that ensued many persons were injured. The wits of the town composed doggerel verses, which were regarded as humourous or slanderous, according as they referred to friends or foes.

David Dunlop was a bookseller and a stationer in the Diamond, and obtained the Corporation records from 1710 to 1792 to bind them in book form. Alderman Copeland, who was informed of this, secured a warrant from the House of Commons to seize them, and the evidence they contained was used in the petition against Admiral Sir John Beresford.

For Alderman Copeland it was contended "that all the freemen of the Corporation were, previous to the Irish Reform Act, legally entitled to vote in the election of members to serve in Parliament, and that, after the passing of the Act, the freemen (subject to the provisions as to residence and registry), and also all other persons qualified under the Act, were legally qualified to vote in the election of Members for the Borough."

The entry in the Corporation Book on 2nd October, 1797, was also put in: "The Right Hon. John Beresford proposed that the thanks of this Corporation be given to Marcus Hill and Hugh Lyle, and to the corps under their command, for their spirited exertions by which the peace of this town and neighbourhood has been so perfectly preserved, and for the attachment they have manifested to their King and Constitution, and that such of the said corps as have not already been made freemen, be made freemen thereof."

A long list of names followed.

For Sir John Beresford the defence set up was that the right of voting in the Borough of Coleraine, before the passing of the Irish Reform Bill, was vested in the Mayor, twelve Aldermen and twenty-four burgesses only.

Mr. Barre Beresford, in his evidence, admitted that fifteen out of the sixteen votes for Sir John Brydges were those of non-residents, and that the whole were either retainers or friends of the Marquis of Waterford, for whom his lordship had paid the stamp duty on their admission as burgesses: that the Corporation rents and profits were received by him, and that he used the same books for the Corporation as for the Marquis: that relatives of the Marquis had obtained leases of part of the Corporation lands, and that all previous elections had been held in a private manner.

The Select Committee decided "That all the inhabitants of the town of Coleraine, and the jurisdiction and liberty of the same, being admitted to the freedom of the said town, were, before the Irish Reform Act, entitled as burgesses of the said town, as well as the Mayor, Aldermen and twenty-four Burgesses, to vote in the election of members to serve in Parliament for the Borough of Coleraine, and that since the said Act, and subject to the provisions thereof, the Mayor, Aldermen and all the burgesses herein beforementioned, and all other persons qualified under the said Act, are now legally entitled to vote at every election of members for the said Borough."

73

The Committee also found that the election of Vice-Admiral Sir John Poer Beresford, Bart., was void, and that Alderman Copeland was duly elected, and ought to have been returned to serve in Parliament. They altered the poll taken at the election by adding to it the fourteen names of those having a right to vote at such election.

The popular excitement caused by this unmistakeable proof that in spite of all their efforts to maintain it, the ascendancy of the Beresfords and the Corporation was waning, knew no bounds, and, in the flush of victory, many extravagances were committed. Nor did the exuberance of the people abate for several years, and the ferment was kept up by frequently recurring elections.

Thus ended this celebrated election petition by which Alderman Copeland's name was made for ever famous in the annals of Coleraine.

Among other marks of Royal favour, it was indicated in its Charter that special privileges would attach to the various trades, and it directed the formation of "Guilds" similar to those existing in London. This direction was followed out to the letter, and Coleraine thus became possessed of numerous bodies banded together in Companies or Guilds.

In consequence of the expected arrival of Alderman Copeland on Thursday 29th September, it was decided by the different Guilds, which admitted men of all religious persuasions, to meet him in procession, with banners, etc., as a testimony of respect towards one who had been mainly instrumental in establishing the rights of the freemen. For several days previously, however, it had been known that Alderman Copeland could not at that time visit his constituency.

Norwithstanding his absence, it was determined by the traders to walk in procession round the town for the purpose of displaying the state of the public feeling on the dispute between the inhabitants of the town and those composing the Common Council. About 1,400 persons assembled at the Bowling Green, and the Guilds first drew lots for their place in the procession, after which Mr. Gribbon, who was in charge of the arrangements, addressed the assembly, and the whole body then set off in the following order:-

First came the boys educated in the Irish Society's Schools, next a caravan drawn by four horses with outriders, and in which was an amateur band chiefly composed by young men from Limavady who volunteered their services to assist the town musicians. After this came Alderman Copeland's election committee, and then the Sons of Freedom, bearing a banner on which was a harp and crown encircled by a rose shamrock and thistle, and the motto, God Save the King, and on the reverse, "We are the Sons of Freedom." Each of these young men wore a blue ribbon in the front of his cap with the same words printed on it. Followed the old freemen who had been admitted by the Common Council of 1897, bearing a banner, one side of which showed a harp and crown, with rose thistle and shamrock, and the motto, "God Save the King," and underneath this "The Hon. Irish Society." On the reverse side, "Gribbon and the Old Freemen." He made the first breach. "Copeland and Liberty are victorious."

74

After these came the Guilds:-

Cabinetmakers, with a banner on one side of which were four hands clasped, supported by the Goddess of Friendship, and emblems of the trade. Motto "United to support, but not combined to injure." Reverse: A chair with drapery and the motto: "We made the chair; let the people make the Mayor."

Shoemakers: King Crispin sitting in state, with a boot in one hand and a sceptre in the other. Motto: "Royal cordwainers Firm to the Last." Reverse: "The Hon. Irish Society and our Worthy Representative."

Weavers: Banner, Weavers' Arms. Motto: "May they wear sackcloth and ashes instead of Coleraine linen who would deprive us of our rights."

Tailors: Banner. Adam and Eve sewing an apron. Motto: "Our trade we can trace from the first of our race." Reverse: "Copeland, M.P. for Coleraine. Merit bears the palm."

The quotation has been ended only after four banners and mottoes have been described of the seventeen guilds, which are recorded as taking part in the procession.

After the procession had returned to its starting point, a crowd of some thousands moved to Dublin Road to meet Mr. Watt and Captain Thorpe, the former being the law agent of the Irish Society, and the latter a friend of Alderman Copeland.

The memorable day ended with its prime movers (about 50) having a lengthy and convivial dinner at Miss Henry's Hotel in Bridge Street.

The next day, more claims were prepared for people whose rights had not yet been conceded, and the following morning, members of the guilds, accompanied by the Irish Society's law agent, and some leading citizens, marched to the Market House, over 600 strong, to present 600 claims and to serve notice on the Mayor to take the necessary steps to exclude nonresidents from the Common Council, noncompliance to be countered by legal proceedings. On arrival, the Market House was found to be closed, with two contingents of armed police guarding the door. No doubt the Common Council was alarmed at the approach of so large a body of men in view of the injuries inflicted during the "disorders" already mentioned and feared that the maintenance of law and order might be in jeopardy.

Coleraine's experience shows the vital role that can be played not only by statesmen but by local citizens, and this Ulster borough set a stirring example by its conduct. In the words used by the writer in the Northern Constitution: "Coleraine was among the first to assert its rights and to fight for them until secured."

Dr. Boyd, the first Mayor of Coleraine, mentioned in this account of Coleraine's struggle for its democratic rights, was a very well known figure in Coleraine. Later, he represented the borough in the Tory interest from 1842 to 1852. In 1852, Lord Naas was appointed chief secretary in Lord Derby's government and, having failed to be reelected in his own constituency of Kildare, was in need of a seat. Dr. Boyd, therefore, resigned, and Lord

Naas was elected to his seat, unopposed.

In 1853, Dr. Boyd was appointed vice consul in Shanghai and was accompanied there by his wife and daughters. George Lyle, son of Hugh Lyle, who became Coleraine's mayor in 1831, was at this time a merchant in Shanghai. His letters home, addressed to "Knocktarna,"[1] Coleraine, are interesting when referring to the internal Chinese rebellion in September 1853 and amusing when mentioning the impending arrival of Dr. Boyd in Shanghai in January of the same year.

"You do not relate, though, how Dr. Boyd, ex-member for Coleraine, is coming out here, and will no doubt bring the polished and lady-like Mrs. B. along and the young ladies to whose arrival the single portion of this entirely (almost) male population are looking forward with feelings verging on the painful, from the excitement of overwrought imaginations concerning the personal and mental attractions of the aforementioned Misses B. Dear me, they will marry them here without giving the fortunate creatures time to collect their senses. . . . The fellows are running after me like a pack of hounds after a hare, to know what I do know and if they are old enough to marry, and come to years of discretion yet, which are two very different periods in human existence."

Unfortunately, a later surviving letter from George Lyle from Shanghai does not refer to Dr. Boyd and his family again, so that no information regarding his daughters' experiences and ultimate fate can be given here.

Later, Dr. Boyd again represented Coleraine, being elected unopposed in 1857, and he remained a member of Parliament until his death in 1862.

Hugh Lyle, who was mayor of Coleraine in 1831, was the son of Hugh Lyle, who has already been mentioned for his services to Coleraine in the Irish Insurrection. The first member of the family to come to Ulster was Hugh Lyle, from Renfrewshire in Scotland, who was an officer in a dragoon regiment. The family had been connected with Coleraine since early in the eighteenth century. Mayor Hugh Lyle was a very kind man whose practical interest in the workhouse inmates was on lines that suggest that in matters of welfare his ideas were in advance of his time. Politically, however, he appears to have been a reactionary, for his decision regarding the election of Sir John Brydges was certainly very wrong.

Notes

1. Now the Vice Chancellor's lodge, New University of Ulster.

The Irish Society, which played such an important part in Coleraine's struggle for its democratic rights, had been connected with Coleraine since the beginning of the seventeeth century.

The association of the area with the Society has been a factor of such importance in the development of Coleraine and the city and county of Londonderry that a passing reference to it is inadequate. Many points of great interest emerge from learning exactly how the city of London became involved in Ulster. Although this means reference back to events in the reign of Queen Elizabeth, the digression is valuable because it covers controversial events and some misunderstandings that even today, in the twentieth century, make their contribution to hatred and violence in Ireland.

Toward the end of Queen Elizabeth's reign, unsubdued Ulster's most important leader was Hugh O'Neill, earl of Tyrone. Rescued by the government when his brother was killed during internecine strife, he was brought up in the household of the Earl of Leicester. Handsome, well educated, and cultured, he spent some time at Queen Elizabeth's court and served in her army before returning to Ulster. At first, sincerely loyal, he supported the lord deputy in all matters and, with his followers, fought against rebel Ulstermen. However, he was a man of great ambitions, aiming to be all powerful in Ulster, "the first of his name and nation." When he realized that the Queen's policy of establishing English law, already nominally accepted but in practice ignored, and otherwise Anglicizing Ulster, he turned rebel. He then fought the Lord Deputy's forces with varying success, spread his rebellion into Southern Ireland, intrigued with Spain, England's most dangerous enemy, only a few years after the failure of the Spanish Armada in 1588, negotiated for the dispatch of Spanish troops to Ulster, and offered to make a Spaniard King of Ireland. Thus, he placed the Queen under the unavoidable necessity of dealing effectively with his revolt, which threatened England's own security.

Spanish troops were eventually dispatched in 1601 but landed near Cork instead of in Ulster and, numbering under 4,000, were too few. The Spanish Commander quickly surrendered without any consideration for his Irish allies, of whom he had formed a most unfavorable opinion.

The Earl of Tyrone's forces were heavily defeated, and, on his knees, Hugh O'Neill, Earl of Tyrone, abjectly surrendered to the queen's representative, the Lord Deputy, who did not tell him that the Queen was already dead.

It was James I of England, son of Mary Queen of Scots, who had to deal with the dangerous Earl of Tyrone, and he was generous. Hugh O'Neill kept his title and most of his vast Ulster estates, while he, for his part, swore loyalty to the crown.

On the September 17, 1607, there occurred the sudden, mysterious "Flight of the Earls" when Hugh O'Neill, O'Donnell, together with over ninety other leaders of Ulster, fled to the Continent in such haste that when Hugh O'Neill's wife, exhausted by the headlong flight, declared that she could go no farther, her husband threatened to kill her if she did not ride on. Another member of the party abandoned his baby son, leaving him behind in Ulster, sooner than miss or delay embarkation.

This deplorable action left the brave and loyal followers of the fleeing earls leaderless, abandoned to their fate. The result was that six counties, the greater part of Ulster, became forfeit to the Crown, for since the reign of Henry VIII, the great ruling families of Ulster had held tenure of their land under the crown, the result of the king's policy of "Surrender and re-grant." Ever since the flight, there has been speculation as to the reason for it, the most probable explanation being that Hugh O'Neill and his friends had been plotting once more, that the Lord Deputy, then Sir Arthur Chichester, had discovered this and planned to arrest them all, the earls being secretly informed of this decision. The real truth of the matter, however, remains unknown.

Hugh O'Neill never saw Ulster again, dying an exile in Rome, in 1616, one of the deluded King Canute's[1] of history, striving to halt the advancing tide of civilization over his ancient but backward and savage land.

In an attempt to stabilize his unruly kingdom of Ireland, still seething with rebellion, King James decided on various measures, the most important being the Plantation of Ulster with respectable, hardworking Scottish and English colonists of the Protestant faith, which was already making some headway in Ulster.

In this project, the King sought the help of the city of London as having the reputation and financial resources to ensure success.

The King had printed "Motives and Reasons to induce the City of London to undertake the Plantation of the North of Ireland," stating that "such an exodus to Ireland would be highly beneficial, that trade would flourish, that the project would prove pleasing to Almighty God, honourable to the City, and profitable to the undertakers."

The Corporation of London eventually agreed, though reluctantly, and only after long negotiations with the Privy Council, and at the urgent request of the King.

The Irish Society then came into being, as is described in a leaflet entitled "The Honourable Irish Society. Its Origin, constitution etc" in the following words:

Articles of Agreement with the Crown were ratified by the Common Council on the 30th January 1610, and forthwith A Company was constituted for directing the affairs of the Plantation, consisting of a Governor, a Deputy Governor, and 24 Assistants, officially styled The Society of the Governor and Assistants, London, of the New Plantation in Ulster within the Realm of Ireland which, after the Restoration became known by the shorter title of The Irish Society. . . . . The Charter of the 29th March 1613 created a new County called Londonderry in place of the County of Coleraine, and a new municipal corporation of the same name founded on the ancient city of Derry. The money necessary to carry out the Plantation scheme, to buy out private interests, to fortify Derry and Coleraine, and to build houses, was raised by assessing the Livery Companies, a very usual procedure in those times.

The Corporation was, of course, not the only body to take part in the Plantation, and some individuals also dealt with the Plantation of other areas.

The colonists introduced into Ulster included some English, but by far the greatest number came from Scotland, as was natural when the close links between Ulster and Scotland are recalled, many of the great Ulster families being Scottish in origin. The Scottish county of Argyle had been colonized in the sixth century by Ulstermen from the kingdom of Dalriada in County Antrim, under their great leader Fergus, son of Erc. At that time, Scotland was known as Scotia (the land of the Irish), and the colonized county was named Dalriada. Both William of Orange and Elizabeth II and many other British sovereigns are descendants of Fergus, son of Erc. Among the Scottish colonists who came to Ulster under James I's Plantation scheme were descendants of those Ulstermen from Dalriada who had colonized Argyle more than one thousand years earlier. The Scottish colonists, therefore, did not bring foreign blood into Ulster but merely one more infusion of the same racial stock that had incessantly mingled with theirs down the millennia.

Inevitably, a Plantation involves much injustice and suffering for the native inhabitants, and to the unhappy dispossessed, the colonists appeared as usurping foreigners, especially when, as in this case, the strong racial links between them were obscured by a religious difference. The majority of the native inhabitants were Roman Catholics, while the colonists were of the Protestants faith. Terrible accounts of suffering and injustice have come down to us, but today some of these are regarded as exaggerated and that a large number of the native inhabitants continued to live and work as and where they did before. To the nomadic portion of the population, however, always on the move, accompanied by their families and all their possessions, the coming of stability and law and order brought the destruction of their way of life. It was natural that there should be fierce local resentment against the Plantation, and, in 1641, there was a terrible uprising in Ulster when barbarous atrocities were inflicted on the unfortunate colonists.

The Irish Society had at first a checkered career, being inundated by complaints and harried by repeated royal commissions, losing and regaining its charter from time to time. In 1635, the city was fined £70,000 for nonperformance of the Articles of Plantation, but as one of the complaints against them was "partiality for the mere Irish, this being the result of the Society's refusal to huddle the natives into small reservations, where they would inevitably have perished from disease and starvation" suspicion is naturally aroused as to the validity of some of other complaints.

In 1641, the city set out in a petition to Parliament details of their activities in Ulster: "The Petition declared that the Citizens had taken part unwillingly, and had only undertaken the venture at the king's most earnest desire, and further set forth that Londonderry and Coleraine had been rebuilt, 15 churches erected or rebuilt, roads made, schools built, and one of the most barbarous places made into one of the most civilised."

The Long Parliament ordered that the Irish Society be reinstated, declaring that the judgment against them was "not only unjust but unlawful."

The Irish Society's leaflet ends with the following paragraph:

> The Society's principal obligation is to disburse the income derived from its fisheries and properties in accordance with the original constitution viz. By the provision of such educational facilities as it may deem desirable, and as may not otherwise be available (i.e. over and above those provided by the State) assisting local administration with developments and improvements, making grants in aid of religious or charitable work etc. independent of the denomination with which it may be connected—in short encouraging and supporting any object which it is considered to be of benefit to Co. Londonderry in general, and its two principal centres in particular, the city of Londonderry and the town of Coleraine.

It is interesting, though idle, to speculate on the fate of the leaderless counties of Ulster had there been no Plantation of Ulster. Would the population then have suffered unending poverty, internecine wars, and abortive rebellions? The answer to this question must remain forever unknown.

It is a matter of fact, however, that the Irish Society has fulfilled the obligations—so surprisingly enlightened—that were set out in its original constitution.

Today, the association between the Irish Society, Coleraine and the city and county of Londonderry is still maintained. Still, periodically, representatives of the Irish Society visit the area, inspect the excellent Irish Society schools and meet their local advisory committee. Still, the area receives financial help for projects such as those outlined in its original constitution.

It is interesting, and perhaps significant, that Coleraine and the county and city of Londonderry have not only benefited greatly in the past as a result of the Plantation of Ulster, so often condemned, but that toward the end of the twentieth century, these areas are still benefiting from the constitution drawn up and the links first forged in London over 300 years ago.

Notes

1. A great Danish King of England and Denmark in the eleventh century. Canute, never deluded, confounded his flattering courtiers by commanding the tide of the Thames to turn back.

19 / 1831—Miss Barbara Young Congratulates Thomas Scott on the Birth of His Eldest Son

Coleraine, May 26th 1831

Dear Mr. Scott
I must tell you I do very sincerely rejoice in the birth of your son. Long may he live and happy may he be. I trust Mrs. Scott is going on well & that you will in reply be able to tell me so remember me most kindly to her I had not heard of the *grand event* having taken place until by chance I met Mr. George Scott in town the other day and indeed I was truly glad tho to the *cut out* of clever little Beadle—I hope Mrs. Scott got her spotted capes in time to put the borders on them. Mrs Carpenter forgot them for some time after I sent them. Give my love to Mrs. Scott and say I hope the next will be better done, I was glad to find you *true blue* at the election in derry but will it oblige you to take up your Q^{rs} at Monaghan.

Tom Richardson is talking of a flight for a short time to England to see Mrs. Layard before she leaves her country for her? *Countess* sister—My people were very glad to return home tho' I think Mrs Richardson liked her

81

visit to Scotland very much—Sir James Bruce is to set off on Monday with his three sisters for the Cove there to leave them for three months to harden them for the winter at Downhill Laura has not been so well these last three days I am going to Down Hill tomorrow to see them off poor things they are very sorry to go or to separate from Lady Bruce and the best of Brothers Mrs. Goulding has taken a house for the summer at Portrush from the 24th of this month and I hear Miss Steele and Miss McCausland are also coming there—I saw Mr & Mrs Ash at portstewart yesterday in the Hotel I think her a very nice Lady like woman I never saw her before. Mr Ash seems much pleased at the birth of *your son* I daresay he would not have any objection to the like but his prospect I think not quite so bright as yours was when I was at Willsboro' What has James Scott got *one*! two! or three! I hope you will join your brother this summer at Portstewart he has I know taken a house on the hill behind Mrs Cromie's—have the furies finished *pounding* your schoolroom and how goes on the young idea

Robert Gye has had his sixth daughter, Lady Bruce her 3ᵈ Mrs Lyle her 13th child within the last month were ever the Ides of March so madning and *I* have a prospect! of an increase to my family you may well say better late than never my *canary* is *clocking* upon 4 eggs!! I shall overtake you yet!! but as I daresay you have not much time to give to nonsense I may as well conclude with every good wish for Mrs Scott yourself and family in which "Susan" joins believe me

My dear Mʳ Scott your very sincere friend *B.J. Young*

Thomas Scott was a son of the James Scott mentioned several times in the Rev. Vaughan Sampson's Survey.

James Scott, second son of William Scott M.P. was destined for the wine trade. He was studying it in Bordeaux when the death of his eldest brother, William, made him the heir and recalled him to Willsboro'. The first member of this Scottish family to come to Ulster was the Rev. Gideon Scott, a chaplain in the forces of William of Orange.

James Scott married Catherine Elizabeth Leslie, daughter of the Bishop of Limerick. They had twelve children: William, James, Joyce, Thomas, Hannah, Edward, Maria, Richard, George, Charles, Jane, and James Leslie Montgomery. James Scott destroyed all his family papers, declaring that it was quite enough for those who came after him to know they were descended from an honest man.

Thomas left home at the age of fifteen and, with an army commission, sailed for Indian in 1798, where he served in the Bengal army. He was with the reinforcements dispatched for Sir Arthur Wellesley's forces that reached him the day after the Battle of Assaye. He was also at the siege of Seringapatan in 1799, during which Tippoo, a sultan who had been negotiating with the French, died fighting. The capture of Seringapatan, Tippoo's capital, was of great significance in that time of intense

Thomas Scott of Willsborough

rivalry between the British and French in India, when Napoleon was in Egypt with a large and hitherto unconquered army, his intention being to proceed from there to India and expel the British from that country where they had been trading since the beginning of the seventeenth century.

The Governor-General of the East India Company, who had been appointed in 1797, was Richard Wellesley, best known as Lord Mornington, elder brother of Sir Arthur Wellesley (later the Duke of Wellington) and a friend of England's Prime Minister, William Pitt. At the Battle of Seringapatan, he and General Harris were in command of the British forces. Both were rewarded for this success, Lord Mornington becoming a Marquis and General Harris a peer.

Lord Mornington's Indian policy—for which he was severely criticized on his return to England in 1806, being accused, though acquitted, of abuse of power—was to destroy French influence in India and make the British the paramount power. This entailed an aggressive policy toward local rulers and transformed the East Indian Company from a trading company into an imperialist body. At a time when Napoleon was at the zenith of his power, Lord Mornington successfully forestalled his designs on India, and this must serve as his excuse for a policy that some may find inexcusable.

In 1806, Thomas Scott's eldest brother, William, a barrister at the Middle Temple, died in London of jail fever. In consequence, Thomas, now the heir, returned to Ulster and lived with his parents at Willsboro' until his father's death.

In 1814, Thomas Scott went to Paris to meet his brother, Edward, who had been fighting in the Peninsular War under Sir Arthur Wellesley and had been seriously ill there.

The Peninsular War broke out when Napoleon, by a mixture of trickery, threats, and invasion, forced the king of Spain and his son to renounce their rights to the Spanish throne, whereupon he made his brother Joseph Bonaparte King of Spain, while Portugal was to be divided between France and Spain. Although both countries were then full of French troops, the people revolted against this occupation and appealed to Great Britain for help. This resulted in the dispatch of arms, money, supplies, and a British force, which included 9,000 men from Ireland under the command of Sir Arthur Wellesley, an Irishman and previously a member of the Irish Parliament. The Peninsular War lasted from 1808 to 1814 when the capture of Paris by the allies and Napoleon's abdication brought it to an end.

Thomas Scott remained in Paris during the 1814–1815 allied occupation of the city, staying in billets with his brother, Edward, who, in due course, recovered his health, left the army, returned to Ulster, and went into the church.

In 1816, Thomas Scott joined his first cousin, Catherine (only child of Sir Edward Leslie), and her husband, Lord Douglas Gordon, traveling with them on the Continent. Lord Douglas Gordon was a brother of the Earl of Aboyne. When the latter became the Marquis of Huntly on the death of his cousin, the last Duke of Gordon, his brothers and sisters were given the rank of Marquis's children. Colonel the Honble Douglas Gordon then became Lord Douglas Gordon. After the death in 1851 of Lady Douglas Gordon, who had no children, a sum of money to which she would have been entitled had she been alive passed to her next of kin, Thomas Scott's children, his residuary legatees.

In 1820, James Scott died, Thomas inherited the Willsboro property and, in 1821, married Hannah Campbell, widow of John Campbell of Limavady, who had one delicate son, Willie Campbell, whose brothers had all died in infancy. After her marriage to Thomas Scott, Hannah Scott had one child, a daughter, Katherine, who died in childhood. Hannah died in 1824.

In 1827, Thomas Scott married again, Anne Lucas, daughter of the Rev. Edward Lucas, by whom he had seven children. The eldest, Elizabeth, was born in 1828, Hannah in 1829, and the first son, James, in 1830, on whose birth Miss Barbara Young sent her belated congratulations to the father.

The clever little Beadle, mentioned in the letter, was Bedell Scott, son of Thomas Scott's brother, the Rev. George Scott.

Thomas Scott was appointed Brigade Major of the Yeomanry of the province of Ulster, a post that he held until the corps was disbanded. It may be to this appointment that miss Barbara Young refers in her letter.

Politically, Ulster had a very strong Whig element in the earlier part of the nineteenth century, but, gradually, with the implementation of reforms and increasing industrial prosperity, the political climate changed, and the province became predominantly Tory, opposed to all liberal[1] proposals for a restoration of an all Ireland Parliament.

Notes

1. Tories became known as Conservatives and Whigs as Liberals.

20 / 1834—To Anne Scott, a Letter of Condolence From Her Sister-in-law, Jane Scott

direct to Post Office
& if writing in uncomfortable to you Thos will
write me a line to tell me particularly about you
Tenby—Pembrokeshire
June 28

My dearest Anne—I should have written to you immediately on hearing of the sorrow it pleased our God to bring upon you, only deferred it as our dear Mother was writing to Thos—a letter from her this morning tells me of her having heard from him—& I am truly thankful ever dear sister to hear what indeed I fully expected that our God of Love was present with you to calm your mind after the first shock had subsided—May He be ever with you in every trial—& truly he will—for his unchanging word says "*I* will never leave thee nor forsake thee"—You have abundant food for consolation in the full assurance that your dear sister was one of God's redeemed children now taken home after a comparatively short pilgrimage—& the time will soon come when those still on their journey will also be gathered in—will bid farewell to sin & sorrow—& be with their Lord—& with each other for ever—blessed prospect—If seen more constantly & more vividly by the eye of faith how much wd it cast into the shade the little trials of the present time—light afflictions when (but truly only when) weighed in the balance of the sanctuary—light as weighed against "Eternal weight of glory—& precious as coming from the hand of Him who doth not afflict willingly & will convert every affliction into a blessing to his children—it was great cause for thankfulness that your dear sisters mind was so supported in the immediate prospect of death—leaving too, those very dear to her—for tho you wd have had no doubt as to her safety, it was another blessed inestimable proof of the faithfulness of Him in whom she trusted—May you & I my beloved sister & all dear to us, *cleave* more closely to that Saviour God who is *all* sufficient for time — for eternity—forgetting those things which are behind, & *reaching forth* for those which are before. May we *press* towards the mark for the prize of the high calling of God in Ld Jesus—poor Mr Biddulph was soon called to experience the utter uncertainty of earthly happiness—May he also be led to experience the comfort of trusting in Him who alone is unchanging—it is when the heart is wounded beyond human cure we learn the full meaning of the emphatic name given by our Lord to the Holy Spirit "the Comforter"—in many cases He alone can comfort—& being God none can be beyond his reach—oh! what a rich portion the very weakest believer in Jesus has even in this life notwithstanding its heart-rending sorrows & often returning trials—without Him—the world would indeed be to many a dreary wilderness which seems to me one reason for His occasionally hiding his face as it were, from his children to keep present to their minds what they wd be

86

without Him—I much long to hear from you again & was indeed relieved to hear of your health continuing (hole in paper here)—I wrote more than half a letter to you just about the time Maria came out finding there was another letter going kept mine, & only tore it a day or two ago—You may believe with what interest I listened to every word Maria could tell me of you & Tho⁵ & the dear children—Charlotte's questions you may suppose were numerous enough—I do hope from all I can hear of your looks that your health is as good as one cd expect in your present situation & that your strength is increased during yʳ confinement. I trust you will find Miss Mackey a comfort for you will feel the children are safe with her— I long to hear if you will have any friend with you at the time—female friend you may well suppose I mean—for your best & dearest friend dear Tho⁵ will I know be with you & as watchful & anxious as man can be—but I shᵈ feel it a comfort to think of someone being on a visit with you at the time—I greatly long to hear from you dearest Anne. I hear Tho⁵ in his letter gives continued favourable account of dear George as heard from & I do think from all the late accᵗˢ we may now hope for a more complete recovery than at one time seemed probable—his valuable life being spared is indeed a mercy to his children, the boon is inestimable—Tho⁵ proved a true prophet in regard to Miss B:—I cd not help feeling very sorry at her leaving them—but possibly an inferior sort of person might do as well & *all* the circumstances many things I have heard are painful & distressing you will know what I mean—but there is one comfort that as far as dear George is concerned all things must work together for good—We much long to know what plan will be fixed on for him—if he will keep to the intention of visiting Clifton—if Bessy & the children will join him if the South of England is recommended for winter—some of the letters spoke at one time of some plan being thought of of his going to the Core of Cork with B & the children—but I do trust & hope that will not be decided on—*even* Balteagh with Tho⁵ within reach wᵈ be better I shᵈ think—but whatever plan is fixed on, we must trust will be directed or overruled by Him whose wisdom & love are both infinite—Charlotte & I came here last Monday for bathing—it was a great step for me to take & latterly brought about quite suddenly—My only fear being the way not being made plain enough—but latterly many little things convinced & our dear Mother taking it up warmly, & speaking to a gentleman coming at that time brought it to a point—I had not been very well for the last six weeks or two months before Maria returned, but still thought it would wear off but after she came back my old distressing symptoms returned stronger than ever, so that I was equal for very little exertion without being ill after it—& as bathing & sea air always agreed with me, she & her dear Mother most kindly joined in wishing me to try it—I at first thought of Clifton, but we heard from every one that it wᵈ not do for bathing, the water not being salt & thick with mud—this, in every way seemed to be the most desirable within reach, & from what I have seen of it I like it greatly—a fine sandy beach—rocky shore & fresh blue ocean dashing against it—the houses are built close by the sea—some of them on the rocks with glass doors from the ground floor sitting rooms leading out to steps cut on the rocks to lead down to the bathing place—the town is very old & built in curious little straggling cross streets which are puzzling to a stranger—we have not yet been a Sunday here—the Gospel is not preached in the Parish Church as I hear, but at a little distance—the poor people I understand are generally in ignorance, but those I have met with are generally pleasing & civil in manner—Much more so than about Clifton & with much more appearance of simplicity—the air feels quite delightful—so fresh & pleasant tho' there has been a good deal of rain since we came—we have bathed twice & began already to have appetites so sharpened by the sea-air, that the food taken to satisfy *must* be nourishing, I trust with God's blessing to return strong & well for I have no one symptom that I had not before—& already I trust dear Maria will get on well till I return, she has the comfort of Miss Lawrence's society, which she much likes & returned from Ireland so different both in spirits & looks, that I trust she will keep up pretty well for a time & between Lynemouth & Ireland she was above six months absent in the last year & it certainly was of very great use to her—it *is* wearing to the mind being in close contact in one quarter—it is great cause for thankfulness that it neither lessens the cheerfulness nor ruffles the sweetness of the one most nearly interested—our dear Mother, I am thankful to say, was quite well when I left her, & hear by her own letter & Marias of today, that she still continues so—the latter promised most certainly to write & tell me in case of any illness coming on that I might return to join her—I have not heard from Canada since the letters you heard of some time ago, but had the comfort of hearing from a gentleman in London today that he had a letter from my dear Father, dated 19th May & that they were all quite well, so I may hope for letters in a day or two—I have written you a long letter dearest, perhaps longer that may be pleasant when y^r mind is occupied with other things—Charlotte is quite well & delighted with this shore—Mr. Greathem of the Crescent & family are near us & exceedingly kind & Capt Ireby who came in the Steam Packet with us, was as kind & attentive as c^d possibly be—he and Mrs Ireby are also here from Clifton—his name you often meet with in Keiths 1st work on Prophecy in company with his brother in law Capt Mangles this long letter must come to an end—give my ever affct^e love to Thos & kisses to the dear children—truly I feel they are dear to my heart—tell Thos we were hearing a great many particulars about a school kept by a clergyman a Mr Birch—a very small number taken— & just as I felt sure it would answer particularly well, we heard he had got a living & was going to give up school—Capt de la Cordamin who married my dear Janet Agnew had been there & greatly pleased with all he saw & heard, but there is no use in saying this now—we may possibly hear of some other that he can visit when he comes over himself if he still intends removing Willy C. I was very glad to know of the latter from Maria & trust he may grow up all that you & Thos c^d wish—may our God of Love be with you dearest Anne I am y^r ever attached sister J. Scott Charlotte sends many loves

Jane Scott (née Farrel) was the widow of Charles Scott, Thomas Scott's brother, who had gone to India, served in the army there, and later was a judge in Ceylon for many years prior to his recent death.

Anne Scott was Thomas Scott's second wife.

Elizabeth, Anne Scott's eldest child, in some autobiographical notes, mentions that the first thing she remembers is being bridesmaid to her aunt, Catherine Lucas, who was married to Mr. Biddulph of Congee House, Tipperary, at Willsboro' in Eglinton Church. Catherine Biddulph died in childbirth, and Jane Scott's letter of sympathy refers to her death.

"Our dear Mother" was the widow of James Scott, and mother of Thomas and Charles Scott, who moved to Clifton after her husband's death in 1820, with her two unmarried daughters Maria and Jane. Maria afterward left home to look after her delicate motherless nephew, James Ogilby, son of her sister Joyce, who had married Mr. Ogilby of Pellipar. Jane lived with her mother until she died and then continued to live at Clifton for the remainder of her own life. No letter from or references to this Jane, Thomas Scott's sister, are included in this collection.

George, who was so very ill, was the Rev. George Scott, the father of "clever little Beadle," who had married Elizabeth Richardson in 1824—the "Bessie" mentioned in this letter.

Willy C. was Thomas Scott's stepson, who had always been delicate, the son of his first wife.

Charlotte was the daughter of Charles and Jane Scott.

Since the birth of her eldest son, James, in 1831, Anne Scott had had another son in 1833. In June 1834, when she received Jane Scott's letter, she was again pregnant, and her third son, Thomas Lucas, was born later in that year, increasing the number of her children to five.

1834—Jane Scott writes again to Anne Scott

4 Paragon, Clifton, Bristol
Decr 26

You will begin to think my letters threaten to fall as fast as dead leaves in Autumn My dearest Anne when you see my handwriting so soon again. I might carry the parallel further, but this will do for the present purpose & in the first place I may tell you that our dear Mother keeps quite well, and I never saw her in better spirits—her deafness is, I am sorry to say *at times* much increased which renders much conversation a little difficult, but it is a comfort that she does not seem to mind it herself—you may suppose I make it a point to see her every day during Maria's absence—she, Maria, writes such accounts of dear George as I think we might *reasonably* expect—that is—not so good as he wrote about himself—but that the improvement sh^d be quite so rapid was scarcely to be looked for—she says he certainly looks stronger and better—but that there is still a good deal of expectoration & great delicacy of stomach—that she sees an evident change in cold weather, for they have had some very cold days—Bessie, she says, is grown very watchful about him, which is a great comfort—She speaks of returning here, the week after next—but I think it very likely she will not come so soon unless some very tempting opportunity sh^d offer—& indeed I sh^d much rather on her own account she sh^d make a longer stay for her spirits sink so low here that it cannot be good for her—but it is time I should tell you the reason for my writing so soon again without hearing from you—it is to ask you to do a commission and I think, my dear sister, kindness will excuse the trouble—could you make enquiries about Miss Styles, Mrs Gough's Governess—it is reported here that she is to leave her in Spring—or rather in June—and a gentleman—the Mr Campbell I think I mentioned to you in my last is very anxious to find out, if she is in *reality* so well suited to his wants, as he hears she is—I have told him of you, and your vicinity to Mrs Gough, and he says he will be quite satisfied to be guided by your judgment as to how far you w^d think she w^d answer for him when I have described to you what he requires—I believe that I told you that he lost his wife in France and has two daughters and two sons—the eldest son a fine young man about one or two and twenty (but with him it is to be hoped the governess would not have much to do) his eldest daughter now about 18 and the younger about 14—so that it would require someone qualified to be companion to the eldest as well as governess to the youngest—& apart from their situation and connections, *manner* is not unimportant but rather the reverse—Miss Styles he heard spoken of as quite a gentlewoman, which under the circumstances of the family having no Mother is peculiarly desirable—he would require her to undertake entirely the education without the assistance of Masters, and a thorough knowledge of music is needful—as they will be certainly in the Highlands of Scotland during the summer months, and possibly occasionally during the winter also—all these matters are easily found out—but I said further that I felt sure my dear sister would inquire particularly from Mrs "G" as to the principles, mind, and disposition etc.—he did not say much as to piety, but although not yet quite a decided character himself, I am sure he w^d wish one that w^d train his daughter up in the way his wife had begun—the young people seem very pleasing—the eldest steady, composed & sweet looking with *some* of her Mother's beauty—it would seem to be a most desirable situation for a superior Governess—he has heard so much of Miss Styles, that he says if you are satisfied with what Mrs G tells you; he w^d feel very much obliged by your engaging her, if she is willing for it—lest there sh^d be any fear of her forming some other engagement—he hears her terms are £100 a year—and if so he w^d give it—but that c^d be ascertained by asking her—his place is in the Highlands of Scotland in Argyleshire—& in case she goes to him in June, she w^d cross over from Ireland to Glasgow—but I think myself that the best plan w^d be, after you have ascertained all particulars & have written to me in return, for him to enter into correspondence with her & form his own engagement—as of course, if she thinks the place desirable on your mentioning it she will not form any other engagement till she hears further from him & Well, dearest Anne, am I giving you a great deal of trouble—I fear I am—but I do hope it may be the means of bringing a letter to me from you very soon—do dear sister tell me particularly of yourself & all belonging to you—I was at the Crescent this morning & was charged with messages of love to you & Thomas & though it is too late to wish a happy Xmas yet it is not so to wish many happy New Years—not as words of course but as the real desire of the heart—give my kind love also to dear Thomas—he seemed to me the last time he was over to be if possible more—I was going to say "in love" but it is not so pretty—more devoted I may say to his wife than ever—for he was almost angry at any of us supposing that two or three days additional absence was not a matter of such very great consequence as he felt it to be—but I believe in my heart I like him all the better for it—& tell me of your dear little ones—& how Miss Mackay comes on—Maria does not say a word of Mlle Adele in her last letter—but in a former one to her Mother seemed to think a gayer place would be more suitable to her so I suppose she will not be likely to remain very long—I go on in my usual course—feeling to enjoy the use of my limbs for a little & then knocking myself up & losing my sleep till I lay by for a little—Charlotte is quite well and sends many loves—have you heard lately from Elizth or Ja^s we have not heard of them for a long time—did they get a governess—give Aunt Jane's best love to the dear children—& may our God abundantly bless you my dearest Anne—& may he lead us both to devote our hearts each day more singly more unreservedly to Him—leading us to live—not to ourselves but to Him who lovest us & gave Himself for us—I am ever your most affectionate attached sister J. Scott

Elizabeth, mentioned above, was Anne Scott's sister Elizabeth Lucas, who had married James Scott, another of Thomas Scott's brothers. They had nine sons and three daughters, two sons and one daughter dying young.

Mrs. Gough, from whom inquiries were to be made about Miss Styles, was the wife of the Dean of Derry.

After 1835—Jane Scott, widow of Charles Scott, writes to her sister-in-law, Maria Scott, in Clifton.

2nd August,
Kingston, Upper Canada

I cannot tell you how disappointed I was to find yesterday that I could not answer your most welcome letter, my dearest Maria, in time for the Great Western; the delay has been occasioned by our being absent for change of air for us both neither being well and this same cause has prevented my writing as I intended before yours arrived, on a subject I know will be deeply interesting to your affectionate heart each day I thought I should write the first settled day, but various things lead us to move from place to place; this is however the first letter I write across the Atlantic on the subject; it has pleased our God that my dear Charlotte should gain the affections of the one in Canada of all I have seen that I should choose for her, if I had my choice, all things taken into consideration. I may have mentioned to you Mr. Givens, an excellent young clergyman, who is stationed among the Mohawk indians in the Bay of Quinte about 40 or 50 miles from this. We first met him about a year ago as he had not been in the habit of coming to Kingston except passing rapidly through, to and from Toronto, but since then his visits have been much more frequent, and as an intimate friend of his, a married clergyman sought for increased intimacy, it greatly facilitated his wish for further acquaintance but somehow it never entered either Charlotte's head or mine that he had thought of the matter from the first time he saw her, but she was surrounded by so many ardently anxious to pay her attention that he having an unduly humble opinion of himself, feared for some time, there was no hope of his gaining her: you may suppose how thankful I was to find on his proposal being made, that she much preferred him to any one she had met with; if I was sitting beside you, I could whisper in your ear some things that would interest and amuse you and which raise a feeling of continued thankfulness mingled with a sort of surprise, on looking back just all they did at the time of occurrence, at the way in which our God guarded and guided and arranged matters with such care in regard to forwarding this event and keeping off some others part of which she knows nothing of herself, and some things occurred just about the time of her acceptance of Mr. G. which there was no use in mentioning to anyone nor is there any use in my saying this to you, only that I am in the habit of speaking all my mind when writing to you which leads me sometimes to rather desultory and wandering; he is son to a colonel Givens of Toronto and since entering into the Ministry has been stationed among the Mohawk indians for the last year or two he had had the rectory of Napanea annexed to his parish of which he does all the duty without as yet receiving any emoluments, though the parish is a very widely extended one and the church eight miles distant from his home but there is hope of another clergyman being before very long appointed to the latter; his house is situated near the water in a romantic and beautiful situation with the Indian church close to it and many indian huts and cottages within a short distance; he is himself a most pleasing person, the general cast of his countenance inclined perhaps to gravity but mingled with great benevolence and sweetness, all of which appear also in manner which is characterized by dignity and calmness brightened occasionally with a degree of liveliness which is very pleasing; he is of decided piety and appears to be looked up to even by those further advanced in years than himself among his brother clergymen; they all seem particularly attached to him and express themselves so delighted with the choice he has made that I feel it quite gratifying indeed, my dear child is not like what she was when you saw her or rather she has the same character softened and sweetened, as I trust and believe by the operation of the spirit of our God; she has still a sort of startling severity bordering at times on bluntness but a something at the same time which has a sort of power of attraction in an unconscious degree over the hearts of some of the most opposite characters and habits of life and mind which I think must be partly owing to her manner having become perfectly natural and open which entirely suited with her sweet open countenance; she refused, as I believe I told you, all large parties such as balls etc. during the winter, but between sewing parties and various other things of the kind, there was still a great deal going on and knowing her disposition well, I thought it better not to restrain her, only constantly offering it all up into the hands of Him who has all hearts in his hands and you may suppose my thankfulness on her determining to give up everything in the way of worldly amusements, finding it so difficult to choose a line and keep within any bounds among young people so bent on making amusement the business of life as those here and this too when she had everything in the way of attention to make going out sweet to her and before she knew anything of Mr. G. indeed nothing would be more unsought on our part than the intimacy with him; the young people used to jest her about being the belle of the navy, from the head down and latterly it has been a "clergy reserve" or a church belle etc. etc. as they say I have been educating her for the church all along in my own shortsighted wisdom I could have wished her not to enter into the marriage state so early but as He who is infinite in wisdom and knows the end from the beginning saw fitting to allow matters to take the course they have done, I feel I ought not to throw any unnecessary obstacles in the way as to time, the more especially as his feelings are warmly engaged in the business that he finds difficult to keep to his daily duties so far away, it will therefore probably take place in September towards the middle or end; we have to be busy getting the fitting out which is a more difficult business here than at home and we have both been ill as I mentioned but now I am thankful to say we are greatly better Charlotte was really extremely unwell the illness I think brought on by cold; she sends her very kindest love and feels that few people will feel such sincere interest as yourself; you can tell dear Mrs. Bowdler with our affectionate love. I well know the kind interest she will feel in hearing of the tender providential care of our God for my child; He has allowed me to see His hand every step of the way I have written unintentionally on such bad paper I fear you will scarce be able to read it and I am grieved to hear of dearest Anne being so delicate but trust from what you say it may turn out something in connection with her present situation; I shall be longing much to hear again. Write soon as ever you receive this. I was still going on with education as the books etc. I sent for would tell you and Charlotte and I were just wondering after Letitia's marriage what would come next to interrupt us. My dear sister K. and Mr. Armstrong feel as much interest as if Charlotte belonged to themselves. Give our kindest remembrances to Mrs. Hayes and Miss Heath and Mrs. Smith. I saw Captain Townsend today who seemed in excellent health and spirits—this is a wretchedly written letter in every way—give our kindest love to all at Willsborough and Balteagh also to Richard and James

93

if you write; give our kind love also to Jane and tell her I am sure she will feel kindly interested and glad Charlotte has met with one so excellent as a companion for life, ever my dearest Maria yours most affectionately J. Scott. Postmark New York 15 August. Stamped "Liverpool Ship Letter".

After this letter Mrs. Jane Scott and her daughter Charlotte pass from the pages of this book for none of the letters or diaries mention them again.

"Dearest Anne" was Mrs. Thomas Scott, who was once more pregnant.

21 / 1836—A Trip to the Continent—Kitty Richardson Writes to her Mother

This letter is addressed to Mrs. Richardson
Somerset,
Coleraine
Ireland
    Via Londres
The first postmark is Schafhausen and dated 16 Jul 1836, the second is London 21 July 1836, and the third and forth are simply A Jy 21 1836, and 4236Y23 1836. There is also a stamp "Suisse par Belfort."

Schaffhausen, Friday evening
near eleven o'clock

My dear Mama, Here we are safe and well, Papa & Henry gone to bed very tired We were delighted to get your letter the day before we left Wiesbaden & I should have written to say so sooner—if I had had the time but we left Mayence (where to our great surprise we had met Mr L & Mrs Lyle of Oaks) on Monday morning at 4 o'clock passed Manheim & spent the night at Leopoldschafen where we were almost devoured by mosquitos—next morning off again spent that day & night & till 4 the next day in the steamer making our way to Kehl/ that was slow work/ the same evening we drove on to Offenberg where we were extremely comfortable & got a nice plan of the best route to see a great deal in a short time from the Innkeeper & hired a Voiture to bring us to Zurich so on Thursday we came by the Black Forest to a queer little village Furstenwald where we had above stairs and the cows below but we were very comfortable. Henry & I were greatly pleased by the Forest the Valley of Kingzuk & the beautiful waterfall of Triburg—but I am

94

sorry to say that the people did not seem to understand our German very well unless we spoke about money This morning we were off very early in order to see the Falls of the Rhine before dark but after seeing the source of the Danube & walking through the Prince Furstenburg's ground & greenhouse when we set off again going up a very steep hill off went one of the wheels & we went very nearly over but not quite the nut could not be found so we waited a long time getting it repaired sufficiently to bring us on so that the sun was set before we got to the Falls but still it was most magnificent. Henry was greatly pleased & Papa confesses he did not do it half justice we are to see it again tomorrow on our way to Zurich Yes, you are very right to get a governess for Mary but still you might send her to play herself a little in April & bring the girls over for three months as Papa wishes so much he has been at me to write this letter but is much too sleepy to say anything, we had so much walking up steep hills & waiting in the sun for the carriage that I am somewhat fatigued myself so pray forgive any small mistakes give my best love to the girls My next shall be to them—good night I tore up all my letters before I left Wiesbaden—so I cannot remember if there was anything in yours that required a particular answer, but I hope not Your affecte daughter Kitty.

Posted from Geneva on 26th August 1836

Monday July 25th

My dear Mama Papa says I must write to you from this to tell you that we have got on very well so far, that we set out for Paris tomorrow—intend leaving it early next week—but Papa says he will write from Paris himself and inform you how soon you may expect to see us. I really cannot begin—here in a hurry, as it is my only day for looking about Mehern—to describe our delightful little tour through Switzerland and it is such a beautiful country I feel quite sorry leaving it. I believe I wrote last from Schaffhausen from that place we took a guide and came by Zurich to the higher mountain in the Canton of Schwartz which we ascended on horseback, no very easy job but quite worth the trouble we spent the night on the top of it and then next day came across the lake of Lucerne to a nice little village called Hypsomach where we spent the night and the next morning crossed another mountain the Brising also on horseback and very tired the master was after these exploits but I would be too happy to go back again over the same route for I never saw anything so beautiful We then came across the lake of Brienz to Interlaken from which we made our excursion to the glacier of Grindlewald but the day was too cloudy and we could not see the high mountains to advantage from Interlaken we came by Berne to Lausanne intending to cross the lake in a steamer, but the day was so stormy we gave up all hopes of its appearing and came here in a carriage on Saturday night & yesterday we went to the English Church and heard a very good sermon—This house is very full & I must go and get ready for table d'hote where there are a great many

English though this year it is said the French are become the greatest travellers—I always like very much to meet them they have so much to say for themselves & say it so prettily. I hope when I get home I shall find you have got a governess for Molly—Papa is quite resolved that you & Fanny & Barbara—at least shall take a little trip here next year he says you did not see Switzerland at all—and though certainly this is a pretty place I hardly admire it after what I have seen but then the weather is so cloudy I do not see it to advantage, I have only got one little peep of Mont Blanc. Most of the English we meet here are either returned from Italy or Stopping short on their way to it for fear of the Cholera which is very bad there now—Papa has been uncommonly well today he seems a little inclined to complain of a pain in his back but I do not think it is of any consequence a pill will set it all right again. I think it is partly an excuse for making me write instead of taking the trouble himself. I daresay you will have heard of us from the Lyles before this reaches you—but only think of our passing Mrs Murray between Schaffhausen and Zurich—Papa called out there is Mrs Murray but we were both going too fast to stop—we afterwards found her name and the Deans in the books belonging to the Hotels—they I suppose will go home by the Rhine whilst we go by France—How often I have wished for you all this last week—how delighted Fanny would have been Henry & I both taxed our powers of sketching but it would not do—Papa has been to the office and is a little disappointed not to find a letter, but I hope we shall find one in Paris—What a fuss you would be in if you could hear me speaking French—but I do not stop at trifles as I think practising is the only way to improve Papa & Henry are out at present & I am busy scribbling on a little till they come in to take it to the post. Give my love to the girls & to the children—I was greatly tempted the other day to take Barbara home a squirrel to make up to her for the loss of her bulfinch (are there two l's in Bulfinch) & I certainly would have done so if I had met with it a little nearer home than at the Glacier of Grundelwald. I suppose Aunt & Gregory are in Rathlin goodbye my dear Mama Your Afec^te daughter

Kitty

Letter addressed to Mrs Richardson. Postmarks dated 8 Au 1836 & 10 Au 1836

Ibbotsons Hotel Monday

Well my dear Mama here we are again in this damp little Island which assumes to itself so much authority among the nations of the world—I bid you goodbye this day week when I was going to church in the Champs Elysee where I heard a very beautiful sermon & where we met Mrs Spencer Knox who has got a very nice house there (in the Champs Elysee) she was very pleasing and kind we spent Tuesday evening with her—& on Wednesday morning we came to Versailles where we walked about for an hour or two—but could not see the inside of the Palace as His Majesty was there & he is rather shy of strangers poor man—in the evening we drove to a little village Maison Lafitte where we slept till wakened by a tremendous thunderstorm & in the morning embarked in a little steamboat & came down the Seine as far as Rouen where we spent the night next morning visited William the Conqueror's castle & got on board La Normandie which brought us to Havre—just in time to step in to the Camilla which landed us at Portsmouth about 8 o'clock on Saturday morning & the same evening arrived here—spent Sunday at the Admiralty & found your letter—one from Aunt Layard inviting us to spend the day at Leamington with the Egertons & a note from Lady Garvagh inviting us to dine, drink tea, or breakfast at Mrs Peters about 8 miles from this—so tomorrow we breakfast with them—next day go to Leamington next evening to Birmingham & Friday to Liverpool in time to start in the Coleraine on Saturday—so if you like you may inquire at what time it is expected to arrive on Sunday morning & send a cart to Portrush for our luggage & we will manage to get up in one of Johnny Shorts cars—Do not send the carriage for it would not carry all our luggage I would write more if my ink were better but I am afraid of you not being able to make out this—Sir T. Troubridge is not quite well but very kind as well as his Lady—Captain Bruce sets off on Sunday evening to go on board the Imogene at Plymouth his daughter is pronounced to be quite well Mr Ponsonby Tottenham has just been making kind inquiries after you—Mr Touchet set off this morning for Southampton I am happy to say—Well I have seen a good deal since I was here last—which I sincerely hope Fanny & Barbara will be able to see with you next year—Papa is lying down in hopes to get rid of a little touch of lumbago which I think is only the effect of having lain uncomfortably in the steamer he had a slight threatening of it at Geneva as I believe I told you after travelling all night—but it went off completely, & he had not the slightest return till today—& I think it will soon go also—as he has taken a little dose—he was very seasick & had not room to make himself comfortable the vessel was so crowded—Good bye Your afec^te daughter

Kitty

"Papa" was the Rev. Thomas Richardson, owner of the Somerset estate, rector of Macosquin, and a member of the Court of the Common Council of Coleraine.

"Henry" was his son, who later married the daughter of Admiral Lord Mark Ker and, in 1838, stood in the Parliamentary election against Alderman Copeland, nominee of the Irish Society, and member of the Corporation of London, who had been the successful candidate in the vital election of 1832. Alderman Copeland was an eminently suitable candidate who had served Coleraine well, but in spite of this and lavish expenditure during the election, he only defeated Henry Richardson by two or three votes. Henry Richardson died in 1844 when just forty years of age.

Mr. and Mrs. Lyle of "Oaks" were Acheson Lyle and his wife, Eleanor, daughter of James Warre of Randalls Park, Surrey.

Acheson Lyle was the son of Samuel Lyle and Esther Acheson.

Rathlin is a small island off the Antrim Coast near Ballycastle. In earlier times, it was one of the islands of the Hebrides and was known as Rahery. Robert the Bruce took refuge there and, according to tradition, was inspired by a persevering Ulster spider to continue the struggle, which resulted in his regaining his Scottish throne. His second wife, Elizabeth, was the daughter of Richard de Burgh, earl of Ulster. Their only son David succeeded his father as king of Scotland.

One member of the Richardson family, Elizabeth (Bessie), had already married into the Scott family, being the mother of "clever little Beadle."

Kitty Richardson, writer of these letters, in the unknown future that lay before her in 1836, was also destined to become a Mrs. Scott, and, as a married woman, will be mentioned again later in this book.

22 / 1835/1838—Extracts From the Journal of Anne Scott

Willsborough April 17th 1835
Good Friday
It is now just 20 years ago since it pleased God to take my earthly father from us & leave us 4 orphans—how awful to think of the lapse of time how unprofitably has my share been spent—how short a portion may now remain—one[1] among us has been taken away the last year (taken I trust from the evil to come) how long shall the remaining 3 be spared May we redeem the time and *all* be brought into God's fold—how often during those 20 years have I been in difficulties in straits in distresses & the Lord has helped, in dangers & he has protected me in sorrow & he has comforted me in pain & sickness & he has supported & restored me As a Father pitieth his child so has the Lord pitied & helped me & what have been my returns—Oh most ungrateful unnumbered have been my blessings temporal & spiritual I have rested in the gifts & forgotten the Giver—buried myself in worldly things neglected those of the spirit—Lord avert from me the consequences of being carnally minded—save me from the consequences of sin blessed be his glorious name. May 12 . . . Indolence I find the bane of all that is useful &

98

excellent in character it especially hinders our walk with God—I feel quite alarmed & almost in despair when I contemplate its effects on my own mind May I be helped to overcome it—but it seems to have destroyed my own character O may it not be suffered to destroy my soul its ravages in my mind are frightful sometimes lead me to fear derangement Lord help me—. . . . Lord do as thou has said remove *this* mountain for me— . . . . . . my darlings all spared often in answer to prayer all sensible all healthy pleasant to my eyes & mind Their father also spared & every year dearer to my heart & more worthy of being so All peaceful prosperous & sweet around me these are my temporal blessings continued through another year & spiritual ones how many also!

1836 Feby 5th First week in Advent—My dear husband left me this morning. May the gracious Lord be his guide his protector & bring him back in peace keep me from repining & loneliness & fear during his absence may I draw nearer to my heavenly husband All things now seem settled satisfactorily the Lord has heard my prayer & provided a Christian for the care of my children & all our family are protestants may all sin be kept from our house May we rule diligently in the fear of the Lord.

November 25th 1837 . . . . . We have returned to our home after an absence of 6 months and have made many changes in our establishment not without prayer for a blessing & direction . . . My beloved husband is in health & my six children thriving around me may all be the Lords and may he keep me from being a stumbling block in their way.

1837 Dec 13th—George & Mr Henderson arrive their visit most profitable chiefly in the way of humiliation I find my heart is proud my mind uncharitable & my nature thoroughly selfish. A long sweet interesting letter from dear Jane from Toronto to George cheered & soothed but convicted me of want of feeling for that sweet Christian sister.

Friday 15th—Mr. Richardson departed this life after a few days illness his death has caused great searching of hearts both in his own bereaved family & among others O may the awful impression not pass away till its work is accomplished drawing us into nearer communion with Him & more earnest preparation for our own summons. Poor Mr R. little expected his in the midst of the battle in which he was at the time engaged I have more reason to contemplate mine O my Saviour enlighten the dark valley that I may be able to dwell upon it.

17th A happy Sabbath much comfort in school Sermon profitable . . . . . enjoyed great pleasure from reading Elijah the Ishbite- great pleasure from my dear little James' love for the Scriptures—

Monday 18th Dec. 1837 Thos attended Mr. Richardson's funeral & saw the afflicted family & also George who had much connection with them rejoicing in the hope of their beloved's happiness he died lamenting his life tho amiable & moral had been too much devoted to the world applied with firm faith to the Saviour & breathed out his soul in prayer "Him that cometh to me I will in no wise cast out" May his family be enabled to keep to their resolve of living to Him & then this sad dispensation will be indeed rich in mercy to them.

On the same day Mr Barre Beresford was summoned away from the cares & Pleasures & business of this life I have heard no particulars of his end may it have been peace through the Saviour who casts out none who come even at the eleventh hour. . . . . So teach us to number our days O Lord that we may apply our hearts to wisdom.

1838 A new Year

18th Two young men went to shoot wildfowl on the water their boat upset at the very moment of laughter & folly one a boy of 13 was providentially saved by a man in a small punt who had room but for one took the weakest the other perished as well as a boatman who had accompanied them the father of 5 children it is greatly to be feared the two taken were in a state of intoxication though not in the habit of giving way to that sin the intense cold tempted to give way to it—O how fearful is sin let no one say this is *the last* indulgence or it is the *first* & there is an excuse in the *act* of it we may be summoned to the bar of God to give an account O let us fear it let us flee from it, let us prepare to meet our God The poor corpse lay in this house all yesterday May the impressive warning be felt by all the bereavement sanctified to his afflicted family in which one has been taken the other most providentially left for a longer sojourn here may he be saved in the end.

Sunday March 11th 1838 I have been suffering both in mind & body but then I know he who hath helped me in *six* troubles can help me in the next weakness restlessness pain & impatience for the end what may *that end* be Lord have mercy on me pardon & help let Patience have her perfect work be strength to my weakness wisdom to my folly bear me up in thine own arms that the floods may not overflow my soul Only to me thy countenance show I ask no more than Jordan thru.

In common with many devout Christians of her day, Anne Scott was obsessed with a sense of sin that constantly plunged her into a state of deep and painful introspection, overwhelming her with self-reproach. In consequence, she suffered from the injurious effects against which William Rathbone had warned his young wife, Bessie, writing, "Do not dwell too much on what you consider your deficiencies. This weakens the mind," and again, quoting the advice of his remarkable and exceptionally well-balanced mother, "Do not let us mistake constitutional melancholy or timidity for contrition, the past is gone and can only be useful to us as regulating our future conduct."

The few extracts from Anne's journal quoted here are revealing and pathetic, but the facts that her husband was devoted to her and that her eldest daughter, Elizabeth, has left written testimony, "as long as my Mother lived we were a very bright happy set of children," suggest that she kept her daily religious torment to herself and cast no blight on the happiness of her household. She never suffered the derangement she sometimes feared.

100

The Mr. Richardson mentioned in the journal was the Rev. Thomas Richardson of "Somerset," who, in 1836, took Kitty Richardson and her brother Henry on a short tour on the Continent.

"Dear George" was the Rev. George Scott, who had married Bessie Richardson.

Barre Beresford was a burgess of Coleraine and chamberlain of the Court of its Common Council.

The "sweet Christian sister," who evoked unchristian feelings in Anne Scott, was Jane Scott, widow of Charles Scott, two of whose letters, written from England, have already appeared in this book.

Since 1834, Anne Scott had had another child, Annette, born in 1836, and, in March 1838, she was again pregnant. It is clear that she looked forward with terror to the ordeal of labor and delivery of her seventh child.

It seems probable that the "indolence" of which she accuses herself was really due to ill health and weakness resulting from her frequent pregnancies, a condition not recognized by the medical science of her day.

The baby, another boy, christened Charles Stewart, was born safely on the seventeenth of March, and Anne Scott survived.

In 1840, Anne was pregnant once more, and here her eldest daughter's autobiographical notes, written in old age, can best describe what happened on that occasion:

After a serious illness our Mother had a dead born child, she was recovering & wheeled into the drawingroom every day. I had just seen her reading her bible in her chair at the fire (in her room) and she said she was coming soon. Her maid found her door locked. My father and W. Campbell (his stepson) burst open the door & found her lying dead on the floor. It was a terrible scene when our father collected his seven children in the school room & prayed with them, it is all stamped on my brain as if it was yesterday, the boys James Willy & Tom weeping silently on the sofa, Charlie carried in, about two years old & Annette about 4, Hannah and I taking charge of them & kneeling with our father at the table. After this our father shut himself up in his office & seemed to be reading & writing a great deal, we found afterwards that he had been brushing up his Latin & translated the whole of Julius Caesar into English, so that he might teach the boys.

In 1919, Charles Scott wrote "My earliest recollection, when I could only have been 2 years & 9 months old, was the scene of my Mothers death." Annette Scott also, when a very old woman, mentioned many times the vivid and terrible memory of that scene in the school room at Willsborough.

1. Anne's sister, Mrs. Biddulph.

23 / 1840/1844—Thomas Scott and His Family

The death of Anne Scott changed the happy, carefree life of her children, previously spent between Willsborough and Portstewart. "We migrated to Portstewart every summer a great undertaking driving over the mountain a cart of hay with a cow tied to it preceding us," recalls Elizabeth and later: "After our Mother's death we had not such a happy life."

For the time being, the three eldest children, Elizabeth, Hannah, and James, continued their education in the schoolroom, taught by Miss Addis, a nursery governess.

Two years later, the whole family moved to Cheltenham, taking a house in Landsdowne Crescent.

We brought over all our Irish serv^{ts} Elizabeth contines: and also our jaunting car & handsome horse called Lady of the Lake because she once saved W. Campbells life by swimming across a lake it was the wonder of the inhabitants James & Tom were sent as boarders to Cheltenham College. Willie (Scott) to a private school he was not strong. It was while we were at Cheltenham that we got the sad news that W. Campbell had died at Gibraltar of fever. He had joined his regiment there it was the Welsh Fusiliers.

Willie Campbell had lived at Willsborough ever since the death of his mother, Thomas Scott's first wife, and the whole family were very fond of him. He was devoted to his stepfather and left Thomas Scott all he possessed, which included property in Limavady as well as money.

The following year, 1843, Thomas Scott returned to Ulster with Annette, Charlie, and their governess, living in a house he owned in Limavady while alterations were being made to Willsborough. "Hannah & I went to a private school in London kept by 2 Miss Stiles who had been finishing governesses. They had only 6 pupils. We often spent holidays & weekends with our Aunt Maria, our father's sister who lived with Mr Ogilby at Ham Common near Richmond Park." Mr. Ogilby, son of her sister Joice, was Aunt Maria's delicate nephew with whom she lived for many years. Here is a letter from Aunt Maria to Elizabeth written at this time:

> I feel a strong desire my dear Lizzy to rise betimes in the morning & with a large shawl on my shoulders & warm bonnet on my head present myself before you & with a hearty kiss manifest my affection for you on this your birthday, wishing that every return of it may find you wiser better & happier than the preceding one, a visit at so unseasonable an hour would however be out of order & would evince more of Irish warmth than English sobriety so I content myself by sending a deputy in the form of a little note to express all I have to say to you Your Cousin Ogilby[1] would have been very glad you & Hannah could have dined with us but he feels it would not be right to ask the favour contrary to the rules of the school & the wishes of your Papa he sends you Keith on fulfilled prophecies a book which combines amusement with instruction (I hope you have not already got it) as a birthday gift, Johnson's little tale is Aunt Marias gift, I hope you will like it it is prettily written—I had a letter since I saw you from Chester, your Aunt Jane gives a very good account of her health her brother also is much better your Aunt is very busy with her two pupils her Welch girl & Cecil, she is teaching them both English
>
> I must now my dear girl wish you good night a very happy day to morrow & remain your sincerely attached Aunt
>
> M. Scott

The Aunt Jane mentioned in Maria Scott's letter is her unmarried sister.

Clearly one Miss Stiles had fulfilled all the stringent requirements set out by Aunt Jane (Charles Scott's widow) in her letter to Anne Scott of December 1834.

While at school, the brothers and sisters came back to Limavady for their holidays

> by a long sea voyage from Liverpool in the "Maiden City"—it took 30 sometimes 35 hours & often stuck in the Lough Foyle just opposite Willsborough—"We enjoyed our holidays spending many happy days at Fruithill now Drenagh and at Roe Park. . . . . . The McNaughtons were at Roe Park while Dunderave was being built by Sir Edmund McNaughton . . . . . no motors in those days but our father always drove 4 horses when we went further than Derry to Bellarene Fruithill or Roepark, sometimes over the mountains to Portstewart or Cromore & made expeditions to Knocktarna & delightful pic-nics.

In 1844, Thomas Scott married Katherine Elizabeth Richardson, eldest daughter of the Rev. Thomas Richardson, the "Kitty" who wrote to her mother from the Continent.

103

1. Robert Ogilby married (1) Mary, daughter of John Morland of Dublin, (2) Joice, eldest daughter of James Scott of Willsboro. Her children (1), Alexander (2) James, born 1812 died 1885, was succeeded by his cousin Robert Alexander Ogilby, grandfather of Conolly McCausland.

24 / 1843—General Sir Edward Nicholls, K.C.B., Writes to Hugh Lyle

The Nicholls family, of which Sir Edward Nicholls was the eldest of seven sons, was well known in Coleraine. His mother was a Miss Cuppage before her marriage, and his grandfather, great-grandfather, and great-great-grandfather, on his mother's side, had all been rectors of Coleraine. General Cuppage of the royal artillery was his uncle.

On one of Wesley's visits to Coleraine, Mrs. Nicholls presented her eldest son to him. Wesley blessed him and, learning of his intention to enter the army, gave him advice that, years afterward, General Nicholls declared he never forgot: "Never turn your back on friend or foe."

He joined the army in 1795, and this summary of his career was published in Coleraine in 1928 by the *Northern Constitution*.

on the 3rd November 1803, he with thirteen volunteers in a boat boarded and captured a French armed cutter from under the guns of Monte Christo at St. Domingo. At the passage of the Dardanelles he captured the Turkish flag, and with a boat's crew boarded and captured the Italian gunboat "Volpe" during the blockage of Corfu. He was present at the reduction of the island of Anholt in May 2, 1809. In North America he raised and commanded a regiment of Indians, and was senior major of all the troops engaged in the attack on New Orleans in 1815. General Nicholls who had been in 102 engagements, and was 23 times wounded, was frequently mentioned in dispatches, and received a sword of honour from the Patriotic Fund. As a reward for his services, he was appointed Governor of the islands of Anholt and Ascension.

In 1843, retired from the army, he had been coaching Henry Lyle, sixth son of Hugh Lyle and Harriet Cromie.

Ireland was at that time in one of its periodic conditions of threatened disorders, and the possible result of Daniel O'Connell's continuing activities was causing considerable anxiety. Daniel O'Connell was still a Southern Irish political leader of great eloquence and influence. He was the first Roman Catholic Mayor of Dublin. Strongly opposed to violence, his peaceful methods, backed by an immense nonviolent following, had already achieved considerable success in the way of reforms, although his aim to restore the Irish Parliament, lost by the Union, had not been successful. His movement was organized and supervised by priests of the Roman Catholic Church. In 1843, O'Connell was an old man, with militant young men in his movement, competing for its leadership with the intention of substituting methods of violence for those of reason. The desire to break the Union had little appeal in Ulster, which had benefited greatly from it, but there was considerable support for the idea in the South. In October 1843, a monster O'Connell meeting was to be held at Clontarf, scene of the Battle of Clontarf in 1014 when, on a rare occasion of unity, all the Irish kings (with the exception of the King of Leinster and the Meathmen who deserted to the enemy) won a great victory over a Danish force that contained contingents from Denmark, Sweden, Normandy, Britain, and Scotland. This Irish success finally broke the Viking power in Ireland, where a Danish king had ruled in Dublin for 500 years. The Westminster Government of 1843 prohibited O'Connell's Clontarf meeting[1] with its emotive place of assembly. O'Connell was tried for conspiracy in Dublin, where he was convicted by a Protestant jury. The conviction was reversed by the House of Lords the following year.

It was against this political background that General Nicholls made the political comments in his letter:

Shooters Hill
Dec[r] 6 1843

Dear Sir

In answer to yours of the 2[d] I think there is no occasion for Henry to remain here as he made a good and fair examination he has worked hard and should have a little play for healths sake he can brush up his french better at home with you, than I think he could by going to Brussels with a youth like himself, I am not partial to Continental educations I have known more harm than good proceed from them. I told Henry that I could not consientiously recommend the Continental trip, of two such young men therefore I think you had better go home in the holidays which he very good naturedly acquiessed in and which I hope will meet your approbation. I do not think you have any great cause of alarm, you have a good and sufficient force to protect the country in general. I do not think O'Connel or his repealers have the least intention of coming to blows that would spoil his *rent* gains, and as to his succeeding in the repeal of the union I laugh at the very idea of it,

105

I hope our Government will do all in their power for the poor in the south as regards the letting of lands and poor rates, but I fear do what they will they will never satisfy the roman catholic priests, nothing but letting them have it all their own way will do for them, and that wont do for us. if they do breake out in a rebellion the only remedy I know of is sending every priest to Norfolk Island, and putting on the old harness on their laity again, No Judges, Privy Councillers, M.P's Mayors, or magistrates, from their fold. but I would always consent their being Admirals, Generals, Colonels etc I never saw my Catholic countrymen fail in their moral or Military duty when we have them away from their Priests and local predjudices I do not wish for a better soldier or sailor than Paddy I have served in more than a hundred battles with them and I ever found them among the foremost—
Give our best regards to Mrs Lyle and your young people
believe me to be faithfully
yours
Edward Nicholls
My son is in the Dwarf goes to Ireland as soon as she is ready for sea.

General Sir Edward Nicholls, in spite of being wounded many times and the hardships of his army career, had a long life. He was eighty-five when he died at Blackheath in 1865.

Henry Lyle, at the age of eighteen, was killed by a fall when rock climbing at Downhill during a picnic in 1844.

In the same year, 1844, Daniel O'Connell's health began to fail, and although he did not die until May 1847, the leadership of his movement passed into the hands of men pledged to destroy the Union by violent means, believers in the bloodthirsty tenets of Wolfe Tone. They became known as "The Young Ireland Party." However, their activities were brought to a temporary halt when, in 1845, an unparalleled disaster struck the whole of Ireland.

Notes

1. The Battle of Clontaaf expelled the Danish invaders from Ireland by force. As it was claimed that the English were also invaders, the implication was clear.

Part II

25 / 1845/1848 Famine in Ireland

In 1845, potatoes were the staple food of the poor in all Ireland. As poverty was widespread, the potato was essential to the health—indeed to the very existence—of the majority of the population.

Periodically, disease, its cause[1] then unknown, produced some failure of potato crops, not only in Ireland. There it resulted in great hardship in the affected areas, mitigated by such methods as government relief work, treasury grants, and private charity.

In 1845, however, as late as the end of July, there was every reason to anticipate a bumper crop of potatoes in all parts of Ireland, while a good supply remained of excellent potatoes from the 1844 crop.

In August, the British Prime Minister, Sir Robert Peel, received news that disease had appeared in the potato crop in the Isle of Wight, the first warning that the disease, then rife in North America, had reached England, where the diet of the poor also depended largely on potatoes, though not to the same extent as in Ireland, where dependence on them was almost total.

At first, while the disease spread to various districts in England and also to the Continent, Ireland remained free of it until September 1845 when it became clear that the Irish crop was not to escape.

Confidential official inquiries were immediately set in train and preliminary arrangements made to deal with distress should it arise, arrangements based on cooperation between the government and better-off citizens.

It is the experience of Ulster that will be concentrated on here, for this is one of the occasions when this differs to a noticeable extent from that of the South of Ireland, due to some ameliorating circumstances that had long existed in this, the northernmost province of Ireland.

The following extracts from "Some Records of the Relief Commission in 1845/47," in the Public Record Office of Ireland, throw light on the situation in Ulster and particularly in Coleraine:

16th September, 1845 D. McGregor. Inspector General Strictly Confidential Circular.

County and Sub Inspectors of Constabulary are hereby directed to make full and immediate inquiries respecting the state of this crop in their several districts, and to report the result of such inquiries without loss of time. . . . . . . the officers will also from time to time transmit to me such accurate information as they shall continue to collect. . . . . . . These inquiries are not only to be confidential but they are to be so conducted as to prevent speculation as to the possible motives for seeking the information required . . . . .''.

There was no delay in responding to this circular. As will be seen from the following extracts, the situation at first not without hope, deteriorated steadily:-

21Sept, 1845

Thomas Thornley sub-inspector, Coleraine . . . . There is not any disease of importance, except in the Parish of Ballyrashand . . . . . N.E. Liberties of Coleraine, and joining the County of Antrim.

25 Sept 1845

George Fitzmaurice, County Inspector, Garvagh . . . . ; in the district of Ballyrashane . . . . . . I understand much loss is likely to be sustained.

13 October 1845

Londonderry Francis Nesbitt, sub-inspector

I feel it a painful duty to report that the disease in the potato crop has shown itself extensively in my district . . . . . . In some instances entire fields have rotted which a fortnight ago appeared to be in a healthy state.

In October a very grave warning came from the Coleraine Work House;

Coleraine 13 October 1845 John H. Babington M.D. Medical Officer, Coleraine Union Workhouse to the Chief Secretary.

Reports in reference to disease of potatoes not by any means exaggerated. Whole fields, looking last week most luxuriant and untained, this week unfit for man or beast. Such being the state of crop a great scarcity of food must be looked forward to attended as a natural consequence by typhoid fever or some other malignant pestilence.

Suggest that means be taken to keep in the country a supply of food, and that the different boards of Guardians afford a simple machinery for carrying out this purpose and that it will be necessary to lay in a stock for two years.

Fears that the pressure for food is not far distant. Places himself and his time at disposal of Government to procure information on the subject.

At this moment also the Lord Lieutenant of Ireland, Lord Heytesbury wrote from Dublin to the Home Secretary Sir James Graham, and also to the Prime Minister Sir Robert Peel, giving the most alarming report of the situation and making it clear that the Government must be prepared for famine in Ireland. The government continued to hope that reports were exaggerated, and nothing of practical value was done, although the Prime Minister gave the situation realistic consideration and came to the conclusion that if the feared catastrophe occurred the only effective remedy would be the free import of food—this would necessitate the repeal of the Corn Laws, something which would rouse great opposition in England and in Parliament.

Serious reports continued to come in.

4th November 1845 Coleraine Thomas Thornley sub-inspector . . . . in some parts nearly half the potatoes dug are diseased, and in other parts one third are diseased, and which has caused a great alarm among the poor class of people . . . . . it has caused oats and oatmeal to rise to an alarming price. There were a great number of carts of potatoes in market here on Saturday last, every cart of which were more or less diseased—so much so that the poor were afraid to purchase in many instances.

In spite of all warnings some ill-founded complacency continued and Sir R.A. Ferguson felt able to write to Sir Thomas Freemantle on the 15th November 1845 as follows:-

. . . . the County of Londonderry I do not anticipate that any scarcity of food will immediately be felt; the potatoes are at present a moderate price in the markets and the disease does not appear to extend itself; and I fear the calling of public meetings *now* for the purpose of establishing local committees or associations would considerably increase alarm without doing any good: and might induce carelessness in the consumption of provisions; our work houses and our hospitals never had fewer inmates

On the fifth of January, Sir R. A. Ferguson wrote to the Chief Secretary:

I have the honour to acquaint you for the information of his Excellency the Lord Lieutenant that I have taken advantage of the quarter sessions of the County of Londonderry to meet there as many of those Deputy lieutenants who by your sanction were joined with me in the inquiry as could with convenience attend, and that it appears that the extent of the injury which has already been sustained amounts to one half of the crop including in that such as have been consumed in feeding pigs and cattle. With regard to the present stock the accounts are most conflicting: generally the disease is believed to be at least checked. With respect to the probability of the supply being sufficient for the support of the people during the ensuing winter and spring, the quantity now seems sufficient but it is most difficult to form an opinion on account of the reckless manner in which the potatoes are consumed by pigs and cattle and of the doubt whether they will be found to keep during the spring as there is a fear that when they begin to bud they will go more rapidly. The reports from the mountainous districts are rather more favourable, the disease affects the potatoes less there than in the rich low lying grounds. We do not at present see reason to dread an absolute scarcity of food, but we think that the prices will be so high in summer as to make it very difficult for a labourer to support his family on his present rate of wages. The oat crop has been very abundant and the starch yards of the farmers are much better filled than usually at this season of the year. There is a fair prospect of employment on the railroads which they are constructing from Londonderry to Coleraine and from Londonderry to Enniskillen, as much as from the embankment and reclamation carrying on in Lough Foyle, should they continue, but in the more inland districts of the county, there is no work of a public nature to engage the labourers and there is little prospect for them of additional employment, which we believe will be absolutely necessary on account of the high price which provisions must reach in summer. To the promotion of such works I trust that the attention of the Government will be directed in the belief that the land proprietors will cordially cooperate with them in this trying emergency.

Although conditions continued to deteriorate, it was not until April 8th that instructions were forwarded to Coleraine regarding the formation of town committees.

Covering Note to Instructions to Town Committees, sent to Hugh Bradley, Chairman of the Town Commissioners, Coleraine
The establishment of such Committees is most essential to the due administration of relief, for it is by their local knowledge that the reality and extent of the distress can be tested; that the most suitable description of employment can be provided, and the most judicious course pursued to obtain, according to their means, the contributions of the community as inseparable from those of the Government.
Arrangements are now in preparation to establish Central Depots of Maize, from whence a supply, to be distributed on the principle of these instructions, may be forwarded to the interior, and directions for the use of the Corn Meal are now circulating through the country.

24th September 1846
Instructions for the formation of Committees for Relief of Distress in Ireland . . . .

(Lieutenants of each County to appoint members to form Relief Committees in subdivisions of each barony in his county, to consist of public officers or functionaries e.g. magistrates, parish clergy, chairmen of poor law unions, principal constabulary officers, principal coast guard officers, officers of the Commissary-General and Board of Works. Each Committee to do its utmost to promote in the baronial sessions improvements in husbandry, the drainage of land and reclaiming of wastes and to supply lists to the Board of Works of persons deserving to be employed on public works. . . . .) "The importation of foreign grain is most properly left exclusively to private enterprise; and to a certain extent the distribution. . . . . . . is left to the same agency"

The Relief Fund will be applicable only to the following purposes -

(1) Providing supplies of Indian Corn, or Indian corn meal, or other food, for sale

(2) Affording relief by employment, if necessary.

W. Stanley,
Secretary,
Commissariat Relief Office
Dublin Castle.

12th October 1846
Babington, Secretary, Coleraine Relief Committee to Stanley:
On transfer of books etc., to the new Committee - There was no necessity here last year for any active operations by the Committee; consequently we had no local fund raised, and the Committee I think only met three times. I wish also to be informed from what source the incidental expenses of advertising the preliminary meeting, printing circulars etc will be defrayed *Answer*: I am to state that there are not any funds for defraying the expenses of Relief Committees except local subscriptions.

In Coleraine John Cromie was the Chairman for Coleraine and Portstewart and Henry Richardson for Aghadowey and Macosquin, relief committees.

In 1846, the situation with regard to potatoes was much worse than in 1845, and, unfortunately, the political situation in England proved much more unfavorable for Ireland. Sir Robert Peel's attempt to abolish the Corn Laws (which kept up the price of corn) and permit its free import failed, his government fell as a result of this honorable attempt to relieve the suffering of the victims of the potato famine, and Lord John Russell, who became the British prime minister, and his chancellor of the Exchequer Charles Wood, were both staunch supporters of the laissez faire economic policy, then widely held, that believed that no interference with the free play of economic forces led to the best results in the end for all. In Ireland, this obstinately pursued theory, which is now discredited, led to appalling suffering, as food continued to be exported from the country, the Corn Laws kept up the price of imported corn, public works were abandoned, and some very practical plans for helping to relieve the distress were turned down in London.

In Ulster, which had survived the first year of the famine without excessive suffering, in 1846, the suffering of the people became very severe, and communications to the chairman of the Relief Commission, Sir Randal Randolph Routh, became more and more urgent in their terms:

6th November 1846—Henry Richardson Chairman of Aghadowey and Macosquin Relief Committee to Sir R. Routh.
The Aghadowey and Macosquin Relief Committee, finding that the daily increasing distress in their district makes it necessary that they shall put themselves in a position to be able to afford assistance (by providing food at a reasonable price etc.) to persons who from age infirmity or other causes unable to earn a sufficient sum to support themselves and those dependent upon them, have resolved . . . . . to open a subscription list for this purpose. . . . They have directed me to apply to you to know to what extent they may look for a donation in aid of that subscription. I regret to say that the distress is greater than anticipated, the anxiety of the greater part of the sufferers being more to conceal their wants, than to clamour them abroad, and nothing can exceed the quietness and good order of the district.

Reply: Donations are made in aid of local subscriptions in the proportion of one-third to one-half of the amount of the subscriptions. The Committee will, however, perceive that all food purchased by a Relief Fund so formed is to be sold at market prices. . . . .

November 1846 H. Richardson, Chairman Aghadowey, Agivey Relief Committee
May corn be sold below cost to families with inadequate income?

Reply: Corn must be sold at a price providing a reasonable profit margin to private traders. Get cheaper food—soup!

November 1846—H. Richardson to Sir Randolph Routh
Sir—I am sorry again to trouble you about the Aghadowey and Macosquin Relief Fund, the subscribers however, and those wishing to subscribe but not yet having done so are anxious to know whether it would be objected to that in cases where a family consists of a certain number and their weekly earnings on being ascertained do not exceed a certain sum which is not considered sufficient to procure them food for all, meal may be sold to them at a somewhat reduced price. I shall procure a copy of the scale they propose to adopt and submit it to you.

114

19th December 1846: Richardson to Routh
We have collected £255 to buy food from local traders at current prices, will send on list of subscribers, please give grant in aid

11 February 1847: Richardson to Routh
Public employments are ceasing or ceased and will not start again for some time. Distress acute. May we find or support or grant or run soup kitchens giving food cheap or (in absence of employment opportunity) gratis.

No reply he wrote on all sides.

20th February 1847 Alex Baillie to Sir J. Burgoyne Aghadowey Relief Committee Appealing for funds before death from hunger occurs or we get as bad as any other place.

6th March, 1847 Robert Alexander, Chairman, Alex Baillie Secretary Aghadowey and Agivey Relief
Distress extreme. Public Employment ceased, £709 raised (list enclosed) but charity ended. Work House full. We have been and are doing all we can, but our funds cannot meet a state of things like this.

19th March 1847 Charles J. Knox Treasurer Clothworkers Tenants Fund to William Stanley
If we get £ for £ we won't need any more aid until next harvest. List of subscribers appended.

To twentieth-century readers, many of the sums of money mentioned will seem deplorably small to those unaware of the very high value of money in those days, which can be realized when it is borne in mind that the average cost of maintaining a pauper in the Coleraine Work House in 1846 was one shilling and seven pence half penny a week.

Suffering due to the famine continued until 1848 and into 1849, being particularly serious in the South of Ireland, where scenes of appalling horror have been recorded. There quantities of food from Ireland were exported while its people starved, there were many heartless evictions, and attempts to relieve the starvation were inefficient and ineffective as well as being seriously hampered by the attitude of the government at Westminster. The situation in some areas got completely out of control, with no food available for the hordes of starving people. Large areas of the country were depopulated as a result of emigration and death from starvation and disease. An estimated one-third of landlords in the South were ruined as a result of their efforts to save their tenants from starvation. Other landlords were pitiless, a particularly scandalous case being that of Mrs. Gerrard in County Galway. She evicted 300 of her tenants, all well housed, hardworking, and able and ready to pay their rents. Her only reason was that she wished to turn the area into a grazing farm. Troops were used to turn out the unfortunate tenants and then to destroy their houses. The case caused such a scandal that it was investigated by Lord Londonderry, a prominent Ulster landlord. He reported to the House of Lords that all the accounts of what happened were true, adding that in such circumstances it was not surprising if there were attempted violence. The many terrible events in the South left behind a legacy of bitterness and hate of England, which had so signally failed to help the people in their extremity.

Ulster, however, had been more fortunate in being the most prosperous province of Ireland at the start of the famine, with few absentee landlords. The tenants were protected also by Ulster custom, which, though not legally enforceable, was generally honored, and by the efficiency, energy, and hardworking qualities of its population, which gave it greater strength, both physical and moral, to withstand the horrors of over three years of famine.

Notes

1. Cause of potato disease is a fungus "Phytophthora," a fact divined in 1845 by the Rev. M. J. B. Berkeley, an English curate and an expert on fungi, but unfortunately not factually established until the twentieth century.

26 / 1845/1848—The Scott Family During the Years of Famine

During these terrible years of famine, Thomas Scott remained by himself at Willsborough, apart from periodic visits to his family, whom he had placed in Paris at the end of 1845. There, in a flat in the Champs-Elysées, his wife, Katherine, her first child, Hatton Thomasina, born in 1845, little Annette and Charles, together with Elizabeth and Hannah, who had now left school, lived for over a year. Elizabeth writes:

We took the carriage, a small open barouche & a pair of cobs. I used to ride with my father in the Bois de Bologne, until one day when the horse threw me. I was not hurt but stunned unconscious for some time, which so frightened my father he would not let me ride again. We had music lessons, my father gave me a harp & I had lessons, Hannah piano & drawing, & of course all had french.

The three older boys, James, Willie, and Tom, continued their education in Cheltenham, spending their holidays in Paris.

In October 1845, James wrote from Cheltenham to his sister, Elizabeth, a hasty, boyish letter. Tommy was their brother Thomas.

October 1st /45
Malcolm Ghur

My dear Lizzie
I should have answered your letter long before but no more of that I am sorry for it and that is all But as to that which you asked me Mille Rodrigue lives at Woodland cottage Rodney terrace I could not find this out much sooner but I could not find out what she had to do but I believe that she attends Miss Auledrigde still I have no more time to write to you but I will soon write again and tell you all the news that I know
Believe me to remain
My dear Lizzie
With best love to yourself and Hannah
Yr affect . . . . Brother
James Scott
Sprott and Tommy send kind regards to Miss Watt and Tommy sends best love to you both.

In January 1846 Elizabeth wrote to Mrs. Richardson, mother of her stepmother, Katherine Scott.

Maison Valin (or Balin)
January 23rd

My dear Mrs Richardson,
As Papa is returning to Ireland, I take the opportunity of sending you a little bag which I have worked for you, and which I hope you will use for my sake. I was very glad to hear from Barbara that you were better and I hope that you will soon be quite well. I would give all I possess, if I thought I could get back to Willsboro' this year, the poor Irish are in such distress, I would much rather that they got our money instead of the French for whom I have no affection. I am sure you would be quite pleased with dear little Hatty if you saw her she is so much improved in looks, and so amusing with all her little tricks, I really do not know what we should do without her. I cannot bear the thought of the boys and Papa going away, we shall be so triste and lonely; but I am going to work very hard, at my music and languages, to make the time pass quickly. I think the next holidays will be spent on the

Rev. George Scott (brother of Thomas Scott)

Rhine. I like all my lessons better than my drawing, for which I fear I have no taste. Oil painting seems to be quite *unlearnable*. Mamma and the children are quite well, and unite with me in best love to you, Barbara and Mary. I remain, my dear Mrs. Richardson

Yours very affectionately
Lizzie Scott

The first half of a letter from the Rev. George Scott to his niece Elizabeth in Paris early in 1846.

Dear Lizzie

I am most thankful to you for your letter—the little delay in consequence of the Doctors coming late would have alarmed us more had we not been convinced your dear Mamma concealed nothing—and therefore we all recollected the various causes that might delay a letter from such a distance—still however the poor little darling had so much febrile irritation acting on her (proceeding very likely from her teeth) that we will all be looking anxiously to you or Hannah to give us intelligence. It has indeed dear Lizzy pleased God to try you all severely—it seems a general time of trial—but we would not if we could take ourselves out of the hands of our Heavenly Father and take our own short sighted guidance instead—yet though this is the truth still Nature must have its way only it is a duty we owe to our God as well as our fellow creatures, not to indulge beyond reason painful & useless regrets—If the recovery of dear Hatty is permitted it will cheer you all—I am sure your Mamma will be pleased to hear that Henry is a great deal better—and if he would take enough of riding exercise and eat *moderately* and simply he would be quite well but he lets himself get ravenous—by long intervals—and then overdoes the business—One of the many officers under whose command we have the misfortune to be at present placed is a great friend of Archdeacon Torrens—a Capt Cromie He is in the district of Ballymoney he told Henry yesterday that poor little Edwd. Chichester is dangerously ill. the Judge went off from Derry in the greatest hurry and had very little hopes. This is a sad thing for them all—but what was to be expected poor little fellow from his constitution

You never saw such busy creatures as Barbara and Mary are—and especially Mary—in preparing and giving out work to the poor girls and women on the property and Parish—it is a happy change from not knowing on earth what to do with the crowds that came for help which it was beyond possibility to give—Now the Hall steps are seldom without 3 or 4—women, girls, or children but they are bringing back their work to be examined—and paid for according to its merit—and you cannot believe how beautifully some of them do it and how quick they are at taking up a new stitch—We have every reason to think the fund may not only be kept up but be an increasing one and they (B & M) have begun to venture on getting material, such as unbleached muslin on a more extended scale than they began upon—the Scotch House who had employ'd many until their House was burnt down was very strict in their fines, and low in their pay—and worse than that their Agents were generally *Public House* keepers or small shopkeepers—who made them take part payments in goods—and threw the young into bad company—still they employ many And we are just slowly creeping *into trade* for the sake of our own people—who are learning many new things—and prefer our pay which is reasonably better than the wretched remuneration they got from the Scotch people If we can but persevere and go on we shall get a ready sale for the work as our prices are

The baby, Hatty (Hatton Thomasina), recovered completely and grew up to marry Henry O'Hara, who went into the church and became bishop of Waterford. His wife survived him, dying in her late eighties, the only one of Katherine Scott's four children to reach old age.

"Poor little Edward Chichester" was the son of William Chichester, who had married Judge Torrens' daughter, Henrietta, the mother of Edward. Edward Chichester recovered from his illness and grew to manhood, but he remained always delicate. His father, William Chichester, inherited the O'Neill estates through the female line, the male line having died out; he also took the name "O'Neill" and was created a baron.

Elizabeth Scott first learned of the death of her young cousin, eighteen-year-old Catherine Scott, eldest daughter of the Rev. George Scott, when her father sent her the last half of his brother's letter to him:

May the Father of Mercies interpose for our relief—Having written this note I hurried back to her room The nurse tender said she was worse I ran to the next room to awake the Doctor & then went to bring in Betsy we found the Doctor leaning over our darling. He beckoned to us to be silent. We kneeled around her in silence for about ten minutes. When we rose up the Doctor exclaimed I never saw the breath leave a dying body so easily We would not believe she was gone—I got a looking-glass and held it to her mouth but there was no mark The immortal spirit was gone from a world of sorrow—pain to a region of rest & security She came up and was cut down as a flower.

It was the Lord's doing He gave her & he took May his name be blessed and our will resigned I know well that for me there is rebuke in this chastening it was needed and I trust it will not be unheeded but is there not great mercy in this that the same event by which I am chastened has secured for ever my much loved child, Through short but severe tribulation she has entered into the kingdom that cannot be moved. I am sanguine in the hope that this event may be richly blessed to our remaining children.

The boys have soon to go forth to combat the temptations of a sinful & ensnaring world and may not this preparatory discipline in the school of sorrow be designed to impress them with deep and salutory convictions. They see that youth and health and hilarity are no safe guard from death and when the last trial comes they see that the only things really valuable & important to the departing sufferer or to the surviving mourners are the evidences which may be found of the soul being brought into a regenerate and saved condition. May such convictions accompany my boys through life and keep them ever sober and watchful unto prayer. You will rejoice to learn that Betsy is well sustained under this trial I am sure she already tastes some of the peacable fruits of righteousness which grow out of chastening for those that are exercised thereby. I hope shortly to devise some means of bringing you into contact with our dear Maria Her loss is preeminently great. Two spirits could not have been more closely united than hers with Catherine's The Father of Spirits has separated them for a season the parting is bitter but it may be the very means which Infinite Wisdom employs to keep them ever with the Lord. We have this day committed to the grave the dissolved tabernacle of my child in the sure and certain hope of a resurrection to eternal life. Among other friends at the funeral was my former fellow labourer Mr. Henderson It gladdened my heart this day by reminding me that I had commissioned him to converse with Catherine previous to her confirmation five years ago, he did so & the impression on his mind at that time was that she had been brought under the regenerating influence of true religion If you think it might be interesting to Lizzy & Hannah to peruse this letter you may send it to them. My Catherine loved them tenderly I feel most grateful to your kind friends for thinking of me and mine in their last moments May the Lord bless them and you

Your attached brother
George Scott

1847—Death of James Scott

In her autobiographical notes, Elizabeth has written of another death, which occurred early in 1847.

My eldest brother James, died suddenly while we were living in Paris, it was a terrible shock, the first death in our family. He was in Cheltenham College, and had been spending the Xmas holidays with us. His father took him back when he was going on to Willsborough, he left him there apparently well, letters followed him to Willsborough, saying he was dangerously ill, he was in high fever & did not know my father & died in a few days. It was the time of the potato famine in Ireland followed by what was called famine fever, it was not in England, they thought he must have got it on the Journey, either in the steamer or on the train.

The famine fever was, in reality, typhus and relapsing fever, one of several terrible health scourges that ravaged Ireland at this time, consequences of the famine. It was very infectious, and many of those trying to alleviate the sufferings of the people, including some of the landlords wives and daughters, who were serving in the soup kitchens, succumbed to it.

1847—the Rev. George Scott writes to his niece Elizabeth.

Balteagh
March 4th

My dearest Lizzie

The first paroxysm of your grief has I trust by this time subsided & left you in quiet acquiescence under the hand of our good God and Saviour.

Mr. Boyd in his letter to me mentioned that your beloved James had been the first in his class (for confirmation) which consisted of sixty four—but he added—his name is now transferred to the catalogue of spirits made perfect.—One of the means usually employed to fit us for that blessed society is suffering.—Of the palm bearing multitude now before the throne there is not one that did not come out of great tribulation

Like them your Mother & your Aunt Jane had their sorrows but now their tears are wiped away for ever—and thus it is we trust with your still dear though departed brother.—His early and unexpected removal has a voice which speaks loudly to you your brothers & sisters—It invites to a livelier faith in Jesus—illustrating the great uncertainty of the life that now is urged to greater earnestness in seeking the life that is to come—Lessons of this kind are continually being taught me by the white rails that enclose the early grave of my beloved Catherine—Often could I stand leaning on those rails & weep—but these were idle indulgences of the imagination—my darling is not there—though not yet risen she is I trust in paradise—the circumstances of that separate state we cannot understand they are not revealed to us—but we have line upon line to lead our thoughts to that bright cloudless day when all who sleep in Jesus will come with him in visible glorious immortal and incorrputible bodies What joy will then brighten every shining face—the Lord himself will then be the supreme joy of all—to him every knee shall bow & every tongue give praise—But gratitude & love to him will not be diminished they will on the contrary be increased by the happy recognitions of reuniting friends and brethren.—Dear Lizzie let us often muse on the sparkling glories of that fast approaching day—is near even at the door, & the contemplation of it should eclipse all other expectations as the sun outshines the stars—What a contrast to this coming glory is the bitter distress of our suffering country—Famine has brought its usual attendant—Disease is more or less to be found in almost every family—As yet we have not a great many deaths outside the poor houses. eleven died there last week.—Tell your Papa trenching goes on vigorously—It is a good investment for his money & with respect to the poor the very best way in which he could possibly expend it—The cry for employment was never so piteous as at present. I am taking upon me to employ at his expense three or four men to enclose & dress the

122

ground about Carrick Church—It is a lovely spot—the Church is beautiful within and without & might be open for service on Easter Sunday—May true worshippers worship there in spirit & in truth.

I wish your father would permit me to enclose for him the wooded bank—I know he intends (& he is right) to reserve it for himself, but it should be secure from trespass which prevents the oaks from rising—

With love to him Mamma & all your circle I remain

    Dearest Lizzie

        Your attached Uncle

        George Scott

1847—Maria Scott writes to her niece, Elizabeth.

                                        March 9th 1847

My dear Lizzy,

I have written to your dear Papa and Mamma since the trial we have all sustained, & have been earnestly longing to address a letter to you & dear Hannah but someway it always happens that I cannot choose my own occupations, something every day seems prepared for me to do that I cannot put off but indeed my dear girls you are often in my thoughts to such a degree that I can at times almost realize your presence, especially at this season when I can so well understand all your feelings, but I know our Heavenly Father is tender of his young children, never allows them to be swallowed up in over much sorrow with youth he gives them elasticity of spirit to aid them in going on cheerfully with their usual course of studies, brings consoling thoughts to their mind, but above all his holy book the common comforter of old & young points out to them the path by which they shall reach those happy mansions where his children who are gone before, are safely housed do you not often find that in endeavouring to comfort & cheer your earthly father you are cheered & comforted yourself by your heavenly parent.

We all go on here in our usual course which you so well know Cousin Ogilby continues much the same as to his legs but in other respects in good health. Mr and Mrs Alexander and Miss Hague are his guests, they are playing their rubber of whist & I have taken the opportunity of gliding into the library to commune with you Miss Hague is engaged to be married to Mr William Bohem, you may remember the young gentleman who unceremoniously broke into the library, all the friends approve of the match they are an amiable couple & I hope they will be happy the match is not to take place for a year

Lady Bryants family are in London not to return for 2 months, the Houghs are all well, Mrs Gibson is a great deal better & is to return to Ham Common in April Capt and Mrs de la Condamin spent a day with us on their way to the isle of Wight to comfort their poor brother Mr de la Condamin on the death of his sister who died very suddenly, you may recollect meeting her here she was a very pleasant & a very good little woman—The Ligons

123

have not yet returned to the common, the Arkinsons a nice young couple occupy their house but I think I told you before all the changes on the common

We expect the Bonhams as usual at Ersler we shall all miss you & Hannah much if it were possible to move your cousin I would try to move him in the spring to meet you at some point but I fear he has got too deeply rooted in this soil to be easily uprooted though he would be better for an occasional change

I have not for the last month been as well as usual frequent nausea over me, which comes & goes, but I hope it will soon take its final departure. I was sorry to hear through Richard the children had got colds. I hope you and Hannah have escaped, the weather has been bitter cold here & I am told Paris is even colder in winter write me a line soon & tell me how you all are. I am a letter in debt to Hannah which I hope soon to pay will you tell your Mama I was much obliged to her for answering my enquiries so promptly & hope to be able to write soon with affectionate love to Papa & all your party

I remain your

affectionate Aunt M. Scott

While the Scotts were in Paris, another baby was born, in 1847, Jane Barbara.

Charles Scott, seven years old when they arrived, retained two particularly vivid memories of this period, which he has recorded.

Among my recollections of my stay in Paris, where we spent a year in the Maison Valin Champs Elysees, is seeing Louis Philippe coming in from Neuilly in an iron lined baroche at full gallop with a large escort, (he had recently been shot at) & another was the entry of the Duke & Dss de Montpensier as a bridal couple after the notorious Spanish Double Marriages, they drove under the arc de l'Etoile in an open phaeton, and four horses with postillions.

He adds: "22 years later I had the honour of leading the cotillon with the Dss de Montpensier as partner at the British Legation, Lisbon, her three daughters dancing in the same cotillon."

There was considerable hostility to King Louis Philippe of France in Europe at this period, as well as much dissatisfaction with his rule among his French subjects.

The Spanish double marriages, which took place in 1846, were major events in the history of Europe and fateful for the Royal House of Orleans, of which King Louis Philippe was a member. The root of the trouble that arose over these marriages lay in past history when a King of France had sought to unite the kingdoms of France and Spain, thus provoking the European War of the Spanish Succession, after which the Treaty of Utrecht was signed by the combatants in 1713. Among other provisions, the Treaty prohibited not only any future alliance between France and Spain but also any member of the House of Orleans ever succeeding to the Spanish throne. These conditions had been agreed again as recently as 1834 by the Quadruple Alliance of Great Britain, Portugal, France, and Spain.

In 1845, the marriage of the very young Queen Isabella of Spain and also that of her younger sister, the Infanta Louisa Fernando, who was an heiress, were under consideration. Eventually, Queen Isabella was married to her dissolute cousin, the Spanish Duke d'Assissi, who was believed to be impotent. This would have resulted in the Infanta Louisa being heir to the Spanish throne, the possibility rendering her marriage of the greatest importance. King Louis Philippe of France (son of the duc d'Orleans, who supported the French Revolution and voted for the execution of the French King, only to die himself by the guillotine), flouting France's treaty obligations, managed to secure the Infanta Louisa as the wife of his eldest son, the Duc de Montpensier, heir to the throne of France. The marriage, therefore, held out the prospect of Spain and France becoming one kingdom and a member of the House of Orleans a ruler of Spain. In consequence, the treaty was repudiated, and Queen Victoria, deceived by a personal friend, was furious.

In the spring of 1847, the Scott family left Paris. It may be that Thomas Scott felt that a change of scene was desirable after the family bereavements of the past twelve months. Elizabeth has recorded their tour as follows:

In the Spring we left for Bonn in Germany, in a large Veturina, a travelling carriage, common in those days, with all our luggage, 4 seats inside, 2 in a cabriole in front, & the driver on the coachbox, & our own carriage which held 4 besides the coachman, an IRISHMAN, Martin Dugan, who had been Willie Cambell's serv* at Gibraltar. He came to us when he died, I believe he had been abroad before with some people and *said* he understood french & German. We spent a winter at Bonn, where we met the Smyly's, Lily Montgomery's Grand mother & Grand Father & their four children 2 girls & 2 boys, the eldest never married the 2nd Ellen, Lily's mother married Mr Newland, Ferguson, the 2nd son married Miss Alexander. Bonn was a great place for schools and colleges.

We drove along the Rhine, it was lovely through the black forest, the castles on top of high hills surrounded with plantations of dark firs.. We came through Switzerland, to Schaffhausen, saw the wonderful waterfall, then to Zurich where we spent some time, went up Mont Bhigi saw the sun rise from an hotel on the top. We generally drove 10 or 12 miles a day, then gave the horses some days rest. We had to look out in Murrays guide book where we could stop & get food . . sometimes it was difficult. The Veturino took a more public way & stopped at Hotels where we generally met &

changed places between carriage & Veturina occupants. from Zurich we went to Geneva where we stopped, then over Mt Cenis, no tunnels at least not under the Mt. We spent a Sunday at an Hotel on top of Mt Cenis a desolate place, we had to get mules harnessed in front of our horses to take us up, we came down to Genoa, a most lovely drive along the Riviera then into Italy by Milan to Florence where we spent the winter in a flat.

We had lessons in Italian, music & drawing. Willie, who was with us, went to a tutor who took in pupils they were all very anxious to join the rebels, who were then rising against the Austrians under Garibaldi. Hannah & I were presented to the Governor or Viceroy or King, I can't remember which, I know he kissed her cheek, an old red faced man, Leopold, Grand Duke of Tuscany at a drawing room in the palace, he was soon after banished, & Italy revolted & made the King of Sardinia, King of Italy.

The winter we were there, our father went back to Ireland and brought out Barbara & Mary Richardson, our step-mother's sisters, They, Hannah & I went with our father to Rome where we spent a fortnight & saw the Pope Pio Nino gathering in the Vatican & afterwards I saw him at St Peters square, where he distributed indulgences to a great crowd in the square, little scraps of paper he threw over the people, he was seated in a balcony high up supported by a Cardinal on each side, all the people knelt, we did not. It was Lent while we were in Rome, all the good pictures were covered up, except the dreadful one of the last Judgement by Michael Angelo in one of the Churches. We went through many of the Catacombs where the Christians hid.

The countries were in such a disturbed state we were advised to return to Ireland at once, a revolution in France where the king Louis was obliged to abdicate & Napoleon III made president, Italians revolted against Austria, & made King of Sardinia Charles Albert King of Italy, so the carriage & horses were sent by long sea from Italy to England & then we came back as fast as we could by rail & river to England where we spent some days & went on to Willsboro' which was ready for us.

In 1848, the Young Irelanders (O'Connell having died), led by Smith, O'Brien, Meagher, and Duffy, attempted a rising in Munster in the South of Ireland that was a complete failure.

The very serious disturbances in Europe when the Scotts left Italy stemmed to a large extent from the situation in France, prime disturber of Europe's peace for the past seventy years, where the existing dissatisfaction with Louis Philippe was intensified by the dangers to which the king had exposed France by the double Spanish marriages, which had roused anger and fear in Europe, by France's flouting of their treaty obligations, and the potential threat posed to the peace of Europe by the possible union of France and Spain. In 1848, the French revolted against their king. Louis Philippe was forced to abdicate and fly from the country

126

to save his life. A republic was declared in France, and Charles-Louis Napoleon, nephew of Napoleon Bonaparte, was recalled from exile in England to become, in December 1848, its first president.

1848—After the Scott family return to Ulster.

Soon after the Scotts return to Willsborough, another baby was born, Katherine Emily.

Although the famine was over, much poverty and distress remained, and private efforts to eliminate and relieve it continued, as is shown by this letter from the Rev. George Scott to his niece Elizabeth, who responded to her uncle's appeal and became a successful saleswoman for the Banagher Industrial Society.

Balteagh
March 16.

My dear Lizzie,

I wish you & your sister to appear at the approaching marriage feast adorned in the chaste beauties of needlework—

And this wish will be gratified if you avail yourself of the opportunity I afford, by sending you from the Banagher industrial Society some beautiful specimens of exquisite finish.—Nowhere can you be so well & cheaply supplied with legitimate & becoming decoration.—Wear them & you will be attired like the beauties who sparkled in Kings courts in the days of David & Solomon.—You will also have the satisfaction of thinking that you owe your adornment not to French or Italian fripperies but to the handywork of industrious nymphs—the daughters of your own poverty stricken land—

It were to stretch beyond my measure if I attempted to define & describe in detail the various articles of rare beauty to be found in the accompanying parcel.

Did finer linen from Cambray ever grace the hand or wipe the face of Bride or Bride's maid than that in the splendidly wrought handkerchief which now goes to you from the mountains of Banagher.—On its hills & in its glens have also been worked by barefooted ill clad & half fed maidens the accompanying set of doilies worthy to be laid on any table even on the festive board at Leicester where congratulating friends may be drinking the health of their bankers bride from the emerald Isle. It is part of your official duty as Bridesmaid to certify the happy couple on whom you are to attend of the advantages they may obtain by becoming customers & correspondents of the Banagher industrial Society—

In haste but much affection
Your attached Uncle
George Scott

27 / 1847—Death of Hugh Lyle

In September 1847, Hugh Lyle died. He had been mayor of Coleraine in 1831.

It was, of course, the nineteenth-century custom to eulogize the dead, unlike the 20th-century preference, which is too often to denigrate them, particularly if they should be at all well known.

A long sermon was preached on the death of Hugh Lyle in the First Presbyterian Church, Coleraine, by the Rev. William Richey. Some quotations from this are given here. There is much praise for the deceased and also a paragraph suggesting that the tributes paid to him were deserved:

> With regard to the departed, it is, perhaps, generally speaking, the safest course to say little, in the majority of instances there is little in the character either very remarkable or very worthy of being held up for imitation but, for this reason, in the case of eminently pious or benevolent individuals, it is right to preserve some brief record, that the remembrance of them may be generally useful

The sermon gave some details of Hugh Lyle's many activities:

> As a landlord he was most assiduous in seeking the wellbeing of his tenantry. . . . . As a magistrate he was unusually conscientious in the discharge of his duties . . . It was his wont, from the bench of office, to follow to his cell the culprit, and there into his softened heart to pour the balm of the gospel. As a Guardian[1] of the poor he had few if any equals. Much of his time was spent in the workhouse, and in planning for its destitute inhabitants. The children looked upon him as a father, and would crowd around him with delight on his entrance. He never repressed this forthflowing of affection, but would sometimes warn them gently not to take such liberties with others. He planned a class for their improvement in singing, and had the gratification of seeing it established. He instructed them regularly himself, and endeavoured to induce others to "do likewise". He united with the more well disposed in a prayer meeting, in which he and they in turn led the devotions. He was careful to keep them supplied with the scriptures, and to furnish with well selected tracts the reading portion. It is pleasant to know that they still speak of him as a father, and regard with deepest sorrow his removal. Those who witnessed the whole of the workhouse inmates drawn up to take a last farewell, as his earthly remains passed to their earthly resting place—aged men and women and little children, all mourning as for a sore calamity, will not soon forget the spectacle.

Hugh Lyle's Sundays were filled with church services, teaching in Sunday School, a visit to the work house, and to the bridewell.

On Sunday observance his views were strict ". . . . . against the running of trains on the day of God he bore his most decided testimony."

He seems to have had a premonition of his own death for "on what was nearly his last evening in public he was led to speak on the subject of death, and the possibility of their never all meeting again on this side of eternity."

It may be significant also that his will, which has survived, was dated September 7, 1847.

Of Hugh Lyle and Harriet Cromie's thirteen children—Hugh, John, James Acheson, Thomas Cromie, George Robert, Henry, Edward Augustus, Godfrey Octavious, Annie Frances, Sarah, Harriet, Ellen J., and Frances L.—all but two were living at the time of their father's death. As already recorded, Henry, the sixth son, was killed while rock climbing in 1844, and Hugh, the eldest, had died in 1834.

The Knocktarna property, therefore, passed to the second son, John, a clergyman of the established church.

Mrs. Lyle survived her husband and continued to live at Knocktarna before and after her son's marriage until her death in 1869.

Ellen Lyle, the twelfth child, has left record that her father was a very kind man and wanted everyone to be happy.

Notes

1. Boards of Guardians were not abolished in Ulster until the twentieth century.

28 / 1849—George Robert Lyle, Fifth Son of Hugh Lyle and Harriet Cromie, First Worked in Belfast for a Firm of Merchants, Wm. McClure & Sons, and a Letter to Them From G. S. Bruce & Co., Refers to Him

London
15th October, 1849.

Messrs. Wm. McClure & Son
    Belfast
Dear Sirs,

We have received your favor of the 13th instant announcing your intention of sending out the Orion to Tenerife and in compliance with your request we enclose a letter of introduction to Messrs. Bruce & Hamilton & Co who will be happy to attend to any instructions from you of which Mr George Lyle will be the bearer

We have no late quotations of the price of Barilla but when the writer Mr Hamilton left Tenerife in June it was supposed that it might be had after the new crop at the price you mention of £2.10 per Ton.

The sanitary regulations at Santa Cruz require that all vessels destined for the Canary Islands must previously go to Vigo to perform quarantine and be admitted to ? pratique We beg particularly your attention to this for should the Orion go direct we can positively assure you she will not be permitted to anchor

We regret that you have not given us more timely notice of your intentions and some information regarding the size of the Orion we are looking out for a vessel to take coal to Santa Cruz and we might have had it in our power to offer you a freight perhaps it is not yet too late

        We are truly
          Dear Sirs
            Your most obedt. Servants
              G.S. Bruce & Co.

We hope Mr McClure will favor us with a call when he comes to London

Be pleased to take note that neither Mexican nor any foreign Dollars are current in the Canary Islands French five franc pieces however are a legal tender at 19 ? vales de villon or 19/20ths of the hard dollar.

29 / 1851/1853—George Lyle Writes From China

By 1852, George Lyle, still a merchant, was in China. The British had had trade connections with China for centuries, although, originally, their activities were dependent on the permission of the Chinese authorities.

At first, the British trade was a monopoly of the East India Company and Canton the only port open to foreign traders, who were mainly British, Dutch, and Portuguese, trading in opium, tea and silk.

In 1834, the British government extended its control over the East India Company, which then lost its Chinese monopoly.

The Chinese had a fully justified complaint that foreign traders had introduced opium into China, and they wished to prohibit its import.

In 1839, the British Superintendent of Trade, Captain (afterward Sir Charles) Elliott, obtained a pledge from the merchants that they would no longer deal in this drug, and the existing stock of opium (20,263 chests) was handed over to the Chinese, who immediately destroyed it. Unfortunately, this gesture, which involved a considerable loss of profit instead of leading to improved Anglo-Chinese relations, merely resulted in fresh Chinese demands that the British found unreasonable and unacceptable. In 1840, the strained relations culminated in the first Chinese war, which lasted until 1842 when Sir Henry Pottinger, representing the victorious British, negotiated a peace treaty with China under which the number of ports opened to foreign trade was increased to five: Canton, Amoy, Fushow, Ning-po, and Shanghai.

In May 1852, George Lyle, from the port of Shanghae, as it was then spelled, wrote to his sister, Sarah Lyle, the letter being addressed to Miss Lyle, Knocktarna, Coleraine, Ireland.

Shanghae
10th May 1852

Please send the enclosed on
to Doppy as they will both go for
1/- allways write by "*Southampton*"
before the 10th of the month and send
a Coleraine Paper some time.
My dear Sally
    I am exceedingly obliged to both your goodself and Ellen for your nice long pleasant & newsy letters by the last two mails, which both arrived together owing to the steamer with the January mail having broke down in the Red Sea, so we were upwards of two months in this solitary corner of

the globe without hearing a word from home either on business, or otherwise. I had also great pleasure in receiving a letter part from Mr Ould & part from Annie, both of which afforded me much gratification. as both are celebrated letter writers & that did not forfeit their characters in that respect this time, particularly Annie. I am pleased always to hear all are well, & that Mama is in good health, what a sad blow for poor John you relate I hope he will not abandon himself to useless regrets but try change of scene, & air for awhile to divert his thoughts & nerve his mind, altho he has more consolation under affliction than most people I know, truly we may say his heart is not now here below.

I suppose you have seen the letters I wrote to Uncle Sam which might be published (at least they are long enough) as a treatise upon China, & the Chinese, by a superficial observer of agriculture, manners & customs etc

How I wish I could draw to give you some idea of the extraordinary figures and faces we see here sometimes, in fact in every individual from the "Coolie" to "the Tautie" or head government officer in S'hae the people appear to me to be feeding (cramming rice & greens down their capacious throats) about half the time, they hold the bowl out of which they eat on the tops of their three middle fingers & the thumb, & with the two chopsticks in the other hand, between the thumb & forefinger, & then between the little, & finger next to it, they place the edge of the bowl against the lower lip, & so stuff it down as far as the Chopsticks will reach—when we were at the play in the city the other day which I told Godfrey all about we had great eating with chopsticks, there was a great spread laid out on about 30 tables in the body of the building, & certainly their eatables consisting of various kinds, vegetables, rice, fruits etc were not to be despised, no tablecloths, no knives, plates or anything else, except bowls & chopsticks, the bowls handed round filled with rice, & the dishes of etc in the centre, rather the tables were actually covered with dishes of various kinds of eatables, everyone helps himself to anything he likes *with his own chopsticks* & places it on top of the rice in his bowl, & so eats away, when the man comes, & brings tea, without milk or sugar, & every cup has a little cover, a pinch of tea put in the cup — boiling water put on the same, after that is finished a man comes round with a great pile of horrid looking coarse brown cloths (dish cloths for all the world) soaked in hot water & the steam arising from them every person takes a dish clout & mops his face and hands with the same then hands it back to the man, & never dries his face at all, which must be horrid, this is all the washing the natives ever do here as they have a peculiar horror of cold water they say it *spoils the complexion*

The country about here is now as pretty as one can conceive a flat country to be, there are a great many trees all about the country, as all the enclosures where the graves of the wealthier part of the population are buried are planted with pine, & balsam trees & many of them kept in very nice order, the wheat is in full ear just now, they have enormous quantities of beans, & mustard plants out of the seed of which they manufacture oil, the peach trees are in full blossom, & the magnolias as high as a house covered with the most lovely flowers, from an elevation the country looks exactly like a carpet of many many colours, mustard flowers yellow, bean blossoms blue, wheat here gold, then green, with patches of ground here & there preparing for paddy (rice) now flooded with water, while the land now covered with wheat will almost all be so by and by. But I do not know whether you take any interest in all these things what are they all when compared with one sight of Knocktarna & a glimpse at old Ireland, particularly about Belfast & Lough Foyle I think very beautiful.

I am very glad to hear Mrs. Fowle is quite well & promise myself the pleasure of writing to her some of these days, her kindness to me when in Liverpool I never shall forget, & wish I had some means to repay. I sent you home a box of Indian Ink the best I could lay my hands upon, it is amongst some little things I sent to Uncle Sam, as well as some teapots for single ladies who love the creature to strengthen them for their dinner—and a card case for Mrs. James all of which I hope will arrive safe & be acceptable.

With my best love to Mama, Ellen, Fan & All including Harriet *Godfrey & McGee & Co.*

I remain your most afft. Brother
Geo R. Lyle

The Boy says "Tiffin" which means lunch is ready, so I must eat it "chop chop" or the other fellows will bolt it all "qui qui"

Ellen and Annie were also sisters of George, the latter already married to the Rev. Fielding Ould.

John (the Rev. John Lyle) was the second son of Hugh Lyle and Harriet Cromie and was George's brother. John had inherited the Knocktarna property on the death of his father in 1847, but his mother and unmarried sisters continued to live there even after his marriage to Elizabeth McCreight, to whose death in childbirth George Lyle refers in this letter. The eldest son of Hugh Lyle and Harriet Cromie had died in 1834 when only nineteen. His name was Hugh.

"Uncle Sam" was Samuel Lyle, son of Hugh Lyle and Sarah Greg.

"Fan" was Frances, the youngest of George's sisters, who had, in 1851, married John Mulholland, son of Andrew Mulholland of Ballywalter Park.

"Mrs James" was the recently married wife of James Lyle of Glandore, Treasurer of Co. Derry. Sarah Mulholland, daughter of Andrew Mulholland of Ballywalter Park, died in 1853, the year following her marriage to James, who was George Lyle's brother.

"McGee & Co" are evidently the prospective employers of Godfrey

133

Lyle, another of George's brothers, who was then an unemployed member of the Lyle family.

"Harriet" was another sister of George Lyle, who had, in 1847, married the Rev. George Vaughan Chichester.

It will be remembered that Hugh Lyle and Harriet Cromie had thirteen children, of whom eleven were living in 1852.

The next letter of George Lyle's that has survived was written to his sister Ellen in January 1853. It was addressed to Miss Ellen J. Lyle, Knocktarna, Coleraine, Ireland, and rubber stamped outside, "forwarded by Still & Co. Hongkong" "via Southampton" "Coleraine" etc., etc. There was no postage stamp and no envelope, the letter being folded, secured with a small dab of sealing wax, and addressed on the blank outer page, as was customary at that time.

Shanghae
January 1853

My dear Ellen

I received your long & interesting letter by last mail dated in Novr. and was very glad indeed to hear you were all quite well and that you had not been rash and indiscrete enough to marry like the rest of the foolish young people we hear of in these degenerate times. Every time I read your letter over I discover some new feature in the originality of the composition & fresh proof of the brilliant even dazling talents of the writer (Ahem!)[1]

I am very glad to hear Mr Jervis has come to the point at last, & as you justly remark all parties are *now* no doubt satisfied. I had also a letter from Godfrey, but so badly written I could hardly make some of it out, but he appears to have a very pleasant time of it, & I hope will get employment soon. Will you ask Mother to be good enough to buy for me 8 pair of the same kind of drawers & 8 flannel shirts *all of the finest description & double breasted* and a dozen pairs of the warmest worsted socks & 4 warm long nightgowns for winter, & charge the cost of all to me or rather get James to pay the Bill, & charge it to me—& send the whole in a small box to care of Rathbone Bros & Co Liverpool & they will do the needful.

We are going on here just in the usual style very busy, & the weather fearfully cold, skating whenever we can get a spare moment—oh! bye the bye tell Godfrey to send me a first rate pair of skates of the best fashion, as he has got mine & I have to borrow. The dry cold here is fearful, my hands are just as dry & as dirty as any old Irish womans I ever saw, no water will clean them, no soap avail. My Proboscis as large as an elephants & lips as a negros all from cold inwardly, & cold outwardly Oh give me the hot weather before this.

On the 8th of next month will be "China new year" & I will try if I am not frozen up entirely by that time to see some novel features in the natives to relate, but for some time I have been so busy I have hardly time to stir out.

I am sorry to hear Mrs. Fowle is still wandering about I wish you would be charitable enough to send her out with Dr Boyd, I am sure this place would suit her remarkably—plenty of servants, sedan chairs — attendance to no end, even the men in summer time have one servant to fan, & another to feed them during dinner. There is great talk here about the rebels in the interior of China, & their progress has upset business totally for a time they are about 600 miles from here, beyond Nanking, & they say 50,000 strong so they are putting the walls of Shanghae city in thorough repair to receive them if they come this way if they do we shall have great fun a shooting of them, sitting, swimming, & flying. I hope you will receive the little box of bronze things I sent per "Mencius" for the family to the care of Mr. L.W. Davies in Rathbone Bros & Co Liverpool who will no doubt forward it all right, as well as the Tea which I hope will be No.1.

With my best love to all I am my dear Nell Your most afft. brother
    Geo R Lyle

I am very glad indeed to hear that Mr. Ould is leaving Liverpool, he must be very tired of it, it is such a dirty nasty place & I am sure Annie will like the society in Dublin much better. I hope by the time you receive this I shall be discoursing with the Dr & the young ladies, dont forget to send Mrs F I'll get a man for her in a week with $200,000

GRL

With regard to the internal rebellion in China, mentioned in this letter, in 1853, Hung Siu-Taiian revolted against the Emperor, nominated himself First Emperor of the T'ai-p'ing Dynasty, which he himself had just proclaimed, and gave himself the title of T'ien-Wang or "heavenly king."

George Lyle gives no further account of the Boyd family or their experience after their arrival in Shanghai; the British merchants of that city had more urgent matters to occupy their minds.

George Lyle's next letter of September 21, 1853 was written to Mrs. Lyle, George's mother, with a short note to Ellen on the same sheet.

Shanghae 21 Septr 1853

My dear Mother,
8 I wrote to you by last mail from hence and have since then had the pleasure to receive your letter by the mail of 24 July also one from Ellen, for all which accept my best thanks

Since I wrote you last we have had very serious convulsions here amongst

135

the natives, & after expecting a row for some days, & nights, on the night of the 7th inst. the Rebels rose in Shanghae, murdered the chief magistrate, burned his house, & divided his effects, his followers in true chinese fashion fired a volley in the air gave a great shout, — ran away leaving the unfortunate man to his fate. Since then we have had to be on the lookout lest they should take it into their wise heads when full of Opium & Samshu, to attack us, as the quantity of plunder they would get down here would be very great indeed, so the Volunteers (of which your child has the honor to be one) were called out, & 30 rounds of Ball cartridge served out to each, & we had to take turns in keeping guard all night, with some of the men from the Men of War, so you may suppose, merchant by day & soldier by night is a little harder work than suits our idea of comfort in these luxurious eastern climes, however we learned to our great satisfaction that the Rebels are in reality more afraid of us than we are of them, & keep a strict guard to give notice of our coming to take the city so that all may have time to run away, which is the first & ruling idea in all chinamen, small & great. However, we are pretty well protected against them, as we have two men of war steamers, & two sailing vessels of war which we flatter ourselves are about enough to take possession of the whole province. Business is to a large extent at a standstill, and no one here, can form the slightest idea how or when these troubles may terminate, or what they may lead to in the end, in the mean time, the people, small & great, are moving from place to place in the greatest consternation, one day moving into the Warehouses of Foreigners for protection & the next, if they hear a rumour of an attack be intended to be made upon us moving away again. Oh! they are the most despicable cowardly crew on the face of the whole earth—I saw about 7,000 of the Rebels the other day & had the pleasure of an interview with the No. 1 great man (who looks about as mean a man as ever I did see) who had all his scarlet clothes nearly sewed over with pieces of tin about the size of Halfcrowns, a regular burlesque of a clown in a circus—just fancy such a lot of semi negro savages armed with everything under the sun except what a soldier ought to be armed with, all with great red cloths round their heads, & waists, & without any attempt at discipline of any kind, turned loose upon a peaceful mercantile town such as Shanghae, but strange to say they do not rob or plunder, & if any one is found in the act he is forthwith taken out into the street, & his head chopped off there & then without further ado—as has happened to some 5 or 6 who did steal.

I am glad to hear you are all quite well & enjoyed your trip to Killarney so much, I am sure there is nothing like moving about now & then for a change particularly when there is anything like the Exhibition to go to see. I hope Annie got her box I sent home in the "Carib" as it would arrive when she was in Ireland. but the Captain promised to take care of it. Please ask her about it & let me know.

The "Mencins" has arrived with my little box all right & i am very much obliged for the nice books & particularly for the pictures of the children

& your goodself which are all duly exposed in my chamber to the admiration of all beholders. I am now deep in "Huc" & like it very much indeed. Mrs. Brown still continues as kind as ever — is very busy fitting up all our rooms for winter for curtains etc etc which will be very comfortable indeed. I have written to James & sent him £500 on my account—which is always something towards making up for former losses. I send you a newspaper where you will see *all* the news. With my best love to Sally & Ellen & yourself & all

Your most afft son
Geo R Lyle

My dear Ellen   Your esteemed favor of the 19ᵗh July was duly received & the contents are noted with much satisfaction, If I can catch a Rebel I can send him home for a husband for you, as I am sure he would soon be well broken in, & submit to the powers that be even if they were enveloped in pettycoats. I am much obliged for all the little knicknacks in the little box, they remind one so much of home, I would rather have one of them than a house full of chinese ornaments.

    Mr. Maltby my friend had not time to go to see you all, or who knows but you might have seen Shanghae yourself. I hope Godfrey is getting on well with the flax & making a fortune.
Yours

Geo. R. Lyle

It may seem to some that George Lyle takes a somewhat insular view of the Chinese people, heirs to a civilization ancient when the British were still savages. In the thirteenth century, William of Rubruk, a Franciscan friar, expressed his admiration for Chinese artistic genius and also for their physicians, commenting in particular on their efficiency in diagnosis by the pulses (the Chinese pulses, not those known to Western medicine) and their expert knowledge of herbal remedies. Acupuncture, the oldest form of medical science in the world, originated in China over 5,000 years ago. It is 700 years since William of Rubruk noted its value, yet it was not until the twentieth century that some Western doctors made any serious investigation of acupuncture and were then forced to recognize its merits. It is now obtainable under the Health Services of France and Germany. China was also a great colonizing nation, but as time passed, few foreigners were permitted to enter the country, which then concentrated mainly on peaceful pursuits and came to despise warlike activities. Soldiers were then looked down upon, an attitude that inevitably weakened warlike qualities in the population.

However, any British contempt for the Chinese was heartily reciprocated, the Chinese view of the British being epitomized by their description of them as "Western barbarians" and "foreign devils." They cherished many erroneous ideas about the British and had no inkling of their formidable strength and skills until the Chinese war of 1840 brought a shock awakening to reality.

After these brief explanatory notes, it is time to return to 1853. The Chinese rebels held the native city of Shanghai from September 1853 to February 1855.

The settlements of the foreign merchants were separate from the native portion of the city. The English settlement, which dated from 1843 when the port was first thrown open to foreign traders, was of a mile in length and was at first separated from the native city by a narrow strip of land, which later was occupied by the French settlement.

The difficulties of the merchants while the rebels were in occupation have already been mentioned by George Lyle. In addition, the customs system of the city was reduced to such chaos during this period that the Chinese authorities asked the consuls of Great Britain, France, and the United States to appoint three officers to superintend the collection of this revenue. This arrangement proved so excellent that when the city was reoccupied by the legal authorities, they asked that it be continued on a permanent basis. H. N. Lang was then appointed Inspector of Customs, and this foreign customs service proved a boon to the Chinese.

Unfortunately, the reoccupation of Shanghai did not put an end to difficulties in China. The rebels continued to operate elsewhere in that vast country, and further unconnected trouble arose between Britain and China.

In 1856, Mr. Harry Smith Parkes (later Sir Harry Smith Parkes), who had entered the consular service in 1842 and had made a special study of Chinese, acting as an interpreter on more than one occasion, was appointed Acting Consul in Canton. His work brought him into continuous contact with the Chinese Commissioner Yeh, whom he found obdurate and obstructive. Finally, in October 1856, matters reached a climax when Yeh seized the lorcha *Arrow* and imprisoned its crew. Parkes's despatch to Sir John Bowring, Governor of Hong King, in this incident precipitated the second Chinese war. Sir John took immediate action, and Admiral Sir M. Seymour captured Canton a week or two later. The war lasted until 1858 when a treaty of peace was agreed to by Lord Elgin and imperial commissioners, which was not ratified in Peking until 1860.

The *Arrow* is always described as a "British" vessel, but a later letter in this collection throws doubt on this point, although in the circumstances it describes, the British action can still be regarded as justifiable.

The two Chinese wars are usually referred to as the Opium Wars

138

and as being embarked on by the British in order to regain the right to import opium into China, but the peace treaties of 1842 and 1858 do not mention opium, although the customs tariff agreed to in 1860 legalized its import.

In 1862, Shanghai was again threatened by the rebel T'ien Wang's, the "Heavenly King's," forces, and British troops were sent to the city for the protection of the British and other foreign settlements there.

In 1861, the Emperor of China died, leaving as his heir a son, then only five years old. In consequence, the country was ruled by two regents, both dowagers. The rebels were still operating in China, and the regents, in due course, took advantage of the peaceful relations then prevailing with Great Britain to secure the services of Maj. Charles George Gordon, a brilliant officer, who had served in the British force sent to Shanghai in 1862. This wise move produced speedy results, and, in 1864, T'ien Wang, realizing defeat was certain, committed suicide, and this, coupled with the capture of Nanking, long held by the rebels, finally put an end to this prolonged rebellion. After a successful career, during which there was much demand for his services, Maj. Charles Gordon, by then a general, commanded the defenses of Khartoum, being killed when the city fell in 1885, the British relieving force arriving too late.

George Lyle's letter of September 1853 to his mother is the last of his letters from Shanghai, although he remained in the city for another three years. He returned to Ulster at the end of 1856, after the *Arrow* incident. Brief passing glimpses of George Lyle in his future life will be caught now and then in the following pages of this book.

Notes

1. The paragraph that refers to the impending arrival of Dr. Boyd, his wife and daughters, from Coleraine is omitted here, as it has already been quoted on pages 75 and 76 "Coleraine Wins a Victory for Democracy."

30 / 1857—The Marriage of Elizabeth Scott

In November 1856, Elizabeth Scott wrote to her father and received the following answer:

Workhouse Londonderry

23rd November 1856

My dearest Lizzie

I read your letter this morning but not the one John Lyle promised to write by same post, you have my full consent to accept his proposal provided his worldly affairs are such as would make it prudent for you to do so, which I have no doubt they are, I know no man to whom I would entrust your happiness with more confidence in his doing everything in his power to promote it—I may now tell you what I never told you before, that Lyle proposed to me for you before you were 16 years of age, my only objection then was (as I told him) your extreme youth, an objection that does not exist now, God bless you my darling child you have been one of my greatest comforts ever since you were born, and I earnestly pray that you may receive your reward in this world in a happy union with this good man, who I am confident will assist you in cultivating the good seed of the word which was sown in your heart by your beloved Mother now a Saint in Glory, and which alone can fit you for that far higher happiness which our blessed Saviour has provided for his sincere followers in the world to come this is the sincere prayer of

Dearest Lizzie

> Your ever affectionate
> and attached papa
> T. Scott

I will write a line to Lyle from Somerset to say that I have not recd his letter and that I will be at Somerset until 1st train on Monday morning when I return to Willsboro. You may enclose him my letter, if you like

TS

Elizabeth's sister Annette Scott has given an account of the wedding that took place two months later, together with some particulars of Elizabeth's life before and after her marriage that she wrote in old age at the request of her great-nephew, Hugh Thomas, Elizabeth's eldest son.

It was on the 21st January 1857 that your father and mother were married in St. George's Church, Dublin. It was a very large gathering for that wedding, the first that had been in our family, and the first break in the home circle for many years. Our cousins the Clements's and Uncle James' family were with us, and also Mr Lucas, a cousin of our mothers, who had then some post at the Castle[1].

The wedding breakfast was in the real good old fashioned style. A splendid wedding cake. No end of speeches (good and bad), altogether a merry bright company was gathered there.

Your mother was a great favourite with everyone, but chiefly with all musical people. She played the piano beautifully, and I never heard any harpist that brought out such a lovely tone from that instrument. Of course it was on account of her talents that we were in the distinctly musical society which was then a great feature of Dublin Society, She was a member of the Philharmonic Soc^y, and also I think your mother was a member of the Ancient Concert Soc^y. Your mother played at almost all the Ph. concerts, mostly as accompanist to Herr Elsner, the violinst, and she and Miss Smyly (afterward Mrs Newland) played duets. In those days there was a great deal more hospitality and entertaining than nowadays. We never went to public balls or theatres, but to many very bright pleasant private dances, and the elders went to many dinner parties which ended up with music, dancing or games (no card games allowed by my father).

At Willsboro' your mother's life again was a very busy, full, one. She liked to devote all, but especially her musical talents, to the very highest aims. The Church music in Faughanvale was very elementary, and your mother persuaded her father to give her a harmonium, which was then a new almost unknown, instrument, and by means of it she revolutionized the music in Church, played every Sunday & taught what became a really excellent choir, with treble, seconds, tenor & bass voices. Many came on purpose to hear it. There was a great deal of poverty after we first came home from abroad, and again your mother took the initiative, & got up a fund for paying for embroidery & knitting done by the people about, sold the things made far & wide, & also got started a Provident Fund for the Parish. At the same time she insisted on teaching Hatty until she was nine years old. She was, Hatty says, the best teacher she ever had. Then she & Hannah rode agreat deal, and each had their own horse. She was very fond of gardening and of *bees*. she and old Willie O'Brien the gardener were most successful bee-masters!

She was also so keen about botany and wild flowers Then the Sunday School which had always been held from time immemorial in the little School-house halfway up the avenue, was latterly managed by your Mother, so her life at home what with music, riding, driving, visiting, gardening, and all kinds of Parish work was a *very* active busy one, and she was sorely missed when she married.

After marriage your mother often came to us at Willsboro' & it was there that you were born in 1858. We were also often at Knocktarna that bright happy house which always was such a hospitable house, and where your father made *us* and all his own relations so welcome. Such a lovely peaceful spot it was & you all were such a jolly set of children. Your Mother at once threw herself with energy & brightness into her new life, so different in many ways to her girlhood's life, but in which she was so happy. She did love Knocktarna, & very seldom left it except to come to her father. Of course

141

with so many other interests & occupations her music was very much given up. But as at her old home she at once took up the Church music & got a harmonium, & taught the choir & the Sunday School regularly until Kathleen was able & old enough to help her.

In addition to her work in the parish, Elizabeth had much to do in connection with her own household. This, at first, consisted of her mother-in-law and her unmarried sister-in-law, Ellen Lyle. Knocktarna was also regarded as home by John Lyle's other married and unmarried brothers and sisters.

Elizabeth bore ten children. Kathleen was her eldest daughter.

John Lyle was Rector of Kildollagh Church, which he had built not far from Knocktarna. Like his father, he was a kind man, and one story of his practical charity has been handed down in the family. It seems that one bitter winter day, John Lyle, warmly clad in a new winter coat, met a beggar on the road shivering with the cold. Without hesitation, John presented him with his new coat, a gift that, rumor relates, did not altogether meet with his wife's approval! On another occasion, having sold a horse, he wrote subsequently to the buyer, saying that, on thinking it over, he thought the horse was not worth so much as the buyer had paid, so he enclosed a check for what he considered to be the overpayment.

John Lyle lived to the age of ninety-five, retaining his health and vigor almost to the end. When nearly ninety, there was consternation at Knocktarna when it was found that John Lyle and a young grandson of about three years of age were both missing. Shortly afterward both reappeared when it was discovered that John had taken his grandson for a row in the boat on the River Bann, which flowed below Knocktarna.

Elizabeth Lyle, who survived her husband, died in 1917. Their eldest son, Hugh Thomas, was the next owner of Knocktarna.

Hugh Thomas Lyle, at whose request Annette Scott reminiscences were written, also planned to write his own recollections but soon tired of the effort and abandoned it. However, his opening is perhaps sufficiently memorable to be quoted here:

> I was born at Willsboro', Co. Derry, on the 24th April, 1858. They tell me my uncle the Rev. Edward Lyle preached a sermon at my christening with the text
> "This is the heir, come let us kill him and the inheritance will be ours".

More prosaically but possibly more accurately, Annette Scott had left a differing account. "Your Uncle Tom[2] was ordained in 1858, and

142

the first clerical duty he had to perform was to baptise *you*, my father's first grandchild, 'Hugh Thomas'.''

Notes

1. Dublin Castle.
2. Thomas Scott, Elizabeth's brother.

31 / December 1856/April 1857—Ellen Lyle's Letters From France and Italy

In December 1856, Ellen Lyle left Ulster for a visit to France and Italy with her sister, Frances (Fan), who, in 1851, had married John Mulholland. He accompanied his wife and sister-in-law on the trip, combining business with pleasure. The Mulholland's family business was the York Street Flax Spinning Co, the largest and most enterprising linen business in the province. The Mulhollands, in 1829, were the first to introduce a steam-driven flax spinning mill into Ulster, the firm then being Thomas Mulholland & Co.

Ellen's first letter was written in December from Paris, and was to her mother:

Hotel du Louvre
Thursday

My dearest Mama

I hope to hear from home tomorrow. We left London on Monday evening slept at a very grand Hotel Lord Warden Hotel at Dover. It is on the station and has steps leading down to the Boat which is very convenient. It is very like a foreign Hotel in size and elegance ladies go into the coffee room The waves were dashing up below my window all night The wind had been very high for a week however they told us it was improving and we went off at eleven next morning. Fan and I had comfortable sofas and were not ill but all the other people the floor strewed over with them were in a deplorable state. John was on deck and as the waves were dashing over it was all wet. We were only three hours. After getting the passport viseèd and luggage searched—They poked out of Fanny's portmanteau a little piece of velvet—half a yard and a few yards of calico and John had great arguing to prevent their charging duty—my box disappeared at Calais—and I have not seen it yet—All the people but ourselves were going on to Paris and it must have gone with

143

them, however I hope it will turn up as a box was left. We had excellent provisions at the refreshment room at Calais but had no power in our feet to see the town so rested till five and came on in five hours to Lille had a little souper there John went off at five next morning for Antwerp and we left Lille at 10 o'clock and came on to Paris which was rather formidable. The country is perfectly flat and uninteresting. The only object you would have enjoyed was a Jesuit college at Amiens and a great rough field in front covered with a flight of the inmates, such disfigured creatures Hervey could not contain herself at the dress and at an old priest mumbling over his paternosters—In our carriage were some Crimean heroes who were telling another gentleman the manners—dress etc of the country but we made no acquaintance At six we arrived and after running in search of my lost box through various caverns we came off without it, and had a long drive in the omnibus to this most superb Hotel—It is on such a scale you can scarcely imagine the furniture like a palace. In our sitting room and bedroom everything is velvet and rosewood—and three immense mirrors in each. The streets are so beautiful. The Louvre almost opposite and the palais Royal at one side, and a long Arcade the other. Everything looks so fresh graceful and cheering after the gloomy atmosphere and solemn parade of London Hervey and I went a little shopping expedition this morning and did not find things near so dear as London. Fan has just been measured by a dress maker and one of John's office boys who is established here John Stevely has gone off to make enquiry about my poor box and appoint an hour with the dentist for Fan—We purpose remaining till Saturday, and do not expect John till Friday. Write me a very full account of everything John's proceedings what Sara and Townley are about and how you are. We have been too hot ever since arriving in London It is quite like summer. Fanny rather tired today but has got on wonderfully. I can walk very little and do not intend to try more. Write to Poste Restante Nice. Piedmont. Italy—The Thompsons and Emily Stuart are there and never dreamt of India. George has lovely weather. Best love to Sara & Townley. Ever dear Mama Your affc. child

Ellen

The Crimean War broke out in 1853 when Turkey declared war on Russia. The war resulted from the ambitions of Nicholas II of Russia, who had determined to extend his already vast dominions under the pretext of protecting Turkey's Christian subjects in the Danubian principalities. Great Britain and France (later joined by Sardinia) all supported Turkey, although, at first, only nominally by the presence of an allied squadron in the Bosporus. However, when the Russians destroyed the Turkish fleet, their action roused a violent outcry of disapproval, and Great Britain, with full public approval, together with her allies, declared war on Russia—in January 1854. Some early successes and the possibility that the Austrian "Army of Observation," 50,000 strong, might join the

Allies brought the war temporarily to a halt. However, the Russian threat remained, and Great Britain and France were agreed that confrontation was unavoidable and that, in these circumstances, it was best faced immediately rather than postpone a conflict that was inevitable. However, those in London responsible for policy and some of those in command on the spot failed in their estimates of the risks and the costs. These factors cost many additional lives and much unnecessary misery and suffering to the sick and wounded before this terrible campaign was finally brought to a successful conclusion, the matchless courage and endurance of the British soldiers being Great Britain's valuable contribution to the winning of this war. It was certainly correct to describe the survivors as "Crimean heroes." It was during the Crimean War that the lethal blunder of ordering "The Charge of the Light Brigade" occurred. It was in the Crimea, also, that Miss Florence Nightingale discovered and uncovered the scandal of the incompetent organization and arrangements for looking after the wounded, a scandal that some people in important positions scandalously attempted to deny and conceal. These despicable attempts failed, and thanks to Florence Nightingale, the care of the wounded in war and the nursing of the sick were revolutionized. It was after the Crimean War, also, that Queen Victoria distributed Victoria Crosses for the first time. This decoration was instituted by her in recognition of the heroism of the soldiers in the Crimean campaign. It is awarded to all ranks in the army and the navy and is given only for some outstanding act of courage or devotion in the face of the enemy. The Crimean War lasted from 1853 to 1856 and was finally brought to an end when the Treaty of Paris was signed on March 30, 1856.

Ellen Lyle had lost a brother at Crimea. Col. Thomas Lyle of the Royal Artillery had died there at the age of thirty-four. Elizabeth Scott, John Lyle's bride, had a first cousin wounded at Crimea, Lucas Scott, son of Thomas Scott's brother, James. Lucas Scott recovered and, when the war ended, went to India, only to die there soon after arrival.

Hervey was the ladysmaid who accompanied them on the trip.

"George" was George Lyle, on his way home from Shanghai.

Sarah (Sae) and Townley were Ellen's sister and her husband, the Rev. Townley Blackwood Price.

Ellen's next letter was to her sister, Sarah.

Hotel l'Europe, Avignon
Dec.18

Dearest Sae

I was relieved and delighted to get your interesting letter on Sunday in Paris. You have no idea how one longs to hear from home when far away particularly when travelling with married people. Fanny has been wonderfully well and strong I have not been very well but am better now. It is impossible to attend to what you say for me at least Fanny is keeping quiet here now for a few days. She has never heard from Springvale and feels uneasy, as they promised to write every few days. We saw very little in Paris from utter inability to walk—one day drove to Pere La Chaise and peeped into Notre Dame but tho two minutes from the Louvre never went in—The horrible dentist required four visits, he is in such demand and charged the most extortionate price—through him we lost seeing the Emperor review the troops in honor of the Prince of Prussia and the Empress present medals and the baby was produced and greatly cheered It was very provoking. I was not sorry to leave Paris. it is such a Vanity Fair and the prices so breaking. On Tuesday we went to Dijon. Three ladies were in our carriage with whom we had some conversation. they are also going to Naples and Rome and seemed well up to pushing their way which is very necessary when there is no gentleman Porters, waiters, Hotel keepers evidently look on ladies as their victims—John manages all such quickly and well We had a nice table d'Hote at Dijon and snug rooms. but the Hotels are all as in Germany opening on a court in the centre and when there is wind one is perished. It was hard frost when we left Paris. quite refreshing after the close unwholesome weather at first. The hot water foot pans are changed often and keep you quite comfortable On Wednesday we came on to Lyons. There is no beauty whatever till coming near it The flat plains of Burgundy covered with vines like rows of dried sticks at this time of year is anything but grand—No trees did I see from Calais to Paris or from Paris to Lyons not one except willows trimmed and little slim ash everything taken off for fire even the bois de Boulogne or Forest of Fountainebleau did not seem to have a tree more than 30 years old. and all trimmed up to the top so as to get the yearly shoots for fire. There was a little damsel in our carriage coming to Dijon rather like Miss Black but dark and foreign looking. I got into conversation with her and found she was a Swiss from Lausanne who has been a year in England, that she had been at Glenarm last summer. and I think she is governess to Lady Antrim's children, she was a very interesting ladylike girl, with a sweet countenance and was travelling all alone from London to Lausanne as her grandmother was very ill—when the other ladies exclaimed at being alone and asked her was she not afraid, she said so simply "Dieu me garde" Near Lyons the banks of the Rhone were very picturesque. The town is all extremely picturesque and houses rising irregularly from the river high fortifications and some old churches and towers. We had to go such a height in the Hotel l'Univers there that we decided not to come down to the Table d'Hote and had a nice little relay of things upstairs. It is amusing first soup then mutton, fish, chicken, veal, spinach & oil pastrys full of mushrooms—artichokes boiled in oil—pudding, stewed pears and dessert and such variety of wines The route from Lyons here is beautiful along the Rhone which is rapid and muddy. one bridge seemed nearly all washed away with the inundations. the hills rise steep and every variety of form studed over with villas or little towns—and many of the steepest cultivated in terraces up to the top all vines.

It is the chain of French Alps where the Albigenses[1] took refuge and Felix Neff lived. After some time we left the mountains and the plains spread out covered with mulberry trees which are very scraggy trees pruned so as to bring forth as many leaves as possible—We passed some groves of olives the green of which was refreshing. The sun shone and the sky was blue and beautiful all the way but when we got out of the train here the wind was fierce and piercing—called the Mistral to which it is liable at all seasons. Our letters are to be forwarded from Paris so I hope to hear and also write to Post Restante Nice I brought Madme Gugon with me. I hope you will stay with Mama and see that she takes care of herself. Very best love to her and the boys. Ever yours affect.

Ellie

We had a very animated little French girl of 4 years old in the train who was whipping her "belle poupee" calling it scelerat and protestant. Fanny will be obliged to you to give Rose one pound the first of February She gave her 10/- before she left.

Springvale was the home of Frances and John Mulholland, who, when this letter was written, had three sons: Andrew Walter, born 1852, Henry Lyle, born 1854, and Alfred John, born 1856, of whom their mother was naturally anxious to have news.

In 1852, Napoleon, nephew of the great Napoleon Bonaparte, achieved his ambition to become not merely prince president of the republic, as he was elected in 1848, but Napoleon III, Emperor of France. In March 1856, the Emperor's son, Eugene Louis Jean Joseph, was born, the baby mentioned in Ellen's letter.

Glenarm Castle in Glenarm, County Antrim, was the home of the Earl of Antrim, of the same family as the Earl of Antrim who was governor of the county of Antrim in 1778 when John Cromie wrote to him on behalf of the local Volunteers.

Felix Neff, a Swiss Protestant, at first served in the army but changed his occupation in 1822, being then ordained, afterward spending five years in the valley of Freissinières, where he combined the duties of pastor with those of schoolteacher, engineer, and agriculturist, being brilliantly successful in all of them. When, in 1826, worn out by his strenuous labors, he was compelled to stop work, he returned to Switzerland, leaving behind him an area and its people miraculously transformed. He died in Switzerland in 1829.

In this letter, there is an amusing illustration of the fact that religious bigotry is not the monopoly of the Protestants in the incident of the doll being whipped by its four-year-old owner for being "wicked and Protestant."

147

Dearest Sae,

Your letter No.2 received at Cannes yesterday was exceedingly welcome not having heard since your letter a fortnight before—we are sitting in Etage No.3 the only vacant apartments in The Victoria Hotel. and delightful they are with the blue Mediterranean not fifty yards from the door and its white waves rolling in under the windows. The sky lit up with stars and the promontories enclosing the long bay from Cannes to Nice with a lighthouse at the point of each like starry eyes watching the entrance to the happy valley—The drive here from Cannes is lovely along the sea with groves of olives—luxuriant old trees and oranges ripe in abundance. aloes wild along the road and cactus—beans half a yard and peas a yard high—There was a little frost and snow on the ground when we left but the air was warm and sky blue and silver the sea the most perfect deep blue, the sun bright and hotter than we generally have in May—the air so light and clear the most distant things appear quite near. The first view of Nice is very pretty at the top of the bay with Maratime Alps behind with their peaks covered with snow. No words could describe the colors, the exquisite shades or the different distances with the sky, the sea and the deep green groves of olives and oranges in the foreground. I will leave it in perfect confidence to your imagination which will do it ample justice.—We left Avignon last Tuesday, the Mistral wind had begun again Our first peep of the Mediterranean was near Rognac a little bay runs up near the railway We passed under an extraordinary aquaduct carried across a valley in imitation of the Romans. it is three rows of arches 262 ft. high We were very tired of the flat plains from Calais to Lyons not a view that is worthy of the name Firing is so scarce that no tree can be left long enough. and the earthy color of the ground at this season with eternal rows of vines like old dried roots however from Lyons the scenery along the road to Avignon and from Aix where we slept on Tuesday is constantly pretty and sometimes beautiful The railway stops at Aix so on Wednesday we hired a nice clarence with a covered drivers seat in front which John and Hervey take alternatively beside the driver So off we set—after breakfast—a lovely frosty morning winding through valleys with Mts. St. Victoria on either side covered with—evergreen oaks and olives—three horses and changed every eight or ten miles—slept at Le Lue the bells chiming incessantly for Xmas. But the loveliest part of our drive was on Thursday thro old towns Frejus where we passed cork trees and magnificent pines the former is evergreen not unlike the olive but a much more yellow green the bark was generally peeled off and the stem usually of a rich deep red brown, contrasting with the foliage was new and pretty. At Frejus we took four horses to cross the Esterelle hills and if you had only been with us to see the said hills—A beautiful road is made winding gradually up in a most serpentine course. the hills are of porphery brilliant colors red lilac green and except where the road cuts through the valleys and hills to a great height are a mass of heath. arbutus and green shrubs—Occasional openings in the hills give splendid views of the sea and snowy Alps. It was too dark coming down to see. We were very tired and remained at Cannes till today—Thank Townley for his kind letter and give him my love—It is very unfortunate about the horses as driving is necessary for you and Mama. I wish she would buy another good horse. At the Table d'hote today there were about 20—Sir W & Lady Codrington among them, handsome oldish pair the latter sent her compts. to us to attend a ball which she gives tonight I suppose struck with our very select appearance—If the chicks are with you give them my love. Write again here I think we shall be three weeks, and hope to see the W. Prices—He is very unfortunate getting cold in his eyes. You know I told you I lost my box at Calais with all my goods—Well I did not see it till today when passing through the douane for examining the luggage on entering Italy we spied it sitting in a shed very composedly all stuck over with bits of yellow and green.—At Calais it set off with other people's luggage to travel in Belgium, returned to Calais, came on to Paris and now is satisfied to return to me I hope by diligence tomorrow. I have been very happy living in Fan's attire when my own failed and had given up all hope of meeting my stray wardrobe again. You might send this document to Harrie which would save postage—I long to see ? Titty ? Aon again, it appears two months since we left home—Tell Jem John expects he will join us before we leave this which he expects will be the 21st—If he leaves London at 8 in the evening he is at Paris at 9 in the morning—he leaves Paris the same evening at 8—he gets to Marseilles at 4 the next day and by diligence on here—I have just recd. your letter of the 23rd We are greatly grieved to hear of dear little Uncle Sam It is no doubt a very happy change for him but he will be a great loss to many—and such a true and humble christian was a light always shining. and it gladdened the hearts of others to see his singlemindedness and steady purpose in following Him who was meek and lowly in heart—Poor Freddy will feel a change in many ways—John does not know certainly whether he will go to Naples or Rome first but I will write before we leave this to let James know where to find us—I am much better since yesterday—but have been variable. Both Fan and I hope the three weeks here will be made useful to both—I wish Mama could breathe these sea inspiring draughts.

Mr William Price and Mrs have just been here paying us a long visit Mr Bateson told them he saw us driving He looks very thin but says he is very much better. it was very pleasant to see them. Poor George must have had a terrific gale. Another vessel as large was almost lost and put back to Portsmouth—I am glad Townley is getting his chicks into order. I wish Mama would get horses She ought to drive often Best love to her and all the boys every dear child Your affec.

Ellie.

Tuesday
If you only felt the sun this morning. John and Fan are very good and we are remaining here that Fans and my health may be able for Naples. I went to the French Protestant Chapel at Avignon and Cannes and heard most excellent and interesting sermons the service is more Scotch than Episcopalian

"Uncle Sam," brother of Ellen's father, has already been mentioned in one of George Lyle's letters from China. In this letter, Ellen is referring to his death, which occurred in 1856. Samuel Lyle was unmarried.

George Lyle's voyage from China is not yet over and has run into bad weather as the ship approaches England.

Croce di Malta
Genoa 26th

Dearest Mama

I only received your letter yesterday which was written the first the stupid porter at Nice can only have asked for letters with John's name so that yours and a note from Edward had been lying in the Post Office ever since It was very provoking as I could not imagine why you had not written and was quite unhappy at not hearing—It was however very pleasant to get them yesterday and to hear good tidings of yourself and all at home. We left Nice on Wednesday morning after breakfast in a sumptuous old English travelling carriage belonging to a nice little Genoese veturrino and his quatre bons chevaux as he called them ever repeating Monsieur Je vous dirai une chose dont soyez bien sur soi J'ai quatre bons chevaux—It rained for some hours while we climbed the hills but cleared up so that we saw some beautiful coast views before arriving at Mentone which is beautifully situated but much more closed up with mountains than Nice—We paid the Monsells a visit who are next door to the Hotel and they seemed delighted to see us. Mrs. M looks very careworn, but is so kind and gentle—her three daughters all looked very nice ladylike well looking particularly the second, John Monsell fat and agreeable as could be. After a long visit he came out took a walk with John while we sat inhaling the cold sea breeze waves quite equal to Portstewart and the gun rock and he came in and chatted till dinner giving us many interesting details of his position and parish—In the morning we saw the steamer with Victor Emmanual on board making its way slowly with rough wind and sea towards Nice. We had met Count Cavour the previous day going by land to meet him. The King arrived we were since told—early—rode on horseback thro' some of the principal streets, and then his followers making way he galloped off all spattered with mud to the Empress of Russia's where gossip says he hopes to win the Grand Duchess Helene.—From Mentone we came to Oneiglia, and had a fine day. The views are so beautiful and grand and always changing. The road winds all the way round one cape after another often out in the edge of a precipice. the valleys covered with olives and orange & lemon trees which are very pretty such bright yellow foliage mixed with green contrasts with the blue green of the olives. Palm trees are very fine and so picturesque between Oneiglia and Savona where we slept the next night. Rome is chiefly supplied from thence during the holy week and carnival for decorations—It is a source of riches the small towns which are innumerable and beautifully situated with their church towers and spires on peaks of rock above the sea or in the centre of olive groves on the slopes are poor looking generally and the people all have an old wrinkled

150

sallow look. The Virgin Mary is the universal Idol. In every niche she is to be seen with a crown and her arms extended as waiting to receive her worshippers, Diana of the Ephesians was no more an idol.and the quantity spent on their churches is extraordinary considering how poor they are—From Savona the weather was much colder—and we arrived here on Saturday afternoon having performed 142 miles from Nice in four easy days travelling, the carriage open. We took some little sketches to remind us of the lovely views, you really ought to see it—there are miles of town along the shore before arriving here—Genoa itself is built up the sides of a beautiful semi circular bay with a very high lighthouse at one side, and all the hills covered with towers—cupolas and campaniles—The houses look mostly like old palaces. This Hotel is one the old Chapel is one of the rooms, the altar made into a fireplace. We look over a raised promenade into the harbour which is full of ships with flags innumerable—All the old streets are so narrow no vehicle can go through them sedan chairs only—two people but not three can walk together in many of them, the houses very high and almost touching at the top which must keep out the sun pleasantly in summer but now there are cold chilling draughts. which make the costume of the people here very out of place It is a lace or net scarf over the head shoulders and arms fastened to the back hair by a large gold pin and is extremely graceful and becoming their hair so neat and the scarf so white—The poorest wear a larger scarf of printed chintz calico—The people all are so much better looking cleaner and more like gentlemen and ladies than the French A gentleman with a very long name left a card on John yesterday having seen us in the street and recollected having met John in Belfast. Murray did not mention any protestant church here and John was quite sure there was none so we staid at home however an American told us since that he was at it and about forty others, It was a great pity one misses it so much—I am sorry Mr Gray is likely to leave I do not see that the reasons you mention are realities—I hope you will give me minute accounts of John's affairs and everything I hope Sarah has returned quite well and Townley from their travels—give them my best love and thank Sara for her nice letters It is such a comfort to me to hear from home John and Fanny say it is the only time I am amiable. It is very sad about poor Mrs O'Neil—John got James letter on Saturday forwarded from Nice. I suppose he may give him up It is very generous of Mr M to offer to assist Godfrey. Do you think so much office business would suit him? I suppose John and Lizzie will take a tour which would give time to have their rooms made nice—How is Aunt Fan? and Ellen. and Cros? We possibly may not leave till this Thursday as a great oriental steamer calls that day and would drop us at Civita Veccia however we may go by a steamer tomorrow and get to Rome on Thursday when I hope to get long letters. When you write to George tell him to write to John at Rome he ought to have written sooner—I hope he has arrived safe—Take care of cold from all accounts the weather is unusually severe at home. Ever dear Mama Your afft. child

Ellen

You might send this to Edward

Victor Emmanuel was then King of Sardinia, though later be became King of Italy. Count Cavour was his very able Prime Minister. Victor Emmanuel's wife, Queen Adelaide, had died the previous year, 1855. Whether gossip was right or wrong regarding his matrimonial hopes in January 1857, Victor Emmanuel never married again.

Mr. M., who had kindly offered to help the unemployed Godrey, was probably Mr. Andrew Mulholland, father of Ellen's brother-in-law, John Mulholland, and of two of her sisters-in-law, her brother James having married Sarah Mulholland and Edward's wife being Andrina Mulholland.

It would seem also that John Mulholland intended to try and help George Lyle to some new occupation on his return from China.

The mention of John's affairs and of John and Lizzie refers, of course, to the marriage of the Rev. John Lyle to Elizabeth Scott, which had taken place in Dublin on the January 27.

Hotel de Londres
Feb 3.

Dearest Mama

I was delighted to get your and Harriets notes on arriving here. Poor Mrs William Chichester what a rapid decline what will become of the poor little girl? I hope Mrs McVicar recovered. Dr McCaldin is a sad man and poor Jane Morrison, was very unsatisfactory when you spoke to her about important things. I hope Wid Blackburn gets on well, she will be very indignant at our vicinity to the Pope. I expect a full account of John's wedding and hope you will write everything. We left Genoa the evening of Tuesday on which it was to take place, in the Vatican a very good, large steamer and had a very calm passage to Leghorn where we landed and breakfasted John and I then made a little expedition to Pisa half an hour's railway and spent two hours seeing the Cathedral, Baptistry where we saw a child operated upon, the Campo Santi a most interesting burying ground covered in except a square in the centre the earth of which was brought from Mt Calvary by an archbishop who was expelled by Saladin. The frescoes and the old Roman and Grecian sarcophaguses are very well worth seeing. The leaning tower is just what I expected. No one is permitted to ascend it since an artist who went lately and threw himself over—We returned to Leghorn dined and went on board again, sailed at five had a very good night, and arrived at dirty damp Civita Vecchia in time for breakfast. It was the first damp climate we had felt.—except the two hours at Pisa (which is a great resort of the English with delicate lungs) we have not seen a blue sky since leaving Nice but no damp in the air until we arrived in the domain of His Holiness—the road very bad and the country up to the very gate of Rome is dreary generally flat and wretched grass. however we saw many flocks of sheep and lambs—ponys, and fine white and grey cattle with long horns. We spied St. Peters great dome 12 miles off but on coming near to it were surprised it did not look so high as St Pauls. There is a delusion in it. the immense size of each part decieves the eye into thinking the top quite near.—The suburb on which it stands prevents any view of the Eternal City. We drove through the Piazza of St. Peters which is very fine a great semi circle of pillars four deep of immense size and an oblisk in the middle—The Vatican with a splendid staircase on pillars at one side. We found very good rooms notwithstanding the warnings every one gave us that we would have to sleep in our carriage from the crowded state of Rome. Every thing is expensive. On Saturday we drove to two Palaces. The Farnesina where with many other things were beautiful frescoes by Raphael and his pupils and the Villa Borghese outside the walls a great collection of old sculptures such splendid salons in different marbles, the floor ancient mosaics. There were three groups we were delighted with by Bernina of David preparing to sling the stone—of Apollo and Daphne, and another also Canovas of Pauline Buonaparte exquisitely chiselled—In the Sistine or Chapel of Sixtus IV in the Vatican covered with Michael Angelo's frescoes John and I spent an hour. they are splendid Sarah would be in a pretty state let loose in such a collection—Certainly the figures are dreadfully in want of clothing which the Pope (for whom he painted) remarked and one of his Cardinals desired they shd be be a little dressed upon Michael Angelo made a likeness of the said Cardinal sitting in the corner of the picture, the infernal regions with asses ears and a great serpent twined round him. and when the Pope desired him to take the likeness away—he said that though His Holiness had power to take out of purgatory he could not take out of the regions beyond—so the poor Cardinal is sitting in the corner still looking very miserable—On Sunday we went to Mr Woodward's church just outside the Porta del Popolo near which we are. It is very large and a great congregation—His sermon was mystifying the sacrament of the Lord's Supper—making it more than we believe it to be though different quite from the Romish doctrine—It is a great pity that a better and clearer preacher is not here, such an important position a lady told me yesterday that he always gets higher as it nears Easter—that after Easter he preaches for some time excellent sermons until the congregation are settled having taken their sittings then gradually he slips off into puseyite nonsense There was nothing in the *service* objectionable except the curates reading too fast. We purpose going to the American Embassy next Sunday—where I believe it is the presbyterian form, and different clergymen preach—Mr. Forbes son of Mrs F of Craigavad preaches now being here with his wife and sister—There are also Blands from Whiteabbey near Belfast—Mr. Hamilton brother of Mrs H of Killyleagh and his bride who gives a party tomorrow to which we are invited but as it is merely for dancing I think we shall not go except John It is curious that two strange gentlemen next to whom Fanny and I sat at the table d'hote one began to talk about the John Maxwells in conversation and the other knows the Gervaises—and had been nearly one of the Sinclair Mulholland and

French party who are gone up the Nile—We dont know the least who either of them are, there are nice looking Americans also, and dutch—such numbers of bridal parties—Yesterday we attended the solemn ceremony of blessing Candles. the only opportunity we shall have of seeing the Pope as we shall not be here during the Easter week. ladies all wore black dresses and black veils and sat on raised platforms on either side near the top. It was an excellent opportunity of seeing the interior of St. Peter's which certainly is a marvel for size and display. The pope's bodyguard uniform is the gaudiest thing—stripes of brightest yellow—crimson and black white rushe round their neck and white horse hair hanging from the top of the hat—all Swiss. The aisle was lined with French soldiers indeed there seem no native soldiers—The priests hurrying along wore silk dresses and white bedgowns trimmed with lace. The guard of nobles took their place on each side down from the altar very noble dress hat with feather and long horse hair behind. white pantaloons boots up to the knee. then came all the different orders of priests some crimson—then white and red—then black then white then Cardinals innumerable with dresses of cloth of gold of different shades. The Bishop of Armenia with a crown and then the old Pope on a gilt chair carried on poles by sixteen men in crimson. Each Cardinal on receiving a candle kissed the pope's hand and knee—but all others—many officers after the priests kissed his hand and toe—then they were all lighted chanting going on and the procession with the old pope again hoisted up and a canopy carried over him, he holding a lighted candle also took a round of the whole aisle and back again—his pointed hat was silvered so that the torch's shone on it—like a star above his head. His hat and dress were changed by the Cardinals for an entirely white and white ivory chair for saying of mass—we soon got tired and came away—Altogether you could not fancy it was intended for religion—the pope is a quiet amiable looking old man and blessed the people diligently with three fingers during his progress. We saw Queen Christina of Spain and her suite—We saw the Pantheon yesterday—such a noble old building like one immense dome on the ground Raphael is buried in it—I hope you take great care, the cold winds are so trying. Will you let Harriet read this and when I hear of Lizzie I will write to her. Best love to all at home. Ever dear Mama Your afft. child Ellen.

When Ellen talks of "Puseyite nonsense," she is referring to the religious views of Pusey, whose brilliant abilities had been recognized in his student days and who, in adult life, became a prominent figure in the Oxford Movement, which produced such a ferment in the Anglican Church, particularly in the 1850s, dividing it into high churchmen, with a leaning toward Roman Catholic practices, and low churchmen, who wished to retain unchanged the Christian doctrine and practices of their Protestant forefathers. Pusey was a high churchman who spent his life striving to bring what he regarded as reform to the Anglican Church by bringing it nearer to the Roman Catholic Church both in spirit and practice, an attempt that was regarded with much disfavor by many Anglicans, whose attitude is exemplified by Ellen Lyle's comments on Mr Woodward's high church leanings. However, Pusey did not suffer from the terrible psychological conflict that the controversy caused in many members of the Anglican Church, of which Pusey always remained a member. More will be heard of the Oxford Movement before Ellen Lyle's trip comes to an end.

Queen Christina, before her marriage Maria Christina of Naples, was the fourth wife of Ferdinand VII, King of Spain, and the only one who had children surviving at his death in 1833. Both were daughters—Isabella II, Queen of Spain and her sister the Infanta Louisa Fernando, both of whom became the center of intrigues and, in 1846, of a political storm, being the brides in the fateful double Spanish marriages, when Queen Isabella, the victim of cooperation between Louis Philippe, Emperor of France, and her mother, Queen Christina, was forced to marry her dissolute and impotent cousin, the duc D'Assisi, while her sister, on the same day, married the duc de Montpensier, son of Louis Philippe. By 1856, Queen Isabella was, inevitably, a miserably unhappy wife, her revolt against her fate making her court the scandal of Europe but producing a healthy heir to the Spanish throne and thwarting the plan of Louis Philippe, who had hoped to see his son, the duc de Montpensier, one day on the Spanish throne through his wife, as a result of his heartless manoeuvers to ensure that Queen Isabella died childless.

Rome
Feb 12.

Dearest Mama

I have been hoping for a letter from you the last week as I am so very far behind now in home news and I get so anxious to know how you are doing and if you have got Florence, I enclose a note to Lizzie as I suppose she is now returned and I am sure she will be a great comfort to you. Do write me a very full account of every thing. I had a very pleasant interesting letter from Aunt Fan but was grieved to hear so poor an account of poor dear Ellen—dont you think she ought to try a change of climate it sometimes has a great effect when other things fail. This air does not agree with many—it is just the opposite of Nice and is weakening and relaxing. Fanny feels sleepy all day but we are all very well at least much better than when we left home; We drive for two or three hours every day and see one or two things—The chief ruins are all very near the Coliseum. and along the Appian Way by which Paul came to Rome as is told in Acts—The old pavement of great blocks on which he walked we drove along—It is only lately cleared from the accumulation of centuries. We paid a visit to the Catacombs of St Sebastian

155

which are interesting as being the refuge of the Christians in the persecutions of the Emperors and where they had their worship. They are narrow passages leading in innumerable directions. Many of the openings are built up as they were made a resort of thieves. The old monk in his long brown coat and cowl with a rope round his waist showed us relics in a glass case the prints of two feet in lava which we were to believe were those of Christ who tradition says met Peter one day near Rome and made revelations to him. There are a great number of remains of mausoleums along the Appian way. one large round tower 19 centuries old to Cicilia Metella the wife of Crassus is the most perfect. The tomb of the Scipios a great large granite chest is quite perfect, was found near it and is now in the Vatican. We went down into three places where the ashes of the dead were preserved called Colombariums. They are very curious rooms with pigeonholes all round in rows with the urn, like a large flower pot containing the ashes—Some of the little arches contained beautifully carved little white marble urns of different shapes—one was to a little child whose ashes it contained and on it was carved a bird feeding its young ones in the nest to show that this monument was raised by maternal love—another was to a dog which was carved and the inscription was The Ashes of the delight of Glycon They were all of the times of Augustus and Tiberius one very large was only excavated within the last few weeks. It is very interesting exploring these kind of places—We found in the little burying place allotted to the English the tomb of Digby Cleaver but no other we knew of. I hope we shall be able to go there again. I suppose Selina Finlay's is there—I should like to see it. We found two priests there when we went I suppose examining that the inscriptions were according to order. Imagine if the English government were to prohibit any sect from putting what they liked on the tombstones of their friends It is extraordinary tyranny. We took tea at the Blands one evening all the parties here are evening ones—and met not a very interesting assemble Some Americans who are not very elegant and are dreadfully snubbed by the English in Rome. but they really bring it on themselves by their presumption and forwardness. We went last Sunday to Church at the American Embassy where Mr. Forbes preaches at three o'clock. he is one of the Craigavad Forbes and has a living in the Isle of Man but was obliged to come abroad for his health and has all his family here his sister Octavia lives with them and is a very nice girl. He is a very good man and preached a very nice sermon on John 1, 12—The congregation was pretty good, it is distressing to think of Mr. Woodward having such an immense congregation every Sunday while he is mystifying their minds—I hope the Chichesters are all well. Tell Harriet I was delighted to get her nice long letter. I suppose Sarah and her party have left you If you sent her this letter it would save me writing to the same effect and I may have something new to tell next week, the Carnival begins on Saturday and lasts till Shrove Tuesday don't forget the pancakes—John intends taking a window in the Corso which is the street for seeing all its operations It is a very long street lined with palaces the chief is Prince Dorias who married one of the late Ld. Salisbury's daughters—Is it true you have had such severe weather the paper says for 30 years there has not been so bad a winter in England or America. I hope you clothe well and keep the house warm. I hope Jem and Edward are quite well. best love to them.

Ever your very affec. child
Ellen

Rome (undated)

Dearest Mama

I wrote to you two days ago in a very nervous state at not hearing and the very next day got your delightful letter so I was sorry I had sent it—but you were too long in writing from the middle of January till the 18 February and I cannot help fretting particularly as this air affects the spirits and nerves so much—Your letter however did me as Solomon says "good like a medecine" and the same day I got one from Sarah which she directed Hotel d'Europe where we never were, as they had no room John and I went to a large party at his banker's last night—which was like the Black Hole of Calcutta for crowds and there was good singing but that was all as dancing is not allowed in Lent—We are to take tea at the Forbes on Tuesday and leave this if all is well on Wednesday the journey is generally done in three days but we intend to take five most of it has beautiful scenery. Terracine and Gaeta particularly. We are trying to see as many of the Palace Galleries as we can before leaving but it would take a whole winter to satisfy oneself with both antiquities and paintings John is buying two or three small ones—We were grieved to hear so poor an account of dear Ellen M—I trust she is in the path of life—her poor little children, what a sad thing if she is taken from them—It is a comfort to hear that Sarah is so strong and George C. better—Fanny is obliged to take things easy and not do anything fatiguing but required to be out a great deal. At Naples it will be easier—here one has to drive through so many odiferous streets before getting to the country. We will write to George it is wrong he has not written to John M—as he promised. Best love from all of us to yourself I hope Harriet is strong I am sure you will find dear Lizzie a comfort she is so sensible and good. Ever dearest Mama your very affectionate child   Ellen

Letter undated but clearly
written in Rome in February 1857

Dearest Sae

I hope you have learned all our adventures hitherto as I asked Mama to send my letters to you—it is no use writing the same things twice when it costs a whole lld. Fanny is not strong enough to do much at seeing sights so we take it very quietly—I hope you and Townley were very much the better of your Northern trips—I am very anxious to hear of you all—when we shall see home and faces again I do not know—the lodgings here are very

157

comfortable—our dinner comes in from a restaurant every day at six and is always excellent—soup, fish, a roast,—snipe and vegetables and pudding—Fresh butter is the dearest thing to buy—Bread very good and tea and chocolate also—John hired a little valet for the month who is quite invaluable. is butler, messenger, bargainer and knows as much about the public places—who the pictures and statues are by and seems to admire them as an artist—he interprets also which as you may imagine is desirable for us; the native Italians seem so very intelligent, bright, and quick compared with the same class at home—and so handsome, splendid eyes—fine brow finely chiseled noses and short upper lip—Their dress is becoming and pictur-esque—The conical hat and cloak with the left end thrown over the right shoulder—or short green jacket bright neck tie and long stockings Poor creatures I believe they are very poor, the number of beggars is extraordinary We sometimes go to the artists studio and have seen several very pretty things—At a Mr Williams were two enchanting paintings just finished but bought—One of Campagna with the ruins scattered about groups of bright figures in front and the sunshine and cloud lightening and shading exquisitely the coloring so fresh and pure Another of an Italian girl with a distaff and a baby sleeping beside her was so lovely Modern painting and sculpture are more to my taste than the old pieces of bodies and dingy things that one ought to be enraptured with—a very few things however I except—viz—the Apollo Belvedere in the Vatican—a group by Canova in St. Peters round the tomb of [2]   We have not seen many of Raphaels productions yet In another where Mr Mulhollands likeness was done we saw a lovely portrait of the Prince Borghese's only daughter of his first wife one of the ladies Talbot who with her three sons died in I believe a week—leaving one little girl she is married to a duke something—and is very interesting looking At the Lateran church today we saw such a beautiful little chapel decorated by the Fordonia family as its mausoleum nothing could be more elegant—Lovely white marble statues were in every niche Gold and white marble with a little malachite and lapis lazuli in the altar is all the ornament—the father of the present prince kept a little shop in the chief street in Rome, became rich and they have married into the Colonna and Orsini families and have a grand palace—We went last Sunday to the American Embassy—The service was very simple the sermon very poor—Indeed Mr Forbes is the only preacher of what is pure and true—We heard Dr Manning Archdeacon he was preaching in the St. Carlo church—There was a crowd of English—the subject "Hail Mary full of grace" I had no idea that they could have not said more for their doctrine Though he is considered so clever and eloquent—his argument was so weak and the texts he produced so glaringly distorted no one who knew any thing of the Bible would be taken in by it—He has a quiet gentlemanlike voice and manner—and has fine small features and very thin—Every time he pro-nounced the name of Jesus, he lifted the little black cap off his head. A russian gave us a short oration previously on the Mission in China. It is a strange language. We have different friends in our balcony each day to see

158

the Carnival Octavia Forbes or Mabel Crawford—The George Hamiltons—and Blands—It is a very curious scene We saw Mr and Mrs Solomon Richards driving about in the thick of it today. When you write direct—Naples as we have this house only till the 4th March—There is rumour of an outbreak there but as it does not prevent others going I suppose it will not us—the weather here is delightful but the odours of Rome which are not refreshing prevent one enjoying it much till the Compagna is reached. The Villa Albani the finest of Roman Villas we explored on Saturday It has a view of the Alban hills with their white tops and the plains of the Compagna—the house is full of old sculptures and the grounds laid out in Italien gardens—hedges of yew and fountains and fine evergreen oaks—I have no account yet of John's wedding except what Mary wrote to Fanny I hope Mama is getting on well Has Florence come over yet? It would amuse her How are the Wards—Best love to Townley and chicks Ever dear child Your affect.

Ellen

"Dr. Manning, Archdeacon" was Henry Edward Manning, one of the most distinguished members of the Anglican Church when the violent religious controversy precipitated by the Oxford Movement first troubled him with religious doubts. After a period of mental torture when he struggled to resolve his agonizing psychological conflict, he resigned his office of Archdeacon of Chichester in 1850, and, in 1851, he was received into the Roman Catholic Church, making the distressing final act of abjuration.[3] Ten weeks later, he became a priest, being then specially selected and trained by Cardinal Wiseman for the task of converting his Anglican brethren. In 1865, he became the Roman Catholic Archbishop of Westminster.

Henry Manning was not the only Anglican to secede in those stormy years for the Anglican Church, some of them being among his closest friends and three being his brothers-in law—George Dudley Ryder and Henry and Robert Wilberforce. George Ryder left the Anglican Church and became a Roman Catholic in 1846, Henry Wilberforce, Vicar of East Farleigh, resigned the living in 1850, immediately afterward embracing the Roman Catholic faith, and his brother, Robert Wilberforce, Archdeacon of the East Riding, resigned his office in 1854 in spite of desperate efforts by his brother, Samuel, Gladstone, Pusey, and other intimate friends to persuade him not to do so. He was received into the Roman Catholic Church in October of that year. The Wilberforces were sons of the great slave trade reformer William Wilberforce, and when the eldest son, William, an Anglican layman, also left the church to become a Roman Catholic in 1863, only one of the reformer's four sons remained an Anglican—Samuel Wilberforce, Archdeacon of Surrey, then Dean of Westminster, and, finally, Bishop of Oxford.

Many other well-known people were lost to the Anglican Church during this period, including John Henry Newman (later a cardinal of the Roman Church), their defections dealing shattering blows to England's established church.

In 1850, the situation was exacerbated by the Pope, overtriumphant perhaps at the glittering list of recent converts. Since the Reformation, Roman Catholics in England had been under the spiritual authority of Vicars Apostolic. In 1850, without any prior notice to the Queen or the British government, the Pope issued a bull that divided England into a Hierarchy of Bishops. Dr. Wiseman, the Metropolitan Archbishop of Westminster, was promoted cardinal and appointed Head of the Hierarchy. The Pope declared that "every day the obstacles were falling off which stood in the way of the true Catholic religion," tactlessly adding "that England was again restored to the number of Catholic powers and that her religious disgrace had been wiped out." Cardinal Wiseman unwisely added a finishing touch; his first Pastoral Letter said, "The Cardinal has desired that the Pope be prayed for before the Queen."

The result of all this was, predictably, public uproar and an intensification of fading sectarian conflict and bigotry. When the queen, her throne constitutionally dependent on her Protestant faith, drove through the streets of London, the cheers that greeted her could not drown the cries of "No Popery." The public alarm and fury was reflected in the House of Commons, where the Prime Minister, Lord John Russell, proposed a bill in 1851, the "Ecclesiastical Titles Bill," that included in its terms, "The establishment of Roman Catholic Sees was prohibited." The Queen was much concerned about this bill, which she considered a mistake. Queen Victoria was a staunch Protestant, with no Roman leanings, but she was not bigoted, and she deplored the unfortunate results of recent events in stirring up a resurgence of religious hostility and bigotry of a bitterness long unknown. The Ecclesiastical Titles Bill was passed after considerable modification, but it was never enforced, and, in 1871, it was repealed.

When Ellen Lyle listened to Dr Manning's sermon in Rome in 1857, it was only a week or two after the death of Robert Wilberforce, who had recently started his training to become a priest. He died in Albano on February 3, 1857, and the following day, Henry Manning had written to Henry Wilberforce to tell him of his brother's death.

Naples
March 26th

Dearest Mama

Your letter of the 10th arrived all safe to my great comfort and Lizzie's was forwarded to me from Rome. Will you tell her how glad I was to get it—and to hear the good news it and yours contained Local, social, and political! It seems as if we never would get home, it is now nearly four months. The trees here are shooting out and have a spring look We had some very close weather and were afflicted with the odours everywhere, but on Monday night a great storm with thunder and lightning cleared the air and deluges of rain since have washed the streets—there have been only three or four days really fine, which was enough however to show us the exceeding beauty of the bay and views around We made a little party one day to Vesuvius Sophia Stuart Octavia Forbes John and me Fanny of course did not attempt it. We set off at 9 o'clock and were not back again till after 8, We drove to Mesina which is built over Herculaneum and ascended two hours from that to the Hermitage, there I took a chair which four men carry on poles, the others walked for nearly an hour to the foot of the cone a gen d'arme came with me for the guides and bearers are such a wild savage set—They talked so loud and yelled frightfully all the way it was quite deafening they had picked up some French and English words which they seemed very proud of Foine view Madam very foine and donner pour boire, dans votre poche came in every now and then. Most of them were very handsome. The Neopolitan is quite different from Italian and not near so melodious We were all except John carried up to the cone a precipice of cinders and no easy work for the poor men. You have no idea what a wilderness of barrenness it is. The extent is very much greater than I expected. On the top it was blowing very hard and bitterly cold. There is a horrible grandeur in the great mouth with steep bright yellow sulphur sides like the jaws of a monster explosions echoing in the hollow cavern and volumes of smoke rolling out—We went down into the smaller crater and were nearly suffocated with the sulphur smoke. The heat was so great while walking on the lava only two feet deep of it was not red hot which we saw by looking down the crevices. We lunched in as sheltered a spot as we could find. and afterwards slid down between two men in a moving mass of cinders and ashes It was the most ridiculous operation the guides shouting out courages madame our hair flying in the wind and feet completely sunk but still sliding on the strata below our little servant Philip who has scarcely any legs found consequently much difficulty in extricating them and with great gravity rolled most of the way. We think of going on to Sarento and Amalfi next week but you had better write here as we intend returning as from this we sail to Marseilles. If you write immediately on receiving this there would be time to get it. John and I jointly wrote a long letter to George which goes today He ought to have written to John. I do hope he will apply himself to the business—which from all accounts will require great energy I hope we shall get to Pompii but it is difficult as Fanny is not up to expeditions and it does not do to leave her all day alone

161

We took tea on Tuesday at the Thompsons who are in the regions of space about 130 stairs They are a merry pair. The party consisted of a Count Nugent, a distant cousin of their own whose family being R.C. emigrated from Ireland when they were under restriction. Their Mother was Italien and had a fine villa on the Bay of Naples. He is a fine looking man and sings very well but is a dreadful sufferer, some years ago he was shot by mistake by his servant and all the balls have never been extracted. Mr. Verner second son of Sir W Verner was also there and not nice A little friend also Mr Ivers who had a quarrel with Wiseman and left England in consequence He did not do us *any harm* being very shy, scarcely spoke—Mr Moore a rather agreeable man and Mr. Burton lieutenant of the English frigate—He took the Thompsons and John yesterday to see the French frigate which is very much larger than the English one The Springvales write that they have given up the idea of leaving home so you will not have the trouble of the children but Fan says she purposes paying you a weeks visit if possible when we get back We hear great accounts of Alfred his being weaned put in short frocks and new teeth etc etc Give our best love to Lizzie and John Jem and Florence Does Jem want coral studs? Perhaps Edward would like to read this I owe him a letter of long standing. I was so glad to hear of the congregation approval and of Mrs. C.O's generosity I hope Ellen M—continues better Give our love to her and Crim

Ever dear Mama   Your affect. child
Ellen

Only the last part of Ellen's next letter has survived. It is also to her mother:

Naples April 1857

We are here in a rich valley of fruit trees John brought in a small branch today with 10 great ripe oranges on it—The roads are all narrow between high walls the earth inside raised to its height—so that the golden fruit hangs temptingly over—while the walls give delightful shade in summer and are covered with delicate ferns and other climbing plants Figs are coming out—the leaf like chesnut and the mulberry—a very light green shaped like alder leaf—on our rides we have lovely views—the sea such a blue as one must see to understand—is still deeper looking through the olives—and orange trees which grow to the edge The white felucca sail is like a snowy seagull with its wings spread dipping to the water—Vesuvius which is opposite our window was blazing very bright last night. but I fear no eruption will gladden our sight. We leave for Naples tomorrow. I wish this lovely clime was not so far from home. You would delight in it for a short run—Will you write to Paris—Monr. E. de la Planche, Rue de Jeuneure, Paris.
    Ever your affec. Child
        Ellen
Best love to Lizzie and all at home.

1. A heretical sect.
2. Name omitted in original letter.
3. Admitting the invalidity of his Anglican order.

32 / 1852/1858—Before and During the Indian Mutiny, Charles Scott Writes to His Father, Mother, and Brother in Ulster

Since Charles Scott's uncle, Thomas Scott, left India in 1806, many changes had taken place on that continent.

The East India Company in London still administered Indian affairs. Its Court of Directors in London still appointed the Governor General, subject to the approval of the Board of Control, which had been established first in 1784. India, however, was a long way off, its history, ways, customs, and conditions little understood in England; it was, therefore, still on the Governor General that the administration and the British reputation in India was dependent.

In the event, the imperialist policy of Lord Mornington, when he was Governor General, had continued in varying degrees under his successors, with the result that by 1852 there had been an enormous increase in the East India Company's territory, power, and influence in India.

In 1841, Lord Ellenborough had been appointed Governor General after Lord Auckland, but his tenure of office proved short-lived, for instead of serving in India for the usual period of five years, he was recalled in two and one-half years by the Court of Directors because they no longer felt confidence in him. There had been much public criticism of him in England, where the government, the queen, and her subjects were anxious that India should be treated fairly and those portions of the country under the control of the East India Company governed in a satisfactory manner. Lord Ellenborough had been sent to India for the express purpose of establishing peace, but an account of his period of office would be a catalogue of wars.

In 1844, Lord Ellenborough was replaced by Sir Henry (afterward Lord) Hardinge, who was followed in 1848 by Lord Dalhousie.

Lord Dalhousie's term of office was punctuated by annexations, some, though not all, preceded by war. The second Sikh war was precipitated in April 1848, soon after Lord Dalhousie reached India, by the assassination of two British officers in Multan, its final outcome being the annexation of the Punjab in 1849. The second Burmese war broke out in 1852 as a result of the ill treatment of British merchants in Rangoon and the unsatisfactory reception of the British protest. The whole valley of the Irrawaddy from Rangoon to Prome was swiftly occupied, and the King of Ava, then refusing to negotiate, it was all annexed under the name of Pegu and added to the provinces of Arakan and Tenasserim, which had passed into the East India Company's possession in 1826 after the first Burmese war. The kingdom of Oudh was annexed in 1856 without war, ostensibly for the benefit of its inhabitants suffering from misrule, an account of the situation agreed to by some historians. Nor does this exhaust the list, for Lord Dalhousie flouted an Indian custom, not interfered with by previous governor generals, that allowed an Indian ruler without a natural heir to adopt one, even on his deathbed, to succeed him. Lord Dalhousie took advantage of such a situation to annex the state, refusing to recognize the adopted heir. He started this practice in 1848, the year of his arrival in India, with the annexation of Satura, an independent state.

Lord Dalhousie was an energetic Governor General, introducing into India cheap postage, the steam engine, the electric telegraph, and many more roads and canals, but these useful improvements cannot disguise the fact that his dictatorial encroachments on Indian independence by constant annexations caused much anxiety and hostility among the Indian population.

Lord Dalhousie left India in 1856, and the next Governor General was Lord Canning, who, before leaving England, made a farewell speech that has been often quoted and might perhaps be taken as an example of precognition:

I wish for a peaceful term of office, but I cannot forget that in the sky of India, serene as it is, a small cloud may arise, no larger than a man's hand but which, growing larger and larger, may at last threaten to burst and overwhelm us with ruin.

It may also be that Lord Canning was better informed and had a more open mind than Lord Dalhousie.

Charles Scott, twenty-three years of age in 1852, the second son of the Rev. George Scott, brother of Thomas Scott, comments freely in his letters home on the governor generals as well as on other matters of historical interest. He is described in family notes as "very clever," a point on which readers can judge for themselves in the following pages.

1852—letter from C. Scott to his brother, Rev. J. B. Scott, dated Feb. 8, 1852, and addressed to Banagher Glebe, Dungiven, Co. Derry, Ireland.

Camp near Cockenudu
Feb 8th 1852

My dear Bedel

I forget when it was that I last wrote to you, but I fear it is now some awful time since, it is uncommon hard to screw a letter out of the utter nothingness of an existence like mine here, so I hope you excuse my irregular correspondence, there has nothing happened here since I wrote by last mail, how could there? I am still at the 'semi-judicial' occupation of canal digging and am in the disaggreable predicament of having to carry on & stand sponsor in a kind of way for the faults, of an exceeding rickety lock, which was begun by my predecessor in the work here, who worse even than the man who built on the sand, built on the marsh & the consequence is that the walls are sinking in all directions, & the jolly lock admits daylight through sundry fissures picturesque in an ancient ruin, but out of place & ill timed in a new lock. But indeed the poor man is hardly to be blamed as he doubtless would have made a good foundation had he had the money, but it is always the way, an estimate goes up to Government & is allways rejected unless it is for about 1/2 of the amount necessary to do a work well: as for the opinion of a man like our chief Col Cotton who has been 30 years at work of the kind they mind it not a straw. Sir H. Pottinger is the best judge, is the answer. Sir H's powers of government having been now pretty well proved, to be about on a par with those of Nebuckadnizzar, in his Grasing State.

You may well imagine what a want of matter I labour under, when I am reduced to grumbling politics.

In your letter you mentioned the marriage of Barbara Richardson, I thought she was the one married to Moor of Bally-Dividy, but perhaps old Moor has been gathered to his fathers & left her free to mate again, they are strongminded women if I remember right, all the Richardsons of Somerset. are they at all tinctured with Bloomerism? for as appears from all the papers "Despotic power in France & Bloomerism in England, are advancing with rapid & appalling (I believe there should be but one p in this) strides. These together with the visit of that "Hungary Adventurer" Kossuth seem the chief news from home at present.

By the way I suppose you heard, that there was great chance of War with the Burmese here the other day, they had actually rigged up a regular army at Madras, infantry, artillery, & what not to go there & we thought they would have sent for two or 3 of us, to go as field engineers, being ready at hand, when the Burmah fellows knocked under & knocked the whole affair on the head. I should like to have gone to Burmah it must be something to see, & a country very little known. Col Cotton who was there in the war of 25 says it is the finest place in the world, there is so much rain there (hes mad on the subject of irrigation is that old man). As I want to do without an envelope I think it is time to stop so with love to all at home, Believe me dr Bedel, ever your afft. brother

C. Scott

Charles Scott was in the Madras Engineers, one of those officers appointed to a civilian post, a practice mentioned later in this correspondence. Colonel Cotton was a well-known figure in India, and the following extract, taken from the Encylopaedia Brittanica of 1928 is of interest:

Sir Arthur Thomas Cotton (1803–1899) English Engineer. He entered the Madras Engineers in 1819, served in the first Burmese War (1824–1826) and in 1828 began his life work on the irrigation works of Southern India. . . . .
Before the beginning of his work Tanjore and the adjoining districts were threatened with ruin for lack of water. On its completion they became the richest part of Madras, and Tanjore returned the largest revenue of any district in India. He was the founder of the School of Indian Hydraulic Engineering and carried out much of his work in the face of opposition and discouragement from the Madras Government though, in the minute of 15th May 1858, that Government paid an ample tribute to the genius of Cotton's "master mind". He was knighted in 1861. Sir Arthur Cotton believed in the possibility of constructing a complete system of irrigation and navigation canals throughout India and devoted the whole of a long life to the partial realisation of the project. He died in 1899.

"Bloomerism" denoted the aspirations of women who desired women's suffrage and women's rights. The word is derived from the activities of Mrs. Amelia Jenks Bloomer, editor of *The Lily*, the first women's paper in America. Mrs Bloomer was also a supporter of women's rights, women's suffrage, and women's dress reform, advocating a short skirt with loose trousers gathered around the ankles that became known as "bloomers," a description that also applied to any divided skirt or knickerbocker dress for women.

Barbara Richardson was a younger sister of Katherine Scott, Thomas Scott's third wife, the stepmother of Elizabeth Scott and Charles Scott.

"Despotic power in France" referred to the activities of Louis Napoleon, then Prince Regent of France, who, in 1852, was desperately intriguing to become the emperor of France and fulfill his ambition to found a dynasty.

The "Hungary Adventurer Kussuth" was regarded then as an adventurer or as an Hungarian patriot. Kossuth was a brilliant orater, rousing strong and violent emotions in the Hungarian public, although there were many responsible Hungarians who strongly disagreed with him. In 1837, he was arrested in Hungary on a charge of high treason and sentenced to a term of imprisonment. In 1847, he was elected to the Diet, where he continued his campaign for Hungary's complete independence with considerable success, becoming in 1848, the President of Hungary and, in effect, its dictator. Power drunk by such success, his demands increased, and he finally declared the complete independence of Hungary in spite of strong opposition within Hungary itself to breaking the link with Austria. Franz Joseph had recently become Emperor of Austria, and, at this point, Russia interested herself in the question. The moves then taken against him by the two emperors forced Kossuth to leave the country and become a fugitive, taking refuge first in Turkey and then in England, which he reached in 1851, both these countries refusing to give him up to the vengeance of Austria. In England, the public received him rapturously as a patriot, and Lord Palmerston, the Foreign Secretary, not only invited him to his private house but also received a deputation of radicals, who described the emperors of Austria and Russia as "odious and detestable assassins," to Lord Palmerston's apparent approval. The public was excited and approving, but the government, the Queen, and Prince Albert, none of whom had been informed, still less consulted, by Lord Palmerston, strongly disapproved, not desiring a quarrel between England and Austria and Russia. Very reluctantly, Lord Palmerston canceled his private invitation to Kossuth. It is of course the duty of a foreign secretary to behave with discretion and not to pursue any course, particularly of an inflammable nature, without the agreement of the Cabinet. On this occasion, violent anti-Russian feelings were roused in the British public, and this has been regarded as one of the factors that led to Great Britain's taking part in the Crimean War.

Sir Henry Pottinger, born in Belfast, of whom Charles Scott speaks so scornfully, was, in 1852, sixty-one years of age and governor of Madras. He had had a distinguished career, having been a Lieutenant General in the Indian Army, Colonel of the Bombay Native Infantry, governor of Hong Kong in 1843 and of the Cape of Good Hope in 1845. He had been appointed Governor of Madras in 1850. It certainly does not appear that his past experience would qualify him to make decisions regarding irrigation. Sir Henry Pottinger died in 1856.

War with Burmah did result in 1852, as described in the foreword to this section.

1852—Part of a letter addressed to Mrs. George Scott, Banagher Glebe,

Dungiven, Co., Derry, Ireland—dated April 7, 1852. Postmark My 21, 1852—from Charles Scott.

Bazmar   You had better wait until you hear further from me, address
to   If one is to believe the papers all you good people at home are in a
great state of fright about invasion from France, if not from Russia & other
amiable continentals. I trust it may prove a false alarm. Certainly I dont think
Louis Napoleon will go to war, if he can help it, it would be the ruin of him,
if either successful, or disadvantageous, to the French. at least if he depends
on the army solely as they say he does, as in the first case they would all
take up with the successful General, & in the second Mr L.N. would come
in for all the blame. As this long epistle of mine will be no joke in the way
of postage I think its best to shut up for the present.
  With Love to all at Home, believe me, dearest Mother
     Ever your afft. son
     C. Scott

  French policy intentions, and the political maneuvers of Louis Napoleon were causing great concern in England. Louis Napoleon's hopes
of becoming Emperor were entirely dependent on the support of the
French Army, so that he could not afford to antagonize it. French military
circles had never forgotten their defeat at Waterloo, still thirsted for
revenge against England, and were in a truculent mood. In 1852, there
was a real danger of a French attack, in the first instance on Belgium.
There was also a possibility of an attempt to invade England, so that for
the time being, Louis Napoleon was in a difficult and unenviable position.
In the end, neither of these warlike projects materialized, and Louis
Napoleon, by methods that roused strong disapproval in England, where
they were regarded as "dubious," attained his cherished objective and
became emperor of France in December 1852. Lord Palmerston, who
had only escaped dismissal over the Kossuth incident because of his
tremendous public popularity, was still Foreign Secretary, and once more
asserted his independence of normal political usage by expressing to the
French Ambassador his own views, which were in direct contradiction
to that of the Cabinet, declaring his "entire approbation of the act of the
President (Louis Napoleon) and his conviction that he could not have
acted otherwise," thus implying that these were the views of the British
government. This proved too much, and Lord Palmerston was at once
dismissed from his post as Foreign Secretary.

  In the case of Russia, to which Charles Scott also refers, war did
come, although it was fought far from England in the Crimea.

Letter from Charles Scott to his brother, Rev. J. B. Scott, dated only

March 5, but from the contents, the year appears to be 1853 or 1854.

Rangoon
March 5th

My dear Bedel,

You see from the heading that I have arrived here all right as my letter to our Father from board the Steamer may have led you to expect, we had a very pleasant passage although rather rough (somehow one is never seasick in India) I left the Steamer at Amhurst at the Mouth of the Moulmien River & came to Rangoon in a country barque which we found ready to sail for this when the Steamer arrived. The coast at Amhurst is very beautiful being bold & high & wooded down to the waters edge with magnificent trees, & owing to the great rise & fall of the tides, 26 feet, you see trees growing in the water at high tide. Here we first saw the enormous pyramidal pagodas of the Burmese who are mostly Buddists, and their pagodas altho they are quite solid in general & have no interior whatever have a much more graceful appearance outside than the Hindoo ones. we did not land at Amhurst but sailed at once for Rangoon where we arrived on the 27th of February at about 6 p.m. the country about the mouths of the Irrawady is not nearly so imposing in appearance as that at Amhurst, being low & the jungle with which it is covered being low & scrubby, but it is a magnificent river, Rangoon is on one of its (some 20) mouths which is a splendid river about as wide as the Foyle at its widest point & 7 or 8 fathoms deep all over. the tide runs at about 6 miles an hour & you can come up to Rangoon or go out to sea at one time, the town of Rangoon is an odd looking place the poonjay houses or sorts of Monasteries in which many of the officers are quartered are queer looking places which more resemble the houses on the old blue plates and dishes than anything else I can think of, they are all raised on poles that is the floor is from 2 to 6 feet above ground as a precaution against the rains, and the houses are all of wood which makes them awfully hot. The weather is already getting frightfully warm & I fear that it will be almost worse than Basmah, however they have cool nights which is a great thing. The town was in a great measure burnt down at the time of its capture and therefore there are only the pagodas left standing in some places as they are the only masonry buildings they are of a very odd description being solid masses of brick and mortar built in this form and stuccoed over, sometimes gilt.

I have here tried to scratch down a sketch of the Great Shoadagon pagoda at the stockade round which the fight took place at the taking of Rangoon, it will serve to give you an idea of what these buildings are like, they are of all sizes the Shoadagon is 320 feet high & stands on a hill about 100 feet high, it was formerly covered with gilding & must have been a most gorgeous spectacle. It is surrounded by a strong wall & might have been a good post had the Burmese defended it properly. The enclosure is full of Poonjay houses all gilt in the inside, too fine to be in good taste, but very striking. The Artillery & H.M.'s 81st are quartered in them, they look a good deal spoiled but still serve to give a good idea of what Solomon's temple must have been

169

like, the whole flight of steps up the hill to the Pagoda are roofed in & the pillars supporting the roof of this covered way and the wood work of the roof, are decorated with gold and vermilion. Almost all the small pagodas & tombs in the town are of the same form as the great Pagoda but some of them not above 15 or 20 feet high, the extinguisher looking cap on the top is a belfry, it is of very pretty open ironwork gilt & the bells hang round the lower ring or base & are moved by the wind but they have been mostly plundered, in fact almost all the little pagodas & tombs have been broken open to get out the little brass or bronze & sometimes gold & silver images which the Burmese brick up in them, this has also been done with most of the big gods built of brick & mortar & plastered over which are scattered about the town, you see several of these deities sitting up, their usual posture, staring you in the face with their stomachs open and their brick & mortar bowels taken out. I think I have now told all I can about Rangoon. the Stockade which was taken at the beginning of the war is a very large one with an earthen rampart behind the stockade & very stupidly laid out. The stockade & rampart of no great height it is being removed.

I should not wonder if I am recalled to Madras & should be very glad to go back after I have seen a little of the country I find that instead of gaining in pay I am a considerable loser by being here, I have done all I can to be taken back to Madras, I hope to be so after a couple of months which will just give me a good look at the country, I am not sure if I will be kept here or sent up country at present I would like to go up to Prome & Meadag but have some fears that the old General will try to get a permanent hold of me if I do he seems to want to keep me in Burmah if he can

Love to all at home
Your afft. brother
C. Scott

Letter from C. Scott to his Father Rev. George Scott. It is not dated and gives no address but is clearly written from Rangoon at the beginning of the Crimean War. England declared war in 1854.

My dearest Father,
Your letter which came out by last mail reached me a few days ago, I was delighted to hear such good accounts of you all, & I have a pretty good one to give of myself this time, as it seems that I have now a chance of coming in for a few of the loaves and fishes of the Service which have been so long in coming, the Commissioner of Pegu having recommended me to the Goverener General as the man to make the road from this to Promu, on a Staff salary of 500 RS, or 50£ a month besides my regimental pay which is also full battu pay or about 2£ a month more than in India, for this I have of course to do very severe work but I am now bound in honour to work my best after having been treated so handsomely. The Commissioner has also

given me the power of nominating 2 officers of infantry as assistants at salaries of 300Rs or 30£ each a month, this puts me in the way of doing a good turn for one of the family, as I am in hopes of being able to get Theophilus who is here with his Regiment and has grown a very nice fellow, appointed, as one of the assistants, I think we will be able to get him on temporarily & then after 6 months or so if he can be spared from his regiment & passes in surveying he will get the appointment permanently, this will lead on to something still better in the course of time. I am about to start by boat up the Lyne river a branch of the Irrawaddie, in order to explore a portion of the country through which the road must pass It is about 40 miles in length distant about 80 miles from here & has not yet been explored by any European. The reason of my going now is that I may see the country under the effects of the monsoon, it will not be the most delightful journey in the world with the rain constantly falling in bucketsfull, but I can put up with it on 500Rs a month. The country is very quiet here now with the exception of a few occasional robberies which were at all times frequent and will be soon put down if they go about it the right way. The King of Ara is now so friendly to our rule here that he has entered into a contract to supply the Comissariat with wheat, he is I believe a new man who lately came to the throne & I suppose represents the feelings of the majority of his subjects. Still I dont think we have much right to the country, & that they had better never have annexed it, as it will cost more than it is worth, if theyd spend half the money they do on roads etc. here, on Madras it would return them fourfold, but it is an ill wind that blows nobody good I would have been long in getting 500Rs a month there—I suppose the good people at home are now in a great state of excitement about the war—There must be something happened by this time, & we all look out for the next mail with great interest, if things dont turn out quite so well at first as they expect I should not wonder if some of us are packed off to Turkey in the panic; it would be worth while to be there to see a country of such magnitude altho of course in such a mass of soldiers all chance of individual distinction would be out of the question; it seems a very strange thing the extreme popularity of the war with almost all parties at home, but I expect when they come to feel the burden of it its popularity will soon go, & people will wish that the 3 poor old quakers whom they laughed at so much had succeeded in talking over old Nicolas; the Sultan must have some odd fish among the numbers who have crowded over to put his army to rights for him, at least to attempt it, the other day we heard of 3 Ensigns who were cashiered by a court martial 2 or 3 years ago who are captains of cavalry in his service now: poor man if he had trusted to his Turkish officers it would have been all the better for him.

In your letter you asked when my furlough would be due, but really that is rather an unsatisfactory subject.

"Old Nicholas" was the tzar of Russia, Nicholas I. His imperialist ambitions alarmed both Britain and France, who combined to oppose his designs on Turkey. He attacked that country in November 1853. France proclaimed a state of war with Russia on the March 27, 1854, and England did so on March 28, 1854.

Theophilus Scott, son of Thomas Scott's brother James, was a first cousin of Charles Scott and two years younger. His father, Rector of Portaferry for many years, married Elizabeth Lucas, sister of Thomas Scott's wife, Anne. He was also Chancellor of Down.

1856.   Pulnez (near Dindegul)
                                                    March 30th 1856
My dearest Father,

Your letter of the 3d November has only just reached me!! together with my Mother's of the same date & one from her dated 14 Dec & one from Bedel of the 17th Novr.

I am afraid from the tenour of some of these letters that some of your letters to me must have miscarried, as I only got your letter on the subject of the robbery a few days before I left Rangoon, or early in December, if I remember right. I answered it at once thanking you for your great kindness in making the generous offer of assistance that you did, but declining it as I was able perfectly to extricate myself without having recourse to borrowing, and I would be hard up indeed before I should think of troubling you, pressed as you must be by so many heavy demands upon your purse. I trust you received this letter, for if you did not, my conduct must seem very strange. I have now to thank you for the very kind letter I am now answering You may depend that I will try to get home as soon as possible & look forward with great pleasure to the time when I expect please God to see you all again at Banagher at which place strange to say I have never been near in my life. But I cannot be too sanguine about the time when I will be able to get away as I must save a little money first, which will be easy enough, if as I have been promised, I get charge of the Madura district on the 1st May next, but at present I do not draw much pay, being only a 2d assistant, as a temporary measure; I hope you got my letter from Madras which will explain that I have left Rangoon & all about my movements.

I left Madras shortly after I had written it, under orders to go to Madura, but when I got to Trichinopoly I got orders to turn off to Dindegul, which you will see on the map about 60 miles in an easterly direction from Trichinopoly, & then to go 50 miles further on to a place where I have to build a bridge over a river called the Amarawutty, which runs in a N & S direction separating the Madura & Cocinbutore, districts—and I am now writing from a place called Pulney, 13 miles on the Dindegul side of my Bridge, where I have come out for a day or two, it is a terribly hot place, but there are some very fine hills in the district some of them within 15 or 16 miles of where I now am, but I am so tied by the leg, that I cannot go there at least for some time; it is a most out of the way place this, the nearest station, Dindegal is nearly 50 miles off, and there the society consists of a sub-Collector 2 or 3 missionaries & a Subaltern Commanding a detachment stationed there. The Collectors & Missionaries, being Masters of their own actions, like sensible folks, betake themselves to the hills during the hot weather i.e. from Feb to June, so the only denizens of the plain now, are the detachment sub, & myself, poor wretches who are supposed to be like the inhabitants of Venus, according to Professor Whewell, and indestructible by heat. I however find myself wonderfully well considering all things—By the way I have just heard that there is a French family of coffee planters at about 50 miles from here, in which there are 3 young ladies, so perhaps you will find me coming home with, a fair coffee planting damsel, picked up in these inhospitable regions; but you need not be too anxious on the subject, as I have not seen any of them yet. By the way talking so much about myself I quite forgot the auspicious event mentioned in my Mother's last letter, of the birth of a nephew, on which happy event I will send my felicitations to Maria and John, they are now getting their quiver pretty full. I am also most thankful to hear such good accounts of George, & hope that ere this reaches you he will have been perfectly restored in mind and body. Bedel gives a sad account of the way in which he has been taken captive in the meshes woven around him, by a Raphoe beauty, of this I look out to hear more anon—give my love to my Mother & all at home & excusing my bad paper believe me my dearest Father

Ever your afft. Son

C. Scott

"Professor Whewell," William Whewell was a well-known British philosopher and historian of science. He was the son of a carpenter and destined to follow his father's occupation, but his mathematical genius led to his gaining an exhibition to Cambridge, where he went from the grammar schools of Lancaster and Heversham. His successes, activities, and the books he wrote are too numerous to mention here.

"Maria," in 1856 Mrs. Rutledge, was Charles Scott's elder sister, who has already been mentioned in this book, at the time of her sister Catherine's early death when Thomas Scott's family were in Paris.

George was Charles Scott's younger brother, who recovered his health, married Annie Colbert, and went into the civil service in England, eventually living at Greystones.

Letter from Charles to his Brother, Rev. J. B. Scott, dated 30th March, 1856.

Pulney near Dindigul
March 30th /56.

My dear Bedel,
Your letter of the 17th Novr/55 has only just reached me having been hopping gaily about sea & land in search of me for the last four months. You seem to have taken a wrong view on the subject of being robbed & obliged to pay up, the rule of the Service being that if money is under a guard, the guard alone is responsible, but if there is no guard the officer to whose department the cash chest belongs is responsible; if he applied for a guard & is refused and anything happens to the cash chest in consequence, the commanding officer who refuses a guard has to pay, this was done in the case of Captn Maddigan of the 84th who was robbed and murdered in the Irrawaddy district last April, Major Codrington who refused to supply him with a guard on his application for one had to fork out the value of the money stolen, but he was only a Major, whereas in my case it was a Major General hence all the difference, so you see I was done down by the authorities I am altogether very glad to have got from under the Bengal Government, who altho they made me great promises at the beginning, did nothing, & whose system of accounts etc are such that if one is not very careful he gets let in for all sorts of things, If you order tools, stores etc from the Arsenal, or any other public property of the kind, you are held responsible for it from the moment of its dispatch to you, — have to make it good whether you receive it or not, whereas in Madras like honest men the Government only debit you with what you actually receive. I consider myself lucky in being only debited with 14£ worth of picks & shovels sent me from the Arsenal at Calcutta to Rangoon which I never received, they having been lost by the carelessness of some skipper between the two places. Of course the skipper gets off because he is not a military man &, cotiris puribus,[1] every case at first sight is decided against a military officer by the govt when a civilian is on the other side. I am in a rather disagreeable position just now being only a 2d Asst. Civil Svr., but have been promised a division in May when the new regulations come out, if I get this Ill have very decent pay & will be able to come home in a year or so. This seems a nice district, there are some very fine hills in it with a good climate and lots of shooting great & small, but I am just now tied down to a confounded bridge that I have to build not much bigger than New Town Limavady bridge, but there is not a soul to do anything at it except myself & a lot of coolies little better than Yahoos. So I lead the life of a slave until I can get matters into working order under some decent native Superintendents. This bridge is one of the hottest of hot places, in fact this existence can only be compared to that of St. Laurence[2] on his gridiron, but it is worse for me for in his case "provision for life" as Sir C. Napier says was included.

Let us hear how you get on with Miss Haughton, I expect you have perpetrated the deed by this time, but I had hoped better things of you, we live in a Vale.

174

I am very glad to hear such good accounts of George, & hope he will be all right before you get this. Bye Bye for the present as I must write to Maria & Rutledge to congratulate them on the additional arrow in their quiver which I have just heard of So believe me

Your afft. brother

C. Scott

Letter from C. Scott to his brother, Rev. J. B. Scott. It is undated and without address, but it appears to have been written about June 1856 from Dindigul.

My dear Bedel,

I received your letter of 26th May a few days ago, & feel for your disappointment, but there are better fish in the sea than have been caught yet, & whatever the personal advantages or merits of the young lady may be, the Haughtons are no great shakes of a connexion, especially without a little gilding.

How the dickens did that ugly little red headed boy manage to hook a 6000 pounder—if he does so well, what ought not his brothers the Crimean heroes with their medals to effect—I am in a bad way & dont see when I am to get home although I want to go for my health which is getting seedy from a 7 year residence in this delightful climate. The new regulations as expected have only had effect in Bengal, but under them a man in my present position would get about 960£ a year—one year of such pay would enable me to go home & enjoy myself I intend when I do go to take a trip on the continent to get civilised a bit after barbarizing out here for so long.

I am afraid that instead of our travels having given Theophilus & myself an advantage over you at home; you'll find us a couple of savages a century behind the age; experience of men is much more worth than that of different countries & I suppose if there is a line of life calculated to destroy all talent in a man it is the East India Service, when you pass your life almost in solitude & have not the slightest incitement to exertion, but rather the contrary, whereas you have been living in a world of men, & must have an infinite fund of talk at all events, from all the practice your sermons give you—in fact you padre's never leave us poor wretches a chance with the females.

I am getting quite sick of John Company's service & have half a mind to cut it if I ever get home, this district is the most stupid one a man can be in, there is nothing of sufficient importance to interest one & I have nothing to do but wander about, & mend old ditches, & write long official letters about them, one might make out projects for large works & send them in, but I have been punished too severely for this excess of zeal, to try it again. There is nothing to fall back upon but shooting for which I cant afford time or money enough to be successful, but it is a fine shooting country for all that, I saw no less than 7 bison one day when on the hills, great brutes from 17 to 20 hands high, & as stout in proportion as the stoutest bull—but not having enough beaters I could not beat the jungle properly for them & they broke too far off for a shot.

Maria & Ruttledge appear to have cut me, they never answered my last letter of some time in March last I hope George continued well I wrote him a long letter by last mail, & that Father & Mother are flourishing give them my love & believe me my dear Bedel

Ever Your afft. brother

C. Scott

Theophilus Scott remained in the Indian Army after the mutiny and became a general in the Madras staff corps. He married Julia daughter of William Alley of Castle Archdale. He is not heard of again in this book.

1857—Letter from Charles Scott to his Brother, Rev. Bedel Scott, dated March 22, 1857.

Madura
March 22d/1857

My dear Bedel,

Your letter of 17th Jan reached me a fortnight since, and I am obliged to have recourse to the hackneyed apology of want of time as an excuse for not answering it by last mail as I might have done. However in continually having to make excuses of the kind I comfort myself with Bulwer's assertion that there must be something effeminate about the mind of a man who is a good correspondent. As regards your kind intention to spend 50£ on a present to me I think you will agree with me that it would be the best way to spend it by taking a trip along with me on the continent or some such place when I go home which I hope to do in about a year, as that would I fancy do you a deal of good after your monotonous life in a country curacy, and as regards myself I have now become quite a healthy individual by having had my pay increased as I mentioned in my last letter to my father. When I wrote that letter we were on the look out for the dispatch of a large force from Madras to Persia, but of this there seems but little chance now much to the disgust of the Madras Army, some regiments of which have been ordered to Bombay to do garrison duty in lieu of the Bombay ones ordered to Persia, the Company of Sappers which left some time since have not yet reached Bushin but are kept at Bombay & will most probably remain there mending old ditches while the war lasts, much to the disgust no doubt of their commanding officer an excentric little man in my corps who had served with the sappers in Scinde, and volunteered for Persia giving up for the purpose of going, an appointment worth 800£ a year Measures of this kind are certainly unpolitic as they will unquestionably have the effect of destroying the military spirit of the Madras Army, which was the one that first of all made John Company what he now is. There is a row in China but that is a place no one much cares to go to and it is thought here that very few troops will be sent from India but instead a force from home if the affair turns out seriously. It seems to have been a chapter of accidents throughout, the vessel seized was not a British craft at the time of capture as the period of her charter had expired but this the Chinese did not know & the rascalls deserve a licking for their impertinence.

There is not much to write about here as usual the papers have some articles about a new 'Black Act' as they call it by which Europeans in India are to be made liable to trial for their lives before the Company's up country courts before a jury of niggers, I don't think much of this, it will fall to the ground before long, but will occasion many calamities, likely enough, before it does. Elevating the Mild Hindoo is the hobby of the present day, and like other hobbies will have to be paid for, not that I am one of those who predict that it will lose us the country because I know well enough that if every Englishman in India were killed off tomorrow before six months were over Jack Nigger would be again in the dust under the heel of Great Britain, but if a man will bring pigs, fowls, rats & other walking flying or creeping things into his home and put them on an equality with his children, the inferior animals will give so much trouble that they will soon have to be turned out again, a more bothersome task than there would have been any occasion to perform, had they never been put in a position for which nature had not fitted them. I have no doubt you will think me a regular brute for expressing these sentiments and I am perfectly content to be called such, because I know that at home people hear such rot about Indian subjects that their minds are quite misled. I have no doubt that you in your clerical capacity hear a deal about missionaries & their effectiveness in converting the natives, now I have known many missionaries, some of them able & earnest men, others humbugs but they have all admitted that they did not think they had made a real convert in their lives, the fact is that such a thing is out of the question the natives of India are not circumstanced like any of the nations who were converted to Christianity in former times. Those people were either utter Barbarians, or people whose ideas of right & wrong were much the same as our own—in fact people who thought & reasoned about something more than the dictates of their animal instinct. Now a Hindoo is neither one, nor the other, he is civilised to the fullest extent of his capability and has been so for thousands of years without ever advancing a step and is so thoroughly wedded to his own customs and ways of thought that you can never get him out of them he is as incapable of going beyond them as a donkey is of winning the Derby, and it is all nonsense to try to make him anything but what he is, not a bad sort of animal in his way, but made to be ruled over by a superior set of beings like ourselves, or the Musslemans, & others, who conquered the country at former times—I did not intent to give you all this jaw when I began, but you can skip it, so I suppose by this time Lizzie is Mrs John Lyle My—if she wont rule him in style, who is the big girl that George is so sweet upon? Someone I suppose that was not out of the nursery when I left home I suppose his attentions to her will somewhat interrupt his wooings of the Muse of the Colerain Chronicle if he has written any letters in that paper could you manage to send me a copy, I fancied I detected some writing of his in the Dublin University Magazine, is it so? I am sorry to hear that you

177

have been so long done out of a better curacy, why dont you intimate to the bishop that you wont stand treatment of the kind I dont mean by writing or saying anything cheeky but get some of the big wigs about Derry to put in a word for you, we should surely have connexions enough about that place to have some influence, and from all that I hear of your esteemed 'father in God' I fancy that considerations of a worldly nature would be the ones to have most influence with him—And it would surely be no great matter to give you a better curacy not to speak of a small living Hoping that we may have a jolly trip over the continent together in some 14 or 15 months time if you havnt perpetrated matrimony before that

I remain
Your afft. brother
C. Scott

India is a land peopled by the descendants of many races, and those belonging to the more independent and warlike of India's various racial stocks made a greater appeal to the British. Nevertheless, Charles Scott's remarks in this letter do not seem quite in keeping with his character as revealed by his correspondence or by the later references he makes to the Indians who served under his command. The word "animal" does not seem to have been used in such a derogatory sense as in the twentieth century, for not only does Charles Scott use the word in connection with the British, but other diaries of the nineteenth century contain such references as that of a father describing his children as "little animals."

If the version of the "*Arrow* incident" given in this letter is correct, then England's conduct, so much blamed, is at least explained. If the Chinese believed that the ship was British at the time of its capture, then to allow the capture to pass without action would, in the conditions of those days, have no doubt meant that no British merchant ship would be safe in that area in future.

The "father in God" was Bishop Higgins, Bishop of Derry at the time of the mutiny, whom Charles Scott's father, the Rev. George Scott, criticized as making clerical appointments on worldly rather than clerical grounds.

Part of a letter from C. Scott to his father. No date, but from the subject matter, it was clearly written in 1857 and apparently from Madura.

. . . . regiment which refused to March sometime since, at the command of their Colonel, was one of many local insubordinations caused by an oppressive and uncalled for order to the men to leave their families behind when they changed their station. If however no ill results come about in the Madras Army, the Government will not have themselves to thank for it, as the state of discipline of the army had been sadly neglected of late, while the sepoys have been harrassed in a very unexpected manner by the vast amount of foreign service they have had to perform since the annexation of Burmah. It is the general opinion out here that the annexation policy of the late Governor general had a good deal to do with bringing about the present state of affairs as it went far to destroy the confidence of the natives in the good faith of the English Government, the way that Lord Dalhousie cheated several regiments into 4 or 5 years of foreign service in his pet province of Burmah, when they had only volunteered to go there for 1 or 2 years must have had a very bad effect and altogether I think it is well for the "Laird of Cockpen" that he got his pension of 5000£ a year before the present rebellion broke out or he'd not have received such a touching mark of the gratitude of the court of directors for his services.

I have had so few letters from home lately that I cannot ask you much about yourselves, but I trust you are all well and wont indulge in the idea so likely to be entertained by people in Europe, that a row at Delhi is at all likely to affect the security of people at Madura some 2000 miles off & among a population about as little likely to rise as hen partridges

Believe me
Your afft. son
C. Scott

The "Laird of Cockpen," to whom Charles Scott likened Lord Dalhousie, was the subject of an amusing and character-depicting ballad by the Scottish ballad writer Lady Carolina Nairns (1760–1845). She was a Jacobite, named after Prince Charles Stuart, and also wrote "Will Ye No' Come Back Again" and "Charlie is my Darling."

The Laird of Cockpen

The Laird of Cockpen he's proud and he's great
His mind is ta'en up wi' things o' the State,
He wanted a wife his braw house to keep,
But favour wi' wooin' was fashious to seek.

Doon by the dyke-side a lady did dwell,
At his table-head he thocht she'd look well
M'Cleish's ae dochter, o'Clavers-ha' Lee,
A penniless lass wi' a long pedigree.

His wig was well pouther'd, as gude as when new,
His waistcoat was white, his coat it was blue,
He put on a ring, a sword, an' cocked hat,
An' wha' could refuse the Laird wi' a' that?

He took the grey mare, he rode cannilie,
And rapped at the yett o' Clavers-ha' Lee,
"Gae tell Mistress Jean to come speedily ben,
She's a wanted to speak wi' the Laird o' Cockpen"

Mistress Jean she was making the elder-flow'r wine
"An what brings the Laird at sic a like time"
She put off her apron, an' on her silk goon,
Her mutch wi' red ribbons, and gaed awa' doon.

An when she cam' ben he bowed fu' low,
An' what was his errand he soon let her know,
Amazed was the Laird when the lady said "Na"
An wi' a laigh curtsie she turned awa'

Dumfounder'd was he, but nae sigh did he gie—
He mounted his mare, an' he rode cannilie
An' often he thocht as he gaed through the glen,
She's daft to refuse the Laird o' Cockpen.

The Indian Mutiny, which broke out in 1857, was due to a variety of causes, some of which Charles Scott has already mentioned in his letters. It was finally sparked off by a rumor.

The new Enfield rifle had been so successful in the Crimean War that it was decided to introduce it in the army of the East India Company. The cartridges for the new rifle had a greased tip to be bitten off by its user. It was rumored that this grease was made from the fat of cows and pigs. Perhaps only those familiar with India and the governing strength of its caste system can appreciate the shock of horror and betrayal that such a revelation would produce in the sepoys, for the cow was sacred to the Hindu and the pig unclean to the Moslem.

In the brief historical background that is all that can be given here, it is not possible to trace the origin or explain the many ramifications of the Indian caste system. It must suffice to mention that there are many castes, from high to low, that their members suffer numerous restrictions and prohibitions, including that of employment. This is the reason for the hordes of servants employed by the British of all ranks in India that have been disapprovingly mentioned by some writers. When each man can only do a single specified task, a large number must be employed to do all normal household work, which in England might have only required one or two.

Many incidents that in England would not be noticed may result in loss of caste in India, regarded as a most serious matter there, necessitating formalities before the caste can be restored. On this occasion, the question of the grease on the tip of the cartridge was treated with tact and understanding by some commanding officers, one at once ordering that the cartridges were not to be used, thus averting all trouble among his men. Others, however, merely declared that the grease did not contain cow or pig fat and ordered that the cartridges be used, failure to obey carrying with it very severe punishment. Although these officers may have believed their own assurances, it transpired that some cow and pig fat had been used in making the grease, an inexcusable violation of Indian religious beliefs, rendered heinous by the savagery of the punishment meted out to those sepoys who persisted in believing what, in fact, was the truth.

The rumors about the cartridges started in January 1857. In February, March, and April, there were isolated outbreaks of revolt in a few places that were easily put down. This period was remarkable for British blindness in high places and a complacency through which no warnings from more intelligent British officers could penetrate. The governor general, Lord Canning, was as obtuse as his advisers and seemed to have left his earlier perspicacity behind him in England.

In May 1857, matters took a serious turn with mutiny and a massacre of Europeans in Meerut, swiftly followed by mutiny in Delhi and other places, accompanied by killings that spared neither women nor children.

The Indian Mutiny, with all its brutality, heroism, and loyalty, its terrible Indian massacres and treachery, and its horrifying British vengeance, really began in May 1857, when Charles Scott, writing to his father from Madura, far from Delhi, sought to reassure his family regarding his own safety.

During the months from May 1857 to September 1857, the troubles in India spread and intensified.

In June, there were mutinies in over twenty-three places, and by the end of the month, disaffection had spread to the Ganges plain, Rajputana, central India, and parts of Bengal. also, in June, there had been a terrible massacre at Cawnpore, in the kingdom of Oudh, when the besieged British and their families emerged from the unsuitable buildings they had succeeded in defending and took to the boats provided, under promise of safe conduct from the Nana Sahib, leader of the mutineers. Very few escaped death.

The disastrous course of events was due in large measure to the unsatisfactory state of the East India Company's army.

The commander in chief, General Sir George Anson, had not seen active service for more than forty years, not since the Battle of Waterloo in 1815. Some of the other generals were in a similar position, elderly, unfit, and ripe for retirement rather than for service in the field. The commander in chief, General Anson, died almost immediately, of cholera, in May 1857, and Lord Palmerston, the British Prime minister, immediately dispatched Sir Colin Campbell from England to take his place. Sir Colin, although he, too, was elderly, had won high praise in the Crimean War, which had only ended the previous year. He had also fought in the second Sikh war of 1848/1849 so was no stranger to India. Son of a carpenter, he had been educated by a rich uncle.

Among the best junior officers, also, the position was not satisfactory, the best of them having been withdrawn from their regiments and employed on civilian duties as Charles Scott's letters make clear. Repeatedly, during the mutiny, the vital role of the officers was made clear, often making the difference between continued loyalty and mutiny. There was also another factor that may have reduced the confidence of the sepoys in their officers. Since 1852, cadets have been selected by competitive examination instead of, as previously, by presentation. While examination was a more democratic method, it ensured an influx of young men from British families, none of whose members had ever served in India and who knew nothing about the country, its history, or the customs of its people, while presentation would largely supply those whose families had such knowledge, which, in all the circumstances was of greater value than facility in competitive examination.

Another defect in the army was that the pressure on British manpower resulting from the Crimean War had reduced the proportion of British to Indians to a dangerously low level. In 1857, there were only 40,160 Europeans to 311,000 Indians, a large number of the latter and those the best educated and of the highest caste coming from the kingdom of Oudh, so recently annexed by Lord Dalhousie, who thus transformed the area from one from which the largest supply of sepoys had always been forthcoming into one of the most discontented and disaffected parts of British India. This situation was further exacerbated by Lord Dalhousie's unfortunate choice of a new chief commissioner of Oudh in place of Outram, who would have been most suitable but, unfortunately, had to resign soon after being appointed because of ill health. Coverly Jackson, who took his place, was a tactless, bad-tempered man and very unpopular. Lord Canning remedied Lord Dalhousie's mistake by appointing Sir Henry Lawrence as the Chief Commissioner in March 1857. He was one of those who had foreseen the mutiny and immediately began to remedy abuses in Oudh, but time had run out when he took up his appointment.

By September 1857, the situation in India was most alarming. Although many Indian regiments remained loyal and fought bravely on the British side, many mutinied, sometimes to the incredulous horror of their officers, whom they murdered in many cases, butchering, also, their wives and children, though some escaped death through the assistance and shelter given them by loyal Indians.

As the Indian crisis became more menacing, beleaguered pockets of British soldiers, hampered by the presence of women and children, bravely held out in many parts of India against hordes of mutineers, who were naturally much encouraged by the apparent inability of the British to relieve them.

The British government, when it tardily realized the urgency of the situation, hurriedly dispatched many units of the British Army on the long, slow journey to India, making what speed was possible to reach their hard-pressed countrymen before it was too late.

Letter from Charles Scott to his father, Rev. George Scott, dated Sept. 11, 1857.

Munnupurg
Travellers Bungalow
Septr 11th 1857

My dearest Father

I take the present opportunity to write a few lines to you as I cannot be certain of my future opportunities of doing so, the fact is that I am now on my way post haste to Madras for *immediate embarkation* for Calcutta to take command of the Company of Madras Sappers & Miners already sailed for Bengal on Service, the order reached me quite unexpectedly last Sunday, when I was on the Pulnez Hill, where I had gone for a months leave to refresh myself after the fatigues of the hardworking part of the year.

I did not see my name in the gazette, until yesterday but I have been able to get off as soon as I have, in consequence of Colonel Fahn the Chief Engineer at Madras, having kindly written to tell me that he had nominated me for the command, his note I received on Sunday—since then I have been able to arrange about giving over charge of the district to my successor, selling my property, etc., and by dint of walking 14 miles going 39 in a country bullock cart — riding 36 have arrived here. Tomorrow I hope to reach Trichinopoly where I expect to get a horse transit coach or palankeen to Madras where I should be on the night of the 15th or the 16th (you see we are rather old world in our means of locomotion in these parts) The duty I am going on, is, as far as I can see, a most important one, and the command has been conferred on me in a most kind & flattering manner by the authorities. I feel the responsibility of it however, and I trust that you will pray that I may have strength given me to perform its duties thoroughly under all difficulties, and to uphold the honour of our name & the Service to which I belong.

The Madras Sappers have ever been the most distinguished Native Corps in the Army, and to command them against the mutinous scoundrels of Bengal is a high honour, I hope they will show the Queen's Army that there are still *some* native troops that can be trusted, but much depends on their commanding officer & I am fully alive to my own defects. The miserable system of the Indian Service which leaves a man in purely civil employ for years & then orders him to join his corps in the field is exemplified in me—and the very utmost that zeal & devotion to duty can accomplish is incumbent upon me to counterbalance want of practice. I have great hopes however that the command, if we are called upon to act with vigour, will be a pleasant one, from what I know of the *men* of the Sappers. I do not know much of my present Company however it having been on foreign service when I was at Head Quarters, and altho I was nominally attached to it in Pegu, I never joined. The names of my *officers*, with one exception I do not yet know!

You see the way we do things out here, but *all that will be changed* when the Mutiny is over, as I hope it will be soon enough not much to retard my return home.

The Ministers & Parliament seem fully alive to the magnitude of the crisis at last—and one sharp cold-weather campaign will leave India as quiet as ever—

Altho evidently an Opposition harangue Dizzy's speech of the 27th July is the best of the lot, I think, that is not saying much as V. Smith's & P. Munzle's answers were decidedly weak—Dizzy has stumbled on a great deal of truth about India, altho the present is not exactly the time to bring forward subjects of the kind—he certainly gives a very true description of Lord Dalhousie's policy, which had no doubt a good deal to do in bringing about the present deplorable state of things, not but that had the Bengal Army been in a proper state of discipline the Mutiny would never have happened.—but both Lord D's policy and the bad discipline were owing to a mistaken economy occasioned perhaps by the greed of the recipients of the dividend derived from the surplus revenues of the country. They could not be content to rule an Empire without pocketing its cash. And when the current expenses of government interfered with their dividend they reduced the expenditure, & employed military officers on duties for the performance of which more civilians should have been interviewed, this took men off from their regiments; Nay held out a premium to them to go; all who were worth much were thus taken from their proper work & discipline decayed—even this would not do & John Company must tamper with the British character for good faith, break treaties, annex the territories of such of his neighbours as were too weak to give any trouble in defending them; then the cant of philanthropists came into play "the Mild Hindoo must be treated like an Englishman"! and to avoid being bothered in parliament by fools, the Indian government gave in to them, and established government Schools etc. presided over by government chaplins at the head of the educational department. I do not think that there was any design in the appointment of the chaplins, but it had a bad effect as it led the natives to suppose that they were to be converted by govt. then all that *bosh* about the torture commission did harm—those who got it up meant well but did not understand the native character. A native we will say pays a shilling a year rent & has £20 a year—he wont pay the shilling

184

coute qui coute unless *compelled* to do so this compulsion consists perhaps, in locking him up in a room of the revenue officer to which he has come with some plausible story to excuse himself from paying his rent, until he disgorges that very rent which he had had tied up in his clothes all the time! and which he considers it a point of honour not to pay unless compelled And this is what Mr Danby Seymour calls dreadful torture.

When I began I never intended to write all this long story about politics but having nothing else to do have gone on rambling as if in idle talk.

I suppose by this time George is a benedict, I am anxious to hear a full & complete account of his Marriage and of your new daughter in law, who I suppose will have too much of a more agreeable nature to do, to write to me—and to whom I am afraid I am too bad a hand at writing to indite a letter.

By the way talking of letters I am most frightfully behindhand in my correspondence with Maria & John Rutledge, tell them that if theyll let me know the name of their new residence in Fermanagh, I will send them letters fresh from the seat of war in India which will I hope be more interesting than this stupid affair—

If I have time I will write again from Madras, and you will probably get that letter as soon as this; for the present, sending my kind love to all at home & hoping that I may support the honour of our family in the wars
   I remain
    My dearest Father Your afft. son
     C. Scott

"The Mild Hindoo must be treated like an Englishman." The belief that people of all races, no matter how different their history and culture may be, are basically similar to an Englishman, and, given the opportunity, will behave like one is a belief that dies hard and, indeed, still lives in England. India is an Eastern country, and bribery has long been practiced there as a matter of course, a practice that inevitably perverts the course of justice. Therefore, the plan to put Englishmen on trial for their lives before an all Indian court in 1857 does not seem either just or reasonable.

1858—letter from Charles Scott to his brother, Rev. J. B. Scott, dated January 22, 1858.

         Camp Allumbagh
         Jan. 22d 1858
My dear Bedel,

You are I suppose indignant at my not having written to you for so long, but I have the same cause of complaint myself, and can plead in my justification a fraternal regard for your pocket, as every letter I write you will necessarily cost you a fortune in the way of postage if my agents at Calcutta do not pay for it, as I have no paper of a less gross consistency than foolscap to write on & no stamps are to be had in camp. My last letter home was dated I think the 18th December, more than a month has elapsed since then & still behold us on our old ground at Allumbagh, not yet having taken Lucknow—how much longer we are to remain in status quo, is still buried in the womb of obscurity; our life now is a complete contrast to the excessive labour of the campaign during the days of our activity & is about the most idle one I have led for years, we have however done a good deal in the way of strengthening our position which is now a very sticky one, & have fought two or 3 scrimmages since I last wrote—the first one which you may see mentioned in the papers, was fought at Gilu, when we attacked the enemy at daybreak & took 4 guns & some ammunition with a loss of only 10 killed & wounded on our side—Outram makes a great story of it—it was a plucky thing enough on the part of the Military train, Volunteer Cavalry, & 5th Fusiliers, who bore the brunt of it but he gives all the butter to the 90th at whom not a shot was fired that I am aware of & I was with them the whole day being orderly officer to Colonel Purcell commanding our next fight was on Tuesday the 12th inst. when our camp was attacked by the enemy in considerable force, but were repulsed with a loss of some 200 men to them-selves & only one or two to us, I was in one of the outlying picquets with the Sappers on that day & came in for the brunt of it. We were in a mudwalled village that we had fortified and had 120 men 2 9 inch, & 18 inch, & 15-1/2 inch mortar with which we played old Harry with the Pandys, who came on with some 5,000 men in a pretty decent line to within 350 yards of us, & pounded into us with their heavy guns in position some 2000 yards off but did not hit a man of us—round shot altho an ugly thing to look at & hear, is not distructive except against close columns, all most all our outlying picquets are constantly being pitched into with it, & yet we rarely lose more than a man a week—to be sure if one does hit you it finishes you & you are nowhere perfectly secure against them at the outlying picquets. I was at one some time since when the room I had to sleep in had had a round shot through it a day or two before I went there & consequently one went to bed with the possibility of finding oneself 2 fellows instead of one before morning having been cut in two during the night—however one gets used to these little inconveniences in time.

Since I began writing this letter a convoy has come in with 5 guns for this force—this, I presume bodes something & we may have to take the city very shortly, I am convinced we can take it with our present force, some 5,000 of all arms, & hold it too, as the rebels have quite lost heart, but we will undoubtedly lose many men if we do so. However I will write again if I hear anything certain as to our operations for the present. Believe me

My dear Bedel
Your afft. brother
C. Scott

"The Pandys"—the mutineers were very generally referred to as

"Pandys," the description originating from Mangal Pandy, a young sepoy of the 34th Native Infantry. At Barrackpore, overexcited by drink and revolutionary enthusiasm, with his musket loaded, he called on his fellow sepoys to revolt. He fired at the British adjutant and the sergeant major, missed, and then wounded both with his sword. The incident ended with the arrival of sixty-year-old General Hearsey, who, ignoring the warning that the sepoy was aiming his musket at him, galloped up to Mangal Pandy, who then lost his nerve, and attempted unsuccessfully to shoot himself. He was hanged the next day.

The rest of Charles Scott's letter and the reference it contains requires the general note that now follows before it can all be understood.

The Siege of Lucknow

The siege of Lucknow was one of the most dramatic and historic events of the Mutiny, covering a long period of danger and suspense.

In March 1857, Sir Henry Lawrence had been appointed chief commissioner of Oudh, his younger brother John being already a most successful Chief Commissioner of the Punjab, which remained loyal to the British throughout the Mutiny. The Lawrences were an Ulster Protestant family from Coleraine, one of those of which Ulster can be unreservedly proud. Both Henry and John, sons of Col. Alexander Lawrence, went to school at Foyle College in the city of Londonderry.

Henry Lawrence, taking up his post just before the outbreak of the Mutiny he had earlier forecast, was fully aware of the problems and dangers of the situation, fortunately for the British European residents of Lucknow. While he immediately began to remedy the mistakes and injustices of the past so far as the Indian population was concerned, he did not overlook the threatening possibilities that menaced the British and Europeans in the city of Lucknow.

Lucknow was a large and sprawling city, the capital of the kingdom of Oudh, so recently annexed by Lord Dalhousie. It contained the palaces of the kings of Oudh. In 1857, the chief commissioner of Oudh lived in the residency, a fine and large three-story building.

On the May 3, 1857, Sir Henry Lawrence disbanded the 7th Irregular Cavalry, an action that is believed to have averted an immediate mutinous outbreak.

In the middle of May 1857, news of the mutinies at Meerut and Delhi reached Lucknow, and Sir Henry immediately applied for complete authority. His request was at once granted. He was promoted to Brigadier and made military Commander in addition to being Civil Administrator.

In Lucknow, there was no outbreak of mutiny until June 1857, and this was successfully suppressed. Sir Henry, however, at once put into effect his plan to combat future trouble, and all Europeans were moved into the Residency, as the area surrounding that building came to be called throughout the rest of the Mutiny. The area, nearly sixty acres in extent, contained a number of buildings, and although by no means ideal for defense, Sir Henry considered it the most suitable available.

Soon after this, on learning that a large body of mutineers was advancing toward Lucknow, Lawrence, against his better judgment, was persuaded to lead a force out to meet and attack them. This attack at Chinhat was unsuccessful, necessitating a damaging retreat and causing casualties that reduced the small garrison, while precipitating the siege of Lucknow on June 30 under conditions far more difficult than had existed a few days earlier. Lawrence considered that their position was now almost untenable and estimated that it would be impossible for them to hold out for more than twenty days at the most.

Fatally wounded by a shell, Sir Henry Lawrence, fifty-one years of age but looking far older, died a few days later. During his dying agony, his mind remained clear, and he dictated to his successor fourteen things that should be done, only two of which were personal. His horse was to be kept and given to his nephew George Lawrence, and his tomb was to bear the following words:

HERE LIES HENRY LAWRENCE WHO TRIED TO DO HIS DUTY MAY GOD HAVE MERCY ON HIM

All the rest were practical instructions in connection with the defense of Lucknow.

Major Banks, who took over command after Lawrence's death, continued in the post for a short time only; then, shot through the head, he, too, died and Col. J. E. W. Inglis took his place.

The siege continued throughout July, passing the twenty-day limit estimated by Lawrence, without the arrival of relief, although it was known that General Havelock had started from Cawnpore with a relieving force that had been originally expected to reach Lucknow before the end of July. Instead, all August dragged slowly by, and the small British garrison still held out under steadily worsening conditions. Rations had to be reduced. Casualties and disease shrank the number of able-bodied defenders. There was much suffering and many deaths, also, among the women and children, sweltering in the hot weather in underground rooms for safety and suffering from malnutrition, the heat, and disease.

After a time, a new and alarming danger emerged—mining, and all were on the alert for the sounds that warned of this underground approach of the enemy.

Gradually, hope, so long deferred, began to die, for it became known that Havelock, far from advancing to their aid, had had to return to his starting point—Cawnpore.

So desperate was the situation that the British officers discussed among themselves whether, in the event of all hope having to be abandoned, they should kill the women and children in order to save them from the ghastly fate suffered by the women and children at Cawnpore, before facing certain death themselves in a "no surrender" last stand.

Throughout the siege, news reached and left the Residency by messenger, sometimes an Indian but also not infrequently a British officer disguised as an Indian. Whoever it was, their journey was a dangerous one, taken at the risk of their lives.

On September 15, 1857, incredibly, the Lucknow Residency had not yet fallen, and Gen. Sir James Outram, with an additional force, joined General Havelock at Cawnpore. Together they started for Lucknow, meeting no resistance until they reached Allumbagh, a pleasure garden and palace of the kings of Oudh, about four miles from the city. This resistance they quickly overcame.

At last, on September 25, 1857, the combined British force broke through the mutineers' opposition and reached the Residency, bringing the first relief to its beleaguered inhabitants, and scenes of rapturous joy followed the deliverers' arrival. Unfortunately, the relief, although it averted disaster and heartened those so long besieged, was not final. Sir James Outram, now in full command, had not sufficient forces to take the next step and evacuate the Residency, still less to recapture the whole city. Everyone in the Residency, therefore, nerved themselves for a continued siege with a larger garrison and a better supply of food.

Nothing further was done about Lucknow until November when Sir Colin Campbell, appointed commander-in-chief of the Indian Army in July 1857, who had on his arrival in India decided that the relief of Lucknow must be his first priority, was at last ready to make a move.

On November 7, the news reached Lucknow that Campbell, with adequate forces, had already started from Cawnpore. On November, 13, the sound of musketry fire roused the hopes of all in the Residency. Bitter fighting preceded the arrival of Campbell and his force at the Residency on November 17. The British troops under Campbell had been maddened by the many reports of the torture and killing of British women and children—some of them horribly true, but some untrue—and, in consequence, they gave no quarter and took no prisoners, their minds obsessed by the desire for revenge. The mutineers fought with the courage of desperation and terror, any cries for mercy being ignored; every mutinous sepoy and, in error, a few loyal ones were butchered.

Sir Colin Campbell's intention had been immediately to evacuate the Residency and abandon the city, leaving its recapture to a later date, while he, having escorted noncombatants to a place of safety, proceeded to deal with the mutineers of Rohilkhand. Outram inquired whether he had the authority to abandon Lucknow, on which he telegraphed the Governor General and received permission to do what he thought best; however, on the arrival of Campbell's tactfully worded dispatch, setting out his plans while indicating that he was the authority on matters military, Lord Canning overruled him on the question of Lucknow, as he considered the political consequences of not giving priority to the recapture of Lucknow would be disastrous and that there was no prospect of peace in the kingdom of Oudh until the city was retaken.

Campbell, therefore, adhered to his original plan to evacuate the Residency, Sir James Outram, with a strong force, was left at Allumbagh, while the women and children, the sick and the wounded, accompanied by Campbell and the remainder of his force, were moved to a place of safety. Although the slow cavalcade was strongly guarded, this was a difficult and dangerous operation, but it passed off peacefully. On arrival at Cawnpore, the women and children, the sick and wounded, were moved down river to Allahabad, while Campbell remained at Cawnpore, pledged to make the recapture of the whole city of Lucknow his next priority. Cawnpore, however, now back under British control, was once more in danger, and Campbell first turned his attention to defeating the Gwalior insurgents and the followers of Nana Sahib, who were a threat to it.

Although Campbell was ready to turn his attention to Lucknow by January 1858, when Charles Scott wrote to his brother from Allumbagh, where Outram was impatiently waiting for Campbell's return, the sixty-five-year-old Commander was one who believed in making preparations that ensured certain victory. January and February passed without further action, while he waited at Cawnpore for further reinforcement of Gurkhas from Nepal and, also, for the arrival of a siege train from Agra. It was not until March 1858 that his leisurely preparations were complete, when the Indian hot weather season had already begun, thus ensuring that the British troops would fight under the most trying conditions, many of them experiencing the intense heat for the first time.

At the beginning of March, Campbell rejoined Outram at Allumbagh, and 30,000 troops with 104 guns prepared to attack over 100,000 mutineers for the possession of Lucknow.

By the evening of March 14, the British forces had won the day. Lucknow had been recaptured. Unfortunately, on this occasion, almost all the mutineers had escaped from the city, then occupying posts that had to be retaken later, a matter that will be mentioned again in a later letter from Charles Scott. It does not require military knowledge to realize that a large force of rebels escaping to fight another day would result in an unnecessary increase in the casualties on the British side. Nevertheless, the recapture of Lucknow brought to an end any doubts as to the outcome of the Mutiny, although some fighting continued for another year.

From Charles Scott's letter of January 22nd, it is clear that he had come to Allumbagh with Campbell's relieving force of November 1857 and had remained there after the evacuation of the Residency, part of the force that, under Sir James Outram, was left there to await Campbell's return. Charles Scott took part in the March recapture of Lucknow.

1858—A letter to C. Scott from General Outram, dated April 4, 1858.

Lucknow,
4th April, 1858

My dear Scott

I leave today & am sorely pressed for time; but I cannot go without bidding you goodbye, & tendering you my most sincere thanks for the zealous & most valuable aid you rendered me during the three months we were associated together at Allumbagh. Upwards of fifteen years ago I knew the C Company of Madras Sappers, in Scinde and Affghanistan. I then considered them a model body of soldiers and most assuredly they have not deteriorated since then. Their skill as workmen, their industry, their cheerful alacrity & general good conduct commanded the respect of all who knew them at Allumbagh, & their coolness & bravery when called upon as they were on many occasions of attack on our position, to act as soldiers, was conspicuous, to them & to their able & gallant commander I shall ever feel truly grateful, & to the latter I shall ever entertain very warm feelings of admiration & esteem

Believe me to be
My dear Scott
Your very sincere friend
J. Outram

True copy
C Scott

Soon after the recapture of Lucknow, much of the excellent effect of this British success was diminished by a proclamation that was issued by the Governor General.

Lord Canning had arrived in India with good intentions and moderate views. At the start of the mutiny, he had strongly disapproved of the indiscriminate vengeance taken by the British in Delhi, and many who believed that very savage measures were necessary disagreed with him, dubbing him contemptuously "Clemency Canning." However, the proclamation that he issued in March 1858 did not err on the side of clemency.

The proclamation confiscated almost all the land of Oudh except that belonging to six named landlords. There was no amnesty. Those rebels who surrendered immediately were assured only of their lives; all else was dependent on the mercy of the British, which, in view of the activities of men such as Colonel Neill and others little better, held out a terrifying prospect.

The proclamation was received with dismay and disapproval by the British in Lucknow as being unjust, far too severe, and well calculated to ensure indefinite continuation of the rebellion in Oudh. Condemnation seems to have been unanimous.

Sir James Outram, who was then the chief commissioner of Oudh, notified Lord Canning that he felt unable to carry out the Governor General's policy. Hence, his departure at the beginning of April 1858 when he wrote to Charles Scott.

The proclamation was unfavorably received in London, also, and it was repudiated by the government.

1858   Lucknow
                                                                   June 30th 1858.
My dear Bedel
    I have been proposing to write to you for many days but from the nature of the climate, the fact of having little or nothing to do, and continual inclination to put off writing until some event should occur worth writing about all acting together on a subject naturally idle in the extreme — infatuatedly given to procrastination, have kept me silent. I write this letter to you in particular but mean it as a sort of epistle general which you can surely make it by reading it out at Banagher I have just received my Father's letters of the 13th 22nd May, by which I am glad to see that my letters from Allenbagh & here have at last found their way home, the way in which they have been delayed on the road serves to show the wretched management of the post office department in India and for this there is no help, as I once wrote a mild remonstrance to the Post Mstr. General about a letter that was sent hunting after me all over India & for which I had to pay 16 times the proper postage, I got a thundering official in reply making out that it was *my* fault that the letter did not reach me sooner! We go on in the old humdrum way here in my last letter I think I mentioned that the enemy are supposed to have been driven beyond the Gogra, & there are two flying columns out now, but a large force is kept Nuwabgunge, the scene of Sir H-Grants last

action about 16 miles north of Lucknow, Since I last wrote, however, Genl. Napier who was Commanding Engineer at the Siege of Lucknow has gained an important victory over the Gwalior fugitives taking 25 guns & 700 elephants, he has gone off in pursuit again & seems for one to be an active pursuing General the very thing we want. Old Sir Colin Campbell has quite lost the good opinion of the Army by his slow & over cautious policy & goes by the name of Sir Crawling Camel! It is reported that the home authorities and the nation generally are dissatisfied with the capture of Lucknow & that we wont get anything more for it than the 6 months Battu ordered by the G.G. if there be a brevet it is feared that it will be a very meagre one, this is unfair, as the Army would have done ever so much more had the Chief let them & Sir Crawling ought to bear the blame; even he does not deserve it all as the escape of the garrison was owing to the misconduct of Brigadier Campbell commanding the Cavalry,.& the old Chief, who is I suppose some 'far & awa' cousin of his, instead of blaming him actually praised him in his dispatch. I am much afraid that we are in for another campaign in the cold weather in which case my chance of getting home this year is knocked on the head I thought to have got a sick certificate; but the worst of my constitution is that without ever being in really good strong health I never get any serious illness & am down one day and up another, this wont do for the doctors. if we have a campaign it will I hope be only a following up, & polishing off, one, as the expected bad news from the Marhatta Country has never arrived & they may yet remain quiet.

What a pity it is that Lord Ellenborough made such an ass of himself as to publish his letter to Lord Canning, the letter was well enough in its way except that it visited Dalhousie's sins on Canning's head which was unjust, but it was one of those things that ought to have remained secret for years—but it is the worst of our parliamentary system that people will insist on making known everything that does not concern them. Lord Ellenborough has cut his own throat most effectively & it is a pity, for with all his faults he is a fine fellow & one in whose knowledge of India & integrity of character great confidence might be placed I hope they will make Sir John Lawrence Governor General the present is just the time we want a man who knows the native & who wont be likely to run into either of the extremes that most men fresh from England indulge in either that of looking upon the natives, who are a most inferior race as the same sort of animals as the European, or thinking them as a set of criminals who ought to be exterminated, the latter mode of treatment they will have quite enough of & the Government ought to protect them from it. I have always looked on the people of India as a set of inferior men whom we rule over because we are superior, just as man rules the inferior animals, the better we treat them after their kind, the better for ourselves, give them any amount of material prosperity, develop the resources of the country & encourage trade, make the people rich & well to do, in fact; but dont let them have a word to say to governing themselves, beyond the necessary powers of the lower class executives "Everything for the people"

193

in fact & "nothing by them" is the rule for India, this we have not observed & while we have been fumbling at doing things by the people we have neglected to do things for them & in this have contrasted unfavourably with the very Native States we have upset, if you go through Oudh you see a country which in spite of the damages of recent war has all the appearance of a most flourishing State, the fields well cultivated, the groves of fruit trees & avenues well attended to & public buildings in good order—while if you go through the C You see all the tops of trees, avenues, wells & halting places (in fact all the little comforts as one may call them, of the country) gone to rack and ruin, in many places, in fact nothing kept up at all except what gives a decent profit to the Government; and in spite of all the talk that is made about recent improvements you often see many fine & useful works of irrigation etc gone to decay for want of a little money spent upon them—all this is because the country is governed by a set of stingy traders who's gospel "a penny saved is a penny got" and who only looked upon this fine country providence had given them to govern as a means of making money—& who rather than really benefit the natives by spending a little money, which would in the long run repay them with ample interest; would permit visionaries and political quacks to try their dangerous tricks of elevating the Mild Hindoo. And yet bad as John Company was, so great a horror have I of anything but a despotic government for these Asiatic people that I would rather see John's power continue than see the country at once given over to the crown. perhaps selfishness has something to do with this as certainly it would be a bad measure for us old Company's servants—altho they are too polite to show it, it is evident that we are not beloved by Queen's officers, whom I take as a sort of specimen of all crown servants. Queen's officers moreover bully the natives much more than we do & have far less in common with them—You are no doubt sick of all this jaw, but a miserable old Lieutenant whose wretched regimental promotion has done him out of the brevet that he might have got for the present campaign is a licensed grumbler & bore—Our Father tells me that he has been speaking for the Church Missionary Society at Exeter Hall while he is on this subject it would I think be well to put in a word in favour of more chaplins for the troops serving in India, there are certainly too few, we have only 2 Church of England chaplins here for a force of (including artillery & cavalry) about ten regiments scattered over a great extent of ground & so circumstanced that hardly more than one regiment can attend services at one place & time there being also large numbers of sick in the different hospitals.

Tell Maria & George that I expect to hear from them sometimes. I have got a cashmere shawl (at least what I am told is such) for Maria, one for Mrs. George & one for my Mother which I will send home, I had intended to take them home, but fear that would detain them too long. I have also some curious swords, knives, & embroidered clothes that I picked up from soldiers & others when the city was given up to plunder but these I think I will keep until I go home—by the way—I fancy what was got on the 14th & 15th March the days on which looting was allowed, & much of which was foolishly given by the finders, to the prize Agents, is likely to be all the Army will get for Lucknow. I bought some things the shawls among the rest, but I got one real bit of loot namely a fine elephant which I captured with the help of 2 of my men in the Kaiser-bagh, I thought to set a good example & gave it up to the commissariat, they cheated me, for they gave me only 100Rs for it in Lucknow rupees which only fetched 80 in the bazaar & soon afterwards I was offered 300Rs or 30£ for my elephant by a private party.

By the way my Father asks if I know a Colonel Sadlier as well as I can make out the name, I dont think I ever met him, he is not in our Artillery at Murehus. While Answering questions of this kind I may as well say that the Scott alluded to in one of his letters, as having been mentioned by an officer of Sikhs in a letter to the Times as having done something at the Secunderabagh action he is not known in these parts—as I was the only Scott of the engineers engaged in the Secunderabagh action & I did not at the time know any officers in the Sikhs, if I had, & he had had a good dinner to offer I should certainly have dined with him—but as it was I was dinnerless for 2 days, except you call a dinner a steak cut from an Artillery bullock that I begged or rather bought for a rupee, from the servant of a commissariat officer, who I found out had been at Addiscombe with me, and he, as commissaries are always in comfort when others are hard up, gave me a bottle of beer! the only one I saw for 3 months—

The Scott of Allenbagh Stacks friend was I rather think, not me, but a man named Scot an infantry officer — an engineer, who is I believe a most worthy man & a warm protestant.

With love to all at home
Ever your afft. brother
C. Scott

There was a great deal of criticism of Sir Colin Campbell in England as well as in India at the time and later.

The escape of a large body of mutineers from Lucknow because Brigadier Campbell of the Bays failed to reach the right place with the cavalry was a disastrous misfortune and necessitated the use of troops to take forts that would otherwise have been unoccupied. His excuse was that he had lost his way. Sir Colin Campbell disagreed with all the blame that was freely heaped on Brigadier Campbell on the ground that an officer who was present and well qualified to judge had told him that he did not think Brigadier Campbell could have done any better. However, a differing account has also been given by another officer who was present. According to him, although Brigadier Campbell was supplied with guides and also had officers with him who knew the area, he would accept no advice or information regarding the route to take but insisted on going his own way, with the result that he went the wrong way and failed to block the mutineer's flight.

Sir Colin Campbell was critical of junior officers who had the temerity to criticize their superiors, but perhaps they were right. At any rate, there were other commanders who took a more active role. In addition to Lord Napier, mentioned by Charles Scott, Sir Hugh Rose conducted a most successful and spectacular campaign, repeatedly gaining victories over mutineers, sometimes against appalling odds, and repeatedly when heavily outnumbered.

Lord Ellenborough, previously a Governor General of India, was in 1858 President of the Board of Control, charged with the task of framing a new constitution for India. Like many other people, he was appalled by Lord Canning's proclamation and instantly dashed off a strong letter of censure. Then, without consulting any of his colleagues, he had it published. The resulting criticism and strong disapproval of his conduct necessitated his resignation.

Other observers have confirmed Charles Scott's remarks about the prosperous appearance of the kingdom of Oudh and also his accusation of the East India Company's excessive concern with profits.

Places memorable in the final relief of Lucknow. (The drawings were not found with these descriptions of them.)

Description of the Drawings

No. 1 Secundrabagh—The hole in the wall on the right hand corner of the picture is the breach through which the leading portion of the assaulting party passed Novr. 16th, 1857, to the left the high building stands over the gateway.
No. 2 Secundrabagh—Bungalow at the north end of the garden, I saw the dead bodies lie 3 feet deep on the floors of the rooms of the bungalow & in the sort of court behind it where 1700 bodies were found—I nearly got cut down going through the 2nd door on the left hand, when the house was full of living pandies, the action here was on the 16th Novr. 1857 & the photograph was taken in April or May 1858.
No. 3—The Shah mujjiff taken by storm Novr. 16th 1857 this view does not show the gateway through which the place was taken but show some breaches made by Peel's heavy guns, the gate is on the left side, facing the building with towers seen in the distance on the left, this building is the 32nd mess house taken 17th Novr. 1857, our loss at the Shah Mujjiff was nearly equal to that at the Secundrabagh 300 men but all men killed outside, as the enemy bolted towards the North, & did not wait for the actual assault.
No. 4—The Chutter Munzil palace on the Goomtee, the odd looking boat like a fish & the frigate built sunken yacht, belonged to the King. The Chutter Munzil was the extreme easternmost post held by Outram & Havelock after they got into Lucknow, they had to fight their way through the courts be-

196

longing to it when they came in to Lucknow Sept. 1857 it is now used as a hospital, & a very bad uncomfortable one it is.

No. 5—A view of the Residency or Bailly Guard held by the original garrison from May 1857 to November 1857, it is the most complete view I could get of the greater part of the position, & yet gives but an imperfect idea of it, the mined gateway on the right led to the Furrud Bux & Chutter Munzil palaces and the minous tower seen through the gateway was one of the corner turrets of the residency house, described in my letter of the 18th Decr.57 the house & the Church behind it were pulled down by the rebels while we were with Outram at the Allumbagh—the large building to the left of the gateway is the banquet hall, used as a hospital by the garrison, the road seen leading up to the residency, on the left side of the hospital is the road by which we went in & brought out the oiginal garrison on the 18th Novr.57 at the lower end of it was the Puilly guund Gate so often alluded to in accounts of the defence, the aspect of the place is much changed since November last, most of the walls & enclosures together with the defences & buttresses thrown up by the defenders having been destroyed, as have most of the houses of the city which closely surrounded the place when the siege was going on. This drawing ought to be the most interesting of the lot. All the above numbers relate to places memorable in the defence or relief of Lucknow in 1857.

No. 6—shows part of the Begum Cotee taken on the 11th March 1858 during the last siege & noted in Sir Colin's dispatch as the scene of the 'sternest fight' that occurred during the siege the fire from the Mosque on the right of the breach was severe & it was here that our principal loss occurred, I was not with the column that assaulted here but with one that got in considerably to the right of the Mosque—did not lose so many ours was the first assaulting column, but there is no picture of the spot where we escaladed the breach was impracticable without ladders & we would have lost heavily had we been stoutly opposed.

No. 7—shows a view of the river just about the 'stour bridge' about which you will have read in the dispatches, I have sent it more in order to show the general character of the scenery along the Goomtee, than on account of any important events that happened here, the Mosque on the high ground has been fortified & forms our principal post to cover the bridge, to the left & in the distance is seen the Large   the finest building in all Lucknow.

No. 8 is a panorama of Lucknow that is to say of the fashionable portions of it which is the *East End* but it does not even show the whole of the kaiser-bagh or principal palace, from the roof of a portion of which the view was taken looking North & East when it is considered that the whole Native City & a great part of the palace lies to the west of the spectator, or behind his back, an idea of the extent of the city which is 28 miles round, will be formed. I have marked in pencil some of the principal objects of interest in the distance. The foreground of the picture is entirely occupied by the courts & gardens of the palace. In the large garden to the right I was under very nasty fire on the 14th March.

197

The buildings in the distance are marked in pencil as follows:—
1. (fixed the residency)

2. (fixed the gateway)
   see plate No. 5

3. fixed Farrud Bux palace
4. fixed Chutter Munzil—see No. 4
5. fixed Motee Muhall, building in distance with 4 white turrets
6. fixed Shah-Mujjiff Gate, the rest hid by trees
7. fixed 32nd Mess House—see plate No. 3
8. fixed Secunderbagh, hardly to be seen among the trees in the distance
9. fixed Ja Murtiniere
10. fixed on the extreme horizon the Dil Koosha House & just under it Major Bankes house.

These drawings comprise most of the points of interest in Lucknow, but I am sorry that I have not got a drawing of the house in which the 2 English ladies Mrs Orr and Miss Jackson were found.
C. Scott

Lucknow. June 8th
1858.

1858—Letter from Charles Scott to his brother, Rev. J. B. Scott, dated November 3, 1858.

Camp Attiar
In the South End of Oudh
November 3rd 1858

My dear Bedel
Excuse the mess a diabolical pen has just made of your name—I received your letter of the 15th September last evening the poor account you give of our Father's health alarms me I do trust you will keep him from working too hard especially in the winter, a man at his time of life cannot do the work of an energetic man of 30 or 40, I will certainly try to get home as soon as I possibly can, and if the worst comes to the worst will be at home by May next, but you may be looking out for me much sooner I trust. once let me get out of this coach & it wont take me long to give Calcutta & Madras my congee & take a last fond look at them in the best point of view they can be seen in, I.E. over the taffrail of a homeward bound P. & O. Steamer.

I have now saved up enough to let me have nearly 300 a year for the 3 years I mean to spend at home & with this & my Captains pay if I get it but there is an on dit that we new promotions are to be done out of this, I ought to do pretty well. Your letter of the 1st September would have been answered sooner if we had been leading anything of a quiet life when it came, but the day after getting it we had a small battle & I was out from 3 in the

198

morning until 6 at night, the fight was not much of a one the enemy getting into thick jungle before we could catch them, however we captured 2 guns with bullocks & ammunition wagon complete with our own ammunition, having one officer & 5 men of our own wounded & being supposed to have killed about 30 of the enemy—Next day we went out to attack a small fort, found it empty & I had to blow it up & dig up some guns we found buried, since then we have been marching daily until Sunday since which time we have been sitting here doing nothing, which is pleasant after the incessant marching all over the country Since the 10th October I am in command of the engineers with this column & suppose if we remain separate from the C in C's force I will not be superseded so that it is rather advantageous for me to remain if possible until our work is nearly done, our General Sir Hope-Grant is one of the most gentlemanly & agreeable men to serve under I have ever met with, & I get on pretty well my two officers & myself keeping with one of the batteries of Royal Artillery the officers of which are a capital set of fellows, who like all their Regiment & the Royal Engineers are much more free from class feeling than any others either in the Queen's or Company's Army that I have met.

It is almost solely a Queen's force but we get on well with all the only ones inclined to sneer at Company's men being the 7th Hussars who look upon themselves as rather swells & are I think too fine for work in this country.

There is a big fort near this which it is uncertain whether we or the C in C whose force is some distance off, will attack, the latter I expect, as just now I heard heavy guns in that direction, we will most likely have but a subordinate part to play if there is much fighting, which I hardly expect now that the proclamation is out; after the big fort is taken, or while it is in the process of being taken, there are a lot of smaller ones to dispose of, & after that we cross the Gogra to attack the Begum's forces in Northern Oudh the portions of the country which we have traversed hitherto being all South of the Gogra. Your letter of the 1st September was a most interesting one, letters of that sort are the ones I like best, if you tell me about your doings I will tell about mine, this epistle must however be brought to a close now or the post office that evilminded institution will charge something enormous for it. if we have more halting I will write at more length again

Ever your afft. brother

C. Scott

The proclamation referred to in Charles Scott's letter of November 3 was that of November 1, issued by Queen Victoria, announcing that she was taking over the government of India and making various promises, including no further annexations, no interference with religious convictions, and an amnesty for all rebels who returned to their homes and peaceful pursuits by January 1, except murderers or those who had willingly harbored murderers.

However, a counter proclamation was issued by the begum of Oudh in the name of her son Birgis Quadr, commenting adversely on Queen Victoria's proclamation paragraph by paragraph, questioning its veracity, and this, no doubt, had influence with some of the rebels in Oudh for the begum's counterproclamation ended, "Let no subject be deceived by the Proclamation."

1858—Letter from Lieutenant Raynsford to Rev. George Scott, dated November 28, 1858.

Hyderghur
Nov. 28th, 1858

My dear Sir,

As I am myself unable to write on consequence of my hand being maimed I have asked another officer to do so in my name—The telegraph will doubtless have already told you of the death of your gallant son before the fort of Rohea.

My words of condolence can be but poor comfort to a father but such as they are I pray you to receive them—I have served under your late son at the Relief of Lucknow and shared his dangers since—and a braver and better man never stepped—The Almighty God has called him to a better world and few here were more fit to meet his God than he. Forgive me if I cannot write long on a subject that is so bitter to me but may He that is above comfort you in this hour of trial—Your son suffered little or no pain as death was instantaneous—he was buried with military honours on the morning following his death and his body lies under a tree about 3/4 of a mile from the fort of Rohea—A letter found addressed to you I enclose. The Committee of Adjustment have kept back from the sale of his effects such things as might be mementoes of one who was so deserving of esteem, and they will be carefully forwarded to your address—I enclose also a lock of his hair that was cut off after his death—

It would be a consolation to you to see how deeply he is mourned by his faithful Madras men who have now served under him for so long a time—If I can be at any time of any service to you in the settling of affairs, I hope you will not hesitate to write to me I shall always be glad to serve you in any matter

Yours very sincerely
F.M. Raynsford

My address is

Lieutenant Raynsford
Madras Sappers & Miners
c/o Messrs Binny & Co.   Madras

Truly do I regret not being able to write but I was sure delay would be perhaps keeping you in suspense receive my heartfelt sympathy for your loss and may the God of Consolation comfort the sorrowful hearts of your family.

F.M.R.

The postscript to Lieutenant Raynsford's letter, giving his address, is in very shaky handwriting, obviously written with great difficulty with the left hand.

After the Mutiny.

In June 1858, the Board of Control and the Court of Directors of the East India Company were abolished. The crown took over the responsibility of government in India. The rebellion finally ended in 1859.

The Mutiny had never spread over all British India. Many Indian regiments had remained loyal, and many Indians had risked their lives to save and shelter British families in danger from the mutineers.

Queen Victoria, now Empress of India, had remained balanced and moderate throughout the Mutiny and had disapproved of the clamor for indiscriminate vengeance. She took up her new responsibilities with a sincere desire to promote justice and the welfare of her Indian subjects.

Various changes were introduced, and among them was the end of the policy of annexations and the regulation that British officers were in future to be kept with their units and not employed on civilian duties.

Lord Canning remained in office as Viceroy. He left India in 1862, his health broken, and died a month after his arrival in England. Sir Hugh Rose became commander in chief.

Sir John Lawrence retired after the Mutiny and returned to England in 1859, his services rewarded by a handsome pension. He became a member of the Secretary of States Council.

Lord Elgin succeeded Lord Canning as viceroy. He died the following year in India.

In 1864, Charles Scott's hopes were fulfilled, and Sir John Lawrence returned to India as its Viceroy. Throughout his term of office, Sir John always showed deep concern for the welfare of the Indian population and also for that of the soldiers.

Later in this book, a letter written in 1905 gives a brief glimpse of India under the crown, nearly fifty years after the Mutiny.

1. "Other things being equal"

1. Treasurer of the church about 250 A.D. When the pope was killed for his faith St. Laurence saved the church's assets by distributing them. The Roman prefect demanded the church treasure. St. Laurence assembled the sick and poor Christians, saying, "These are the Treasure of the Church." For this, he was condemned to be roasted on a gridiron with a fire underneath.

33 / 1857—The Scott Family Suffers Another Bereavement

Since the family's return from the continent, Katherine Scott's two younger daughters, Jane Barbara and Katherine Emily, had died, and, in May 1857, Katherine Scott and her two elder children, Hatton Thomasina and Henry Richardson, were in Thomas Scott's house in Dublin. Hannah was also there. The two Scott boys Tom and Charles were students at Trinity College Dublin.

Annette Scott has written of her stepmother, "Our Stepmother was invaluable, she took such a deep interest in the brothers' studies, and encouraged us all to use our talents (such as they were) to the best advantage."

On May 21, 1857, Katherine Scott wrote to her stepdaughter Annette, who was staying at Knocktarna:

Thursday
Morning

Dearest Nette

I owe Lizzie two letters, but I suppose I owe you half a dozen—so I must tell you your letters were a great comfort & pleasure to me but most days I have had three or four to write & I knew you would understand better than many how hard I find it to write much—You have heard by this time what shocked us so terribly yesterday the death of Mary Macnaghten your Father's letter I send to you—I trust the poor parents may be comforted—

Tell dearest Liz I am much obliged to her for her satisfactory account of Maria Clarke—I have engaged a laundry help—& am leaving Brit to choose her own underling—We still hope to be passing thro' Coleraine on Saturday 30th & to find you & Betty on the Derry side tickets taken & luggage on board & some one to take back Thompson & two trunks 1 as large as mine 1 small. I daresay you can pay yr own ticket & Bettys & settle with me when we meet Lizzie can send me by you any money she owes (she

202

asks me what to do with it). We are all quite well but all greatly shocked—Poor Miss French you may suppose is much distressed Tell Lizzie Hatty was to have written but may not have a brief ready for post

Your very affecte Mother
K.E. Scott

In Annette Scott's handwriting, there is a note on the top of this letter "May 21st 1857. She died on May 26th just 5 days after."

Annette and Charles Scott have both recorded the tragedy of the twenty-sixth of May. Charles Scott writes in his autobiographical notes,

After gaining high honours in Classics in my freshman years I was encouraged to enter for Scholarship, & did so in 1857, but at the last day of the examination on stepping out of the Exam^n Hall I was met by my brother Tom with the crushing news of my stepmother's sudden death that morning soon after I had left her in apparently her usual health. He himself was leaving at once for Holyhead to meet my father who had been telegraphed for from London, & my sisters were alone in the house to which I rushed off. I was deeply devoted to my stepmother—the only Mother I ever knew.—My exam having not been completed by the last two hours I was disqualified. . . . .

Annette Scott writes in May of the same year:

Whilst I was paying my first visit to your mother at Knocktarna, we were suddenly shocked by receiving a telegram from Dublin telling of the sudden death of our stepmother. I had had a letter from her that morning telling me that the next day I was to meet them all at the station and go home with the rest of the family to Willsboro'. It was a terrible shock to us all and especially as my Father was in London on some business and only Hannah and Tom were in the house except the two poor little ones Hatty and Harry. It was long before we could realize the loss for long years we missed her. She was a true mother to us all & especially to Charlie and me. My father took us all home & we never came back to Eccles St. again but the house was sold. It was a sad lonely house we came to, it was never the same again, and my father cared little for going about or seeing many people.

Since her trip on the Continent, Ellen Lyle continued to live at Knocktarna with her brother (Rev. John Lyle), his wife (Elizabeth Scott), their children, and her mother.

Ellen seems to have kept a diary most of her life, but the one covering 1863 is the first of those surviving. A number of pages have been torn from the beginning of this diary, and it seems certain that these contained details of an experience referred to in this and also in a much later diary.

Extracts from the first Diary:

10th March 1863—Prince of Wales married—George went to Coleraine to see illuminations did not return till morning

15th—George had headache all day. . . . .

19th—Mama and I lunched at Cromore—took picture for Mary F. to copy—Flo got letter urging her to go home—Fan writes poor accounts of Louisa—Letter from Edward—Heard that poor Eleanor T.[1] is put under restraint near Dublin—£200 a year paid for her.

20th—Read Philosopher in town and country on beginnings and ends—Importance of dividing time into distinct parts so as to begin fresh and feel only the *present* pain—practised an hour at Church—saw old McElrarys—in filth and wretchedness—Surely no blessing can rest on children who desert their parents in their helpless old age.

22 Six girls in my class—felt much interested in teaching and they most attentive.

23 Felt sad and nervous all day—How painful memories reign at such times self reproach—past errors of judgement or mistakes from want of sense or observation are raked up and cut more keenly than actual sins—My yearnings for a strong and good guide on whom to lean and a kind true heart to understand and sympathize with my peculiar nature are checked and disappointed when apparently on the verge of being satisfied. I wish I could *always* feel that God's will is the best—sometimes I do but it is hard when results seem to have followed one's own mistakes.

26 . . . . . My mind has been disturbed today thinking over and regretting the past I have erred in many ways from peculiar temperament and would perhaps act as foolishly if in the same circumstances again . . . .

27 Blowing March day . . . . . John read Russells North & South aloud It gives one quite the feeling of having witnessed the scenes . . . He describes also a sail in a strange little steam affair. which was in such danger. Russell recommended returning without reaching their object The Irish sailor said on their landing "Weel ye'r weel landed for if we had gone on ye would neer have come back". On being asked why he had not said so before "Oh and I didn't like to spoil the trip!

30th The Eccles. Com[r2] add £45 yearly to the income of this parish which enables John to give 100 to a curate if necessary—Mr Steuart and he rode to Dromore in search of Hannah Kilpatrick who is sent for by her sister in America—I fear she will only bring disappointment to everyone who is concerned for her Poor Annie has been a kind sister She was such a wild irish looking girl when she used to be in my Sunday class—Emily's[3] interview with Widow Blackburn amused her greatly "She had got the beauty of the family"—and "Its no wonder he fancied you for you're a beauty" "Ye had a good Protestand name" etc She and James rode up. . . . .

April 1st Heard poor Aunt Fan had renewed her cough in Dublin—going to visit Eleanor Thompson—found her comfortably placed a maid sitting working in the room, spoke sensibly on many subjects and nicely on religion but launched out against Miss Adair who she said was a murderess—but poor innocent Fanny Cromie she would speak to her—

Ap 4 Heard from Fan[4] poor little Louisa not better. the boys in measles at Brighton and John not very well. wants me to go up on Monday. . . . .

May 4 How little I thought when I last wrote in this what would happen before the next time—Deep have been the lessons of the last month—On Monday April 6th Craigavad—felt a strange unwillingness to leave home.—almost turned back from Coleraine, was it presentiment—. Louisa recovered during the week. She is certainly an unusual child. Her bright large eyes. full of light and changing expression, brilliant auburn hair, and coaxing little way—With a strong self will and obstinacy—pride and sensitiveness. . . . . .Heard such bad accounts of poor little Willie Chichester I wrote to say I wd go & help Harriet[5] to nurse him—. She begged I would go and help her, George C met me—Felt quite overcome seeing the dear little child Sat with him his last night—His restlessness was distressing limbs cold disliked greatly taking any nourishment except milk. It was affecting to see his little wan face and large blue eyes undimmed and wonderful strength—. I called Harriet at near 5 o'clock to come and see if he shd take some barley brandy which the doctor ordered. She had not sat one minute beside him when he suddenly closed his eyes laid his head back and a smile overspread his face—I ran for George, a few long quick breathings and he was with his Saviour When Harriet had been with him an hour or two before, she whispered to him "Would Willie like to die and go to Jesus"—he said "Yes" About a fortnight before his illness. he said to her—"I love Jesus so much I would like to die and go to him"—He delighted in hearing the little book "Ada" read. one of her sayings "Jesus died stead of us"—Harriet wishing to know if he understood it said "What did Jesus do". With a very earnest grave face and voice he said "He died on the cross for us"—A short time before his illness—She was walking in the Park with him. He was playing some way behind with the dogs and throwing stones for them—suddenly he stopped and called out Mama come here On coming to him he said whisper—so she leant down. he said "I dont want God to hear. Is it Satan tempts me to be disobedient?" On Tuesday Edward came & he and I drove with poor Harriet to the grave yard and chose a quiet spot where he is to rest. It was a sad struggle to part from that lovely precious little creature, even after death he looked lovely such a noble brow and head like pure marble—so calm the expression. . . . . . . I wrote to little Edward knowing how he would feel it. . . . . On Wednesday 15 Ada[6] and Helen[7] came with me—to Knocktarna . . . . . . Felt very unwell for two days—Staid in bed on Saturday & sent for Dr Lathom—He thought it a badly ulscerated throat, burned it with caustic stick—said it was not infectious to children—When we were coming G to avoid all risk told Ada and Helen in the train they were to be kept entirely separate from the children here but. on arriving Lizzie said she was not the least afraid and that Hugh had had it a little time back—. Lathom used caustic again on Sunday also fluid on Tuesday and Thursday It was great pain even swallowing liquids for a whole week—a gargle of Borax alum. port wine and water was very useful and inhaling steam of vinager laudenum & hot water. Took no medecine except fluid Magnesia & found brandy Negus very hot. hurt me less than anything. Lizzie very kind and attentive few there are like her to be depended upon Oh how little I thought of the cloud ready to burst on our heads.—Dear little Ernie[8] had been looking thin & small. and saying "He dot a told" for some days, however nurse thinking it was his teeth as he was cutting two double teeth—took him out in the afternoon when there was bright sun and cold wind, his throat was sore on Wednesday morning—evening Carson sent for On Thursday I sat with him. while he sat up in bed. rubbed the paints and looked at pictures—Friday he was very unwell—Lathom sent for Saturday morning early croup cough began lasted incessantly all the day Lathom blistered the spine—gave tartar emetic—It was wonderful to see a little creature not 3 years old show such spirit—seizing his medecines and swallowing them down. Dear little child he was so loving—putting up his little face to be kissed & saying "GOOD BOY"—in a voice as of asking Am I?—Sunday afternoon he took a long sleep with his dear little head on my hand, and seemed better when he awoke eat some jelly—but soon the sinking began the doctors said his lungs were filling the cough subsided but painful breathing continued—restlessness—he spoke about "Daddle" wanted to see him to tell him "Sucky"—and said "I am going away" John came in He said Pappy take me when he had him in his arms he said "Give me 'ucky' "—poor John went for lozenges—He talked about his little garden and where he and Hugh had been planting primroses—and "Ernie little cart"—The precious little darling continued until near four o'clock breathing painfully but not otherwise suffering and passed away quietly. Another lamb gathered into the fold—I wish I had told him about Jesus.—though his mother did teach I should have done it too. My own little godchild, but my foolish worldly heart

Rev. Bedell Scott (Son of Rev. George Scott)

was distracting itself with other things and fretting after things denied me in His wisdom So opportunities slip by . . . . I have prayed that dear John may be comforted and his loss more than made up to him in God's own way He has borne it in such a sweet humble spirit—to him a most severe wrench he did so dote on Ernie—What a wonderful thing it is to see—A Christian at such a time No murmur. No rising up against the blighting stroke but meek submission. and patient cheerfulness tho' the heart is wounded and bleeding—. Dear Lizzie also so kind and sympathizing with others grief. I was glad the Major took her to Willsboro on Monday . . . . James Emily and George[9] came up on Tuesday. It was the first scene of death to Emily. It seemed to shock her. The precious little creature tho' so changed looked fair cold and calm I had made a little wreath of moss and primroses. some of them out of his own little garden. and it lay on his bed. I took George in at night to see him, he seemed affected by it & I prayed that the sight might do him good—.

Today 6th Ernie was laid in his little grave at our own Church . . . . . It is like a dream of pain which I can only realize now and again . . . Dear Lizzie wrote that she had been greatly comforted by her Uncle George.[10]—He thought it sinful to look back and blame anything in the chain of circumstances.—Either what has been or might be have been God works and brings round what he wills and we dare not question. either what he does or how he does it. . . . .

July 30 The last seven weeks we have been here in the Crescent have passed so quickly—. . . . . . We had the Chichesters the first three weeks. Richards illness of Diptheria was very trying to them and us after what both families had suffered so lately from the terrible illness. . . . Our tea party on Tuesday went off pretty well—I do not much like having games when people are grown up and plenty of interesting conversation might be. . . . . Gardiner Young making strange faces—He is good natured but unlike a clergyman should be. . . . . Bedell Scott has been spending the last few days with us, I never liked him so much—He has many nice things in him—so unselfish and original. . . . .

It is not known whether the Eleanor Thompson mentioned here is the daughter of Sam Thompson who wrote to John Cromie in 1783, but in view of the date it seems unlikely.

Hugh Lyle, son of John Lyle and Elizabeth Scott, writing in old age, says, "One of the first things I can remember is the marriage of the Rev. Bedell Scott to my Aunt Ellen. I remember the wedding breakfast in the diningroom at a T shaped table." Hugh, the eldest of the family was, in 1863, five years of age.

Notes

1. Eleanor Thompson.
2. Ecclesiastical commissioner.
3. Emily Ward wife of James Lyle of Glandore, John Lyle's brother.
4. Frances, sister of John Lyle, wife of John Mulholland, later Baron Dunleath.
5. Harriet, John Lyle's sister, wife of Rev. George Vaughan Chichester.
6. Sister of little Willie Chichester.
7. - ————— do ————— -.
8. Second child of John Lyle and Elizabeth Scott.
9. George Lyle, Ellen's brother, who had been in China.
10. Rev. George Scott, father of Bedell Scott.

Part III

35 / June 1859/March 1863—the Making of a Diplomat. Extracts From the Private Diary of Charles Stewart Scott, Attaché to Her Britannic Majesty Queen Victoria's Embassies at Paris, Dresden, and Copenhagen

Charles Stewart Scott, first cousin of the Charles Scott killed in 1858 during the Indian Mutiny, was the youngest child of Thomas Scott and his second wife, Anne Lucas. He has already been mentioned twice in this book: when he was a child in Paris, in 1846, and when a student at Trinity College, Dublin, in 1857, he missed the last part of his examination because of his stepmother's sudden unexpected death.

In autobiographical notes written in his old age, Charles Scott tells what happened to him after his disqualification for not completing the examination in which he had been expected to gain a scholarship:

The next year I was urged to compete again, and with unpardonable levity I did so without sufficient preparation, relying on what I had done the preceding year. The result was ignominious failure, and, as a matter of fact, I did not return to college again-the prospect of a new career having unexpectedly opened for me.

I had been proposing to work-before my scholarship fiasco-for the Indian Civil Service Exam., a decision which W. Tyrell who had been bracketed with me Senior Classical Honourman in our Freshman Year, had also taken. However in the summer of 1858, Sir Thomas Bateson (later Lord Deramore) suggested to my father to try and obtain for me an appt to the Foreign Office. The Diplomatic Service had lately been reorganised and made open instead of a strictly patronage service in which the junior members recd neither pay nor commission. Sir Thomas thought that the new system wd be a lucrative one! Neither my father nor I had any idea what the Diplomatic Service or its requirements were, but I was fascinated by the idea of a life of foreign travel, and I strongly pressed my father to entertain it.

The 3rd Marquis of Londonderry, a friend of my father and his family, was my godfather, and he had told my father at my christening to let him know when I grew up what I was going to be, and he would give me a commission in his regt or do what he could for me. Lord L. was dead, but his widow, Frances Anne, who still kept up her friendship with my father, readily consented to ask Lord Malmesbury for a clerkship in the Foreign Office for me. He replied that there was no vacancy at present in the office, but offered me a nomination as Attaché in the Diplomatic Service.

After studying for some months in London, I passed the test exam before the C.S. Commr with honourable mention in December 1858 and entered the F.O. for preparatory training in January 1859. After three months work there, I was sent as temporary extra hand and unpaid attaché to the Embassy in Paris where there was an unusual stress of work owing to the tension of relations between France and Austria.

The Ambassador was Lord Cowley, and the embassy staff was unusually large, headed by Lord Chelsea,-father of the Earl Cadogan who was afterwards Lord Lieutenant of Ireland-his was a purely political appt and ceased on the fall of Lord Derby's Govt.

Charles Scott arrived in Paris just as a dangerous situation involving Italy, Austria, and France was reaching its climax.

Italy, hub of the controversy, posed problems that were both ancient and modern in origin.

In 1859, Italy had never been one nation. The peninsula, frequently a battleground, was divided into small kingdoms and principalities. It included the papal territory, ruled by the Pope.

For a long period, Italy had been mainly dominated by Austria and the Bourbon-ruled countries of France and Spain. In 1746, the armies of France and Spain were fighting in Italy against the forces of Austria and her ally, Sardinia, a small island off the Italian mainland, adjacent to Corsica.

When the Corsican, Napoleon Bonaparte, the most brilliant general of the new French republic, became the ruler of France, Italy suffered with most of the rest of Europe from his compulsive, insatiable lust for military conquest and for the advancement of his relatives. After French victories, a number of Italian rulers were replaced by Napoleon's nominees or married to members of his family. Napoleon himself was crowned king of Italy.

After Napoleon Bonaparte's defeat in 1814 and the return of the Bourbon monarchy to France under Louis XVIII, the victorious allies were faced by many problems created by Napoleon's aggressions, some undertaken under the hypocritical pretext of "liberation." The major victors convened the Congress of Vienna in September 1814 in order to come to agreed decisions, appointing as their plenipotentiaries Lord Castlereagh (England), Prince Metternich (Austria), Prince Hardenberg and Baron Humbolt (Prussia), and Count Nesselrode (Russia). In Vienna, after discussion, dispute, and negotiation, the Congress reached its final decisions. As they did so, the news broke that Napoleon had escaped from the Island of Elba to which he had been banished. He reached Paris, was rapturously welcomed by the French Army, Louis XVIII fled, and Napoleon once more led France. His brief period of freedom and restored power soon ended, however, and, in 1815, he was finally defeated at the Battle of Waterloo, and the decisions of the Congress were duly implemented.

In Italy, generally speaking, the original rulers were reinstated. The papal territory was returned to the Roman Catholic Church, and the Pope, driven into exile by armed force, returned to rule in Rome.

However, the French Revolution, whatever it did or did not achieve, effectively publicized the theories on which it was based. These theories attracted many people in many countries—humane men of liberal views, undernourished peasants struggling to survive those suffering under brutal and unjust governments, and ambitious men craving for the power and luxury that reward successful revolutionary leaders no matter how incompetent and unsuitable they may be to rule a country and lead their trusting followers into the promised land—so easy to promise in rabble-rousing speeches and so difficult to deliver in real life.

In Italy, the growth of nationalism and the longing for democracy grew steadily after 1815, their appeal strongest to the mass of the people. Rulers, haunted by the specter of the French Revolution and all its attendant horrors—a silent presence at all their deliberations, often influencing their policies—tended to support the status quo, although some embarked on reforms.

By 1857, Italy was full of secret societies, including the Carbonari, their aims "Expulsion of the Foreigner and Constitutional Freedom." Armed revolutionaries, they desired the unity of Italy under Victor Emmanuel, King of Sardinia, the only native Italian ruler at that time.

In 1857, a small group of Carbonari were in England, traditional sanctuary of political refugees from other lands. In January 1858, four left London for Paris with their leader Orsini. The English police notified the French authorities of their departure, their destination, their intention of assassinating Louis Napoleon, Emperor of France, and also supplied detailed descriptions of them. Nevertheless, they reached Paris safely and, unmolested, posted themselves outside the Opera House. When the Emperor and Empress arrived, they threw their bombs. Ten people were killed, and 140 injured. The Empress's gown was splashed with blood, but she and the Emperor escaped with trivial injuries, his a scraped nose. Both went on to attend the performance at the Opera House.

The conspirators were arrested. Orsini was condemned to death. On the eve of his execution, Orsini wrote the Emperor an impassioned appeal to help Italy. The Emperor, himself a member of the Carbonari in his younger days, was touched and with difficulty dissuaded from pardoning Orsini.

The French public were furious to learn that the assassination had been planned and all preparations made in England, their ally and, therefore, supposedly a friendly country. Nor was it the first time that something similar had happened. Some French officers, strongly supported by the French public, vociferously demanded war with England.

The British public was equally enraged at the idea of France presuming to dictate what their policy should be, particularly as their own Emperor, Louis Napoleon, had spent his years of exile in comfort in England. For some time, also, there had been rumors that France was planning to invade England, a fact that exacerbated the situation. The British public was wholeheartedly in favor of a war with France. So violent were the feelings roused on both sides of the Channel that at one time it was feared that it would be impossible to avoid war.

The French Emperor, Queen Victoria, and Prince Albert were not in favor of war. French ministers reproved "the Colonels" and the French press. In August, Louis Napoleon, to cement the alliance with Great Britain, invited the Queen and Prince Albert to visit him at Cherbourg, where he welcomed them warmly and entertained them lavishly, the only tactless note being a display of naval strength, the growth of which was a source of anxiety in England, lending color to rumors of invasion plans. However, the visit ended on a note of friendship and affection, although afterward Prince Albert, the shrewdest of political observers, recorded that he had noticed a change in the Emperor. This has since been attributed to the fact that the Emperor was already negotiating in secret with Victor Emmanuel, a fact that he refrained from mentioning, believing correctly that Queen Victoria and Prince Albert would disapprove. Great Britain's influence at that time was devoted to preserving peace in Europe.

By January 1859, King Victor Emmanuel had built up the Sardinian Army to war strength, its soldiers ready and eager to fight for the freedom and unity of Italy.

In April 1859, Austria, determined not to lose her Italian possessions tamely, sent a truculent note to Sardinia requiring immediate demobilisation and laying down a brief time limit for compliance. The note was ignored. On expiry of the time limit, the Austrian Army attacked and, at Montebello, suffered a defeat that, of course did not affect the war, which continued.

In May 1859, Louis Napoleon announced his sympathy for Italy's cause and declared war on Austria.

At the beginning of June 1859, the British Ambassador in Paris was still Lord Cowley and the Head of the Embassy Lord Chelsea, while the British foreign secretary was Lord Malmesbury. However, in June 1859, Lord Derby's government fell, and Lord Palmerston once more became the British Prime Minister. He appointed as his Foreign Secretary Lord John Russell. The French Foreign Minister was Count Walewski.

On June 10, 1859, when Charles Scott, then twenty-one years of age, began his private diary, the war was still going on, and he records much of historical interest as well as details of his personal life.

EXTRACTS FROM THE DIARY

33 Rue de la Madelaine

PRIVATE   PARIS

June 10th 1859. At 12.30 A.M. I began my diary, forming a resolution (with, however but little hope of keeping it) to write something in it every night, of what has happened to me in the day, and to make a confidant of this small book, so if any evil-disposed person should have laid hands on this diary and have so far trespassed on another man's property as to rob my confidant of his exclusive right, let him drop it like a hot potato for this is PRIVATE AND MOST CONFIDENTIAL.

June 17. Friday I found some difficulty in opening my eyes at 10 a.m. and when I succeeded in doing so found them fixed on Durand's garcon, arranging my breakfast, my conscience painfully reminding me that I owed him 60 francs for breakfasts and that each day I had promised to pay his little "note" demain. I closed them again and answered his "Monsieur est servi" (said in a hesitating tone) only by a low grunt, and he departed . . . I did not go to fence, but booted slowly down to the Embassy (We only moved into our new pig-stye of a chancery yesterday) . . . Later in the day there came in news of a conspiracy in Athens to dethrone King Otto, and the intelligence was sent in cypher to the F.O.[1] It appears that the conspirators have called themselves the Italian French Society, and tried to implicate the French Minr. Very important news arrived of the state of the Prussian policy drawn from a convn of Fch Minr in the Schleinetz. General opinion in Chancery that Germany wd join Austria before the end of the month . . .

I wrote to Conyngham about the £4.10 (travelling expenses) asking him to send it to me. I am in a fearful state in the way of finances and I am afraid to tell the Governor, but what am I to do. This is the 17th. Quarter does not commence before the 23rd of July and I have only this £4.10 with lots of debts . . .

Letter from *Tom.*[2] More cheery, is going to be priested-Parish matters-good advice etc.

Lizzie[3] State of religious excitement in North-to my weak mind this looks like a d---d humbug, that is the effect of living in the same uncivilized spot, without new ideas, that has made everybody so superstitious. However, Liz seems rather to believe in it.

I feel rather maudlin and sentimental in fact in low spirits tonight—the state of my funds. I have been a great fool. Durand's and other debts weigh on me like a nightmare, or an overfeed. I am doing nothing to get myself on in my profession, and instead of improving my mind, I think I am stupifying myself more and more every day.

June 18th Saturday . . . . . . The Austrians seem to be in full retreat from the Adda. A letter from Claremont is dated Covo. The Emperor, it appears is at Grevighe. Claremont expresses surprise at the ease with which they advance, the Austrians never molesting them in a country which he describes as most favourable for doing so.

The Ministry is formed and we are most anxious to find out what sort of a F. Minr Ld John will make . . . . . .

Laurence and I lunched at Guerre's and then strolled through the Tuileries. I was greatly surprised to Meet Mr. C.O'Neill and Annie in the Rue St. Honore. They are stopping at the Hotel Westminster. I shall go and see them. I saw some very pretty faces in the Champs Elysees, one particularly so in a carriage . . . .

We all dined at the Taverne. My dinner was 3.45f. Afterwards I went home, dressed and went with Laurence to Lady Elgin's where we met Lady Gray and Mrs Colonel Bruce (Mrs. B. is wife of the Guardian of the Prince of Wales). She is a nice agreeable person and soon set us at our ease. Lady E. is quite a fixture, can't speak, and altogether paralysed she seems quite odd and this makes one feel very awkward. Lady Gray is a very agreeable person, something like Miss Finlay.

After this L. and I walked home . . . . I was "de service" but there was nothing to be done. Our work is certainly getting milder than it was when I came.

June 10th Sunday. . . . . By special messenger desps from Naples. Affairs at Naples are beginning to look up. A general amnesty has been proclaimed. A Minister has been appointed, a Prince-(I forget his name), who is strong for reform and liberal concessions. The surveillance of police has been withdrawn. A Demonstration, however, took place on the occasion of the French and Sardn Minrs illuminating their houses. The police interfered with much brutality, the King has promised to dismiss the head of the police which Elliott says will give great satisfaction.

. . . . Cowley wrote some desp^s home upon the feeling of Emp^r at conduct of V.E. and Sardn troops (most conf.) the other on the opinion of Fch officers on the effect of the new rifled cannon on the Austrian fortresses.

I went to Church in the morning. . . . A messenger (Wright) went this evening. What a hard life those messengers lead. Here has this unfortunate man been travelling three days a week and three nights every week. He arrives early in the morning form Calais and packed off at 7 at night back to Calais. . . .

June 20 Monday. . . . Kennedy and Laurence called for me about II and we went to Ruas's and had a good fencing lesson. I got to the Chancery at 1.30 . . . Desp. from Claremont dated Trevigliato, the whole line is advancing, but the Desp. contained nothing interesting. I expect we shall hear something decisive soon on the Nuncio.

Mr and Mrs Torrens that are to be came in, they are the same people we had a marriage applied for at the Embassy the other day Miss T. is very nice looking, not very pretty but amiable and clever looking. I took a fancy to her at once.

A let: in cypher came in from Mark, rather confused, about some Comm^g Officer of a ship which he does not mention who it appears has spoken about the object of the squadron's visit to coast of Spain, what that is I really don't know, but I suppose we shall soon hear. Tel: later in the evening from Ld John, who has accordingly commenced his duties as F.S. Kennedy was "de Service" and I did not hear the contents. Cowley went to dine with the Empress at St. Cloud. Laurence and I dined at Voisin's (8.50 a good dinner) I went on tick. That infernal blackguard Leopold has been enquiring about me from Kennedy who properly told him that I belonged to the Embassy and that that ought to be enough for him, the brute dunned me the morning after I bought something from him.

Laurence and I were looking at lodgings, we enquired about some in a very nice "maison" opposite the Embassy. They were 260 a month. We saw others opposite the Russian Embassy of rather a bawdy shop appearance 300 a month. These were a "grande appartement" for two. I did not like the look of the house.

June 21 Tuesday

I did not feel at all inclined to get up this morning. I managed to do so however, at ¼ to II o'clock and got to the Chancery at 12.30. I copied some letters from Ld H. de Walden about Mr Hayman's flax. There was no news of any kind today. . . . . . . We dined at the Taverne. Afterwards I went to the Levenson's where we met some Miss Burnetts, one very nice looking indeed, we had all manner of games and dancing. I felt awkward and stupid and did not add much to the evening's amusement. . . . We walked home at a little before 3 o'clock.

Another day gone and I have not written to the Major. I feel so ashamed of my poverty, I really do not know what I shall do if it lasts much longer.

I had a letter from Hannah[4] they have gone to Portstewart, it is about a year since I was there. What a change in my life since then! What a different life! I can scarcely think changed for the better, yet what a miserably slow existence that was, nothing new, no excitement. Now in a perpetual state of excitement, debauched, and in a state of abject poverty. What shall I be this time next year?

June 22 Wednesday

I was not able to pay Durand. Conynham, the wretch, has not sent me my money. . . . . Went to the Chancery at 12 and found lots of work going on. . . . . Despatches of some interest from Naples Florence and Claremont . . . Claremont seems to think that the allies are not so sanguine about the coming engagement as is supposed. There is some talk of the Austrians holding out at Montechiari, which Claremont thinks foolish with the Nuncio on their rear. it appears also that great jealousy exists between the Sardinian and French troops. . . .

June 23 Thursday

In the Chancery at 12. A Desp: from Claremont dated Brescia 20th Inst: the Austrians have evacuated Montechiari & Castiglione The Hd. qrs. to move at 21st to Casletuedolo. The French must be within 20 miles of Mantua and less from Peschecra. I half expect to hear of the seige of the latter town today. But no news has arrived. Sandford and Kennedy stayed out most of the day so L and I had to stick to the Chancery until 4.30 when we went a walk. . . . . The Luxembourg Gardens I admired very much. They were crowded with dirty looking children playing that insane game of ball they have here.

Laurence and I dined at Voisin's. Kennedy came in after we had finished. He lent me a Nap:[5] We stopped there until he had dined and then walked up the Champs Elysees. There were lots of pretty women out. We were snubbed by two English-women (ladies maids I think) Afterwards I returned to L's rooms where we played double dummy but were interrupted by a summons from Cowley to the Embassy to put a desp: into cypher. It was to the effect that an article would appear in tomorrow's Moniteur declaring the dictatorship of the King of Sard[a] in Italy was only temporary and wd not influence future arrangements.

I wrote a long letter to the Major on the state of my funds. I wonder with what effect. It was a painful but necessary proceeding. K, S and I seriously discussed the pecuniary state of H.B.M's Chancery, and came to the conclusion that this sort of thing could not last. Violent steps must be taken. I am seriously thinking of applying for another station. I should be very sorry to leave Paris but I do not think I shall be able to live on my allowance. However, I have bought experience with a vengeance this quarter and I hope it will have a good effect next quarter.

June 25 Saturday

I got up very late having suffered terribly from toothache. On my way down to the Chancery at 12.30 I saw an "Affiche" giving the news of a great battle dated Caravine June 24th 9.15 in the evening to the effect that the Allies had engaged the whole Austrian army in a line of 15 miles, taken all the positions and captured several guns, flags and prisoners. The details have not yet been given. It appears to have been a very bloody affair and I should not wonder at hearing a very different version soon. Farquhar had arrived. He handed me £4.10.0. which Conynham had given him for me and which, as you may imagine, I was glad to get. . . . . . Sandford and I went to the Taverne and dined. Afterwards we went to Nortons. The whole town was illuminated and "pavoisé" They seem to be confident of having won a tremendous victory. Madame is not at all pretty or young, but very nice. Middleton (Attaché at Madrid) was at N's rooms and seems a great friend of Madame. She had insisted as an Italian on illuminating the windows with the Tricolour for, as she said "Maintenant nous seront libres". Norton and

Laurence played chess and Madame and I talked. She is very intelligent and seems to be well enough educated. I am all anxiety for the news tomorrow. The French must now be crossing the Nuncio and in the Quadrilatère. Canards[6] are going about of the losses of the Austrians speaking of them as 35,000 and 75 guns, also that the French have entered Mantua. Cowley seems to be excited by the news. He did not go to Chantilly as he had intended.

June 26th Sunday (Fete de Dieu)

I breakfasted at the Cafe de France and on my way to it I went up the Madelaine steps to see what I could see of the Fete Dieu procession. I found myself among a bustling, hot, dirty crowd most of them strangers and distinguished a sort of lugubrious music produced by drums and a small brass band, and at last was fortunate enough to see the greasy heads of some priests and choristers carrying banners, crucifixes, flambeaux, some blowing large ophicheides, walking at an absurdly slow rate. I did not appreciate the sight and as the crowd was too great to indulge any hope of getting inside the church I took myself off. . . . . After dinner we did the coffee and liquer dodge at the Cardinal, and while we were there the newest telegram was posted up stating that the Austrians had left 1,500 prisoners in the hands of the French 30 guns and 3 flags. On one side of us when the news arrived were some Italians, on the other Germans. The effect on the respective parties was worth seeing. . . . . We played Vingt-et-Un and Buckerer till 4 o'clock in the morning with an entracte of lobster salad Champagne, chicken and strawberries.

June 27th Monday

I paid dear for last night's amusement in the way of toothache I was suffering so much that I had to go to the Chancery without breakfast. I could not manage to eat anything. When I got there Norton stuck a long confidential Desp: from Cowley to Ld J. into me. He however softened the blow by giving me some creosot for my tooth which deadened the pain, but made me feel very sick. At 3 I breakfasted, at least eat an apology for one and returned to my Desp: which took me more than two hours. It was one of great interest. Cowley anticipating a proposal on the part of Russia to set on foot an armed negotiation, examines with great accuracy and tact the probable phases the negotiation would assume. The interest of each of the Belligerents in the war and what they were likely to cede and accept respectively. I think I should be scarcely justified in going minutely into so important a Desp: as this marked *Conf*[1] it was clear and well written and put matters in a true light and while he admitted the wrongs of the Lombards showed the dangerous policy of allowing such an enormous state with considerable strength in the Adriatic and Medit[n] to fall into the hands of a Power under the influence of and indebted to France. It also mentioned what C. thought likely to be put forward as combinations.

Tuesday June 28

Toothache still bad but better than yesterday. Mr and Miss Torrens were married at the Embassy at 9 o'clock, it was too early an hour for any of us to witness it. . . . . Claremont sent a Desp: and private letter from which it appears that the Battle of Solferino must have been a most desperate affair and that the fighting on both sides was most plucky. He describes the heat as so intense that he could scarcely sit his horse, the sun made him so ill. The Emperor was on horseback 14 hours and behaved very well, exposing himself almost too much. C. has only seen 3 flags taken from the A^{us} one of which was without the colors, a simple flagstaff. He describes the effect of the rifled guns as most satisfactory where the Austrian guns are harmless.

June 30 Thursday

I got up at 7 breakfasted at home, coffee and strawbereies from Cafe de France and then went to the Chancery. There was nothing except a Desp: from Claremont and from Cadogan giving further particulars of the late Battle. At Caravina they seem short of necessaries, the Austrians seem to have deprived the villagers of all sort of food etc. I called on the Levesons and found a large circle of them with Mrs and Miss Burnett. The latter is very pretty . . . After dinner went to the O'Neills where I met Miss Torrens' I enjoyed myself greatly. The Miss T's are charming. I devoted myself to Miss Constance who is a very fine handsome girl. We had some singing and afterwards table and hat turning. The sensation of sitting with my fingers on Miss T's over a hat was pleasant. The tables turned most successfully. I hope I shall meet these girls often again.

July 1 Friday

I breakfasted late and went straight to the Chancery. To my great delight I found Laurence had got his allowance and that I could have someone to borrow from. I got a letter from Stavely about Agencies etc., which I answered by return of Mess^r . . . I borrowed 100fs from Laurence and went to fence, had an assaut with a Frenchman of course I could do nothing it being only my second assaut. Afterwards I met Craven, went with him to the Guerre's, and then to hear the band play in the Tuileries, where we saw such a lot of pretty women, the Miss Torrens in the distance. We met Heppesley and talked of plans of fun with the Leveson's tomorrow. I returned to the Embassy and found a letter from Papa evidently in very low spirits as to the state of my finances and talking of my giving up the profession. This I could not think of doing, but I must really look out. He promises to send me £35 at once.

Saturday July 2

I got up very late and when I got down to the Chancery Norton rowed me an stuck a long Consulate forwarder with various things into me. . . . . The French have crossed the Nuncio. Peschiera is being attacked. Gladstone's election still doubtful. . . . . At 6 joined the Leveson's party with Craven, Kennedy and Heppesley to the Bois-the heat was almost unbearable. We went to the Chalet on the island. Nothing could have been more delightful. . . . We dined soon after seven on a balcony in the Chalet . . . K's health was drunk and he had to respond. Afterwards we rowed by lamplight on the lake. The chalet and all the boats were illuminated and the effect of the lights as they were reflected on the dark water was charming.

Sunday July 3

Was awoke by the sound of drums, etc., and on enquiry I was informed by my breakfast waiter that the De Deum for the victory was to be sung today at Not. Dame and that the music came from the troops who were going there. . . . .

Monday July 4

I got to the Chancery at 12.30. There was rather an important Desp: from Ld. John relative to the Perugia atrocities; he desires C. to read the Desp: to Wal:[7] and in it he expresses his conviction that the Papal Government is a crying evil in Italy and that at any future negotiations it would be desirable to take steps to deprive H.H. of all temporal power. C. wrote an important conf: Desp: home upon the rumoured agreement between France and Sard[a] respecting cession to former of Savoy. He expressed a wish that gentlemen of the Chancery should not speak about it to anyone. It appears that steps have been already taken towards negotiation by Prussia. She has made porposals at London and Sard[a] to England and France to join her in settling bases. Austria wished Prussia to act alone. Prussia will not assent to do so. Claremont writes from Valleggio the Sardinian Army are besieging Peschiera, the Emperor seems to have turned his attention to Venice . . . I felt so indignant at myself for not having read anything about the Papal Govt: or the Govt of the Italians when everyone was talking about them. I must get up in history soon. Exiles have been recalled at Naples.

Tuesday July 5th

We had despatches from Turin and Florence; at both places there seems to be great indignation about the atrocities said to be committed at Perugia. At Florence the people wanted to make the Sard[n] Comm[r] declare war against the Pope. Cowley wrote home today the result of his communication with Walweski on the same subject. Wal: excuses the Pope, 1st because the accounts have been much exaggerated, 2ndly because the inhabitants were themselves much to blame in not quietly admitting the troops but firing upon them, and then driving them into a state of fury was to render them quite unmanageable.

Wednesday July 6th

My money did not come this morning so I felt rather in a swearing humour. I wrote out a forwarded for Desp[s] from Naples. It appears from one of them that Filangieri has resigned on account of the King having made some exceptional clauses in the political amnesty which look as if he intended to follow in the steps of his father's policy. Charlemont sent some desp[s] in which he describes the French positions as perfect. They form a semicircle resting on the Nuncio, the right a little in front of Peschiera, the centre point being Goito which secures their communications from attack from Mantua. An attack has been expected from Villafranca and the French movements made to meet it. Pcs. Nap. has joined with upwards of 20,000 and forms the 5th Corps. From the Moniteur it appears that a mutual exchange of wounded prisoners is to take place. Cowley sent home a telegram to the effect that probably at the moment the Pope had excommunicated the King of Sardinia. I don't think he will mind much.

Norton is to be promoted to Secretary of Legation somewhere or other, he does not yet know where. How we are losing our best men. I called on A and brought her what she wanted this afternoon. We then dined with Kennedy at Durands. We (Craven, Nunse and myself) made promises of writing, etc., and drank in iced champagne to our next merry meeting. Poor K. how sorry I am to lose him. I was beginning to like him so much. Afterwards Craven and I went to the Concert Musard where we heard some charming music . . . We beered at Hill's and I got home soon after 12.

Thursday July 7th

When I got down to the Chancery a little before one, Norton rowed me for having deserted them yesterday when there was so much work to be done. . . . I was kept busy over Desp[s] one about the treatment of Austrian prisoners in France. It appears that Loftus has got hold of some canard[8] at Vienna to the effect that the Austrian prisoners here are paraded before the people and are to be set to hard labour in Algeria, he wrote to Russell about it and he to Cowley. Of course Wal: indignantly denied it. The Austrian prisoners from all accounts are most kindly treated. Some were taken to Algeria thinking Wal: says, they would prefer it, but are to be the first exchanged. Another long Despatch fell to my share to Wal: enclosing the accounts of the expenses incurred by the Allies in supplies to the Ottoman Army and to Russian prisoners, etc., I dined alone at the Taverne and on my return to the Embassy found a tel: from Crampton which, as Laurence was not there, I decyphered. It was about the proposed conference at Berlin. News had just arrived of the *"Suspension of Arms"* in Italy. A Tel: was at once sent to the F.O. Late in the evening another Tel: at length came in from Crampton in which Gov: regrets the refusal of H.M.G. to accede to Prussian proposal for a preliminary negotiation. . . . I wrote today to Papa in answer to his of the 1st inst.

Friday July 8th

. . . . A paragraph in the Moniteur warns the French not to count too much on the Suspension of Arms in Italy with a view to peace as it is only a temporary relaxation of hostilities . .

The Pope, it appears, has declared to the Duc de Grammont his intention of never submitting to interference in the internal Govt. of the States of the Church and said with much excitement that he was ready if necessary to become a Martyr but that he would be cut in pieces sooner than agree to the conditions it was thought likely to be required of him. His encyclic address to the Clergy which appeared in the Moniteur the other day was strongly against V.E.[9] whom he has excommunicated, tho' this is not yet officially announced.

Chelsea bade us goodbye today, he is off tomorrow. . . . . . . My money has not yet arrived.

Saturday July 9th

Imagine my feelings-no letter-no money. I am left alone in charge of the Embassy and Cowley has given me strict instructions as to what I am to do. I only hope I shall not make a bungle. There has been a row at Naples; One of the Swiss regiments has revolted, but after employing cannon, it was overpowered by other Swiss and Neopolitan troops, 40 killed and the rest taken prisoners. There are no more details respecting the Armistice. The emperor was expected here but had not yet left the army. Ships are to be allowed to cruise unmolested in the Adriatic under any flag . . . I was not able to go to Enghien with Craven and Mure which put me in a grumpy humour.

Sunday July 10th

Conyngham had arrived from London on his way to Naples. . . . I like C. very much, he seems a clever fellow. He described Vienna as a slow place where one did nothing but drink beer and listen to Straus's music. He seemed delighted with the thought of going to Naples. I left him at 4 and went down to Asmeters in the train I suddenly remembered that I had not posted the Desp^s: I got to Asmeter, met H's party with Alice Adeline and Anna and then I returned posted the Desp^s: and joined them again at dinner at Asmeter at 7. . . . . I got rather jolly and came back in a fiacre between Adeline and Anna, spooning Anna to a great extent. I lost the key of my rooms during this day's amusement, where I do not know.

Monday July 11th

. . . . . An article in the Moniteur gives the emperor's "ordre du jour". He intends to return at once to Paris and is to have an interview today with the Emperor of Austria at Villafranca. Claremont is to return with him. A letter from C. says he had an interview with the Emp^r who is highly pleased with the Armistice. C. informed him how acceptable the news would be to England at which he seemed pleased. Cowley wrote off a heap of Desp^s: one on the contemplated invasion of France by Germany in which he shows folly of such an attempt and how popular such a war would be in France as compared with the Italian, from its being defensive instead of agressive etc. The Pope has not excommunicated the King of Sardinia by name but in an act of Excom^n against all those who participated in or aided the insurrections in the Legations. C. also wrote another long desp: on the motives which are supposed to have weighed with the Emp^r in pressing an Armistice independent of the desire of peace.

Conclusion of Peace of Villafranca'' Tuesday July 12th

After a campaign of 2 months; at 11 o'clock last night the war was ended. The cannon of the Invalides was the first announcement we received of the conclusion of a Treaty of Peace between the two Emperors. We were sitting writing in the Chancery when all of a sudden the cannons were heard and we knew something was up. We had not long to wait for a Tel: was soon despatched by Cowley in these words-"The canons are announcing the conclusion of peace. I do not know the details''- not long after at 2 o'clock the following Tel: was despatched-"A Treaty of Peace has been signed by the Emperor of Austria and myself. The basis are 1st. An Italian Confederation under the honorary presidency of the Pope. 2nd. The Emp^r of Austria cedes his rights over Lombard to the E. of the French who resigns them to the King of Sardinia. Venetia remains in the possession of Austria while forming a component part of the Confederation.-General Amnesty-''. This was all that was officially made public.

Cowley had an interview in the afternoon with Wal: when he obtained further information which he communicated to Ld. J. in a conf^l: Desp:

The Emperors met at Villafranca as arranged at 9 on Monday night and spent the greater part of the night in discussion, separating in the afternoon to meet again for a final interview in the evg. and at 11 the Treaty was signed. The Emp^r of Austria refused to cede Lombardy to Sardinia, but agreed to do so to France as she had conquered it and she might do what she liked with it. Venetia as an unconquered country she refused to make terms about. She also refused the points strongly argued as indispensable to peace by Napoleon, the sanction of the Powers in a Congress. Nap: was forced to yield this. "This ended the War" (so Cowley concludes his Desp:) "undertaken with the object of drawing the Austrians out of Italy and restoring the Italians to freedom and independence''.

The question now seems to be will this satisfy the Italian people, and have they gained their object by this war. Some say No-others Yes. They have gained a Confederation, now they have got it they will be able to satisfy their wishes. The Emp^r is confidentially reported to have been urged to make peace so soon by the rapid strides made by revolution on the Continent. He has indeed done more than was expected by anyone and by a brief and glorious campaign and the moderation and disinterestedness displayed in the conclusion of a peace he has raised himself in the eyes of the World to a higher level than I venture to think he ever hoped to attain. The streets were beautifully illuminated tonight and our Embassy and the Russians joined in the rejoicings for the first time and I dined at my diggings and walked about to see the illuminations. The effect of them in the Place de la Concorde was something glorious. The "Cercle Imperial" Ministere de la Marine, etc., on one side and Corps Legislatif and Aff: Et^s on the other were very fine. On the quays the Spanish Embassy, legion d'Honneur and one of the Ministeres beat everything else to fits. The Rue Rivoli Place de la . . . . and Palais Royal were the finest public rows of light, and the Place Vendome were well got up and even some of the smaller streets. The heat was worse than any day I have been here yet.

Wednesday July 13th

A messenger arrived with Desps: from Naples. The mutiny of Swiss troops seems to have been more serious than the first accounts seemed to make it. The pretext given was the National emblem of the Cantons being taken out of the drapeaux of the regiment. All those who wish to return are to be discharged and sent home. 3,000 they say will avail themselves of it. Cowley had a long conversation with Walewski. It appears that Austria keeps the fortresses. The news of peace appears to have been received with great applause in England. Cowley went to St. Cloud with the diplomatic body to present congratulations to the Empress. In a Desp: he sent home he expresses his intention to attend Te Deum unless he receives instructions to the contrary. C. believes that bases must be sanctioned by some European Act. . . . . On my return I found a letter from Papa saying he had sent me £25 on the 29th June it has not made its appearance. My letter oddly enough arrived as I was going to dinner, with the money. It had been in the P.O. since July 1st . . . . . . King Oscar of Sweden died some days ago-succeeded by his son.

Thursday July 14th

. . . . The Constitutionnel of this morning has an article supposed to be official which states the considerations which may have operated with Emperor in concluding peace to have been the revolutionary aspect of the Continent and the threatened extension of the war by the attitude taken by Prussia. C. adds in his dispatch the apathy of the Italians in their own cause, the desire to spare Venice and distrust of the King and Cavour. The Augsburg Gazette say that the E. of Austria has declared he was obliged to yeild having been deserted by the Allies on whom he counted. Letter from Claremont gave some unimportant details respet. of the interview-the E. of French rode to meet the E. of A. As they were entering the house chosen for the conference, they each wished the other to go first at last the E. of the French went in saying as he did so, "Eh bien, Je passe le premier puisque vous etes chez vous". Claremont dined with the E. just before the day of the interview. The E. appears to have had some conversation with C. on the probable effect the Armistice would produce in England. C. assured him he did not doubt but that his moderation would be highly appreciated, at which the E. seemed pleased. C. says the Italians are behaving badly. Garribaldi's Corps are very unmanageable and the Tuscans totally undisciplined, and that the Italians altogether evince no desire to fight for themselves. This must disgust the French. Cavour has resignedd-Hrese has been called upon to form a Ministry. . . . . . . Webster, Laurence and I took a carriage and drove to the Bois and dined at the Chalet. We got an execrable dinner but the air was delicious. We afterwards drove to the Pre Caletan with the intention of going to the Fête there for the "Blessèes de L'Armée d'Italie" but as the Entree was 10 francs we drove home again and finished the cooling by a rubber of whist at Norton's when I won 24 francs.

Friday July 15th

Cowley wrote a heap of despatches today. . . . There appears to be some chance of Russia coming forward and proposing the ratification of bases by a conference in order to help France out of her difficulty. C. wrote a Desp: Rel: to reported extraordinary armaments at Brest, in which he ventures his opinion that if England would put an end to the rivalry of the seas she must take such measures as will render it impossible for her to be equalled in Navy by France and her Allies. He expresses his conviction that the E. has never seriously meditated an invasion of England, but that the French nation do not see the danger and importance of the undertaking in the clear light which the E. does. The E. is expected at St. Cloud Sunday or Monday. He defers his public entry till he shall be able to make it at the head of the Armee d'Italie. . . . A Despatch from Odo Russell says the Romans are greatly dissatisfied with the conclusion of the peace and loathe the idea of the Pope's supremacy over a regenerated Italy. News from Milan represents the Milanese to be also dissatisfied. They seemed anxious as to the reception the E. would have there; however it was a most flattering one. The King of Sardinia was with him and accompanied the E. to Susa.

Saturday July 16th

Phillip Currie of the F.O. passed through Paris on his way to the Pyrenees to day. He says London is in a dreadful state from the heat and stink of the Thames. We got two private letters from Claremont dated Milan and Turin. He says that the peace is most unpopular in Italy but that the Emp^{rs} reception has been good at both places, the E. he says sends agents on before him to give out that he has concluded the peace under pressure from England, Russia and Prussia. The people are so bitter against these countries that C. was told that if he and his Russian colleague went about in uniform they would be insulted. I should consider this was a slight exaggeration of the state of feelings. Claremont also says that a very strong and unfavourable impression has been made by the speeches in the House of Lords on the chance of a French invasion. The E. talked of this feeling in England as an epidemic he could not account for. In the afternoon Norton, Laurence and I went down with the Cadogans and Cowley to Chantilly by the 5.30 train-heat intense-we arrived about 7, dined and had coffee on the "Terrasse". There was a beautiful moonrise and the air of the country was charming after Paris dust.

Sunday July 17th

L. and I were up at 8 and went out in deshabille to bathe in a small hole which we found in the canal. It was a mineral spring and icy cold. At breakfast Webster arrived from London He gives a description of the heat and stink there everyone is leaving it, they say. When the others were at Church we sat out in front of the house reading till 12 when we all amused ourselves by cutting our names and devices on a lathe kept at the chateau for that purpose. After luncheon we drove in a bus to the pheasantry. The Forest looked nice and cool but the sunny parts we had to pass through made one expect to be shrivelled up . . . Cowley has 3,000 young birds this year, they seem to thrive splendidly with him. We dined at 6.30 and L. Cadogan and Lady Adelaid started by the Mail for London. We sat out on the balcony over the Moat, feeding the carp and trying to make the swan drunk by gorging him with bread soaked in cognac, to no purpose.

Monday July 18th

I was awoke by Laurence at 5.30, who was suffering from a violent cholic. We tried to relieve him by putting hot cloths and plates on his stomach . . . seemed in a bad way. Norton and I sat with him. Webster and I breakfasted alone, Laurence not being any better. We went for the Doctor

228

who came just before we left and ordered him not to move before tomorrow. We left him there in charge of the Maitre d'Hotel, and went up to Town. . . . The young Queen of Portugal. has died of Angina Pectoris, poor thing. She was so much admired and liked when she passed through London. Cowley had an interview with Walewski today. A Convention is to take place at Zurich between Austria and France to sign definite Treaty of peace. . . .

Tuesday July 19th

This morning Laurence made his appearance having nearly quite recovered his attack. We had lots of work today. In the first place I had to copy a long despatch from the Chambre de Commerce at Orleans on the state of the vintage. Soon afterwards Cowley sent me a long Desp: of 8 sheets giving the substance of his interview yesterday with Wal: on the subject of the peace of Villafranca. By this it appears that the fortresses of Perschiera and Mantua remain in the hands of the E. of Austria. The E. of A. also gave Nap: his word of honour that Venitia should have reforms with which she wd be "non seulement heureuse, mais satisfaite". He agreed with the E. in the necessity of advising the Pope to grant the same reforms, but refused to join any power not R.C. in advising it. A new and startling feature in this affair was brought to light by the account given by Hudson of his interview with Cavour and the King. The former condemned the terms most severely, said that Sardinia was dishonoured by agreeing to a treaty by which after fighting for the independence of Italy, she obtained only a slight self-aggrandisement, that he had advised the King not to accept Lombardy and that the K. not wishing to abandon the Lombards, had tendered his resignation . . . The K. said to Hudson that he had remonstrated warmly with the E. and had bitterly condemned the bases; that the E. had replied that he made peace under force and fear of losing his throne and from the urgent remonstrances of a great Foreign Power. In contrast with all this is Wal:'s repeated statement to Cowley that the King of S. not only approved but urged the Peace as well as the Armistice on the E. At Leghorn and other places demonstrations against restoration of Gd Duke of Tuscany and Duke of Modena have taken place. The difficulty now is to replace these princes. The E. Napoleon refuses to allow French troops to be employed and also prohibits their restoration by Austrian troops. The E. seems very anxious for the expression of opinion of H.M.G. . . . Cowley is in great excitement about the Desps: from Turin. A Desp: from Cadogan gave the same account of the dissatisfaction of King and people of Sardinia. The statesmen there say the peace will ruin Sardinia that they will have to keep up fortresses equally strong as Mantua and Peschiera with forces on a war footing. There is also a difficulty as to Lombardy having to pay her share of the Lombardo-Venetian debt . . . This morning I received an order for £50 . . . . The E. gave some promise about the immediate release of Austrian prisoners but he now finds this cannot be done until they have been condemned at Prize Courts.

Thursday July 21st

I was in the Embassy at 11.30. Cowley sent down an angry minute with a request that some of us should be in the Chancery every day from 11 till 7 and that we should be on duty by turns. He and Norton went in full tog to

229

St. Cloud where the Emperor received the Corps Diplomatique, the Nuncio made a short speech expressing the pleasure of the Corps at his safe return and the speedy re-establishment of peace. The Emperor replied with some little asperity in his tone that Europe had been unjust to him at the commencement of the war, that he was glad now to have an opportunity of proving that once the honor and interests of France were satisfied he did not desire to provoke further confusion or a more general war. A very important telegram from Rome passed through Paris this morning, a measure of reforms has been received by the French Ambassador at Rome to be submitted to H.H. The Pope is in secret negotiation with Spn Min^r to reconquer Legations. In case of distress he will probably retire to Spain. I was talking to Claremont this morning, his opinion is that undertaking the war was a mistake, but that the Kudoz? was that when after a series of successes and the prospect of further ones the E. discovered his mistake he had the necessary strength of mind to stop short and make peace. The mistake he says was counting on the Italians-that there were muskets enough for the Lombards in the French Armee and they never asked to lift one in their own peculiar cause . . . . . . Another Desp: of Cowley's states that a plan of reforms has been dictated by the Duc de Grammont to the Pope. The Pope is not willing to grant any reforms but those which are valueless. Wal: does not seem at all as sanguine as de Grammont of the chances of the Pope being induced to grant requisite reforms.

Saturday July 23rd

. . . . Cowley wrote a long despatch home on the discrepancies between the account given by the K. of Sardinia of the interview at Valeggio and that of the Emperor. One thing that goes to explain some inconsistencies is that the E. employed Plompton as his medium. We went down with Cowley on the 5.20 train to Chantilly.

Sunday July 24th

. . . . Breakfast at 9.30. . . . then joined the others in launching the small double boat contrivance. After various successful expeditions by Pennefather and Sandford S and I tried to get on together but in a few seconds found ourselves in the green water of the moat, which strongly resembled a thick peasoup in colour and consistency. We got very wet and uncomfortable to shore. I had to figure the rest of the day in a costume which was a sort of mongrel between a Mute's dress and an evening turnout.

Monday July 25th

. . . . Another Desp: referred to the language of the E. to the Corps Diplomatique which has given great offence to them. Odo Russell writes an interesting and amusing Desp: on his conv^n with the Pope-Pope's complaints of E. statesmen-explanations-warnings-this Desp: is marked Secret. Cowley has cancelled yesterday's Desp: about the discrepancies in accounts of E. and K. of Sardinia. . . . . An article in the Times on the freedom of the press gives Lord Palmerston a tremendous tongue-thrashing. A letter to Laurence from Kennedy gives his account of Austrian women.

Tuesday July 26th
An article in today's Moniteur institutes a comparison between the war and naval budgets of France and England in different years and shows that England has no cause for apprehension from the present attitude of France. This article looks ominous, ends with the remark that France has given England no cause for arming. E. must then have some other object in view. Such an article in an official paper reminds one painfully of the commencement of the rows with Austria. . . . C. telegraphed home to know what sort of a Treaty would be acceptable to England between France and Austria; the one preferred would be a Treaty confirming the preliminaries but guaranteeing the non-intervention of the contracting powers for the future in Italian affairs. Austria has refused to admit a Sardinian plenipo: to the negotiations. This seems to me to be the beginning of a series of difficulties arising out of so hurried a peace. The Patrie has this evening rather a bitter article against the English dread of invasion, alluding to article in Moniteur.

Wednesday July 27th
I spent most of the day in reading Adam Bede. This book fascinated me in a wonderful manner. I shall feel miserable for days. Hetty Sorrell interested me to a wonderful degree. I could have cried like any baby at her fate and I could not bear after I had read it to finish the book. It is a very weak point in this child's character to get so excited by ficticious joys and sorrows. I wonder is the effect a beneficial one. I felt that in Arthurs place I should have done exactly the same. What unthinking brutes we all are.

Cowley wrote home a good many Desps: I had to concoct one about a Rev. Mr. Hamilton which was approved. It appears from one of these Desps: that the Emperor has despatched M. de ? with an autograph letter to the E. of Austria to try and induce the E. to smooth the difficulties raised to the terms of the negotiation and strongly pressing a conference. Desps: from Odo Russell represent the Pope as obstinate as ever about allowing any interference on the Legations, but willing to grant some reforms. He has received the Emperor's letter. Cardinal Antonelli is the great bugbear to reform, according to Russell, and detested at Rome. . . . The English papers seem to have been thrown into great excitement by the article in yesterday's Moniteur. They look upon it as warlike. C. wrote a Desp: about it in which he states the comparison is not a just one, the statistics probably incorrect, the fair comparison would have been between the numerical forces of the two Countries not the cost of the armies. England pays her conscripts, France does not. E. keeps up forces in her colonies and besides has had an Indian war.

Thursday July 28th
There was an article in the Moniteur today giving notice of the Emperor's intention to place the army and navy on a peace footing; if this is really carried out, it will be a stopper on the fears of invasion on the other side of the Channel. This announcement is said to be the result of a Privy Council meeting, who on the suggestion of de Persipy to do something to appease the fears in England, met yesterday to consider what course they should take.

This, it is to be hoped, is the first fruits of their deliberations.

Friday July 29th

. . . . News has been received that the Pope accepts the greater part of the Reforms suggested by the Emperor. He is willing to introduce laymen into the Government.

Monday August 1st

I decyphered a long Tel: from Elliot this morning to the effect that the Neapolitan Government had been informed that Garibaldi with 12,000 men meditated a descent on some part of the Neapolitan States and had engaged steamers at Genca and Cagliani for that purpose. The Government of H.S.N. wished to know whether H.M.G. would protest against Sardinia permitting this expedition and if H.M's Fleet would allow it to be carried out. Cowley asked Wal: whether he had received any intimation to the same effect. He said he had been applied to by the Neap^n Govt. and had accordingly written to Sardinian Govt. but he did not believe there was any foundation for these apprehensions. . . . The Russian and Prussian Govts. are beginning to back out of a congress and say they have serious doubts whether it is advisable. Ld. J. seems inclined to join in it on condition that he first sees the Treaty of Zurich and that the Emperor of Austria takes part in it. He seems to expect that the Congress will not confine itself to the preliminaries of the Peace. . . . I was all day deep in "What will he do without it?" I am greatly interested in it. . It has had an effect on me, as it opens my eyes to the beastly inactive life I have been leading and I made strong resolutions to begin and work.

Tuesday August 2nd

. . . I finished "What, etc" today. . . . I could not help asking myself "What shall I do with out it?" when I thought of the chance I had got in entering this profession What I have done with it is precious clear. I have done worse than nothing . . . What a beast I am . . . I looked over some lodgings today with some thoughts of changing mine and trying to economize. I saw some very cheap but also very nasty. I shall go and look up some more today. . . . . I had a letter today from Lizzie who has been to Craigavad and the Prices. There is some talk of Tom's moving into the Derry Diocese. I wonder is that fellow really happy?

Wednesday August 3rd

. . . Bowyer Smyth, the new attaché, made his first appearance. He looks a decided muff but it is hard to judge a man by appearance . . . Some Despatches arrived from Rome, the Pope has been greatly hurt by a Tel: sent "en clair" by the Emperor to the Duc de Grammont in which the E. styles the Pope's answer to his letter as "derisoire". This has created great excitement at Rome. It was provoked by the obstinate refusal of the Pope to admit reforms into the Legations. Cowley and Wal: say the Emp^r sent off this tel: without consulting anyone and now regrets having done so. . . . Capital dinner but enourmously dear, 18 Frs a head. Afterwards we played Loo and I lost £16. My state of mind is something awful. I could hardly sleep a wink all night and vowed I never should play a gambling game again.

Saturday August 6th

. . There was very little work and Laurence and I got away at 5 and went down to dine with Lord Gray at St. Germain. We had a good dinner and enjoyed ourselves as much as we could have expected dining with two old people.

Sunday August 7th

. . . . The preparations for next Sunday are on a magnificent scale. The Place Vendome is to be turned into one enourmous amphitheatre and the Rues de la Paix and Castiglione ornamented with triumphal arches &c., Windows in these are going at 1000 Frs each. . . . .

Monday August 8th

. . . . I stopped most of the day in the Chancery, wrote out some Desps: in the correspondence book which is still 1200 in arrear, tho' Smyth is getting it up in fine style. He does nothing but write in it all day and never opens his mouth by any chance. . . .

Tuesday August 9th

. . . . Work very dull this morning. Bold British subjects dropping in every now and again for tickets for the Fete One I had the honor of an interview with has the coolness to wish to join the Emperor's staff next Sunday. He has brought his uniform for the purpose and expects the E. will furnish him with a horse. I told him he might apply to the Chef d'Etat Major if he liked, but told him that we had nothing to say to it. . . . I sat in the afternoon with Tota. I was disappointed in not meeting then as she told me I should the girl whose photograph in her rooms I have fallen in love with. She did not come. She is so pretty and, I believe, rich. She is now in a convent and she went to take the vows as a nun. . . . .

Wednesday August 10th

. . . . Cowley came up at two o'clock and Webster arrived soon afterwards. I lunched with the latter-(he has promised to lend me £25)- and then went to Chancery where I found lots of work. Cowley wrote a lot of Desps: by one it appears that Austria no longer refused her friendship to Sardinia. Sardinia is no longer under any obligation to adhere to the Treaty founded on preliminaries Conference at Zurich; they are not expected to last long. Great difficulties as regards to Duchies, the Fch. Govt. exerting all their moral influence in persuading the Duchies to consent to restoration of Arch-dukes. . . . L. received a Tel: in answer to one to Hammond asking for leave. H. desires him to proceed at once to Madrid; he seems rather "triste" about it.

Thursday August 11th

Laurence went down to Boulogne to see his people before starting for Madrid and so Adams and I are left almost alone in the Chancery as Smyth devotes his energies to the Correspondence Book, and Sanford never makes his ap-pearance till 4 or 5 in the afternoon.

Friday August 12th

Currie and Alderson made their appearance. They have come up for these fêtes. Applications are pouring in thick and there are very few tickets for

233

anyone. . . . Everyone is going out to St. Maur to see the camp which I hear is wonderful sight, but which I have not been able yet to go and see.

Sunday August 14th

Up at 7, dressed in white tie and tails and down to the Chancery at 9. There I found Lord C. and Atlee in morning coats, so I went back to the Place de la Madelaine, changed and got to the Place Vendome at 9.30. The Place had a most gorgeous appearance, one enormous amphitheatre packed tight with well-dressed ladies and gay uniforms (among them an Irish Militia uniform-probably Patric!) above us in front of the Ministere de la Justice and facing the column, the Imperial Balcony covered with crimson velvet and shaded by a crimson velvet awning. This was crowded with the members of the Court, among them Prince Jerome, Princesse Mathilde, Walewski, Hamelin, Hould etc. . After a short time the Empress's carriage drove into the Place amid the most enthusiastic cheering. She made her appearance some minutes afterwards in the Balcony with the Prince Imperial, the latter in the uniform of the Chasseurs de la Garde. He is a pleasing looking little child, yellow like most French babies, with pudding cheeks. His mother looks very nice, it was the first time I had any chance of seeing her to advantage. She has such a charming expression and was looking her very best. After this there was a long pause which I employed looking round at my neighbours. I was in the diplomatic gallery, Lord Cowley and Dusseleff below me, the Swedish Minister behind, some Persian attaches beside me in full uniform, and the American Mission a little in front. On the next tribune, the Duchess of Montrose and Lady H. Graham and lots of charming English faces, everybody nicely dressed and as happy as possible under the hottest sun I have felt for some time. Soon a rustling of dresses and a number of impatient and excited explosions of "les voila" made us all strain our eyes towards the entree by the Rue de la Paix, and in a few seconds the Emperor, at the head of the Cent Gardes and surrounded by his Staff, cantered into the Place on a beautiful charger. I shall never forget the magnificence of this sight, his horse prancing and rearing, the Emperor with a beautiful seat on horseback, his hat off and bowing right and left and everybody standing up and shouting at the top of their lungs, while the small prince stood up in his mother's arms with his drawn sword and saluted his Emperor Govr: who took up his position under the balcony.

And then the whole army passed before him, the wounded leading the way, these last caused great excitement, and the Empress and others seemed deeply moved by the sight. It was certainly a dreadful thing to see one of them, a young officer, walking in front of his men, with both his arms in a sling, others limping along on crutches and some scarcely fit to crawl along with their wounded colleagues. The rest of the proceedings was very monotonous, the troops took nearly four hours to march past and during this time we had some very heavy rain which did not seem to have a very good effect on the ladies dresses or tempers. After they all had passed the Emperor, with the Marshalls at the head of the Cent Gardes with the captured Austrian Colours and the decorated Colours of the regts: As he rode off, a sudden burst of sun lit up the scene and had a most stunning effect on the uniforms and Colours. It was a most successful thing altogether, and if one thought of nothing but the fact that an army was making its triumphant entry after a short campaign in which it had fought gloriously and gained some great successes, into this native town, with a victorious Emperor at its head, there was nothing wanting to the brilliance of this day's festivities, but unfortunately there were some things that one could not forget even in the gaiety of this dazzling scene.

Monday August 15th

Today was the great Paris holiday and a holiday it certainly was in the widest sense of the word. The whole of France seemed to have gone mad and to have rushed frantically up to Paris, every place is as full as it could hold, every body good humoured and apparently at peace with all mankind. Here the French Bourgeois, his wife and red faced family, there a Garde Nationale, painfully uncomfortable in his uniform and not knowing what to do with his musket. there a thorough-going Parisian fête hunter and there an unmistake-able British snob, everybody jostling everybody from morning till 2 or 3 o'clock in the night. We tried to dine at Voisin's with Gray who has just arrived and seems to be a very nice fellow, who does not think he compromises the dignity of the Secretary of the Embassy in associating and dining with unpaid attachés. . . . The evening's amusement finished up by our finding ourselves very happy and contented in the middle of a sea of other happy people carried on through the Rue de la Paix and Place Vendome and I must confess that till now I had no idea what illuminations were. To describe it would be out of the question, the effect upon one's mind was that of inspired admiration and wonder at what the deuce could make a nation spend so much money on their simple gratification. The Avenues in the Tuileries were beau-tifully lit up with coloured lamps in the most perfect taste, the Place de la Concorde was one blaze of light and sea of heads. . . . Alderson joined the Duchess of Montrose's party and drove round the town.

Wednesday September 7th

Here is a slight break in my unfortunate journal which has been slightly neglected since the 15 August. I am again reduced to the same miserable pauper state I was in when I first made the resolution to write a diary. Want of money brings me home at more rational hours and to more rational pursuits. Well, I have enjoyed myself these last weeks . . . A little more experience perhaps bought at a heavy price both in purse and happiness. I have none of the old tastes I had this time 2 years, or even this time 1 year. I am looking forward to seeing Papa and the girls on the 20th. They talk of spending only a week or 10 days in Paris, it will be something to me to have them here even for that short time. How I should enjoy it if I had not these difficulties which must come out and which will fuss the Major so much. I am afraid he will think I am quite done for and that he is the principal cause. God knows my resolutions to economize were sincere when I made them, but I believe He never made a weaker mortal than me as far as keeping them are concerned.

I have just come from seeing Norton, poor fellow, he is done for I am afraid. His secretaryship will be of little use to him. He could scarcely speak and looked so ill, it was such a melancholy sight to see such a handsome fellow lying pale and helpless on his bed breathing with pain and difficulty and evidently suffering terribly from weakness. He told me he owes his illness to Lisbon and warned me strongly against exposing myself to wet &c when I go there (which I hope to do soon), Tota takes such care of him. She must be a charming nurse, she never leaves him and is so fond of him.

As to political news-the great question seems to be what is to become of the Duchies? Austria made it a "sine qua non" now in the Preliminaries that the Archdukes should be restored. The Duchies, and surely they have a right to be heard in their own cause, wont hear of their restoration and call for Annexation to Sardinia. France is thus in a fix-it is true that she has given her word that the Dukes shall not be restored by force, but she accepted the clause in the Preliminaries for their restoration. The only course that seems at all possible is the reference of the question to a European Congress, to this Austria is not willing to accede. Naturally-for it seems tolerably sure that a Congress would give it in favour of the Annex[11] and to this the Palmerston Govt: seem inclined. Yet I think that one should hesitate before making Sardinia one of the most powerful nations in Europe, for this she must be if she obtains Lombardy and Tuscany with all the Tuscan ports on the Mediterranean. Prince Metternich has repeated interviews with the E. on this subject and proceeds tomorrow to Vienna. In the meantime the Conference at Zurich are at a standstill. In Italy the Pope seems more inclined to accept reforms though the negotiations to induce him to grant a separate administration to the Legations have failed. Some talk of the introduction of some sort of modified constitution with the Govt. of Naples.

Differences have arisen between Spain and Morocco and the Spanish Garrison at Ceuta has been reinforced. Spanish subjects there have been outraged by the Africans and it has been seriously taken up by the Spanish Govt: This received more importance than it might otherwise have done from the fact that the Emperor of Morocco was supposed to be dying and his death would have been the signal for disturbances in Morocco respecting the succession which could have given a great chance for foreign intrigues on the African coast, a state of things which our position at Gibraltar would not have allowed us to overlook.

I am thinking of changing to Lisbon. I have been spending too much money here and as Sir A. Magennis is appointed Minister at that place and Grey his greatest friend has offered to recommend me strongly to him, I have thought right to accept Grey's offer and have written to Papa about it. . . . . Another book I have been reading, "The confessions of Rousseau", there are some charming pieces in it perhaps a little too "emascule" as Pennefather says, and effeminate but still charmingly written. . . . . . My lodging is unpaid, and bills come every morning. How I wish I could manage to live like a sensible being and at some reasonable rate. I am afraid I am rapidly "going to the devil" by the stale old road that many a fool has gone before and which one knows pretty well by heart from the warnings and experiences of our elders. However, weak beasts, we are never satisfied till we have found it out by experience and then the devil is to get back again to where we started. As for me, I am afraid I shall never accomplish this but have a dreary prospect before me.

Now, goodnight and pleasant dreams to all good friends.

September 8th to September 15th

. . . . Poor Norton is not much better. The change in the weather can have done him little good for it is now cold and wet and we have strong symptoms of winter. . . . I am, of course, getting poorer and poorer; today (friday) I had to borrow 60 frs. from Adams 20 of which went to little A who is also hard up. Matters are coming to an interesting crisis, and a new European mess is brewing and this time on a very respectable scale. 1st in China, the French and English Ministers proceeding up the Reilco in order to ratify the Treaty, were fired upon the 20th June and three gun-boats were lost, 460 men killed and wounded, and the Ministers forced to retire to Shanghai. This was the first telegram which came to our hands and a startler it certainly was. The details soon followed telegraphed by Rumboldt, who was on his way home with Desps: It appears that the P.P. arrived on the 24th at the mouth of the Pielco which they found blocked up with stakes and booms; that the PP ordered Adml. Hope to force the passage which he succeeded in doing, when all of a sudden the batteries on either bank were unmasked and a slashing fire poured on them. The batteries were manned by Mongols, an enemy we met for the first time in the field. Attempt to land some of our marines in gun-boats was signally unsuccessful, the banks being formed of soft mud in which our men sank up to their middle, exposed all the time to a desperate fire. Adml, Hope is wounded and the affair is altogether a most signal disaster. Various conjectures are being made here as to the prudence of the attempt with the force in hands; the more sensible defer their opinion till the full details are known. All bear witness to the gallant conduct of Admiral Hope. The Allied Govts: are about to concert measures for teaching a lesson to these Chinese savages. God help them!

The second mess would be a more serious one, it is thought, if the first did not exist. It is the result of the death of the Emperor of Morocco and the excesses on the Spanish and Algerian frontier committed by the Moorish rebels which give a good pretext to the Govts: of France and Spain to enlarge their territory in those parts. This we declare we could not permit. The question is can we prevent it? Or shall we be forced to lump it? In the meantime Walewski pretends to treat the matter with indifference and carefully abstains from all expression of opinion on the subject.

As to the Duchies, Italy is working well and pluckily in the cause of freedom. France is, however, deserting her, and acknowledges the justice of the clause in the preliminaries for the rest[n] of the A. Dukes. Meanwhile the Conference at Zurich are at a standstill and the French Govt. are waiting anxiously for the return from Vienna of Ple. Metternich for the latest answer from Austn. Govt.

As to domestic matters I expect Papa and the girls on Monday. How

237

glad I shall be to see them. I hope there will be nothing unpleasant in the way of money matters. An answer has arrived from Magennis-no vacancy at Lisbon and if there is he is under obligation to Thurlow, but as Thl is anxious to return to Paris, a change could easily be effected.

September 15th to October 2nd

Since I wrote last we have had from Rumboldt more accurate accounts of the Chinese affair. R. states that Bruce acted up to and within the letter of his instructions; the affair was certainly most disastrous and the attempt extremely rash. We shall some day learn whose fault it was. In the meantime, poor Hope, who seems to have behaved most gallantly, is being pulled up by the English papers with not much mercy. He is I believe in a very dangerous state; his wound is more serious than was imagined.

The results of Ple. Metternich's mission is not yet made known tho' we have heard it confidentially. The article in the Mon^r has produced a favourable impression at Vienna. The E. of A. seems very anxious to arrange matters but insists on the restoration of the G. Duke of Tuscany, making the reforms in Venetia conditional on this. In the meantime the Tuscans have proclaimed Victor E. King, and carry on the Govt. in his name. Lord Russell seems to be inclined to the opinion of non-intervention, that a nation is free to choose its own ruler. Ct. Richberg comes down upon him with the Ionian Islands.[10] Ld. John will not have anything to say to a Congress which is to force a ruler on Tuscany without her consent. Austria asserts her rights of reversion and says she can never surrender them. Conference at Zurich at a standstill.

Morocco question in a more promising state, tho' Spanish Govt. are making new demands on the Moorish Govt. who are willing to make all reasonable concessions.

Lord Cowley has gone to Biarritz to discuss with Walewski Chinese Question, Regis Contract, Italy and Morocco. He has taken Atlee with him.

We are in daily expectation of poor Norton's death. He is now in a hopeless state and can last but a few days more at the most. What a scene for a death-bed. A father and mother separated for the last 6 or 7 years meet at the bed-side of their dying son. His mistress, poor Tota who has nursed him and kept him alive these last few years and who, I firmly believe, has done more for him than either of his parents who have been adding their family disputes to all his other trials. . . . Papa and the girls have been here for the last 10 days and I have been constantly with them. I do not quite know how they liked Paris. I bothered them tremendously about their dress which was very uncivilized, and I made them buy bonnets, gowns and mantles. . . . My people are gone. They went by the tidal-train, Monday October. 3rd. I was up at half-past five that morning to see them off. They intended going straight through London to Ireland via Fleetwood. I gave them an idea of our dinners by taking them to Durand's and the 3-Freres. The Major had a long talk with Grey about me and the result seems to be that I am to stop here as long as I can, he undertaking to help my allowance to keep me. He was very jolly and advanced me £25 of my next quarter.

Poor Norton received the last sacrament yesterday and was not expected to live through the night. We look up every morning to the windows half expecting to see the shutters closed and know that all is over.

Papa made me a present of Wheaton's Elements. I have some wild scheme of getting it up and also of making a precis of the Italian question, and have written to Dusayn for advice.

November 16th Dresden

I came here on the 6th of this month appointed unpaid and Antrobus moved to Vienna. My first feeling on hearing of my appointment was sheer disgust. Now that I am here and beginning to know the place, I am far happier than at Paris. Strange enough, Dresden is to be twice as gay as Paris. Comparatively nobody there here I flatter myself I am somebody, as I am the only other representative of H.B.M's Legation, after Murray, my chief.

The first day I came I spent the greater part in bed as I was pretty well done with 36 hours on end in a railway carriage, the rest in dining and looking about me for I called on Murray and Anthrobus and did not find either of them in.

Nearly a year afterwards in October 1860.

. . . . I begin my diary again. I wish I had kept it during the past year. It would have been curious to have compared my everyday life at Paris with my life here. I am very happy, in far better health than at Paris, occasionally hard-up; and continually haunted by thoughts of unpaid bills. I have been very gay all winter. The spring and the beginning of the summer I spent in Ireland, and have now settled down in charming lodgings which I have furnished and where I give occasional suppers. On the 11th October I began my journal again.

Thursday Work

The King of Sardinia is supposed to have closed the frontier and the Pope has refused proferred indemnity and it is thought will demand Peter's Pence. . . . . .

January 1862

. . . Three years since I began this diary and the negligent way it has been kept, or rather not been kept, is a true enough indication of the sort of life I have led.

The year that closed a few days ago has, I have no hesitation in saying it, been the happiest of my life. A year carelessly and fruitlessly spent like the rest of the years that are now dead, dead in all but the result that they have left, the ties that they have strengthened, the chains of habit that they have fastened round me, a year begun with laughter and dancing, ended in the midst of death and mourning, begun in the company of the dearest of friends and ended in comparative solitude, a year which, tho' it has done but little in the way of strengthening my character or developing any little good there may be in it, has done much to teach me its faults and bring me to a knowledge of myself. . . . . Many of my old tastes have been revived and improved by intercourse with kind and congenial friends, particularly my taste for poetry. . . . . I detect with horror a gradually growing coldness of heart and ingratitude towards the first friends of my life. Home ties are weakened and early principles are gradually being effaced.

In a worldly point of view, I have perhaps gained the last year. I have got rid of the awkward shyness I had at first, I have made many friends, I have acquired knowledge and I hope I am in a fair way of acquiring more. In German I am wonderfully improved, so much that I can now read the literature with intense pleasure. . . . . .

As we are in deep mourning for the Prince Consort, I have been but little in society and have kept away from the theatre. This Court is also in mourning for the Duc de Bija, the 3rd of the Portugese princes who has died in the last month.

Each day may bring us the important answer from Austria. I fervently hope such an unnatural war may be averted. . . .

The news from America continued to be pacific.

I took down, half by chance, from my bookshelf "The Diary of Machintosh" given me by my dearest Mother the night before she died; this affected me not a little. O, that she were still with us. She understood me and my temptations, I feel, and might have done much for me.

Duff and I are to act "Box and Cox" on Wednesday. I don't half like the idea as the piece is far beyond our powers and will be a failure I am sure. It is a melancholy souvenir of our acting last year. . . . .

Monday January 6th

. . . . . A telegraph has come in to the effect that the Privateer Sumptor has made some prizes, has sunk them and run into Cadiz-pretty warfare this for the 19th century.

Sunday January 12th

Our acting went off far more successfully than I could ever have expected. I was astonished at my own success and I verily believe my good friends think I am an actor. . . . The Yankees have given up the Comm^{rs11} with as good a grace as they could. I do not understand why they did not do so at once, it would have been far more politic. Another similar case has occured which I hope they will arrange in the same way. . . . . I had a nice letter from Lizzie in the good accounts of all at home, also a charming one from miss. F. from Paris, and a few lines from Fred G. who has become junior partner in a house of lawyers. I am very glad of it as it ensures him a good income. How I should like to be earning some money like him . . .

October 16th 1862

Little prospect of a peaceful settlement of affairs across the Atlantic. Lincoln's proclamation emancipating the slaves not only an uncivilized but a useless and impolitic one.

Prussian affairs looking bad. The lower House has unanimously refused to vote the Military Budget 'in toto' without details. The Herren-haus sides with the Govt. and the chambers closed. I do not see how the question can be settled. We have also had a meeting of deputies at Weimar and the National Verein at Coburg. Both seem bent upon restoring the Reichsterfapung of '49. the 1st favour of exclusion of Austria.

Quant a moi. I have gone through a good deal lately and passed my examination and will be entitled next January to draw on H.M.S. Treasury. for £150 p.an. I spent 4 months in London and Ireland. Saw old friends. All over with A.

October 18th Saturday

. . . In Prussia a report that Bismark has suggested to the K. to submit the Budget question to universal suffrage, a report that seems scarcely credible as we have no reason to doubt the popularity of the Deputies . . .

Friday October 24th

Just returned fro a rout at Ctss, Colloredos. Duke George of Macklenbg. there, a fine handsom man but very deaf; was presented to him. A pleasant party . . Mme de Cramer there and Mme de Blome and a lot of other pretty women. . . . Saxony desires a settlement of the relations with Austria on basis of Treaty of '53 and only accepts the Treaty on condition the Zolweirin is continued, otherwise not inclined to join Prussia unconditionally.

Dreadful storms in England. The Queen delayed three days in Belgium unable to cross.

2 new battles in America account as yet confused-Confederates said to have retreated. . . . 3 pleasant letters, one from Laurence in Madrid-souvenir of old times. . . . another from Tom in ante-matrimonial difficulties . . . Yesterday conversation at Club on travelling and eastern nations. Remark on similarity between words in Java and the Slavonic languages, e.g. word "mountain"

Saturday Oct. 25th

A telegram this evening to the effect that King Otto has abdicated, and gone no one knows where. Revolutionary Govt. named. Athens quiet. . . .

Sunday Oct. 26th

Went to a Jewish wedding-music good and ceremony very interesting. The bride remained during half the ceremony in an inner room surrounded by her bridesmaids and friends where she received an exhortation from the head Rabbi. The bridegroom meanwhile was led in state to the altar and placed under a canopy. After some time the bride was brought into the church preceded by torches and children strewing flowers, and placed beside the bridegroom, after which a long exhortation on the duties of married life was delivered to both of them and then after several rites of which the principal was drinking out of a cup, the blessing was pronounced and they returned to the inner room again in procession. The congregation, a most curious assemblage of Jewish faces in which the hooked nose was the most characteristic feature-altogether much interested.

Thursday October 30th

K. & Queen of Greece arrived at Venice. Mavrocordate, Prest. of Prov[l] Govt., D. of Leichtenberg, P[ce] Alfred and a son of K. Emmanuel spoken of as likely to be elected King (P[ce] Alfred-absent) Suppos[n] of Russian intrigue. An English and French fleet sent to the Piraeus. . . . . .

Cobden's speech on Maritime In~ Law proposes to exempt private property from capture at sea and prohibits blockade of con~ ports. The raw material of our food and industry come from America. The only three powers

w. whom we cd. go to naval war are France, Russia, U. States, France cd. always make use of Hamburg and the free ports and from Russia and the U.S. we draw our principal imports. In the Crimean War, we purposely abstained from enforcing a blockade until we had imported sufficient grain from the R^u ports. Deputation from N. of England showed what a state we should be reduced to if we strictly enforced the blockade of the Baltic ports.

Duel at Paris betw. D. de Grammont Caderousne and Dillon of the Jockey Club. Dillon killed. G. escaped. . . .

Papers full of the Greek revolution. The Gt. Powers did not guarantee the B^{n12} dynasty, but only the independence of the G^{ks} and their sovreignty-(1832). . . . An article in the Mg. Post reminds the Public that the Gt. Powers, Parties to the Treaty of London[13] stipulated that no members of the Royal families of any of the contracting powers shd. be eligible to the throne of Greece . . .

The D. of Leinster marries Miss Bridgman. He is 72:- the old fool. . . . .

Another speech from Cobden-old story telling the Manchester operators that they are the victims of the right of blocade, accused Lord P.[14] of being the staunchest of Tories and the most extravagant-he says that Lord P has held up the bugbear of F. invasion without any cause and thus involved the country in useless and absurd expenses and that they must not expect to gain any advantage if England were to go to war to get cotton, the cost of such a war would keep all the Lancashire poor for 19 years on turtle and venison.

Ld. Rt. Montague[15] married to his kitchen maid and sent her photo^{ph} to Mr. Cromie (!)

No more news from Greece; all quiet there apparently Times says that Duc. of Leichturtz cannot be elected unless a new Congress is held to set aside the article excluding members of Rl. families of Contracting Powers from the throne. Hopes that jealously of powers will not interfere with the interests of Greece.

November 12th

On Sunday mg. I received my orders to proceed to Copenhagen. A pleasant announcement particularly at this moment when Mr and Mrs M. return and the winter promised so well. However, "l'homme propose le F.O. dispose",-I must put on a pleasant face and go. Wrote to the Major for £60-pleasant for him. My successor is Labouchere, an original who studies in the hospital and buys up "les morts et les mourants" (a story of Pf's). . . . . .

The Prince of Wales coming of age was not celebrated anywhere officially.

The King and Queen of Greece recd. enthusiastically at Munich. The Queen cut-up, constantly in tears; the G^{re} Maitresse and jewels saved by the help of Digby and Drummond. The former was shot at and the latter attacked by a gendarme with a bayonet. Spirited conduct of a little Ct. Demoisselle d'Honneur of the Queen's, when called upon to give up her mistress or her country, she chose to stick to the former, saying that as she had attended her in happiness she would not desert her in her misfortune . . . Another story is that the King, seeing the Royal flag hoisted on an island exclaimed "I have still some true subjects left" and proposed to the Captain of the English steamer to land him on it. The latter is said to have refused to land H.M. anywhere but on Corfu, Malta or Trieste (a story of Mdme de Gise) on some authority. Fch. Minister behaved abominably our Minister admirably.

December 21st Copenhagen

I arrived here on the 9th having left Dresden on the 5th. My first day's journey was to Berlin where I slept . . . I started at 11 o'clock that evening for Hamburg where I arrived early the next morning. . . . On Monday started via Kiel and Coraver for Copenhagen where I arrived on Tuesday after a disagreeable journey. My first impressions most unfavourable cold and wind intense . . . . Next day paid my tournee of visits and the evg. went to a concert at the Queen's where I was introduced to all the Royalties and swells.

On the 17th I got into my lodgings which are far from comfortable. This place is certainly no pleasant residence in winter.

I wrote out the Dft. of the P^{ce} of Wales' marriage treaty. She is to have £10,000 per annum pin money and £30,000 a year in case of his death.

Here I find the other side of the Holstein-Schieswig[16] Danes indignant at Earl Russell's proposals-the idea of dividing Schleswig quite impracticable, only prop^n likely to be accepted is that of a common constitution in wh. the German element is to be more taken into consideration, but this must come from Holstein Chambers. We are to go into mourning for another year for the P^{ce} Consort.

January 1863

The New year has opened more peaceably than one could have expected. It has found the Federals in a worse state than ever, the accounts of the late battle at Fredericksburg are terrible and the loss almost unparalleled.

The affairs of Greece remain in the same unsettled state. England and Russia have declined to allow any member of their reigning houses to accept the crown and King Ferdinand[17] has refused it. England agrees to surrender the Ionian Islands when a legitimate monarchy has been established.

Here matters are by no means improved. The Holstein States are to meet on the 24th but nothing favourable is expected to result from this. D. had officially declined to accept Ld. Russell's advice, tho' backed by the approval of Russia. The Holstein States seem by no means inclined to meet the Govt. on their side half-way. No good can be expected as long as the present Ministry hold their seats.

The Marriage Treaty proceeding slowly . . . . I have been presented to P^{ss} Alexandra, our future P^{ss} of Wales. She is lovely and graceful, natural and charming in her manners and will certainly have a great success in England. I saw her first in a "Tableau" at the Landgraf's. It was the Landgraf's birthday and the princes and princesses had arranged a series of tableaux vivant, each subject to begin with one of the initial letters of his name. . . . . Afterwards we danced til 12 Xmas Day.

We had a ball on the 7th January at the Nicolay's (Russian Leg^{tn}) Very pretty and animée. A dinner on Thursday at our Legation.

PRINCESS ALEXANDRA

Without being a great beauty has one of the loveliest faces and expressions I have ever seen, lofty open brow, large clear grey eyes, a beautifully shaped nose and mouth with the most perfect and dazzling white teeth, chin strongly marked but by no means detracting from the symmetry of the lines of the face which form a perfect oval, the head admirably set on the most graceful neck and shoulders, not a fault in the figure, the expression full of life, nature and maiden modesty, the bearing princely, at times a little shy. I have seen her dressed in the most trying colours and her lovely complexion stood it amazingly well. Sometimes she is very well dressed, but not always. I danced with her twice, once at Mrs Paget's and once in the Cotillon at her father's P^ce Xian.[18] She dances well and seems passionately fond of it.

Tonight I have just returned from the Queen Dowager's fresh from a most touching scene and one that I am not likely ever to forget. It was a concert given as a farewell to the Princess. The last piece performed was "The Farewell" composed by Dr Bach, set to the music of one of the oldest National airs of Denmark. It consisted of a solo and chorus; the whole company consisting of the parents, relations, and the Court Society, mostly friends of P^ss A's childhood, stood during the performance and in the last verse, where her country is supposed to take leave of her praying her not to forget little Denmark in all the splendour of her new Kingdom, the whole of the Society joined in the chorus, and nearly everybody was touched to tears. P^ss A. herself was much effected. It was one of the most touching things I have ever seen. It was no empty court paid to the P^ss of Denmark, the future P^ss of Wales, it was the expression of the genuine sorrow of her oldest friends and dearest relations, of her countrymen and countrywomen, among whom she had lived and been loved in the most liberal sense of those words, (for here the limits that separate Royalty from their subjects are far less defined than in any other country and seem only to spring into existance on State occasions) at losing the brightest, loveliest, dearest jewel in their Country. God grant her lot may be as happy as we all pray it may be and as we all feel she deserves. She leaves Denmark in tears and will find England awaiting her with smiles and English welcomes.

The Royal Party leave this on Thursday at 3 o'clock and are to arrive in England on the 7th March. Paget accompanies them.

With this account of the touching Danish farewell to Princess Alexandra, Charles Stewart Scott's private diary ends.

To her contemporaries, the glittering marriage of the lovely Princess Alexandra from tiny Denmark to Edward, Prince of Wales, so socially attractive and heir to an empire "on which the sun never set," may perhaps have seemed a Cinderella like romance. The reality was very different.

The early marriage of Prince Edward was regarded by his parents as essential. Queen Victoria disliked her eldest son and considered he would never be fit for his future responsibilities. His sister, Crown Prin-

244

cess of Prussia, was very fond of her brother. Nevertheless, in letters to her mother, she said she thought he was not capable of warm and lasting affection and that, much though she loved him, she did not envy his future wife.

With the hindsight of later generations, free to read confidential letters of the time, the marriage will appear to many as a tragedy. Princess Alexandra's mother's fears, roused by gossip, were allayed by Queen Victoria herself, who told the Crown Princess what was to be said to the anxious mother and by whom. This included the assurance that Queen Victoria and Prince Edward had never disagreed and that the Queen was very confident that he would make a steady husband. Queen Victoria wished these assurances to be conveyed by Lady Paget, wife of the British Ambassador at Copenhagen.

The marriage took place in England on March 10, 1863. The following month, on the April 25, the queen wrote one of her incessant letters to the Crown Princess saying that B.[19] had not improved since she last saw him, and his ways and manners were very unpleasant.

Charles Stewart Scott, whose private diary ends here, will appear again several times in this book.

Notes

1. Foreign Office.
2. His brother
3. His sister Elizabeth, Mrs. John Lyle.
4. His sister.
5. Napoleon—French money.
6. Rumors.
7. Count Walweski, French foreign minister.
8. Rumor.
9. Victor Emmanuel.
10. Under British protection since 1815. In 1859, there was agitation for union with Greece.
11. American warship forcibly removed four Americans (two Confederate envoys and their secretaries) from a British ship. Only the tact of the prince consort's amendment to the British note averted the serious risk of war with America.
12. Bavarian.
13. Great Britain, Prussia, Austria, and Russia. Treaty of London, 1840.
14. Lord Palmerston, originally Tory, was at this time a Whig and the prime minister.
15. Lord Robert Montagu, son of the duke of Manchester, had first married John Cromie's only child, Ellen.
16. A long-standing dispute with Germany that ended in war in 1863 when Prussia and Austria invaded Holstein. Denmark, unaided, was defeated. Prussia took Schleswig and Austria Holstein.

17. King Ferdinand, who refused the crown of Greece, had married the queen of Portugal in 1836 when he was prince of Saxe Coburg. He received the title of king in 1837. In 1862, the queen was dead, and he was free to accept the crown of Greece had he wished to do so. Greece would have liked Prince Albert, Queen Victoria's son, and offered him the Greek throne, but he was barred from acceptance under the Treaty of London. Greece then asked England to nominate a suitable candidate. England suggested Prince William George of Schleswig-Holstein-Sonderburg-Glucksburg, brother of the Princess of Wales. He became king of Greece in 1863.

18. Christian.

19. The Prince of Wales was known to his family as "Bertie."

36 / 1867—George Lyle Writes to His Sister Ellen, Now Mrs. Bedell Scott

Glencairn
Craigavad
29th May, 1867.

My dear Ellen

I am always very glad to receive a letter from you, you write with such a warm heart in it, & I always put your letter in my waistcoat pocket to warm my cold heart. As you seem to take an interest in our gettings on here, I will tell you all about it. We have breakfast at 8 sharp go into town by 9 train, & there is I am glad to say plenty to do. come home by 4.30 train take a walk along the shore or about Craigavad till 6.30 *then dress for dinner* always. at 7 o'cl.-after dinner light the horrid cigar, set the beautiful musical box agoing, sprawl in armchairs and read the Quarterly, Saturday or such like till 10.30 then off to bed. You will say not a very interesting or exciting existence. However that is only in quiet times. We have had James and his wife here Edward Ward and Capt. W. Ward for a week or ten days at a time. The Hon. & Revd. Henry W. off & on ever since I came here nearly. I have only been one night alone in the house as yet. I like it very much being quite independent, go & come as I like, quite Bachelor fashion. It is lovely here in the evenings in fine weather or indeed any time, the Steamers & Ships going past & the view so pretty, there is always variety. I do not feel melancholly now the way I used at Knocktarna, quite out of my element, an idle man in a Parsons house. Godfrey says I will be quite independent *yet*.

We saw poor Uncle John[1] on his way through Belfast, he looked very thin but not very bad-not half so bad as I have seen George Chichester look times out of mind-Mrs. C. was not of course nearly so cheerful as she used to be, but if he gets better she will come round again I see the fun still in the corner of her poor eye. She is a regular brick when all is well. I am glad you are going to Portstewart; it will be good for you and the little one-I long to hear it talk, her eyes always looked as though she was full of it, as no doubt she was poor thing & now her time has come maybe she wont let it out in volumes. It is a wonder Bedell survived the walk over the heather, he says to me "Stop, Stop, not so fast, *you* did not preach yesterday" They seem to have had a pleasant party at Knocktarna last week, with Ned[2] & the Chichesters-Lizzie says Mother is very low in spirits & even Ned and Harriet could not stir her up & she wants *me* down to her, I can keep her alive she says, so next week if possible I mean to go. There is nothing new here as you may suppose-not even a fine day, or rather a day without rain-I am afraid the farmers are in a bad way, particularly up in the mountains, the Hotelkeeper in the Highlands writes me to say it is winter *there* yet. It is little better here. I wish you would tell the young lady you spoke of that I am likely to retire on a large, small, fortune, & am quite young yet-younger than Uncle John when he married anyhow. but dont fix the day or hour, just yet. I saw Ned just a minute passing through Belfast-Sarah I have not seen or heard of yet. James & wife are at Bangor Castle & intend I hear going to Kircubbin on a visit for some days next week. Excuse this scrawl, give my best love to Bedell & the little one & believe me as ever

Your most afft. Br.
George.

On George Lyle's return from China in 1856, he stayed at Knocktarna until it was decided what he would do next.

Eventually, he went into partnersship with Frederick Kinahan, one of the fifteen children of the Rev. John Kinahan, Rector of Knockbreda. George Lyle and Frederick Kinahan had both been apprentices of William McClure & Son at the same time. Together they founded the firm of Lyle & Kinahan, wine merchants in Belfast, which proved to be a very successful venture. After the death of its founders, the firm of Lyle & Kinahan was carried on by the descendants of Frederick Kinahan.

In 1867, George Lyle was 46, and Ellen Scott had one child, Aimée.

"Uncle John" was John Cromie, who was married four times and was 75 in 1867.

George Lyle never married.

About 1867—Frances Mulholland writes to her Sister Ellen Scott.

Poole April 20

My dearest Nell,

I received your letter a few days ago in London where we have been in lodgings for nearly a fortnight The boys joined us the beginning of this week but the weather has been so unsettled that we preferred remaining in London where there are evening amusements, to going to Bournemouth as we had intended, We started however on Thursday, encouraged by 2 fine days but here we are shut up in a stupid inn with the rain coming down in torrents We came here direct that we might have our heavy baggage on board the Egeria in which we hope to have a cruise next week and as we are within an hour's drive of Bournemouth we mean to go there when the day clears up a little. The boys are all looking extremely well and most pleasant and agreeable, the girls are also with us as both their governess and maid are gone for a holiday so we are a goodly party 9 in all-Andrew and Harry go to Eton on the 8th of May and I think it likely we will keep Alfred at home for a term until we find a desirable school for him as he does not return to Brighton. Our plans are still between returning to Ireland and going to Hissingen. If war breaks out it will decide us, but if not I have no idea which we shall do. We are much disinclined to travel so soon again but the Waters of K were so useful to John last year and he is rather out of order now that it is a great inducement to go We enjoyed our tour in Spain extremely notwithstanding the little annoyances inseperable from travelling there. One of the most trying is the extreme *dolessness* of the people their want of punctuality and all the other every day virtues and their apathy on all occasions when they have been most provoking. Indeed the chief requisite for a journey there is a boundless supply of patience. I wrote you from Valencia all about our pleasant stay in Majorca. We did not enjoy our stay at Valencia so much partly because neither of us was so well and partly because we did not at the time know exactly what to see or do. You know of old John's dislike of starting after breakfast for a days sight-seeing. Now at Valencia the town has few objects of interest (except a fine collection of pictures by Ribera or Spagnoletto as he is generally called) and the thing to do is to go a few miles by train when there are charming hills ruins and other beauties to be seen, We saw some of these from the Railway to Madrid the country for about ten miles is rich beyond expression, just like a very productive kitchen garden but almost at once you leave all this and enter the most barren dreary hilly country which lasts almost without variety until you reach Madrid. I was interested in seeing on every farm about Valencia its little plot of nice ground, all a few inches deep in water which the men with a very primitive looking plough drawn by a mule or ox were turning up the mud. At one side of Valencia near the sea there are extensive tracts of rice in an old swamp but the government limits the quantity grown in the inhabited parts as it is so unhealthy a crop Cotton has also been grown in the neighbourhood but not hitherto with much success, The irrigation is one of the wonders of Valencia It was all done by the Moors long ago and is very ingenious Our first view of Madrid was in the early morning as we travelled all night and I wished so much I could have sketched it but we whirled by and I found that view was the only one at all suitable for a sketch. The city when you are in it is not at all imposing There are scarcely any fine buildings and nothing very noticeable in any way. There is one fine square in which our Hotel was which is always crowded with people chiefly men which gives one a great notion of the idleness of that sex in Spain All Spaniards have such an amusing way when you complain of the wretched way things are managed of shrugging their shoulders and saying C'est l'Espagne which is supposed to explain all deficiencies-The pictures are the pride of Madrid, the collection is really splendid almost all chef d'oevres of the first masters. I went 5 or 6 times and never enjoyed anything so much We spent day at Toledo which is a most interesting town. It was the old capital for a long time and contains remains of all the different races which have predominated in Spain as I had not seen Granada I was much interested in the Moorish remains, the Cathedral is most beautiful and the cloisters adjoining it I shall never forget. We got a few excellent photographs which I hope to show you some day. We joined a very nice American family on this excursion, whom we liked extremely, they were Northerns but the very opposite of all the Americans I had met before, they were, however, desperately prejudiced against the South The most interesting excursion we made was to the Escorial It is about ½ hours by train all which time you are ascending and when you reach it such a scene of desolation surrounds you The place is about 4000 feet above the sea on the slope of the Guadderama mountains the hills are close behind the monastery and still capped with snow, beneath is a great expanse of barren moor as far as the eye can reach thickly strewn with blocks of granite in all manner of strange shapes & often of great size, Imagine in this desolate spot an immense building composed of great blocks of granite dark & cold and ever in shadow, almost uninhabited and giving the idea in its immense halls and solitary galleries of a gigantic city of the dead, it contains under the Church a large Mausoleum of great height like the Panthion at Rome surrounded with niches containing marble sarcophagi in which are the bodies of Charles V Phillip II and their many wives and other kings and queens the Escorial to me stands separate from all the other things I have ever seen before as peculiar and interesting to the greatest degree I am afraid I have bored you with this long letter but you are the only person I know who likes descriptions so I reserve them for you. We met several persons at Madrid who knew Charlie Scott[3] and all spoke in the highest terms-Our address will be for some time Yacht Squadron Castle Cowes Love to Bedell & kiss to the babe You dont tell me a thing about her

Notes

1. John Cromie, brother of Harriet Cromie, George Lyle's mother.
2. Edward Lyle, brother of George Lyle.
3. Charles Stewart Scott, who was transferred to the embassy in Madrid when he left Copenhagen.

Feb 11th 1869-Mr Scott says he never remembers a year which has appeared to him so long as the last-I suppose it was from being so eventful. in things he was deeply concerned about-the way our Church was attacked-the injustice and virulence-seemed to bow him down at the time, and the resigning the parish-cost him much thought-Bedell dined at Mulderg today-Presbyterian Ministers but no priests, they are so busy with the Jesuit Fathers at Clady. The public House keeper there says that the money that has been spent with him is wonderful he did not know there was as much in the country-Many Protestants went from curiosity to see their services-The money is to build a great Chapel at Clady-Mr Galbraith of Comber came while we were at dinner and staid till after 6. . . . . Aimee amused us with the fuss she was in to see the strange gentleman and to get on her mauve frock-When he asked the names of her dolls she told him-Louise-twins & penwiper.

1869 June 11th . . . . . Mrs S in todays letter says Dr R is gone over to a great Manchester demonstration against Mr Gladstone's bill Last Saturday the 5th many important events were occurring-Our Derry meeting-about 70 from this parish went in-About 4 or 5000 at it good speaking-Mr Boyd of Kilmacool the Times say was the speech of the day-W. Sims a young Belfast man made a very eloquent speech-Willie Scott a very pithy one-Tom Scott seems disgusted with t he orangism of Derry people-The evil bill and debates on it have stirred all the poisoned elements of strife on all sides Orangism is a power on the right side and in self defence may be most valuable. though it is sad the party bitterness that has become resussetated-The Lords met on Saturday to consider whether the will of the Commons was to be resisted and a large majority 70 or 80 agreed to give battle. May they be given courage and strength-Our little prayer meeting last night was a happy one. Bedell addressed them on the story of Moses during the battle with Amalek-and showed how similar the present attack has been-and what God thought of Amalek's conduct then. Prayer was Moses weapon-H urged the people to hold up the Ministers hands by their sympathy and prayers The decision of the Lords as far as it goes an answer to prayer-Our petition of 534 names the secretary said was to be presented immediately and wished as much care and trouble was taken by others.

Last Saturday also John Mulholland won a cup £100 by winning the yacht Royal Club races on the Thames The Prince of Wales presented it-the news sent by Atlantic cable 1000 words would appear as soon as in the Times at home.

June 25th-Edward Chichester and the three girls left us today after a most pleasant visit of ten days. They are such sweet good children, sensible and anxious to do right-I hope Aimee and Georgy may be such. They were so delighted with our pic nic to the Glen with Mr Walker who was the Irish Society deputation-a wonderful little soldier of a man quite a worthy descendant of his ancester of Derry celebrity His encounters with priests whom he withstood to the face. were very exciting-The quiet and simple way the society works merely paying any R.C. countryman who can read to teach others-giving a lesson to a man at his plough or anywhere they may be-Our day at Ardmore and the Lodge was very pleasant-but Aimee has been so unwell with a feverish stomach attack since-She had complained occasionally of pain in her stomach for some time back and was fretful, if I was out of her sight but I thought it was only being a little spoiled. She had a headache coming home and became dreadfully flushed and feverish in the night-We gave her a warm bath and a little senna. Dr Moore in the evening came and ordered a grain of calomel. and antimonial wine, 15 drops every four hours till cool-*a plunge into warm bath* for *half a minute* after which she cooled greatly. and slept well. Senna at four in the morning-her stomach very sick which relieved her. a warm linseed poultice in flannel to her stomach when pained.

Oct 12th-Our school feast at Ballagh about 60-We sung some hymns in Church. Emily Ould played the Harmonium Fanny & I leading-then the feast and great games afterwards at Banagher During dinner Fanny got a letter from-Henry giving a very bad account of their father, a matter of days-it is a sad shock-the accounts had been rather better-since his return from Malvern. he had got a bath chair and was able to sit out in the garden-Emily says latterly-spoke much of his death being near and made every arrangement accordingly, and requested of them all to choose what remembrance of him they would like-his patience and gentleness also great-and love of reading his Bible-

May 1870-Bushfoot-

God has answered all my prayers for my little pet. As I sat beside her little cot every night before going to bed I said "Lord I gave her to thee before she was born, and ever since she was born She is Thine-Make her one of the Saviours lambs-give her Thy grace and Thy Holy Spirit from her infancy" Sometimes the thought flashed into my mind as I did so-God sometimes takes those who have this grace-early to himself-but then the thought came I will trust him nevertheless I must have her saved-He is loving and merciful. and I thought He would not as it were requite my prayers that way-I wanted to make him as it were responsible for her salvation by giving her life to him. First felt unwell Dec. 8th died 14th

17th . . . . When she was three she and baby were sitting on my bed while I was dressing and I listened to her while she talked-"Little brother do you know who gave you everything? God-He gave us Grandpapa, and our papa and Biscuits and everything" I had said to her when she came into my room in the mornings-Who makes the beautiful sun to shine? and she came in other mornings with the same question to me-and then I think its God with a loving smile. . . . . One night when she was not going to sleep for some time after being in bed I heard her repeat two lines to herself "From his shining throne on high comes to watch me where I lie" and the same lines I heard her repeat during her illness. One night in the Autumn when I took her up to bed.

Before she undressed she stretched up to whisper some question to me in a very low voice about Grandmama Lyle. I forget what it was but I said "I dont know dear". She then whispered "May I ask God when I go to Heaven" One day while walking with her Grandmama she said "Grannie Jesus has'nt blessed me" alluding to his blessing little children and Grannie said Oh yes at your baptism he blest you and she was quite satisfied.

Her Grannie said one day to her. When the poor beggars come hungry to the door Mama will give them bread and she added and Doty will put jam on it-. . . . . Her truthfulness was quite wonderful. One day she had thrown some milk on the floor in the dining room. and I met her and Granny coming out of the room and I said What is all this-Grannie wished to screen her and said Oh she did'nt intend it at which she said earnestly Yes Mammy I did intend it-When she had been naughty and I set her on a chair She was sometimes out of temper for a moment but very soon she had her arms around my neck—During the first days of her illness she said one morning I think Mammy ought to be a little punished I said Why? Do tell me. But she would not. - I did not know what Nurse afterwards told me that the Sunday before her illness-she had been left with Nurse while we were at Church. She took some little piece off the plate Nurse told her not-and Nurse gave her a little slap on the hand. which distressed her and she cried-A little after she went over to a chair and knelt down where she staid a little while-When she came back Nurse said What were you doing-"I was praying to have my naughty head taken away-I want to go to Heaven" Nurse said Oh Yes when you grow up and then you will have a home of your own "Oh no she said I will never leave my own kind dear Mammy-I want Mammy and Pappy and little brother all to come to Heaven Wont it be joyful when they find me there and her eyes filled with tears When she came down to dinner-she said to me Mammy I was a little naughty and a little selfish when you were at Church But Na Na punished me so you need not. When her cousins Emily and Fanny were summoned away on their Fathers illness-She prayed every night-God bless my dear cousins and comfort them-After she had risen from her prayers one evening she looked earnestly in my face and said But they wont be *very* sorry. . . . . . Minnie Rutledge wrote that the last Sunday she was at Banagher she took little Amee with her to Church. . . She said to Minnie This is the happiest day of my life, the only sorrowful thing is that Mammys not here I would like to go over those mountains to see Mammy-Minnie said But you might lose your way What would you do then?-I would pray to God and He would point with his finger out of Heaven and show me the way—Another time "Mammy-will I be afraid to see Jesus?" I said "Oh no. He looks so kind and loves little children" But then the bright light round his face she said so bright you know to look at-I said "it won't be too bright because your eyes will be made strong to look at it "and she was satisfied. . . . Two different times I said to her "Would you like to go to Jesus"? She said "Yes" . . . During the last hours she was very restless but quite calm and collected-not an expression of fretfulness or discontent on her countenance to the very end She saw us all about her-all she loved-and then said "I would

252

like to see little Sonny" She felt sight failing for she said to me twice "Light a match" which her Papa did and she was satisfied-She said near the end "I am very sick" and "Now we'll all take a nice little sleep".

Each year since her birth 1£ given as thankoffering to the Ch Miss Socty[1] Her last birthday was kept by having the 8 little orphans to tea.
1870 Bushfoot.
June 23rd-Yesterday Mr Scott drove over from Craigdhuvarren. . . . I said "Mrs Maguire told me Lady M had said to her 'This is the happiest time of your life while your children are young and you have them with you' He said 'The happiest time I think is when you are near the haven and have a clear knowledge of God's character. This is ground confidence in his character. Nothing in ourselves. we are weak sinful creatures' ".
1870.
Dec 11 Sunday. This day last year our little darling was ill. . Have I learnt the lessons this sore stroke was sent to teach? I do earnestly seek more real faith-and humility-Oh I stretch up to reach nearer to that beautiful place where my little pet is now and feel Oh so thankful to my dear Jesus for what he did for her and in her to bring her there-Lord give me humble submission and thankfulness.

Mrs. S. was Mrs. George Scott, Ellen Scott's mother-in-law. She and her husband were staying with the Rutledges, who had a house on Carlingford Bay.

Willie Scott was the father of Kate and Annie Scott.

Tom Scott, a brother of Willie Scott, was, in 1867, a curate of Derry Cathedral. Later, he became Rector of St. Augustine's in Derry.

The Orange Order, the most important of a number of secret societies in Ireland, is a Protestant body, taking its name from William III, who was Prince of Orange. It originated in Ulster at the end of the seventeenth century. Its aim was the maintenance of the Protestant ascendancy in Ireland. Orangemen formed a powerful defensive force at a time of extreme sectarian strife when many excesses were committed on both sides. In Ireland, the past is never forgotten. Danger, though sometimes dormant, always lurks beneath the surface. These facts kept sectarian bitterness, distrust, and fear alive through continuing generations. Religious bigotry's terrible death throes toward the end of the twentieth century torture Ulster as these words are written.

Mr. Walker's "ancester of Derry celebrity" was the Rev. George Walker. He was one of the thousands who took refuge in the city when James II, with his southern Irish supporters and his French allies, besieged that city in March 1689. As food ran out in the overcrowded city, thousands died of starvation and disease. Lundy, the Governor, prepared to surrender and ordered the gates of the city to be opened. Twelve apprentice boys closed the gates with the full support of the weakened and suffering garrison, inhabitants and refugees within its walls. The Rev. George Walker, already commanding a regiment, and Maj. Henry Baker took over command from Lundy. They refused to discuss any terms for surrender. In spite of appalling conditions, the city was eventually relieved, but not until the thirtieth of July. The Protestants of Ulster had saved their province for King William and themselves from probable annihilation. Ulster has never forgotten the Apprentice Boys of Derry. Their action is commemorated each year with a march of their modern successors. Each year, also, Governor Lundy is burned in effigy as a traitor in the city that he was prepared to betray to its enemies.

The "evil bill" of which Ellen Scott writes was Gladstone's Bill for the disestablishment of the Church of Ireland presented to the House of Commons on March 1, 1869. The bill also included the confiscation of all the Church property and its redistribution in accordance with the terms of the bill.

Gladstone had long been interested in Irish affairs. He suffered from a guilt complex regarding British conduct in Ireland. He was particularly anxious to see the disestablishment of the Church of Ireland. He maintained that the church only ministered to one-eighth or one-ninth of the population. The actual position was that the Church of Ireland ministered to a large majority of the population in Ulster and a minority in the rest of Ireland. In 1867, Gladstone was leader of the Liberal Party at Westminster. In December 1868, he became Prime Minister after an election fought and won on the church question. Declaring, somewhat optimistically, "My mission is to pacify Ireland," he immediately set about the attempt, the "evil bill" being his first step. There was much opposition to the bill in Parliament and in the country, the Liberal Party not being united on it. However, the Commons passed the bill. At first, the Lords rejected it by a large majority. Later, the Lords passed it. The Church Act became law on January 1, 1871. From that date, the Church of Ireland became a voluntary body, and the legal connection between the Church of Ireland and the state came to an end.

This was a breach of the Act of Union. The Church Act was the start of a long struggle on Gladstone's part to achieve his worthy aim. Whether his efforts contributed to peace or merely intensified Southern Ireland's permanent political instability is a matter readers can judge for themselves.

Notes

1. Church Missionary Society.

When I was at school, between the age of 13 and 14[1] it was the time of the war. Reserve regiments were sent to Ireland and one was quartered at Ballyshannon—Extraordinary set they often were—one story told by a labourer—gives an example he had seen one of these soldiers going into a shop. buying a ½ dipt candle. scraping the tallow down and spreading it on his bread.

When I was at Torquay I heard of a person of the name of Lyle[2] being clergyman at Brixham near-Torquay-He heard I had been enquiring and called on me . . . He had 1500 in his Sunday School at Brixham—Adults came to his school. He said fruit came in at first by dribbles but afterwards by armfulls The day I called to return his visit—(he kept pupils) he had Lord Cranbourne with him. He was blind. He told me his sense of touch was so obtuse that he had great difficulty in teaching him.—Bedell was a little fellow at the time and he asked to feel him. he was a son of the Marquis of Salisbury—Lyle told me that he often wished his father could make his next brother eldest son as he felt his own infirmities made him unfit—He lived to be a man and was very clever.

When I was at Balteagh there was a farmer Boyle by name. He was the only farmer a Church man of any extent I found him sitting by the fire without clothes with a blanket over him He had been so for ten years—he was a very pleasant man to sit and converse with except on the subject on which he was demented. He spoke with such pleasure of the former times when he said he used to sit at a good fire. He had an impression that everything was going to be sold out and that he would starve. His wife could not give him his clothes as he would have wandered away. so he sat with a blanket round him. One time she had to pay the rent and she went for it but it was gone. She asked him but he would give her no satisfaction—She did not know what to do. At last after several weeks (She knew he prided himself on his honesty) she accused him of taking a pound out of the rent at which he fired up and said to her pointing "Take that stone out of the wall" She went and found it. I said to him one day "Do you believe that I speak the truth?" "Oh if an angel from heaven were to come in at that door I would not more believe him"—"Now if I brought you an assurance from Mr. Beresford the agent that he will not turn you out would you believe me?" He said "to be sure I would". I went to Mr. Beresford and got the assurance and brought it to him He got quite well in mind from that time. He received the truth and died some time after in humble faith. His wife fell into a desponding state of mind after he recovered and was in a spirit of consternation thinking that she was lost—

One time I was living at Portballintray and I heard my landlady with whom I had lived at Dungiven for many years was ill. I reproached myself for not having seen her for some length of time. I dreamt I saw her lying lifeless on the floor. I saw her smashed as one would see in a dream in some way—French was staying with us and I said to him at breakfast I had an extraordinary dream about Mrs. Adams last night—When the letters came in I saw one from Alex Ross—It began "we are in terrible distress about Mrs. Adams attempting to destroy herself". Her mother lived at Magiligan—she had also a dream about her which made her very unhappy. She got up and begged her son to saddle the horse and ride over. He pooh poohed her and sent the old woman to bed but she either dreamed it again or was so unhappy she insisted on him going and he said as the next day was market he would go and get his business done. He got up rode over to the cottage knocked at Mrs. Adams door but could not get in After waiting some time he pushed open the door and found her in the very act of committing suicide—just being in time to prevent it. She did go out of her mind or must at the time have been so and went to an asylum. On one occasion she fell over a tub and hurt her hip—she fancied she was the Patriarch Jacob until the Governor said to her It is not fit for you if you are Jacob to be in the women's ward. This opened her eyes to see the absurdity and she gave up the notion.

At that time we had a diocesan Home Mission 30 years ago—I was out upon it and Stack was with me One of the places was Gorten six miles from Omagh—It was a fair day & the sermon was arranged for 10 o'clock I took a sermon which was on my mind on "Wist ye not that I must be about my Father's business"—It was a plain practical sermon opening with the narrative We are to regard God as a Father and our work as being about his business—I felt it was a cold congregation and came away not happy I heard no more for 15 or 20 years. McPherson was on his way to Tuam and to stop at Castlebar where his bed was ordered. He felt lonely and asked for the clergyman's house and invited himself to drink tea. He found him a very intelligent good man he began to talk to him about this country and asked if Mr. Ross of Banagher was still alive. Who is in his place? McPherson said Mr. George Scott. to that he said "that was the first man gave me a new thought about the Church of England Till I heard him I thought the church was all orange lodges—and nothing of reality—but there was an ardour and earnestness about Mr Scott and I felt differently from that It was the turning time in my life".

Capt Pringle with his brother and Jeffries and Erskine who wrote afterwards when converted a beautiful book on "Internal Evidence" were a sceptical clique in Edinboro'—The brother of Capt Pringle was in service in India as an engineer officer. He was so clever at engineering, he was brought home from India when the Statistical Ordinance Survey of Ireland was being completed to see that it was all right. When he came back some of his sceptical friends met him in Edinboro' and said to him in a scoffing way "Do you know that your brother Tom has become a saint and was called upon to expound Scripture to a party of ladies the other night"—The reply of Capt

Pringle's brother was—"Well whatever Tom does he will do well"—which silenced the scoffers.

General Oliver was brother of the good Lady Lifford and he was the person who first led Pringle to examine the Scriptures—Finding Pringle obstinate in his sceptical views "Well remember the Proverb Pringle 'There is a way that seemeth good to a man but the end thereof is the ways of death' ". He looked and found it twice repeated It was fixed in his mind He entered on a course of Scripture reading which resulted in a total change of his views and of his character. When Pringle was on half pay he came on deputation to Balteagh for the London Hibernian Society—afterwards he was called to service again and was quartered in Ballymena and he came all the way to Balteagh to see me and we had two very happy days—One day at Mess in Dublin, some officers engaged in profane conversation and Capt. Pringle offended by some remark and was challenged—It was then thought a cowardly thing to refuse but Capt Pringle stood up at Mess and said—You all know from your knowledge of me I am no coward but I will not fight a duel for I fear God. He rose and left the room—Two young officers encouraged by his conduct rose and joined him, They three knelt down to thank God for making them to so act—When the Regimental accounts were being looked over later by the Duke of Wellington he observed this account of Capt Pringle's conduct—It made him resolve to put an end to duelling and after a time it was made illegal.

Notes

1. 1804 or 1805; Mr. Scott was born in 1791.
2. Mr. Scott had been at school with him at Portora. This Lyle was not related to the Lyles of Knocktarna.

39 / 1876/1877—Extracts From Ellen Scott's Diary

Aug 8 . . . . Bedel thought that praying for everything wd not do in all cases.—
When we got to the boat Princess Wales every cabin was engaged . . The previous days had been so stormy that there were a crowd of people. The old man who kept the book of Berth Bedell & I spoke to & when he heard our names it seemed to occur to him we shd be attended to so after whispering with the stewardess a gentleman was asked to vacate a cabin & M & I entered in it with joy. Poor M.[1] was sick all night. She is getting experiences of life . . . Arriving in London ⅛ past 3—drove to Huttons—waited an hour. Fine strong goodtempered looking man—took M's feet in his hands—looked steadily at them—said there is dislocation your foot is all wrong—Bedell

257

seemed greatly afraid of being taken for a patient—explained over and over that he was only one of the party—Hutton appointed us to meet him at ½ past 9 next morning at Dr. Bailey's 9 Cavendish St. . . . Next morning an old lady went in to be operated on before us—& in about six minutes they came to Minnie leaving the old lady to recover from the gas—M sat back in an armchair Dr B put a pad over her mouth to which a tube was attached communicating with a great black indiarubber ball full of the gas (Chloral ether)—after about a minute he signed to H who jerked the foot up and down & sideways till the joint came in with a crack—M awoke quietly with a look of wonder—saying Oh what a lovely dream—It seemed like ages Dr. B said ''Have you read George Elliotts books It was under laughing gas she got the subject of her last book 'Ronda' ''read it''—Hutton prescribed ice to be applied for ½ an hour. then friction with the hand—then linen dipt in brandy & water & covered over for an hour—and again at night—plenty of hand rubbing—I had no money! & H told me you give Dr B 2 guineas. I said when he came in for the fee—Will you allow me to send it? He looked a little suspicious! but shewed us out civilly.

Wotton Rectory

Augt 11th—The son & heir born at Wotton at 12 o'c today—''Our little Aimees birthday''—May he be born to the same glorious inheritance as she was—Bells ringing all day.

Aug 12th . . . Yesterday when we arrived George[2] had his pony carriage at the door . . . We drove thro' a stream and up a green mound to the post. left the carriage in Dorking took a fly met numbers of people returning from Holmwood Vicarage Arriving. we got out & thro' an arch. into such lovely grounds covered with beds of flowers and a terrace commanding a grand view—Mr Steere member for East Surrey with some clergymen were making the little boys run races—some children were blowing bubbles—Mr Wickham a most benevolent elderly gentleman was looking very happy & busy—he gave us some cider—& we walked thro' the gardens to a lovely sloping hill where were some swings going. It was altogether a perfect picture of English country scenery—and the happy meetings of neighbours and schoolchildren.—The church quite close to the house. In the evening Mae and I. Bedell — M^r N Moore walked to see the Bonfire—across the park to the slope near the house. The sky was lightened by it. and a crowd were enjoying it—a band playing. Arthur & Alfy[3] had been forbidden by their tutor—but they slipt off and were watching. to avoid being seen by him. All of a sudden the people turned round and cheered and we knew M^r E had come out to speak to them—G.V.C. was with him and he says M^r E was shy about speaking. saying he did not know what to say—G told him that what he had just told him viz that there had not been an heir born in Wotton for 200 years would be interesting to say however he thought it safer to say for very many years—As Mae and I walked she reminded me of snakes which are common and a gentleman had been bitten by one on Leith Hill lately—of which he died—a gentleman had told her they were about his house and even came inside—We saw some stars fall. Harriet drove out this morning—all going on well Frances[4] quite cool—the baby—a fine little thing—brown hair—dark blue eyes not very short upper lip—Frances sent her love and that she was delighted we were come . . . . found letters here from Mad[lle] and got one today from her and little George—Poor little boy—he was so disappointed we did not wave from the train—He had put on his red cap that we might know it was he—he wept a little but has been happy and very good. He put his boat to sail in the bath saying Mama is on the sea so my boat must be sailing too In his prayers he added Do keep dear Papa & Mama safe.

Augt—12

George & Bedell drove me over & left me at Wotton—No carriages allowed within the enclosed part—I walked to the great door which was open pulled the bell several times but no one came at last I walked in to the foot of the stairs & fortunately saw Harriet she took me to the nursery—it and Frances room belonged to John Evelyn and had not been occupied for long but a door now leads—you go down into the room by a flight of steps—The cradle. lace and pink was placed on the bed and Mrs Love presided. The dear little sleeping babe little knew all the thoughts it had raised Mrs Love shewed us a card M[r] E had sent up to her—M[r] Liardet to see the baby if possible W.A.E.—so M[r] L saw it and quite approved—M[r] E also writes to Mrs Love that he will pay the nursery a visit at ½ past 8—I think it was every morning. . . . Mr E came back and sat down beside me and talked so pleas-antly—He said I can scarcely realize this that has happened—he spoke so nicely and kindly—Harrie went up to put on her hat and returning said Frances would like to see him at ½ past 7—He had other arrangements made but said he would give up his ride in order to see her then—H & I walked thro' the shrubbery and sat down in a summer house M[r] E has made lately—she told me all about Ada's affair Every step of its progress and how nearly they broke it off in consequence of a letter—The family history well written would be more than ordinarily interesting—I told Harrie there that I had had a letter from Mrs Hamilton in which she said. The Chichesters are I think instances of "Seek ye first the Kingdom & all other things shall be added" Harrie said Well I do think it has been our desire I reminded her of on one occasion when they were at Campden a great struggle of mind she had written to me about when the girls had no prospect of seeing any society Temporary duty in a strange parish and without acquaintance that the O'Neills[5] and Mulhol-lands[6] invited them urgently to send the girls to spend some months—when there was to be company—Harrie wrote to me. that she and George after much thought had decided they would trust the case in God's hands rather than to send them into worldly society alone. Harrie said "I do remember it is in my diary. . . . . .

Sunday 13th. . . . . In afternoon George drove me & the evangelist M[r] Harris to Broadmoor a pretty drive thro' long private roads thro' several gates. passed a lovely spot with lake and grand trees and a lodge where the Duke of Norfolk used to come for shooting. but now has let it.—a few men—were seated under shelter of a high hedge—and a few women and boys gathered and some chairs were ranged and M[r] H first prayed. then we sung a hymn then spoke a long time on 22 Psalm Very nice and well expressed. Easy to understand and earnest a good deal of repetition chiefly on Come to Jesus as you are—for pardon for holiness for heaven—ended with prayer The people were very attentive—Bedell was greatly pleased more than I expected and thought what M^r H said wise and free from objectionable extremes—

Augt 16th . . . . . Harrie appeared in the waggonette immediately after breakfast and hurried me off. with her & George to meet Ada at the train. A young Miss Florence Braithwaite with her—both were in the pale cream silk with fringe very cool & pretty—Ada looks strong but her complexion not good i am glad she is married and well married . . . In evening we met . . . . & a doctor who had been in the French army—a little boy Bernard Arkwright sat next me and talked very pleasantly about Harrow. He drank sherry and glass after glass of claret—It frightened me to see a boy of 12 with a taste beginning so early—he seemed very clever—plays classical music and paints. . . . . Next day Tuesday . . . up before 7—off at 9—Took a fly at station not knowing that the driver being dressed in blue wd make us have to pay double. . . found Huttons room full of patients We after waiting about 20 minutes were shewn into a small room behind He received us kindly—then looked at M's foot worked it about said bones all right—made her walk three times across floor without crutch said it was a very successful case—I said the pain in her side you were to examine—so he placed her on her back on a sofa—made her leave her leg quite loose then bent her knee up and jerked it suddenly to see if there was anything wrong with the hip bone then said the pain must be muscular—the foot is to be bathed in vinager and water with strong salt in it seven times a day and next Tuesday to see him again in London and have a rubber—Back at Wotton at 9 o'c . . . This afternoon drove with Bedell & G.V.C. in the Wotton Wagonette to Albury Lady Rok-wode Gage's—she with her sister the Duchess of Northumberland were daughters of Mr Henry Drummond. The Irving etc. & member for Surrey She was waiting to welcome each visitor A delicate looking plain featured old lady. not a happy expression She has had great sorrows—George says Her husband Sir R.G. a R.C. treated her very cruelly and she had to get a separation. She introduced us to an old gentleman and asked him to show us a wonderful old chesnut This was as Mr Adams told us afterwards Mr Hoare married to Miss Cardale prophetess and speaker of tongues—I think he said she had been the chooser of the 12 apostles and at their death the coming of the Lord is expected. They are all dead but two Mr Adams told us. Mr H Macneile preaching when a young man at Albury originated the Irving heresay here—itwas taken up by Mr Drummond and there is a considerable body of them now. their church is beautiful. They disown Irving calling themselves Church of the Holy Apostles They hold a spiritual real presence in the Sacrament Their hourly expectation of the Coming keeps them up as Mr Adams said to a high degree of faith—The Duke of N. has adopted their views—There was a military band—aviary full of silver pheasants and doves—besides cages of green paroquets and canaries. A great number of well dressed ladies—Lady Antrim, a son and daughter—Plenty of refreshments ices etc.—tea—fruit—claret champagne. . . .

Mad^{lles} story of little George. She reproved him for nibbling his nails—to which he answered I have been told that the Chinese let their nails grow so long that they can tie them round their arms with cords. Would you like Mama to come home and find my nails like a Chinese? . . . . .

18th—Harrie came in Wotton large carriage took G Helen & me to call at Deep Deane. Mrs. Hope's about ½ mile other side of Dorking—a lovely place. such trees—such sward—such pretty lodges. spangled with flowers—Her daughter the Duchess of Newcastle married to a dissipated young man just for a title they are little together Her eldest son a boy of about 12 was let fall by his nurse when a small child—and his arm only being broken was badly set—some years after he was taken to Paris—to a surgeon there—who said he must break it to set it again—the poor boy's strength was unequal to bear it and it has destroyed his health . . . Harrie George & I had a long talk today—very interesting—One thing G said Mr E had said to him the other day "I have had a very unhappy life with my brothers. but Frances has brought an interval of calm and happiness" Certainly she has been a blessing to him in every way—Many other things.

Sunday Aug 20. . . . . Had a quiet happy day. Long talks with H She complains of her head not being equal to teach now as formerly and her memory not so good & felt very unhappy about it. I told her it was the usual and common state at her and my age—and would pass away after a time which comforted her . . . . . . she told me much that grieved me about H.M.⁷—Worldliness and vanity—selfishness & heartlessness—seem nurtured in her by those who should earnestly check—It is very strange how a person of F's observation and many wise qualities should act about her children as she does—We sat some time with Frances—in her large picturesque room with a large bow at one end—she looked so pleasant and her playful laugh was cheering—the dear little babe drinking his fill May it choose for a better inheritance as well as that to which it is now heir—M^r E was very agreeable he liked the Greek Church better than the R.C. and told us when he was in Cephalonia—a Greek priest was very civil & took him about shewing him what was interesting & introduced him to the Archbishop told him it was customary for those of his own religion to kiss his hand but he wd be excused however Mr E did it—and when he was parting with the priest—he gave him the kiss of peace.On Saturday H & E & G—drove into Dorking—brought Ada & the elder Miss B⁸ from the train—They went to lunch at Wotton— We went over in the afternoon—Mr E sleeping in the armchair—Miss B sitting up beside him mute Mr Braithwaite soon arrived and we took a little walk thro' the shrubbery to the bathing place. Mr B. does not seem nice enough for Ada There is no mistake about it He gives me the idea of not having much mind or any thing interesting—rather conceited and very delicate however Ada seems satisfied and that is the chief thing. . . . . Mr E talked a great deal at lunch about the picture of Duchess of Devonshire by Gainsboro that had been stolen & said the jokes of the Club attributed it to Lord Dudley himself—or Lord Derby's kleptomania at which

261

he laughed heartily. Afterwards I was sitting with the baby on my knee after F nursed it—it looked so nice Mr E came in . . . . sat down beside me and looked intently at it saying I have had little experience of babies & I must confess it puzzles me. he catches at every word said about its looks or healthiness and seems to think by day and dream by night about it He told H he dreamed that the baby had been taught to catch mice and his brother Charles caught it up and glared at it fiercely at which he himself rushed at him saying "Give me my child" . . . Mrs Love cannot understand the absense of enthusiasm in F[9] about the baby and it quite offends her. London. Fords Hotel—Aug 23† . . . Took Handsom to Hutton—waited some time about 10 people in his room—Told me to bring Minnie as there was one thing he required to look at which was the muscle below ankle—found rubbing woman with her . . . H looked at her foot worked it up & down in a sudden jerk said it was all right & he was to send his bill. . . . Aug 24 Train just left Crew where we had excellent coffee & lamb, potatoes biscuits Mad[me] Bye . . . met us at Euston Station I was surprised she is nicer looking than I thought gentle good face. Had to go out in tug steamer. An hour in reaching Thomas Dugdale—nice cabin open at top—Md[lle] knelt down to pray before going to her berth Found Imperial full went on to Royal—Left Md[lle] and came off to search for B.—arrived at boat He called from the deck "Number One" in a business manner & I found the luggage was only being got out The Captain finding the boat was going aground swung her round which stirred B. greatly . . . took our luggage to N.C.R. station., the children & Mad[lle] waving on the sand-hills—so thankful to find all so well. . . . .

Aug 27th Dr Hannay preached good sermon on Marriage in Cana . . . Sunday Sept 3 Banagher . . . Yesterday morning left Portrush at 8—Mad[lle] came with me to train Certainly her affection and grateful remembrance of kindness—is not common—& most attractive person and fine character she will be a sad loss—Yesterday there was great excitement at the junction—prisoners being sent to jail for rioting at Downhill such agony of parting what drink brings—Rather disturbed meeting James & Emily driving from H. Lyle's Lodge She is so artificial & insincere in manner . . .

Saturday 10. . . . Spoke to G papa this evening. . . . the Rutledges dividing between Pellipar & this—Maria being so delicate & unable to manage— I do desire to act right about this. . . . . . Mad[lle] Turin left on Tuesday last. . . . Looking back for the last two years I cannot perceive a fault in her conduct—great attention & care of the children—never seeming weary of them though often having them with her for six hours together always making them happy and good—She writes from London that she is very sad about Albertine Portal who tho' so ill has engaged herself to a young Frenchman whom she does not care for but only accepted because the other girls called her "une cruelle" . . .

Sept 12 Craigdhu—Mrs McMeehan came in to me to the drawing room—very serious and told me—the master[10] has had an upset—come in & see him—I went—he was lying on his side on the couch—they were applying lint dipt in salt water to the part just below the shoulder which looked bruized—He was exclaiming the shoulder is off—it is certainly off—It will take an experienced doctor and so on—We cheered him as well as we could by telling him we did not believe it was off and that he shd have the best advice I went up and told Mr Scott He agreed to telegraf for Latham, then after sending it I went into the drawing room and Minnie said she had been told he was no surgeon so I went to Mrs M and said which do you think best—to send for Miller or Latham She thought for a moment and said Miller so I sent a second telegram By ½ past six a telegram came from Miller saying just returned from Country will go by 7 train morning By 7 a telegram from Latham—cannot come till 9 morning so if the accident had proved more serious and a bone been broken what shd we have done Dr Moore was sent for and pronounced his opinion that the bone was not off or the collar broken—At first he seemed to feel much pain when moved but less towards evening and eat his dinner when fed . . . The accident occurred when H hastily pulling the one wheel on the raised side of the road He liked one a little higher than the other but—done hastily it went over—He has agreed with G to confine himself to B . . . Sept 14—Dr W Miller came for breakfast pronounced that the collar bone was fractured but the parts not separated this with the bruize is all It was the shock from the bruized part hurt the collar bone A cushion of cotton wadding with oil silk round it is placed under the arm and it bandaged tight to its side—It is quite wonderful how calm & cheerful he was reading his paper when I sat with him after it. . . . The other morning George awoke saying "J'avais un si triste reve oH si triste Je revais que je J'aurais Mad^lle Turin encore" He came into my bed but seemed too ready to weep to speak—Again thro' the day he said "C'est si triste de retoruner a Banagher et de penser Mad^lle ne sera pas avec nous oH si triste. . . . "Bedell preached a very lovely sermon on "Thanks be unto God for his unspeakable gift" G'papa & Grannie sat in Kings seat, both heard well and seemed greatly delighted He said to her. I dont know when I have heard such a sermon—and coming home he said to me. I think that is the best sermon Bedell *ever preached* at least that I have heard. . . . I dont know what makes little Thomas Wall look so cross at me He evidently thinks I have wronged him somehow. Poor little John Wall has been the last two Sundays with us. . . G'papa said I have often told the story of the martyrs who when asked by the Sherriff Should we pray to the dead said No Master Sherrif there is no warrant in Scripture for that Again the Sheriff said Do the departed pray for us—I do not know Master Sherrif but if they do I will be praying for you in half an hour—Mrs Jeffries so like her sister Margaret Paton and look also of Elizabeth—she spoke several times of being glad to meet me—that she has so often in her sisters letters heard of us—that she had spoken of her great happiness and great affection for her husband—How it brings back the past—more sadness &regret in this than any other feeling She says Anna has gone to Stutgard—that she speaks in her letter of very interesting preaching she hears there that latterly there is more of a religious tone about than formerly that her brother John whom I remember so well is now in Columbia where he holds a very high position next to the Governor

263

wants Anna to go out to him, as his wife who was a pretty little widow Mrs
St. George with some property deserted him seven years ago to see after her
affairs & has never gone back—not liking colonial life Duties must sit
light. . . . . Heard this morning from Louise and also from Bedell of little
Ada Scott's happy flight from earth and all her care and sorrow and
pain . . . What a world of change and contrasts it is—A paper comes from
Wotton with a great account of the christening of the little heir—such
joy—such congratulations—such affectionate addresses from
cottages—workpeople—household—tradesmen—. . . . . . . Lizzie brought
little Tom here yesterday to see Dr W Miller—He has the same opinion as
Latham—the danger of the inflammation at the bone—injuring it so that it
will supporate and come away—He shd keep it always up. . . . Heard from
Lizzie from Tarbys Nassau St—Had seen Surgeon Porter—satisfactory old
man quite understanding Toms foot—is to be brought forward by poultic-
ing—Just what Latham and Miller wished to avoid—I do believe it will be
the beginning of long suffering and perhaps lameness—Wrote to beg she
would have other advice first—Dublin close and noisy—poor little
Tom. . . Miss Mary Ross came today to dinner Mr Ogilby came into the
drawing room and was so agreeable and pleasant—so clever and piquante in
remarks and playful—He began to tell her of his accident which she had not
heard. . . . Mr O is greatly interested in Evelyn's Diary the last few days.
Such a nice copy in 4 volumes—with portraits of the eminent personages—some
of them from paintings at Wotton—Grandpapa was greatly pleased today at
a very grateful nicely expressed letter of thanks from Mr R.E. Ogilby to his
cousin James who has given him a handsome gift . . He does seem an amiable
man who has encountered vicissitudes—Minnie had walked a couple of
hundred yards the last two days & not suffered—I am sure it is her health
& not sprain now. . . Mad^lle says the children are tres sage—Had a long
account from H.E.C. of the dinner given at Wotton to tradesmen of Dorking. . . .
Knocktarna Oct. 7. . . . . Went to see some of the people—Mrs H Campbell
folded her hands and shut her eyes and shook her head saying Oh you're
greatly changed so I was rather surprised by James saying You look better
than when you were married Am I really better? Sometimes I think quite the
contrary—
Oct. 8—Sunday—Took Lizzies class and enjoyed it . . . John taught all the
other classes I played harmonium and during service felt tears often rising
so many memories it recalls. . . Called to see Old Mrs Spier—very warm
always in her welcome. Mr Bell Rector of Banagher in Kings Co come as
deputation for Jews—a very attractive earnest looking man. . . .
Oct 28th—Lovely weather still—Trees beyond imagination tinted . . . George
and Bab were examined before their Papa for the first time—and he says they
did so well—Certainly Mr McG has a very pleasant way of getting them on
all as pleasure . . . Mr Scott spent four days this week visiting on foot for
hours each days in different parts of the parish—taking sandwiches.
Nov 7th Tuesday . . Had note from Lizzie—Still poor little Tom not well—Dr
L has twice probed the foot & it is trying—Then she says John was looking

264

poorly worried—It is a life of perturbation—Then she has had a painful correspondence with the lady in Paris who sent her little Marie The girl has turned out badly and she is blamed Certainly it would have been right to put such a child as she was under some one dependable servant as both Nurse & Fraulein disliked her and were always stirring up Lizzie against her—Little Sarah Murdochs mother came on Friday staid the night and left on Saturday I allowed the little girl to go with her mother to Dungiven—tho' it was sweep day and she was as cross and odd the whole evening. This morning M.A. told me she would teach her no more that she had said to her "Dont speak to me you that was brought up by the P.O. Society[11]—I called her in and gave her notice & wrote to her mother—

Nov 17th Friday. . . . . I staid in bed with bad cold this morning—Minnie told me that at breakfast B said "I wish I had taken post cards with me it is always hard to write every day" little George said "Oh yes I wish you had On Sunday Mama was quite nearly mad not getting a letter—but the morning she got your letter with "It was saft but not too coorse and saying you were not a bit scrapy Oh she was in such joy" . . .

Dec. 9 Saturday. . . . . I paid poor John Lockhard a short visit—His starting eyes and short breathing show what is at work—Yesterday we drove in Croydon to Killaloo—Margaret Lyle came to meet us and young Mr Brown of Comber who with three brothers live out in Nicaragua Central America—He gave a fearful account of the ignorance and superstition of the people. . . .

Dec 14th . . . This morning I had a letter from G.V.C. telling of his sufferings—Last Monday night I awoke suddenly in the night after a vivid dream—I thought a number of us together I observed looking out of the window a light like a star darting hither & thither and was conscious it was an omen of evil—then a gigantic female figure appeared in the room silent & shadowy and meeting us as we walked across it—waved her hand and pointed to George Chichester—I felt his hand grow cold in mine—I did not feel anything more of fear or sorrow but ran backward and forward holding little Aimee in my arms saying "My baby & I" I told this dream at breakfast and once or twice again saying I never had a dream like it and thought it must mean something—& saying I wish I could hear from Wotton. . . . On Wednesday . . when we returned a letter awaited me from Mad^{lle} Turin—beginning Mr Chichester a beaucoup suffert—de son bras—and his letter of this morning tells of it all—A week of great pain in the right shoulder treated as rheumatism or neuralgia, then submitted to a doctor who found the bone dislocated—under chloroform put in by two doctors His nerves so shaken as to make him feel very near death especially one night at one in the morning he has lived on teaspoonfuls of liquid for ten days—and it gives him pain to write the letter . . . B & I drove in Croydon after dinner to see Willi Thomson of Fincairn poor old man—groaning with great sickness and very weak not having taken food for a week—very anxious to live—had an attack a year ago. The warning I fear not taken to heart. His son a pleasing looking young man came with us to get beef tea & brandy & magnesia but I fear they will not be much good..

Dec. 15 Poor Mr Thomson died this morning . . M's dislike & want of sympathy about our little meeting Ihave felt much—She told me so—and that she also hated teaching the S. School but she always tried to do it as well as she could . . .

Jan 3 1877—Yesterday we all went to Pellipar for a Xmas Fete—George had not been looking well crying in his sleep swelled jaw & gum so I gave him a grey powder which has been very useful—and the change to Pellipar seemed to do him great good . . . At Pellipar Charlie, George & I took him to see what had been kept a great secret only darkly hinted at, so as to fill him & Bob with curiousity viz a little cart waggonette gardiner is making for the donkey to draw It is so nice in George that whenever he is given any present his first word is nearly always "How very kind it was etc. ."Had a letter from Sae[12] . . . says she is sorry to hear that Harrie is feeling great weakness Jan. 30 . . . Heard from Helen M of Andrews intended marriage to Miss Amy Harriet Lubbock

Feb 10th Saturday Heard from Harriet today—in London with Ada—who she describes as very happy—Reginald devoted to her and filling her sphere so well The Evelyn baby still suffering from rash but lively and merry—She says Andrew Mulholland had only known Miss Amy five days when he proposed—so it is rather a risk—Sir John Lubbock is author of a clever book on prehistoric man—Harrie says she was going to have a long seance with Lady Macnaughten whose sermon is being printed . . . Miss R told me she had been much surprised at the way c talked when she was present about three weeks ago—against the way—wealth and poverty were distributed. such foolish talk she said that she thought perhaps it was the disease affecting his head—Curious. Yet not curious as I had asked to be guided what to say at our little meeting I spoke so much about our ingratitude to God and that it was the great feature of our natural heart—also what return have we made for benefits countless ever since we were born— . . . . . . The other day Jemmie Thomson brought in two little young rabbits he had caught for George—so they were in the crochet room for two days, but wd not eat or drink so little George called me up after he had been some time in bed to beg I would let them out for their Mama will be looking for them—so next morning the children got Jamie to let them down the rabbit hole in front of the door—Yesterday we left George in the afternoon with J.T. in the garden soon after he came in exclaiming I do so love Jemmie Thomson he is such a nice man—he told me so many secrets and shewed me a hens nest with three eggs in it . . . . On that Saturday G'papa felt chilly and could not shake it off—In the morning of Sunday when I went in to see him he spoke with difficulty, said you need not mention it but I believe my time has come—he complained of great pain in his side close to the heart—and the phlegm in his chest would not come up Mrs Scott was in the room afterwards when he said to me "You can tell her afterwards that I know whom I have believed and I am persuaded that he is able to keep that which I have committed unto him" I happily had linseed meal and mustard in the house and applied a large poultice to his side and gave 10 drops of Hippo wine which caused slight wretching & both were of use—He desired to see Mr King after Church and also to be prayed for in Church . . . . Mr King came & I heard G'papa say to him "I think this is likely to be my end" Mr King however came out from him saying that his voice and altogether did not appear to him like death and that he had finished by saying "I will see you tomorrow at Pelliper"!! at which he could scarce keep his countenance Mr W Miller came about six and was very satisfactory. He said it was an attack of slight pleurisy—that the skin was too hot and ordered a medecine to act on it and also aperient pills He brought with him an expectorant mixture with pills to be used with it. and ordered me to continue the poultice. sprinkled with mustard—Louisa & I called on Mrs Ross yesterday she looks wretchedly—& Canon Ross worn out and old—Robert—whose intended going off to California (which is breaking his parents heart and health) seemed quite easy and unanxious—wearing the gold chain & locket with inscription presented to him the evening before by members of the cricket club at an entertainment given in his honor—His companion going is a son of a sadler—Magee by name!—They told us that poor M'Clelland who had lost seven children a few months since had fallen into melancholy and had committed suicide. His poor wife had at first consented he shd be sent to the asylum but the neighbours persuaded her that he was all she had left and not to part with him. so like the cruel kindness of neighbours:—

March 28—Took children in to Derry—Gillies talked a great deal about the danger of drawing teeth even when the new ones are growing behind as there is such a tendency in the jaw to contract would not touch Georges told me to bring him back in three months recommended oatmeal stirabout to make bone—white bread very un nutritious that even cattle were not fed so as to make good wholesome meat forced grasses etc.

Ap 2nd Easter Monday—The children have been acting April Fools all day—quite excited at their success

Apr 13th. . . . John R told us J O'Hara had written to his father advising his son not to join with the other clergymen who were to sing at a public concert in Coleraine to get funds for a rowing club—I scarcely understood the matter thought J O'H had taken up an idea that concerts were wrong. and I rather laughed at it all as a foolish notion—but Mrs Ross seemed to think it was not quite the thing and when I began to consider it. I quite felt that the young clergymen. were far better out of such secular and public entertainments so I will write to Mrs Ross & tell her so

Apr 16 . . . . B & I sat some time with G'papa He is wonderfully well but his voice weak.

Henry Drummond was the son of a banker and was himself not only a banker but also a writer with particular interest in religious subjects. He took a great interest in politics. In 1847, he became member of Parliament for West Surrey and continued to represent that constituency until his death in 1860. He voted conservative and made a close study of all political questions. He was one of the founders of the Catholic

Apostolic Church and, as he grew older, became more and more involved in its work. He became one of its office bearers, went to Scotland as one of its "Apostles," and while there, was ordained as an "Angel."

Dr. Hannay, who "preached a good sermon" in August 1876, was for a time a rector in Ulster. He was also a writer under the nom de plume "George Birmingham," one of his best-known works being the novel *Northern Iron* set in Ulster.

"Emily is so artificial and insincere in manner." Emily Ward, daughter of the Hon. and Rev. Henry Ward of Killinchy, had married James Lyle, a widower, in 1861. She was then eighteen and he was forty-three. Handed down in the Lyle family is a tale that James Lyle had not intended to marry Emily Ward but meant to ask someone else to be his wife. Emily, however, misinterpreting something that he had said, rushed to her mother and told her that he had proposed. Extracts from the diary of Emily's sister, Caroline Matilda Ward, throw some light on the situation. Caroline Ward was staying with her married sister at the time, Arabella (Araby), who had married Robert Edward Ward, First Secretary at the British embassy at the Hague. Louisa, mentioned in the diary, was the eldest and seems to have been the beauty of the family.

The Diary.

Thursday 27 Dec. 1860   Heard the most astounding intelligence from Mam about Louisa which shall not be written till it proves itself neither mist nor thin air.

Mon. 7th Jan '61   Heard from Mam concerning the tragical end of what I noticed last Thursday week, and which in consequence shall be buried in my bosom.

Fri 18th Jan '61   Heard from Mam all not quite over

Tues 19 Feb '61   Heard from Mamma the J.P. tragedy finally impossible for 2 years on one side no engagement on the other—so it's over.

Fri. 12th Apr '61   A letter from Godfrey[13] to Araby in which he orders her not to teach me to flirt but engages to conduct that part of all our education himself Made a promise to Araby to marry Jas. Lyle! If he ever asked me!!!!

Sun. 16 Jun '61   Heard from Emily an amusing rhapsodical letter the summon substance being that Jimmy had returned and that Louisa having refused she herself intended to walk into her shoes and captivate his fancy and 'Fections'.

Fri. 21 Jun '61   Heard from Mam an account of the picnic she is still sanguine about Louisa and Jimmie! owing to a sentiment he let loose while moving a briar out of her way "I believe I could smooth your path thro' life Miss Ward". . . .

Fri 5th Jul '61   A letter from Mam with an account of the Shanes Castle picnic. The principal features of the day were Alice and Capt. Calcott sat in the rumble for three mortal hours and in fact stayed together the whole day Louisa and Capt. Harrison ditto. Emily's dejection was also remarkable for she sat under a tree the whole day reading poetry! A trip to the Giant's Causeway is proposed for next week. Bangor Lyles and Kills[14] to live between the hotel and James' house at Portstewart, all sounding very inviting.

Thur 11th Jul '61   Mam wrote to Araby with astounding intelligence that he proposed to her on the Cliff at Portstewart.

Wed 17th Jul '61   L's[15] 25th birthday . . . They parted at Portstewart each firmly convinced they would never meet again. Shadowy insinuations and visions of the trousseau He arranged so that his visit to Papa should be next week after the Assizes.

Fri 19th Jul '61   A letter from Mam. James has been there and got Papa's formal consent and the trousseau is underweigh. . . . The Wedding

Mon 11th Nov '61   Great fervour of favours and card directing. Spent the evening making garlands with Em and silver paper roses Waiters scurrying about in all directions. Dining Room looked dreadfully breakfasty.

Tues 12th Nov '61   A fine day. Breakfasted a la wedding in hall Emily as well as anybody. Dressed ourselves quietly and got up an excitement of bridesmaids in the vestry the usual dread of being late . . However we did follow her up the aisle before 12 o'cl and she was married. She behaved beautifully neither fainted nor even cried . . Bridesmaids were Louisa and Ellen Lyle, self and Alice? and Nina Price. Best man Henry Head Esq. M.D. Edward Lyle married them—when the first detachment of bridesmaids returned to the house they found them kneeling calmly before the fire. The seating card? MUDDLE THEN BEGAN OVER WHICH WE HAD GREAT FUN. Actors Jimmie Luisa Alice Godfrey Head and self. Had Edwd Lyle at breakfast who is amusing. Godfrey's toast was "The Treasurer[16] and his Treasure" Cromie gave "the Bride and Bridegroom. Godfrey "the Bridesmaids" Head "the Army and Navy and Durrant the ladies of England and Ireland . . "The table held 36.

The couple had three children: Henry, Sidney, and Alice. Henry became a judge in the Indian Civil Service and married Lucy Higgins. Sidney married Fanny Spotswood Ash and became agent for the estates previously managed by his father-in-law. Alice married Denis Pack Beresford of Fenagh, Co. Carlow. James Lyle died in 1900. Emily, his widow, remarried. A copy of a letter to Ellen Scott, undated from E. Hamilton, refers to Minnie Ould's treatment by Hutton. "I hope your niece had quite recovered the use of her foot ere this—I own I have some faith in the work of *bonesetters* so I trust she has got benefit." As already recorded, Minnie Ould was cured by Mr. Hutton.

Notes

1. Minnie Ould, daughter of Ellen Scott's sister, Anne, wife of Rev. Fielding Ould.
2. Rev. George Vaughan Chichester, husband of Ellen Scott's sisterr, Harriet.
3. 3rd and 4th sons of George Chichester and Harriet Lyle.
4. Frances Harriet, 5th child of Rev. George Chichester and Harriet Lyle. She married W. J. Evelyn, descendant of John Evelyn (1620–1705), the English diarist.
5. Lord O'Neill was George Chichester's brother.
6. John Mulholland's wife, Frances, was Harriet Chichester's sister.
7. This appears to be Helen Mary, daughter of Frances Mulholland, a sister of Ellen Scott and Harriet Chichester.
8. Braithwaite.
9. Frances.
10. James Ogilby, son of Thomas Scott's sister, Joice, first cousin of Bedell Scott.
11. Protestant Orphan Society.
12. Sarah Ellen Scott's sister, wife of Rev. Blackwood Price.
13. Godfrey Lyle, James Lyle's brother
14. Killinchy Wards.
15. Louisa.
16. James Lyle was treasurer of Derry.

40 / 1877, May to August—Ellen Scott's Diary Continues

May 1st 1877. . . . . . I had spent all yesterday at Pellipar settling accounts & wrote a long letter to Papa on the subject he had asked me a question about a few days previously viz What do you think will become of J. Ogilby when I leave him? At the time I said that B & I would not undertake more than a necessary supervision of his household and would not have any responsibility or power over financial matters—Some days after much thought & talking it over with B—I came to the conclusion that influence over the household could not perhaps exist without some power—also that Maria's family & George's would be left badly if Mr O's help was withdrawn I wrote this to G'papa and he said Mr King had asked him what he proposed and if B would take his place with Mr Ogilby to which he said no! he thought not but that he thought I would. B taking care to fill the chaplain duties. He also spoke strongly about his views that he wished J.O's Mother's family to be about him and have the care of him as it was altogether their interest to preserve his life. the other side naturally had different feelings about it—He said that when he was dismissing Mrs H. he gave as reason that the influences and associations which he wished should surround Mr O. were not those that she wished. Mrs McMichan and also his relations by his Mother. Grandpapa told me to ask Mrs McM to shew me over the list of things Mr Ogilby was accustomed to pay himself. He also said he was trying to get some large things transferred to Mr King to pay—Mrs Hillier as one—Mr King he said thought it was too large but—

May 9th Wednesday. . . . This afternoon I was told a woman wanted to see me in the kitchen—There stood a tall rather good-looking girl—dark—when I said I do not know your face. she smiled brightly and said looking round to see that no one was near—I'm Dan Kane's wife. and I want to consult you about my health—I brought her up to the study and she said I did not want any of them to know who I was. Catherine my sister in law came with me part of the way but she did not know I was coming here—I would not like Dan to know, he is very proud—on describing her symptoms I told her they were nothing serious only natural—she told me she had been married two months—that she had as a girl been at School in Dublin for some months I said you have not the accent—Oh no she said they laughed at me and I put it away—She thanked me very much and shook hands—I promised to take her some rhubarb—which she fancied but no one is to know so it wont be easy—It did seem so strange her coming to me—said she had not even told her mother that she felt ill—

May 13th. . . . . Poor old John Miller was in the house with his hand bound up—he said he was pretty well considering

May 20. . . . Our little Cluster meeting each Thursday—. . . Old John always there—the last cancer in his thumb had come out the last day—The quack who cures so many has been wonderfully successful with him. . . .

June 5th—A letter from H.E.C.[1] "I suppose you heard last week that the Mulhollands were in some anxiety about Andrew who was laid up in Paris with Roman Fever Last night a telegram came saying he was worse An hour later another saying '*All is over*' Oh dear Elly you can well imagine the unutterable anguish of poor dear Fanny and them all". . . . .

July 3rd—George and I came with Grandpapa over the mountain on Monday Poor little George—I do not know what to do to make him less fearful of pain—His imagination exaggerates so terribly that it was a painful scene today at Gillies[2] in Colerain I chatted to him and kept him amused looking out at cows and horses till the moment arrived. but nothing we could say or do would make him sit back in the awful chair or submit—He said he would let me pull it—but he feared Gillies and his pinchers so terribly—Poor Gillies' patience was tried. If I only knew how to give him more resolution and courage but from experience I know. the effects of an over vivid imagination and its terrifying exaggerations—I spoke to him seriously this evening he makes no excuse does not appear to feel remorse but only content to be out of reach of Gillies and the pinchers. . . . . Grandpapa preached twice on Sunday attended the funeral of Rachel Craig on Monday—the poor creature has died under very painful and distressing circumstances—Her brothers boiling with anger at the treatment that had brought her so low and occasioned her death threatened revenge—so Grandpapa thought he and Bedell attending the funeral would have a soothing effect. . . . . . . Mr Fred Clarke . . has 1000 ch. population and has very good attendance I asked him how it is there are so many Episcopelians—in a colony originally Scotch—He said that a former rector Hamilton by name—would not keep a tenant on the three Glebe townlands who did not come to church—so they all became church people . . .

July 12th—Mr Ogilby wished to see the Orange procession. Grandpapa told the children that his great great Grandfather Gideon Scott chaplain to King William read prayers at the Battle of the Boyne.

July 20th . . Came to Banagher to be at Confirmation next day Ada with 15 others from this parish were confirmed and seemed thoughtful—Took tea here before leaving—the Bishop gave a very earnest interesting address. . . . . Minnie & I also Bedell lunched at Canon Rosses' the Bishop talked in an amusing lively way—and told some stories—One subject interested him greatly was the deliciousness of the little roast pig!—I am sorry he was amusing as Mr Manning was opposite and he thinks and talks profanely—Minnie seemed distressed too after the solemn service we had had Bedell says It is the law of reaction and when he spoke to John about it He quite agreed it was natural. B & I were very sorry to hear from George Scott that the boys had a disagreement coming home and behaved badly—I suppose reaction is the excuse—

Aug 1st. . . . Louise and I called on Capt and Mrs Robinson—He alluded to the late Duke of Marlboro having married his Aunt Miss Flower and her tragical death—after her baby was born her mother and she differed about something and she took a fit and others followed till she died—Her daughter grew up and tho' only 24 has been married twice . . . Yesterday was our school feast . . . The day passed off very well—B—had to reprove James Mullan for using an oath. I fear from his look he is getting coarse and selfindulgent—It is so sad—We were astonished to see John Clarke and George Scott such good friends and competing amicably in races leaping etc. after the latter having made bitter complaints of the former so as to say he would not come to the School if the other came Miss Reins remarked to me quietly "It does not do to mind boys"—

James Ogilby was Bedell Scott's cousin. His Aunt Joyce (or Joice) Scott had married R. Ogilby. They had two children: Alexander, who married Miss Kirwan and whose only child, Isabella, married Lord Ellenborough, and James of Pellipar House, who never married. James Ogilby was always delicate and from an early age had been looked after by his Aunt Maria, who, in 1877, was still living with him. She was another of Bedell Scott's Aunts. Now Bedell was an old man, and Maria was feeling her age. The next owner of Pellipar would be an Ogilby.

The cure for cancer mentioned in the diary may still be in use in Ulster. Some years ago the writer of these notes was told of a cure for cancer similarly described, which cured some people. It was said that some doctor had wished to buy the prescription, but it had not been sold by its local owner.

Andrew Mulholland was the eldest son of Frances and John Mulholland. According to the family letters exchanged on this tragic occasion, Andrew Mulholland possessed all the virtues most admired in Victorian times. He was on his honeymoon and had just come from Italy when, in Paris, the illness developed from which he died. His death was wholly unexpected and a most crushing blow to his parents, rendered the more tormenting because he had recently confided in his mother that he "wished he could believe" his bride Amy (Lubbock) was heartbroken and wished that she, too, might die. She chose to live with the Mulhollands rather than return to her own family.

The "Orange Procession" commemorated King William of Orange's victory at the Battle of Boyne in 1690. It is held every year, and there is no thought of discontinuing it. The defeat of James II, aided by France, is too often regarded as solely an Irish battle. It was far more than that. Certainly it saved the Protestants in Ireland; but it also saved Ireland from becoming in reality if not in name a province of France as well as saving the Protestant Church in Europe. That it was so regarded at the time is indicated by the fact that every Protestant state in Europe sent a contingent to fight in King William's army at the Boyne, proof of the international implications of the struggle. The French massacre of Protestant Frenchmen on St. Bartholomew's Day in 1572 is just one of the more terrible examples of the dangers of belonging to the minority religion in those times. William of Orange was, however, in advance of his time in being tolerant on questions of religion. It is interesting to know that the Pope, still feared and hated by bigoted Protestants of the twentieth century, was anxious for the success of William of Orange, not approving of any further growth of French power. The Pope had earlier given excellent and humane advice to James II about his treatment of his Protestant English subjects, which, had he followed, it might have saved his throne.

Notes

1. Harriet Chichester, Ellen's Sister.
2. The dentist from Derry all the family attended.

41 / 1882—Charlie Lyle Becomes a Midshipman in the Navy

The time had come for the five surviving sons of John Lyle and Elizabeth Lyle to enter some profession or find some occupation.

Charlie Lyle entered the navy at the age of fifteen. His sister Kathleen Anette Lyle, records this event in her diary:

> July 23rd 1882—Charlie has passed for the Navy & come home on leave. He did fairly well and will be a middy in about six or seven months. . . . . August 17th O dear me how am I to write all that has happened in this short month. First part is bright—Charlie so merry funny—like his old self. . . . Suddenly we hear C appointed to the "Agincourt" & must be ready to start any minute. Everything confusion telegrams about clothes Uncle Edward to go with him etc etc. The app—very good a flag ship in the Channel Fleet off Alexandria just where the fighting is. On Wednesday order to sail from Portsmouth on Sat 19th must leave tomorrow. Monday C & I spent the day walking about with At Hannah he got endless presents. Went out to Willsboro between trains saw A^net & Mrs Stuart & now today he has gone, O it has been such a weary weary day but he went off with Father very well Twins Herbert & I saw him off dear little boy I miss him so *fearfully* tonight he always came into my room or I into his and we had such fun with lanky Tom too. . . . Mother has borne up bravely but she would not see him off . . . Sat August 19th Charlie sailed today in the Malabar at 2½ from Portsmouth Thinking and praying for him.

The following month brought a letter from Port Said.

H.M.S. Agincourt
Port Said
September 6th 1882

Dearest Mother

I am sorry I did not write before, but I could not get any Egyptian stamps. We got here last Saturday. We stopped a day at Malta, there is very little to do there except eat fruit which is very cheap, grapes are only three halfpence a pound. We stayed about 12 hours at Alexandria, it is all in ruins, all the decent places are burnt down. A Colonel somebody was asking about me at Malta I believe he wanted me to dine with him, I think his name began with a T. This is an awful hole, I have been on shore once & I dont want to go again, it is a beastly sandy place. There is not much chance of us having anything to do, we are expected to come & pay off as soon as the war is over; I daresay I shall get some leave before I go out to the Northampton. I suppose Jack & Herbert have gone back to school. What is Tom going to do. We have to turn out at half past six every morning, & do half an hour's

Charlie Lyle (son of Rev. John Lyle)

gunnery or something like that, then we have breakfast at 8, divisions & prayers at 10, then we do about an hour's work with the Naval instructor; on some afternoons we do seamanship. I wish we would hook it from here, it is so awfully stale. We saw the iron clad train at Alexandria. Tell Aunt Nette I thank her very much for the writing desk, it is very useful. Where did Father & Uncle Edward go after they left Portsmouth, who preached instead of father. I dont think I will get any shooting or fishing out here, did Jacky catch any more fish at the Bar mouth. Please send me Hugh's address, has he got to Dumdum[1] yet. We are sending a party of blue-jackets ashore today to patrol the canal, two midshipmen are going with them, one of them is a fellow who was in the same term as Sinclair. There are seven ships here now, the Northumberland, Monarch, Alexandra, Superb, Inflexible & the Teneraire. Tell Kathleen & Florence & Harriet to write to me & direct their letters to H.M.S. Agincourt, Alexandria.

    Give my love to everybody
        Your loving Son
          C.A. Lyle.

    The brief war in Egypt in which Great Britain was engaged in 1882 was the culmination of troubles in a disturbed and unstable area. Egypt had ceased to be a French protectorate in 1801. Since then, there had been aggression from Turkey and many internal struggles for power. In 1867, an eyewitness gave a vivid description of the poverty and misery of the people. Ruined by the burden of innumerable taxes, added to daily, many were fleeing the country to escape the impossible situation from which no effort on their part could extricate them. In 1869, an ambitious project, the Suez Canal, was opened. Egypt's financial situation became so appalling that shares in the Suez Canal were sold to the British government. This led to a British Inquiry into the financial state of Egypt in 1875. The conclusion was that under its existing administration national bankruptcy was certain. This led, without armed conflict, to some European control over the situation with the agreement of the Egyptian ruler. However, soon after declaring himself satisfied, Ismail returned to his old ways and resumed his gallop to financial disaster. In 1882, it became clear that there was grave danger of a very serious rising in Egypt and that only military intervention would save Egypt. In May 1882, British and French fleets arrived at Alexandria. After a local massacre, the British Admiral bombarded the forts. The Sultan of Turkey, given the opportunity, refused to act. The British government then decided to do so and sought the cooperation of France. France refused, and Great Britain then turned to Italy, which refused, also. Great Britain then acted alone, and the war was soon over. After the Battle of Tell-el-Kebir, Lord Dufferin, the British Ambassador at Constantinople, was appointed High Commissioner of Egypt. He prevented much revenge killing and insisted on a reform of the administration. At this point, France desired the cooperation she had previously declined, and England, very reasonably some will think, refused her belated desire to assist.

As the Egyptian war ended, Kathleen Annette Lyle's diary continues:

Charlie got leave as soon as he reached Portsmouth & started at once on Saturday coming round by Cork 3rd class because he had not enough money & arrived Monday evening. *So jolly* on 30th October Wednesday 8th November Charlie & I went to Willsboro I went shooting with him everywhere . . .
Friday 17th. . . . took the donkey cart His piercing shrieks filled the air. Drove to Coleraine with Charlie. Great fun in evening fireworks gambled for sweets Lovely *Northern Lights* Very happy. . . . .
Bought Charlie a text book tried to extract a promise to read it. . . . . O Monday terrible Monday . . . Monday 20th Nov. This long dreaded day is over & I am thankful in a way. It was even worse than I expected I could not keep up. We all went to the station after great packing at ½ past 11 we got to Colerain Twins C & I in the cart. Mother looked terribly white but she was quite cheerful the tears would come into my eyes and I had such a cry when I came home the twins have been quite jolly the whole time I dont understand. . . .

Postcards from Birmingham and Devonport told of his safe arrival, without losing anything on the journey. One more letter from him survived, written 1883.

H.M.S. Northampton
Bermuda
March 31st

Dearest Mother
Thanks for your letter, I daresay Mrs Simons saw me, she came on board to sing at some readings we had at Halifax; there is a Mrs Ramsey at Clifton too the wife of our paymaster, she went home from Halifax about last November. Is Herbert growing at all, I hope not, I dont want him to be any bigger than me, 5 ft 4 in. is quite tall enough for any respectable person. Please send the money, as quickly as possible, as my leave is stopped till it arrives, if you send me 7£ I shall probably be able to pay off at once without waiting till the end of next month or borrowing any, I think I can keep about 4£ from my pay at the end of this month as it is the end of the quarter, & we get 8£.16 instead of only 5£.3.
What does Father do with himself does he ride a bicycle; I must learn as soon as I get home. Hugh seems to be just going on a fortnights or 4 months leave shooting, no wonder he likes being out there, I wish we could get leave when we liked; How are Flo & Ta getting on with their violins,

can they play anything yet. I hear that Tracy is rather a wild sort of fellow, wasn't it him that shot another fellow in the arm on the Northumberland. I wish my leave was good, they have just got a brand new billiard table at the club, & that is about the only thing to do in this place, except going out in the boat. Is there anything of a theatre in Bristol, is there a decent river there, I forget the name of the affair, but it did not look up to much when we used to pass it in the train from Dartmouth. I spent a very jolly couple of days with the Heavens, you might write to Mrs Heavens—she asked me to be remembered to you—and thank her for asking me up there, I think they are up at their other house, up in the mountains now, but if you directed your letter to "The Ramble" Ramble, P.A. Montego Bay
Jamaica
the letter would be forwarded alright, they have got lots
of ponies
Give my love to everybody
Your loving son
C.A. Lyle.

Although there are no more letters from Charlie Lyle, there will be more news of him.

Hugh, Jack, and Tom were all brothers of Charlie who were starting their careers at the same time.

Hugh, the eldest, went into the army, the Welch Fusiliers, and was sent to India soon after Charlie Lyle sailed for Bermuda. At the same time, Jack went to Coopers Hill and became a civil engineer in the Public Works Department in India. Tom went to Canada, and letters from him will describe his work there. Herbert was the youngest son and still at school.

"Uncle Edward" was the Rev. Edward Augustus Lyle, brother of Rev. John Lyle.

1882—Tina Scott writes to her sister-in-law Annette Scott.

British Legation
Colburg
August 25th

My Dearest Annette
Are you *too* much offended with me, to read this letter, if you are, then put it in the fire, and say nothing about it, if you are not then read it & answer it some day *soon*—What are you all about at Willsboro Willie Kate & Annie & all of you I don't know what I would give to be back there, playing lawn tennis and leading the happy life we did two years ago but now with four children *thats* an utter impossibliity indeed I dont believe we shall *ever* go to Ireland again, unless its to take up a pig farm when we cant any longer

struggle on in diplomacy, and then I suppose you will *cut* us, even if you do however, perhaps you will buy our hams, if they are good but joking apart four Babies *are* a struggle there is so much wanted & so much to be done to keep them nice, indeed I have almost given up trying to keep them clean & tidy—I am going to have them Photographed the day after tomorrow if it is fine, and then I shall send you some, Charlie & I had ones taken when we were in Gotha & I will send them as soon as any of them arrive, I had caught a very bad cold at the Races and that accounts for the rather woollen appearance about the eyes and nose.

The Duke & Duchess of Edinburgh arrived here yesterday, but as she is of course in deep mourning, I dont suppose it will add much to liveliness of the place—

My mother and sisters are going to Dresden for the winter. I shall miss them awfully, but I suppose its best for them to go somewhere they will see pictures & will have good masters and all that sort of thing—My housekeeping does *not* improve, indeed I begin to despair of ever being able to manage well, & then we have a bad cook who uses a great deal & sends up the most horrid things sometimes, we had a very good one at one time but she left as soon as she heard the Edinburghs were coming, as she had always been their second cook, now Charlie is sometimes quite ill with the greasy food we get—Have Kate & Annie long dresses now & do they look nice in them, give them both my very best love and tell them that I think they might sometimes write to us, I know that I am a very bad correspondent, but then I have a great deal to do & they are comparatively speaking idle, and now that our family is increasing so quickly, I begin to think we shant ever be able to go to Ireland, so that if we dont all write to each other sometimes you people in Ireland will soon forget that you have a brother & family abroad. I know just as well as possible what you will say when you read this letter— "Oh its all very well for Tina to write about forgetting each other but she is the worst of the lot". *When* you say or think that, please also remember that I am simply *over-run* with Babies & have very little time to myself because of course I must pay visits & receive them and that also takes up a good deal of time even although this is a small place—Vera is growing such a big girl & quite a companion at times, but I fear they have all rather bad tempers which is rather a pity, but perhaps they will grow out of it in time.

Charles Edward Stewart is getting on nicely now but of course is *very* tiny for his age. Willie's godchild is the fattest of the lot & much more like a boy than Master Charlie is. I fancy Miss Alice & the boy will be like each other both very small & fair—

Poor Lizzie what a sad parting she must have had at Portsmouth, I felt so much for her when I read all about the departure in the papers.

Give our best love to everyone &

Believe me dearest Annette

Yr very aff^ate sister

Tina Scott

How are Betty & Pat & Martha & all the rest of the Willsboro establishment getting on.

Charles Stewart Scott had married, in 1865, Christian Crawford, daughter of James MacKnight, writer to the Signet of Edinburgh.

Notes

1. Dum Dum is near Calcutta.

42 / 1883—Annie Scott Visits London and the Continent

Annie Scott was the second daughter of William (Willie) Scott, who had inherited Willsboro' in 1872 on the death of his father, Thomas Scott.

Willie Scott, though very clever, was always delicate. At the age of eighteen, he took first of first honours at Trinity but suffered so much from eye trouble that he had to leave college soon. As the eldest son and also because of his health, he entered no profession but always lived with his father at Willsboro'.

His wife, Georgina, died unexpectedly two months after the birth of her third child, George. Willie's younger sister, Annette (Aunt Net), then came to live at Willsboro', where she remained until Katie, the eldest, was old enough to run the house and act as her father's hostess.

In 1883, Annie was nearly twenty, and a small black leather-bound notebook of hers still survives. On the flyleaf, she wrote, "Annie F.E. Scott Given to me by my Aunt Hannah to write an account of our first visit to London and the Continent." From this little journal, the extracts that follow have been taken:

May 11th 1883

The Grand Hotel London. We have just arrived here, it is horrible so uncomfortable. A great deal of splash and show about it but not a bit nice, the charges are enormous 9/6 for a miserable tea and 10/— for each bedroom, we are going to leave it the first thing tomorrow morning for even the most uncomfortable lodgings would be better than this abominable place, one could then do as you like but here no word is strong enough to express my disgust. I wish I could express it to Mrs A. Bowen for recommending us to come here it is not our style at all. . . . . . The Hotel was more bearable next morning but still we stuck to our decision & after breakfast which was in the "Grand Salle" a splendid room full of little tables with people at each all busy eating, we started in the Underground Railway from Charing Cross

Station for South Kensington. We just reached the platform in time for up whizzed a train, in we three stepped & off we went under the mighty city, the only disagreeableness being the close air but we were not in it long enough to mind it. I cannot imagine how the poor engine drivers and guards live in that atmosphere it surely must be very bad for them On reaching sth Kensington we hired a cab for an hour and set off to look at the lodgings recommended by Dot Alexander, the 1st ones were all full but Katie spied a notice in an opposite house & went to ask about the rooms. They turned out to be just what we wanted so we settled to take them at £4.14.6 per week. It is rather dear but at this time of year all places are expensive. We returned to the Grand Hotel with much lighter hearts knowing that we had only a short time longer to spend under its roof . . . . We said Farewell to the Hotel with no very sad hearts at 3 o'cl. . . . .

Today Whit Sunday we donned our new peacocke dresses and proceeded to St Paul's Church. It turned out to be very low Church lower than we are accustomed to as the clergyman preached in the gown. . . . . In the afternoon we sallied forth for a walk . . . at last we found ourselves in what is either Hyde Park or Kensington Gardens . . . Such lots of different people as we saw & some of them such swells it is really quite a different world from poor Ireland here everyone seems rolling in riches & dressed in the richest of materials.

Whit Monday

May 14th

. . . . After lunch we set off for Westminster on reaching the Kensington Station we found such crowds we almost wished we had not gone however as we had taken our tickets we did not like to lose them. On the platform were several of the fish women from the Fishery Exhibition they were all dressed in costume & looked very picturesque. I think they must have been Boulogne fishwives, they each wore white caps, long gold earrings short dark dresses a small bright shawl around their shoulders & long coloured stockings & shoes. They had also curious shaped bonnets decked with ribbons in their hands Some of them looked rather bewildered. I wonder how they liked being gazed at as everyone did. . . . we went on to the Abbey . . . We afterwards found out the preacher was Archdeacon Farrar[1] whose sermons I have read and liked much. He was not a bit what I had imagined but was very commonplace looking round fat and reddish grey hair. . . . . I need not try & attempt to describe the Abbey for I could not it is far too beautiful. . . .

Tuesday May 15th

We have had great days outing & enjoyed ourselves immensely. First of all Katie & I did a little shopping here close to this Street . . . At ¼ to 1 o'cl we started for the Beaufort Gardens arrayed in our best we got there just as the clock struck 1 so we were in good time. After lunch we three & Dot started for the Academy. . . . Nell Alexander met us in the carriage at 4 o'cl & took us both with them to call at the Larbins Harley Street, Mrs

281

Trench Queen's Anne Buildings & we ended up with the Heygates where we found Papa they were very friendly to us & we had great talk especially with Mabel and Maud. Mr Bob H. did not appear. He was busy packing as he & Capt H. start tomorrow for a short tour in Holland. The Alexanders drove us home they were most good natured and kind to us shewing all the places of note as we drove past. Among other things we saw the window in Whitehall where Charles 1st was beheaded. London certainly is a splendid place.

Thursday May 17th

I did not write yesterday as I was really so footsore & tired when we came in that I could do nothing but rest. In the morning we made our way to Harvey & Nicholls in a buss we ordered hats to match our dresses as the milliner advised us not to get bonnets Papa then took us on to the Park to see the ride, such a sight as it was, hundreds and hundreds of people riding & as many more driving & walking, the marvellous thing is where all the people come from. After lunch we went by train to the Zoological Gardens we had to walk all through Regents Park to get there & it was quite a sight in itself crowds of people but scarcely any of the upper class, numbers of poor children were seen in all directions playing under the trees & on the grass. It must be a great boon to all the people having such lovely parks in the centre of the city. When we at last reached the gardens we were nearly roasted alive the sun was so very hot but the animals amply repaid us for all our trouble, they all look so happy & so well, such a contrast to those in Dublin. . . .

Today we went by train to Westminster walked along the Thames embankment & saw Cleopatras Needle we then went to the National Gallery as it was Student's Day we had to pay 6d but it was much easier to see all the pictures as of course there were not so many visiting as usual. There were a great number of people copying & it was very amusing seeing them all. . . . The pictures were really beautiful especially Turners. . . . . We have succeeded in getting rooms for Auntie just at the other side of the street. I think she will like them as they seem very clean & comfortable, she hopes to come up next Thursday.

Monday May 21st

. . . . . On Saturday morning we set off to see the first Meet of the Coaching Club it was a great sight seeing 27 coaches all with very fine horses driving passed. We got out on the road so as to be able to see better, but we rather regretted it as 1st we were nearly drived over by the Duchess of Connaught & secondly a dreadful panic took place for one horse in a coach got restive & I believe both leaders turned round however everyone fled & we were crushed up very near the royal carriage it was dreadful but in a moment the Duke of Connaught[2] called out "Its all right there is no danger" or something like it. It was very nice of him as everyone was in such a dreadful fright. He is so *goodlooking* tall rather fair & well cut features just the picture of a thorough gentleman. The Princess of Wales passed later on but we did not

282

see her the carriage was surrounded by such a crowd After lunch we made our way to the Albert Hall to hear a concert. We got 4/- places which were very high up but we heard everything. . . . We enjoyed the whole concert thoroughly it was an especial treat as we had not heard any good singing for such a long time. . . . I had no idea people would have been so kind to us in London they have all been so very friendly to us asking us to go to them etc.—This morning Papa got a card from Mrs K. Scott asking us three to go to them for supper on Sunday night . . . Papa started soon after breakfast to meet Mr King about the Woolwich business & we went at ½p. 11 o'cl. to the Albert Memorial where we found Etta & Lady Heygate waiting for us in their carriage. We drove to the far end of the Park & then got out & walked about & finally sat down to watch the riders & the walkers, it was very amusing looking at all the different styles of dress some very pretty & others most extraordinary. We passed the Prince of Wales his two sons & the ? Princess riding I only saw their backs which did not look very remarkable. A. Heygate consoled me by saying I had no great loss in not seeing them any nearer as they were not much to look at. . . .

Wednesday May 23rd

Yesterday Papa went off early in the morning with Mr King to see Woolwich on Mr Ogilvy's affairs Katie & I took a cab to Harvey & Nicholls & there tried on our travelling Dolmans I bought a black parasol & some other little things Auntie's liberal present of £10 each is very useful now. I do not know how we would have done with only our quarter. We called on the Alexanders on our way home & found Nell & the Bishop Mrs Alexander was better. . . . . Mrs Campbell called but did not come in Mrs Mulholland also came, she came in & asked us to go to her for lunch some day before we leave.

Saturday May 26th

. . . . . We saw so many monuments etc. that really it is impossible to choose which to mention I know I shall find I have not mentioned the most important but I really cannot help it for it is impossible to remember everything. . . . . Auntie dined with us I am afraid London is too much for her she does not seem up to anything On Friday we took her to the Fisheries but it tired her so dreadfully we gave up all hope of going round it & came away again without seeing much. We met the Heygates just as we came out & then we three went to Mrs Senior to tea.

Monday May 28th

Yesterday morning we went to St Peter's Church . . . We & Auntie then had early dinner & then started for the Abbey . . . we heard a distant Amen being chanted & then the great organ began to resound through the whole building It was beautiful so indeed was all the service the boys voices were so wonderfully sweet & clear they sounded more like what one would imagine Angels voices. Archdeacon Farrar preached a very good sermon. It was rather hard to remember but the leading thought was "That it is only one out of thousands leave traces behind them & even the greatest seem to fail in their object but this is no reason why we the less richly endowed with talents should hide our one talent, there is work for each of us however poor & humble we may be & let us do it not thinking of ourselves whether we ourselves will be remembered or not what does it matter if *we* are forgotten so long as the work remains—there is someone else to carry it on."

Saturday June 2nd

. . . All Thursday morning was taken up at the Stores where we got a nice little basket to hold our lunch & some sketching materials. In the afternoon we finished our packing & at ¼ past eight we started for Victoria Station. The train was very full & we had some very amusing fellow travellers 1st of all at the far end was a large jolly man who had evidently travelled a good deal. He informed us we would have a very good passage as he had telegraphed to know how the sea was & had heard it was like glass. Our spirits immediately rose & we felt much happier—then came a thin little greyhaired man very fussy "Oh dear me there was not enough room he could not bring a lady in there" However he changed his mind & soon re-appeared with his tabby cat or rather wife. Last of all came a tall thin man & a fat bignosed man rather like a Jolly Presbyterian Minister he had evidently made up his mind to enjoy his trip & to get every opinion & advice he could but was very nervous about crossing He was most amusing very talkative & ready to take notes in his pocket book. He tried to make Papa talk but I think he did the most part of it We got on board about 10 o'cl & we had to pass through the Customs House & had a very good passage we scarcely slept at all as it was so hot but we were not sick until just the end when we were getting up We landed at Flushing at ½ past 6 o'cl. & we had to pass through the Custom House In about an hour we were on our way to Antwerp Our travelling companions were a young German I think who was very civil & helped us when changing carriages at Rossenach the other two were English on their way to Berlin The Dutch are very odd people we saw lots of women coming home from market in blue dresses white caps sabots & white stockings the men all wear caps & dark blue blouses & look very untidy The country is dreadfully flat & all the trees are pollarded which make them look like Noah Ark trees not pretty but *very* neat & all planted in straight rows In this Hotel l'Europe everyone speaks English so we have no trouble except in asking our way when we loose ourselves in the town. Yesterday we went to Plantin's House the first printer in Antwerp it is a beautiful old house built round a courtyard & covered with an old vine that twines all over the house We went through some beautiful old rooms full of old Manuscripts we also saw all the different types & Plantins printing press just as it was left & looking ready for use Such an interesting old place as it was we walked through the rooms some of which had such quaint furniture We saw the bedroom & old bed in it, the drawingroom nursery & Libraries & also a long corridor that looked as though it had been a picture gallery besides lots of other rooms all very interesting. After Table D'Hote . . we all took a drive or rather Promenade in an open carriage. We saw all the Quays with their fine iron sheds & also the Boulevards some of which were very nice & shady . . . . The most interesting of all however was a fair we drove through there were boothes down the centre of the Boulevards, all looking so gay some were full of toys & fancy goods, but the most of them were little theaters & peep shows or else Restaurants It was very amusing driving down the Boulevards & looking at all there was to be seen.

At 8 o'cl. we were left at a concert or rather Band in the open air the porter of this Hotel gave us a ticket so we got in & heard a very good Band play & watched the people walking about all chattering French as hard as they could they are all so much more lively than the English.

Sunday June 3rd

Immediately after breakfast we made our way to the Cathedral High Mass was going on . . . We did not see much of the building or pictures as we did not like walking about during Service although indeed the people did not seem at all in earnest & spent most of their time gazing about. We went to morning & evening Church. What a difference there is between our Service & the R. Catholic ours all seem so much more in earnest. I certainly was disappointed in the Cathedral Service for I thought it would have been very solemn & impressive but it was quite the reverse.

Hotel Royal
Monday June 4th

Today we went out early and saw St Pauls. . . . We next made our way through a broiling sun to the Cathedral a guide took us round it & shewed us everything very well. . . We have bought some photographs which will help me to remember all I saw. . . . . We three had a nice little dinner at ½ past 3 o'cl. after which we said Goodbye to Antwerp & started for Gand. We drove to the station where we found a Steamboat waiting to convey us across the Scheldt from the deck of which we got the last glimpse of the dear Spire we have been looking at for the last few days . . . After about an hour & a half in the train we reached this. We were all three nearly roasted alive the heat was something terrible & it seemed to get worse & worse. This Hotel seems much more French than the one at Antwerp we had quite a long conversation with the femme de chambre we made a few blunders but managed to make her understand, she seems a bright merry woman. . . . Goodnight it is bed time . . .

Tuesday June 5th

This morning at 5 o'cl. we were both awakened by hearing a band playing it was evidently the "Reveille" it sounded so very pretty & cheery & was played with such spirit I suppose the soldiers marched round this square as it is called La Place d'Armes. We had breakfast at half past 8 o'cl. & then went out for a drive. . . . It seems a much larger & more flourishing town than Antwerp it is all intersected with canals, the houses rising up at each side, they with their red tiles & odd painted gables have a very picturesque effect the barges or boats are also very quaint & the bows are all painted with different bright colours. . . . Such lots of dogs as we saw drawing carts they were harnessed just like horses poor things some of them looked so very hot & miserable. If the load is heavy you see three dogs all pulling it when they all match in size & colour they look very well, but so many look so miserable I don't like seeing them. . . . . A great cannon something like the roaring Meg we saw too also several other Churches We came in after our drive & had lunch . . .Just as we were sallying out again we heard English voices & what was our surprise to see two of our Antwerp fellow travellers they seemed to be doing the sights like us for we met them just going into the Cathedral as we were . . . We saw the font in which Charles V was baptized a very ugly structure a blue globe surrounded by a gold serpent & supported by Cherubs.

June 6th Wednesday

We paid such a very pleasant visit to Bruges this morning We were called at ½ past 6 o'cl. and started at ½ past 8 o'cl. We reached Bruges in about an hour We made our way to the Hospital de St Jean. . The Cathedral we went through. . . I am afraid we did not inspect this Church very closely as we were decidedly tired of Churches . . . When we had seen all these we went back to the Hotel & had a very good little lunch of veal cutlets. Today at Table d'Hote we were quite alone & such a sumptuous repast as we had, we had courses to no end, & at last finished up with a dish of cherries. There is a great puppy in the garden here which is a great amusement to watch he & the page boy play together all day.

June 8th Friday
Koln

All yesterday we spent in the train we were up at cockcrow for our train started at ½ past 7 o'cl. We had only to change once the whole time & that was at Brusselles from where we had a Coupee all to ourselves. From Liege to Veviera we passed a very pretty country all sides of mountains well wooded with picturesque houses every here & there It was such a relief to ones eye seeing some hills again as all the rest of the country we had passed through had been so flat. The 1st Germans we saw were the Customs House officers such solemn looking individuals I could not help laughing when I saw their grave faces it was such a contrast to the vive & bright Belgians We reached this Hotel du Nord in a thunderstorm I am glad to say everyone speaks English as it is so very confusing trying to speak German after the French A French word will always come in instead of the right one. Such a large table d'Hote as we had it was very amusing but very long I had a very agreeable elderly gentleman as neighbour & he made himself very talkative to us. Now for an account of the Cathedral which we visited this morning. I can truthfully say it exceeded all my expectations which were by no means small. . . . We also went to the Treasury most interesting The shrine the skulls of the three Magi

286

was beautiful all carved gold & ornamented with precious stones The three skulls which we saw through the open door have diamonds all round them A Shrine containing the bones of Bishop Englebert was also gold with figures all round. Such costly relics as we saw one little one covered with pearls & precious stones is said to contain two thorns of the Crown Jesus wore We also saw two links of the chain with which St Peter was bound. . . . .

Sunday 10th
Hotel Bellevue Coblenz

We left Cologne yesterday morning . . . Such a fine large steamer as it was; the deck was all covered with an awning & we could sit up there & see all round . . . we saw the Druchenfels with its ruined castle the great masses of red sandstone of which the mountain consists gave it such a picturesque appearance We also saw Rolandseck with the one arch and the only remains left of a Castle at the foot of the mountain in the Isle of Normansworth Oh! it was all lovely so graceful & beautiful. . . . We reached this at 3 o'cl. the Hotel is not 2 minutes walk from the landing stage so it is very convenient. Our bedroom is in front & we look out on the fine rock of Ehrenbrietstien an immense German fortification it is attached to Coblenz by a bridge of boats which is constantly opening & shutting to let the steamers etc. pass Such numbers of soldiers as there are great detachments of them are always passing this which makes it very lively. . . . Today we went to the English Service but did not enjoy it much as the clergyman was very high Church went on with such antics besides reading the service at such a rate it was hard to follow. . . . such a thunderstorm as we have had. We have had thunder each day at 4 o'cl. since we reached Cologne so we are getting quite accustomed to it by this time.

Tuesday
Bingen
Hotel Bellevue

We said Goodbye to Coblenz yesterday afternoon It was lovely coming up the Rhine . . . The Lorelei Cliffs were simply splendid such bold dark gray crags rising straight out of the water at each side the grandeur of them was over-powering & as the whole thing looked gray it added an almost eerie appearance to the whole place . . . We got here after 7 o'cl. this Hotel de Bellevue is by no means 1st class but it will do us very well for two days. However I must say for it our room is a *very* good one poor Papa has not fared so well & we were not treated to a table-cloth at breakfast. We spend such a pleasant day at Weisbaden today. . .

Eisenach
June 15th Friday

We left Bingen yesterday & were by no means sorry to see the last of the Hotel which had been very German the food almost uneatable. We had an hour to wait at Frankfort & got a little dinner there. It was very hot in the train & we were very tired when we reached this Hotel, a great change from the last it seems very comfortable the only drawback being the trains which are quite close & keep on whistling all night . . We half expected Aunt Net & Kathleen[3] to turn up today so we put off going to see the Wurtburg until the afternoon but they did not appear so we three took a carriage by ourselves We first went up to the Wurtburg we went over it with two Germans a father & daughter the latter was very shy but managed to speak a few English words to us. It was such a nice old Castle at the top of a mountain which was all wooded to the top, there were lovely views the whole way up & we tried to imagine Luthers feelings when being led blind-folded to the Castle not know-ing whether he had fallen into the hands of friends or enemies. It was in this Castle St. Elizabeth lived in a narrow gallery we saw frescoes all illustrating her life some were very well painted The Private Chapel was very nice a vaulted ceiling painted blue with stars on it & old seats for the knights with stools in front for their pages Luther must have preached in this very spot. . . . We then passed out into a much older part of the Castle detached from the rest & after going up a staircase found ourselves in Luthers room, the table on which he had written, his chair, bed etc., were all there it was most interesting. . . we walked on & on until we saw a Big A cut in the rock & then we knew we had reached the Annathal suddenly we found ourselves in a very narrow path with great cliffs meeting above our heads—towering up to an immense height they were all covered with moss. . . .

Lubenstein Hotel
Bellevue
Sunday June 17th

We were up before 6 o'cl. yesterday as we intended driving over here early . . . This hotel is a very pretty one with such nice gardens at the back & there are walks all through the wood which is close behind. It is a very German place not another English person here & scarcely a word understood in the Hotel, this makes us feel very lost & lonely . . Papa was going down to post a letter when he spied our trunk, were we not glad to see it we two rushed at it & brought it into our room ourselves! At Table d'Hote a German next to me tried to speak a little advising me to eat some apples with roast chicken! which I would not do. . . .

June 22nd Liebenstein

. . . . We were feeling very lonely & we two were standing out in our balcony on Monday when we saw the porter in the garden looking up & waving a letter at us with a most beaming countenance. This turned out to be a telegram from Aunt Net saying she & Kathleen were coming here that afternoon. Oh was that not joy I could have cried I was so glad. . . We have had such a pleasant time since it made such a difference being all together. . . . Aunt Net left on Wednesday morning as she did not like leaving Newhof for long as Uncle C. was getting rather nervous about Aunt Tina but Kathleen stayed on with us & we are still a very jolly party. . . . There are some rather nice people here I *think* they are Russians A Mother & son & a brother & sister they all seem one party but are relations cousins I think. The Mother is such a pretty middle aged lady & looks very nice. Then there are very pushing people opposite (friends of Kathleen) a Mother & daughter & a little child that looks very ill. My neighbour is rather interesting but I think she is decidedly cracky, her husband has left her here alone. But now I must say something about our expedition to the lower regions, for it certainly was nothing more or less. We four with two tourists were conducted by a guide down into a dark passage in the side of the rock. Two little boys with candles went before us & the guide walked beside us bearing a light. It was a most peculiar & weird place we passed on down this vaulted passage which brought us to great caves or rather vaulted rooms which the guide lit up with Bengal light which made all the surrounding rocks appear quite red. In the largest cave after going down a slight slant we came to an underground lake we found a boat moored to the rock & we were all soon seated in it & rowed round this extraordinary place at each end of which in sorts of grottoes were quantities of flowers some of which our companion visitors pulled & presented to us 4 when this grotto was lit up with Bengal light it looked very well but it all was most weird & looked as if it was the place where all the ghosts & imps of the neighbourhood dwelt & I don't think any of us were very sorry when we found ourselves in the open air & sunlight.

Coburg
July 14th Saturday
Schless Neuhof

It is a very long time since I have written in my Diary . . . but since we came here I have felt so lazy I think the great heat has a good deal to say to it. However now I must write down a little of what we have been doing since we stopped at Liebenstein until June 30th my birthday Aunt Tina had another little girl much to everyone's grief as they now have 5 girls and only one boy. Uncle C. came to see us when we were at Liebenstein & cheered Papa up greatly he had not been looking at all well nor in good spirits he confesses now he rather wants to go home!!

We got up very early on my 20th birthday & I was given such pretty presents. Katie a beautiful Eisenach jug blue & gray, a brooch from Papa of very pretty stones, terra cotta jar with painting of black on it from Kathleen & an amber cross from Aunt Net also a beautiful nosegay of roses from the two K's. We had breakfast & left Belle Vue at ¼ of 8 o'cl. We were all very sorry to say Goodbye to it but soon the beauties of the drive drove away all our sadness. The Drussenthal waterfall was lovely such a quantity of water pouring down the side of a very high cliff. We got out of the carriage and went a little way up some steps cut in the rock & got covered with spray. A great herd of cattle were slowly wending their way through the valley & all had bells which made the whole thing most romantic. . . . After some time we reached a pretty village full of quaint houses the horses rested here & we strolled about the streets & talked to a woman who lived in such a quaint house that has been built in 1600, we told her where we came from

289

etc. & she was greatly astonished that we had come from so far . . . We reached Friederidroda at 2 o'cl. very hot & rather tired . . . After supper we three girls sat in our room talking nonsense to some dance music which was being played by a good band at the Kur Haus close by. Sunday we read the service together & then went out . . . At table d'hote which was very large the waiter gave us a card of "Julie von Pererif" who had called on us when we were out, friends of Uncle Charlie, she left us a message for us to be sure & go to them at 5 o'cl. that afternoon. The people were most amusing they all drank the health of a Pferwwoiw & his wife at the foot of the table & they had a great jollification together. When we had dined we went upstairs & got up the waiter to explain what Miss Pererif had been. he had just left us when in came a very solemn darkhaired man shut the door noiselessly behind him & began to gabble something in German Kathleen who was nearest to him 1st discovered it was a message from the Shachs asking us to drive with them in the afternoon Katie & Kathleen gave some kind of answer & Papa gave an emphatic "Ya" & the solemn man rapidly disappeared. We all went into fits of laughter as our faces had been one more horrified than the other when the man 1st appeared as we could not imagine where he came from or what he said. If we had had our wits about us we ought to have written a civil little note, but however it all came right for the Schachs turned out to be very nice people after the 1st formidable introduction Katie chattered away in German to Mr & the girl who took us for a lovely drive talked English perfectly & was so nice. Such a good guide as she was she knew all the places so well. . . . The next Monday . . . . . . we drove to Schmalbraiden where we got into the train & reached Coburg at 8 o'cl. Uncle C[4] surprised us all by getting into the train at Meiningen where he had gone to hire a pair of dun coloured ponies & a very nice carriage. Katie's 21st birthday was on the 12th she got a great number of presents & we all drank her health at dinner.

Sunday July 29th Neuhof

Just fancy we have been to the Rosenau[5] and *spoken* to the Duchess of Edinburgh & played tennis with the Grand Duke Paul! But now for a real account of it. Katie Kathleen & Uncle Charlie all went into Coburg on Saturday the two girls to do shopping & Uncle C. to receive the Duke of Edinburgh at the Station They did not come home till 3 o'cl. & then came with the news that Katie was to go to the Rosenau that afternoon to play Tennis with the Grand Duke Paul. Such a fuss as we were all in & we had great work dressing Katie in her cream nuns veiling dress & hat with feather to match She went off looking very well but decidedly nervous I believe the 1st words the Duchess said to her was "oh you are a great deal too swell you will certainly spoil your pretty dress" & she was not a bit formidable in fact none of them were alarming personages the Duke of Edinburgh[6] being very shy himself & the Grand Duke Paul only about 23 & rather shy too. Katie played tennis very well so Uncle C. said & seemed to have enjoyed her evening very much. The Courtseying is the worst part of the business as you have to courtsey twice to all royalties. Kathleen & I had great practising.

On Monday the G.D. Paul & Baron Schilling & another came to play Billiards. I was presented to him & taken up to play Tennis Lady Harriet Grimston the Lady in Waiting is very nice & was very kind to me In the middle of a game of Tennis up came the Duchess & I had to be presented to her Oh! WASN'T I frightened but I managed to make my courtsey all right & it was soon over She is fair & rather fat, not pretty but has a very sweet face & not a bit formidable. I did not see the Duke of E. this time as he was out shooting. The Grand Duke is very goodlooking tall dark & peculiar almond shaped eyes.

Tuesday July 31st

He is very nice & not a bit stiff, sometimes it is very hard to remember he is a Prince & to say Sir or Monseigneur as he always speaks French. We three girls & Uncle C. went twice Kathleen got on very well & liked it very much. She & Katie went again yesterday & had some very good games We all got great compliments on our playing They are all extremely bad players except the Duke who is really beginning to play very well now poor Baron Schilling makes a very bad attempt at it, his serves are most comical such skyers he is so proud when they manage to get over to the right side of the net. The Grand Duke remarked he had a great hole in his racquet. I thought it a very grand joke as he misses every ball.

Sunday August 5th

I see I last wrote on Tuesday 31st the day Katleen left us. we were all dreadfully sorry to loose her & miss her greatly at first I was always going to knock at her door but now we are getting more accustomed to it. Papa escorted her to Frankfort & the next day he gave her in charge to the Smylys & came on to Bamberg at 12 o'cl. in the night where we two & Aunt Net were in bed We had walked to Oeslau Wednesday morning the coachman carrying a little bag, our luggage! as one pony is so lame it cannot be driven. We reached Bamberg at 2 o'cl. & got a very good dinner & then off we walked towards the Cathedral. . . . Thursday morning we walked all about the town & showing Papa all we had seen & bought photos We left after 12 o'cl. & had a dreadful fuss about tickets we ought to have paid something extra for coming back in a fast train. The guard evidently thought we were cheating but some civil Germans in the carriage made it all right for us. Unfortunately the Duchess of E. & the Grand Duke Paul were in our train but I hope they did not see us running frantically about the platform. Uncle C. met us at Coburg & I & he went on to Oeslau while the others drove out in a hired carriage we arrived in much the same time & were just able to get dinner & then off we started for the Rosenau Aunt Tina going with us I did not enjoy it as much as usual I felt much shyer going with Aunt Tina & then I did not play very well I think I was too tired, however the Grand Duke was very nice & we had some good games. Friday was the Duchess namesday so Uncle C. sent her a lovely basket of flowers & we went up arrayed in our best for L.T. the two eldest children going with us The Duchess received us this time & poured out tea for us herself we had tea under the trees close to the T. ground Eliza von Reuter & her little sister were there The Duke of Edinburgh also favoured us with his presence & of course the G.D. Paul was there It was a very pleasant day & we all enjoyed ourselves very much We did not get home till 8 o'cl. poor Papa & Aunt Net have rather a dull time but as neither of them play tennis they have not been asked to the Rosenau. I close this book with an account of our visit to the Rosenau

July & August 1884

which in a few months will feel like a dream.

Notes

1. Archdeacon of Westminster in 1883, writer of many important religious works as well as of *Eric or Little by Little*. His daughter, Lady Montgomery, was the mother of Field Marshall Montgomery, victor at Alamain.

2. Prince Arthur, son of Queen Victoria.

3. Kathleen Annette Lyle, Annie's first cousin, daughter of Willie Scott's sister Elizabeth, and also the preserver of the letters and diaries on which this book is based.

4. Charles Stewart Scott, still in the Diplomatic Service, was in July and August 1883 working in Coburg. Later that year, he was transferred to Berlin as H. M. Secretary of the Embassy there.

5. The Prince consort was born at Rosenau.

6. Prince Albert, second son of Queen Victoria, who had been offered the throne of Greece in 1862 at the wish of the Greek people. He was duke of Saxe Coburg Gotha. Queen Victoria called him "Alfie." The duchess of Edinburgh was Princess Marie, only daughter of Alexander II, tsar of Russia.

43 / 1882/1887—Diary of Ellen Scott

May 24th. . . . I answered H.E.C.[1] who has decided to come to Ireland for one month Rectory let to Honble Mrs Holden Maid of Honour to Princess of Wales—Ada B.[2] to have great musical party—100— . . . We went to Pellipar for tea. Smith's finger bitten by Oscar seems very nervous. . . . I telegraphed to Mills New York 16/— . . . we met poor Ballydun Kane woman she wanted us to take her children said the neighbours would know nothing about it—Bought shawl for her . . . 26th Friday Did Pellipar books . . . visited poor Hampson who has been thrown from his cart—spine hurt in two places, legs paralysed—seems so patient—poor little wife in a very delicate state—said she had been very suffering all spring & wished much to see me but did not like to come up—called at Dan Kanes on way back . . . 28th Whit Sunday . . . Drove to Pellipar—no Bank being Holiday—Party gone to Coleraine—I came back by McCormicks—He standing about outside with an umbrella & his eye tied up—All the blisters had no effect until he put on three leeches. got immediate relief. . . . . All evening Beatrice was chilly—& went to bed early—very hot & feverish. . . . Dr John came on Friday evening. I looked at her throat & found it swelled—wrote in for Dr John to bring carbolic application & telegraphed for Sir William—Dr J came found the throat little ulcerated—put the carbolic on—came to meet Sir W at 3 who at once pronounced—diphtheria who at once applied much stronger carbolic—very strong quinine every 3 hours and iron preparation every 3 hours — beef tea & milk alternately—Dr J. found her better on Sunday. He took Sir W. down to see poor Hampson. and he gives little hope. . . . 12th . . . nice letter from Georgie—Alfie[3] going to Switzerland and then with Mr Moss round the world! Old Mullan met us and said Dr Miller had told him that a man called Hutton might cure his leg. so we are to enquire about him— . . . 16th . . . Walked with Bedell to see Scott & Moores who have lost all their hens with a disease . . 17th . . . Found Bess cherishing two little chickens in a teapot. . . . June 27th . . . Very nice letter from little George—greatly liked his fly book I sent him on his birthday—We sent off a box of cards etc to Mr Ogilby as tomorrow is his—June 28th Mr Ogilbys birthday he is 71—Just as we were starting by a car for Coleraine a note came over to say Mrs O'Hara would like to see me so I went—Had a very delightful visit—she is so bright—so full of interesting information—We spoke about the remarkable effects of the persecution of the Jews—Only last year a complete survey of all the Land of Palestine was made—so that every acre is down—Then Five & Six Building Societies are at work & have been for more than a year in Palestine—The money subscribed in England. is to enable the Jews to go back & 70,000 are going from Russia A speech of Ld Shaftesbury he says from interviews with the wealthy Jews in London that they have no wish that their people shd go back—I did not know before that Lady Roseberry has ceased to be a Jewess—& when she sent the usual present to the Rabbi at the Passover He sent it back. She heard from a person who had been in the Rothschild family that they were most liberal to all their household and generous—but that the Baroness dressed in the oldest & shabbyest things—

Mary Cooper told me that Mrs Shuldham gave a wonderful account of the Queen's ways at Mentoni—She dressed so very shabbily—The King & Queen of Saxony came to visit her & the latter entered dressed like a peacock—but soon after came out & beckoned to her coachman. a bandbox brought out of the carriage and before all the soldiers & guard she took off her bonnet & put on a little hat out of the bandbox—then stripped off her gorgeous mantle. which was folded by the footman and laid on the seat—then caught up her grand mauve silk dress round the waist inside out—and put on a waterproof. It was that they were going to climb a mountain "John Brown" attended the Queen everywhere & an attendant behind him—

Mrs K. Boyd came in to see me—Two sons in Texas & they write that the influx of emigrants has been such that it is difficult to get an acre now. Sat a little with Kearny—she told me an anecdote of a journey she took at one time by train going to Malvern—two farmers leaving the carriage said to a gentleman still in it "if this weather goes on much longer we may give up our crop" She remarked "If those gentlemen would apply to Him who regulated the weather, they might perhaps save their crops"—The gentleman said in astonishment "Do you really believe that would have any result?" She entered into conversation with him, then he said to her "Could I assist you in any way? I wish I could" "If you ladies knew how much influence a few words in season may have you would not waste the opportunity" "I was one of the greatest swearers—never spoke without an oath & a lady in the carriage with me offered me a tract once 'The swearers prayer explained' and spoke to me a little on the subject. Since that day I have never willingly used an oath"—

7th. . . Nice letter little George 29th . . . I went to meet George in Coleraine not arriving early train Charlie Lyle drove me out to Knocktarna with twins met next train George & I were at home about ½ past five—The Prices had come on the 19th the Chichesters on the 20th . . . Charlie & George great cricket and tennis

1884

July 12th. . Great special train of orangemen just leaving Portrush station . . . B & I left early for Belfast sailed in Duke Connaght very rough—& ill— John Lyle with us—found H⁴ lying out on couch on veranda bright & cheerful—was surprised as her letter had alarmed me spoke of her mind at peace, had comfort from a long talk with Mrs Hill . . Tuesday . . . Very warm—hot sun—Harriet took an hours drive in afternoon—seemed rather faint when we returned home—she has sickness oftener—more restless nights—fidgets—says she feels an increasing pressure on the digestion . . . Frances talked to me about her—H—shewed me her portrait by Sant which I greatly like . . . Edward spoke about the anxiety he felt about his father if left—not knowing how he would ever get on—August 1st Very lovely hot day dear H had good night—Yesterday evening she had a fit of sickness—before going up to bed—as she lay in the bookroom on sofa G came in & crouched down beside her She said to him something about going to Ireland as Frances had urged in the morning He said Oh not till you are better—She said "I will never be better"—Yesterday while I sat out on the veranda with her after Frances had come back to urge G. going at once—She said "I have thought that I had only a few weeks at most. but Dr H. said it might be a few months"—I knew that *after* George would require a complete change perhaps for a few months and if it was only a few weeks for him with me it would be better for him to wait but perhaps if he goes at once there would be time for him to get a little change—She said again after lying quietly—"I think now I have peace" Last Tuesday B. & I went to London—train being late I had some interesting conversation with Miss Fox Young—B also with Mr Wickham—who was of the opinion the H. of L.⁵ & Lord Salisbury will be most wrong in refusing to pass Mr Gladstone's franchise—so cowardly for fear of disestablishment—Friday evening Dear H—has been free from pain or much uneasiness all day—She kept George up to the plan of going with Fanny tonight. He vacillated much. We feared the heat might knock him up if he staid till Monday . . . Frances & Johnny & Ada came in the afternoon on their way to a school feast at Mr Wickhams Johnny came up to his grandmama in his very dignified manner and after kissing her said "I hope grandmama you are better" and then seated himself close to her for conversation. He in his kilts . . . After they were gone Edward rode over from Denbies—he also encouraged his father to go & not wait . . . He gave an interesting account of a meeting at Okely yesterday. Some literationists came down to hold a meeting to inveigh against the House of Lords & the Church—A Church defence advocate was telegraphed for. Mr Chambers and a great crowd collected The literationists were hooted and would not be listened to—very nearly got a ducking in the pond and the people shouting What brings you here—We dont want any of you. Get out of this—duck them etc. Mr Dusatoy their rector advanced full of indignation waving his stick protesting against them coming without his leave or knowledge to invade his parish—it ended in a ch defence address. from several persons present Harriet lay out quite in the open air after George had left . . . she was so bright and like herself all evening telling anecdotes of Alfred when he was a little boy. Once when he was eleven near Poynton near Buxton a parish. He was very naughty and when reproved said very angrily "I'll not put up with this kind of thing—I'll leave the house"—marching with his hands in his pockets down the avenue His mother quietly followed him. compelled him to come back & locked him in a room until he would apologise. When food was sent he threw it out of the window—At last the tutor was sent to tell him if he did not apologise the schoolmaster from the village was to come up & whip him This brought him to his senses and he humbly apologised—Aug 3rd. . . . Ada came down and staid with her mother. Frances carried me off in pony carriage—very pleasant lively woman Mrs. Edwd O'Brien sat beside me and opposite was her husband very plain not pleasant man with hideous wig . . . and an old very handsome Mr Stanton a schoolfellow of Mr Evelyn. . . . Johnny had got his face and knee greatly scraped by a fall—F said he was so brave—never minded blows & scars. Certainly he has not had many . . . Had tea & an animated talk with Mr Stanton He defending Mr Gladstone & the franchise for Ireland—I shewing the ignorance & what the consequences wd be. Bedell had also a great discussion with Mr E O'B also a Home Ruler[6] and Fenian[7] they say!! He might be anything with such a face & wig . . . Mrs E O'Brien who is an American told me she knew of a child who was so ill of diarhea & no power to assimilate food—seeing some tomatoes begged to taste them & the nurse gave a small bit & it was the first thing retained & assimilated—another case of raw beef pounded very fine answered when all else failed—once when measles would not come out the patient begged for cold water and tho forbidden was taken and immediately the eruption came out beautifully—They thought nature often required what a patient took a longing for Aug 6th . . .dearest Harriet had a restless night the first part . . . In the afternoon as she lay on the couch on the verandah—She said "I have such causes for thankfulness everything to alleviate sickness—and such an inexpressible comfort to have you" I said "If I could only help you in any way"—She had risen from the couch while I was away for some minutes & sat on the stone edge of the verandah looking very ill and weak—I put a pillow under her & she began to say "I wonder if there is any way by which a person of George's character could be made happy?" "I was just thinking how his life had been one long moan" "I have often looked out on those lovely green hills and trees and thought of the wonderful goodness that places us in such a beautiful spot but George's one cry is 'If I was anywhere but here' How I envy the Prices"[8] I said "No matter where he is it is his way to think he would be happier somewhere else His want of happiness consists in his trying to please self!" Aug 19th R.[9] had consulted me coming down about renting a house on the other side of London as Ada was so anxious I said it might be months this illness might last but that a gradual decline was quite perceptible . . . The day after the last entry Bedell & I went up to London . . . On our return to Wotton Rectory we met May with a telegram from Maria "George hurt leg by fall" It was trying leaving dearest Harrie. She was so poorly. I wd like to have staid with her but it was not to be—Her tenderness & sympathy and thought for others was wonderful. . . . we started next morning Never had so sad & anxious a journey in my life on arrival found George had been leaning over the bannister—overbalanced came down on side—top of thigh broken—A miracle of mercy that his head did not come down first—For seven weeks he lay. and his general health did not suffer . . . The crutches at first were difficult and one day feeling rather weak he attempted to come downstairs. when they gave and he fell down. The first flight on his other side—It was another special mercy that he was not injured . . . At XMas 84—had a card from darling Harrie with farewell—May it only be for a time—She lingered on until May 26th and sank peacefully.

1887

March 4th—Weymouth . . . Great numbers of Home Rule pamphlets we have got from London & G.V.C.—to distribute this evening to people who come to a radical meeting. to be held at Burdon Hotel—this evening Mr Conybeare member for Cornwall to speak at it—a violent Home Rule Radical—Lizzie has just been in today. Charlie pretty good night but beginning to feel pain in side what Dr Smith seemed to expect. . . . The earthquake at Nice on 25th gave such panic that some ladies arrived at Paris en chemise and some in their ball dresses. It was bad along the Riviera and even to Rome from Cannes—Edward writes that he was awakened by the shaking of windows, jugs & basins—jumped up to see if chimneys were falling—found all the household outside but went to bed himself and slept soundly— . . . saw Charley in his room. thinner each time . . . March 14 Gerald Ovens came for a minute—he is trying to get revisionist Liberals to take part in the meeting on Saturday. . . . March 25 Charlie Lyle not so well quite. We staid with

296

him all the afternoon while Kath went up with Tom to say Goodbye to Lucy and the Andrews. Poor Tom goes tomorrow . . . March 28 Monday. . . . Tom left on Saturday—saw him off—A card today tells of his safe arrival at Liverpool & spend Sunday at Chester Had letter from Harry Mulholland enquiring about Jack[10] hopes to use interest with Lord Dufferin[11] to have him moved to a healthier place—. . . . Emily Ould sent two interesting letters from Flo[12] from Cairo. . . . Left Weymouth April 5th Left London 12 train April 7th Went off without our heavy luggage—B. not patient! arrived in Chester—next day Good Friday After Church went to Oulds—Emily[13] very well & agreeable. Dear little Annie[14] full of plans for Edward rather imaginative. . . . Next started 11 for Dublin—via Kingston. The Ireland fine boat the only boat a difference is made between first & second class passengers—I had to pay 3/—extra for lying on a sofa in the 1st saloon. . . . 25th Sara & Turnley came this afternoon—Kirkpatrick gave me a receipt for gingerbread which I copy

¾ flb Flour sifted
½ lb butter "rather rich"
1 teaspoon ginger
½ do soda

egg spoonful baking powder pinch of cream tartar less than ½ lb sugar Rub flour butter & sugar well together till all crumbly—Add treacle and one egg till nice dough—put on board Knead—divide in two roll out cut with tumbler or tin lid pretty hot oven.

6th May Heard from Lizzie that they have taken the Preston Vicarage for two months Hugh & Alice join them. Poor little Charlie is no better, weaker . . . W Cowan gone with his son to America leaving his parish to whoever can be got for Sundays. June 25th. . . . We had an illumination of 96 candles. All the side towards Dungiven, three great tarbarrel bonfires and a few fireworks and firing of guns etc. The Castle was illuminated and a great bonfire on the top of Benbraddagh. Our people from all round came and enjoyed it; Charlie had flags up on his high trees and four on our roof which are there still. There was an attempt by disloyal persons to take down the flags on the castle but finding someone had a gun protecting it, they desisted. A large detachment of loyalists and police had to guard the bonfire on the top of the mountain the night before. The disloyals had rolled down the tarbarrels. Wonderful times we live in. Arthur Chichester[15] writes from the South that things are left to themselves, Government doing nothing. Healy making frightful speeches so that Arthur feels radical. Our jubilee[16] morning was spent at the Castle with the Youngs, a cricket match going on. Splendid lunch in the Castle.

August 27th. . . . . . Some riddles Mary Cooper has been giving us I will write down "What is the difference between an Irishman and a Highlander on the top of a mountain" "One is kilt with the cold, and the other cold with the Kilt". "What is the difference between a duck and a doctor" "In the

one the bill produces the quack, in the other the quack produces the bill''
''If the sea were to dry up what could Neptune say?'' ''I haven't an ocean
(a notion)''. ''Why is Neptune like a man looking for the Philosopher's
stone?'' ''Because he's a sea king (seeking) what never was''.

Tom Lyle left for the United States.

Harriet Chichester died of cancer.

Charlie Lyle was living at home because he had contracted consumption, that scourge of the nineteenth century.

''Edward'' in the earthquake at Cannes may have been Edward
Chichester, Edward Ould, or Edward Lyle.

Arthur Chichester, son of Harriet Chichester, who wrote from the
South of Ireland that things were left to themselves, the Government
doing nothing, while Healy made frightful speeches, referred to a situation
which has occurred more than once in Irish history. The English, constitutionally unable to understand the Irish character and temperament
have sometimes tried to solve the problem of Southern Ireland by restraint,
reason, and reform under which violence has spread like a forest fire.
Extreme severity, of course, hands verbal ammunition to violent men,
although it sometimes restores law and order. Healy, a supporter of Parnell, was a former railway clerk, journalist and barrister. He made extremist speeches. At one time he was Parnell's secretary.

Mr. Gladstone, whose political activities are mentioned several times
in this diary, had never wavered in his views on Ireland, or in his de-
termination to bring peace and reconciliation to that turbulent land.

In 1870 Mr. Gladstone's first Irish Land Bill had been passed. This
Act legalised ''Ulster Custom'' in all parts of Ireland. Hitherto only
tenants in Ulster had received the voluntary benefits granted by Ulster
landlords, one of these being payment for any improvements made by
the tenant on the termination of his lease. The 1870 Irish Land Act
contained more than the provisions of ''Ulster Custom.'' For example—if
a tenant was evicted for any reason other than non payment of rent, the
landlord was liable to pay him compensation. In some cases compensation
might be as much as seven year's rent. It was natural that landlords did
not welcome this Act which appeared to them—quite correctly—as the
first step in a policy of spoliation. Unreasonably, however, Southern
Ireland's tenants did not welcome the Act either. Ignoring its benefits for
them, they complained that it did not grant *all* their demands.

From 1879 to 1882 the Irish Land League agitation, led by Parnell
and Davitt resulted in very serious disturbances and a great increase in
crime in Southern Ireland. The aim of the Land League was the dis-

possession of existing landlords and their replacement as owners by their tenants. In 1881 the situation had become so serious that a Coercian Act was passed at Westminster to enable law and orderr to be restored. As evidence of his kindly intentions towards Ireland Mr. Gladstone, in the same year, steered his second Irish Land Bill through Parliament. The terms of this Act included dual ownership of land by landlord and tenant, and the appointment of a special court to fix rents in the event of dispute. Rents so fixed were to remain unchanged for fifteen years. These provisions hastened the dispossession of the landlords by making it preferable for them in many cases to sell land so controlled.

In 1882, when this extract from Ellen Scott's diary started Gladstone came to an agreement—known as the Kilmainham Treaty—with Parnell, leader of the Irish Party at Westminster. By then Mr Gladstone was more convinced than ever of the justice of Home Rule for Ireland, and that those demanding it were the true voice of the Irish people.

In 1882 Earl Cowper, the Lord Lieutenant of Ireland, resigned and was replaced by Earl Spencer. With the express purpose of ushering in Gladstone's new era of reconciliation, peace and prosperity in Ireland, Lord Frederick Cavendish was appointed Chief Secretary and Mr. T.H. Burke Under Secretary. On the day they arrived in Dublin Lord Frederick Cavendish and Mr. Burke were murdered in Phoenix Park. The murders produced a very unfavourable reaction in England, and a very severe Coercian Act was passed at Westminster. This was effective in restoring law and order. Mr. Gladstone's convictions on the problems of Ireland remained unshaken. In 1884, under Mr. Gladstone, the franchise was greatly extended in England, and also in Ireland, a measure which Ellen Scott believed to be undesirable for Ireland because of the ignorance of the people.

Violent controversy was provoked by Gladstone's plans for Home Rule for Ireland, an issue which split the Liberal Party. Ulster was unalterably opposed to Home Rule, having many reservations and fears about the outcome on their own peaceful, prosperous and loyal province. Gladstone, however, thought it quite unnecessary to provide any safeguards for this peaceful area in the various Home Rule bills which he periodically introduced at Westminster in the coming years, whenever he was Prime Minister. More will be heard of Mr. Gladstone and the Irish question before the end of this book.

Notes

1. Ellen's sister, Harriet Chichester.

2. Ada Braithwaite.

3. Alfred Chichester, son of Harriet.

4. Harriet Chichester.

5. House of Lords.

6. Home Rule Movement, founded in 1870 by Isaac Butt, a Southern Irish Barrister.

7. The Irish Republican Brotherhood, also known as the Fenian Movement, founded in 1858, its sole aim Irish Independence.

8. Sarah Lyle, sister of Ellen and Harriet, had married the Rev. Townley Blackwood Price.

9. Reginald Braithwaite, Ada's husband.

10. Jack Lyle, brother of Tom, Kathleen and Hugh.

11. Viceroy of India.

12. These two letters and others from Flo are given after this extract of Ellen's diary.

13. Emily Ould, sister of Annie.

14. Annie Ould.

15. Son of Harriet, Ellen's sister.

16. Queen Victoria's golden jubilee.

44 / 1887—Letters From Flo Holme

1887—Letters from Flo Holme to various relatives (all copied from Ellen Scott's diary). Harriet Florence was the eldest daughter of Anne Lyle, sister of Ellen Scott, and the Rev. Fielding Ould. She married Samuel Hill Holme, a merchant of Liverpool.

Hotel d'Europe, Algiers
Jan. 27
We enjoyed Algiers very much and are sorry to have to move on. We start at 5 in the morning for Constantine a very interesting place 18 hours by rail, with Roman remains, and go on to Tunis, sailing from thence to Malta where we shall probably stay only a few days. Will pick up a steamer for Alexandria. We have had a long walk today to see the Government House and old Moorish Palace and the walk back looking down at sunset on Algiers was too lovely.

Hotel d'Orient, Constantine, Algeria, Feb. 1st.
Dear Edward[1]
I saw a lovely girl, would suit you, Pauline Bucknall, 23 daughter and sister of an architect, brother nice, father at Port Said doing something to the Gordon Memorial there. The Jewesses here are such objects, bare arms up

to shoulder, no stays or waists. Grey sunless day, *very* cold. Tomorrow we stay at a place, South Ahras, where St. Augustine was born. "Jaguste" of the Romans and where he lived such a wild fast life.

Direct French say Mon^{sr} not Esquire.

Ellen Scott's Diary—March 1887:

Emily Ould writes that they have heard from Flo from the first Cataract—had had a lovely sail up the Nile, had met an interesting German, who had been there during the war told particulars of Col. Stewarts death. Flo expects to be at Jerusalem for Easter.

Again, in March 1887, Ellen Scott wrote in her diary:

Emily Ould sent two interesting letters from Flo from Cairo in which she says:
"No word can tell how amusing this place is, you want your eyes all round your head We had a feast of mummies at the museum—All the heads, necks, breasts exposed indeed there was an indignant article in the paper that the great Rameses II should be so indecently swathed Pharaoh of the time of Moses birth is jet black (kind of embalming) with little rings of curls of jet black all over head & forehead Rameses II who oppressed the Israelites has a small rather weak head is not black at all, has high nose and a bunch of light sandy hair at each side of the head Marenptah the Pharaoh whom Moses withstood we have not seen yet Many of their teeth white and perfect One a princess with her tiny babe at her feet is still wrapped in lovely creamy crapy stuff with pale pink lines has never been disturbed tied round with pieces of itself in loose knobs—perfectly fresh There are chairs bushels eggs & seeds of the time of the patriarch so we see what Abraham sat on. A perfect wooden figure or statue of a man most life like 3 ft high of 1000 years before Abraham We drove to the Pyramids on Saturday a good road trees all the way overhead We explored the Sphinx and the granite Temple lately uncovered, built of such enormous blocks, smooth perfect walls as if just finished and it is older than the pyramids then to some curious tombs with perfect carving (bas relief) of all they did all over the walls We climbed to the place they enter the large Pyramid & had some idea of the fatiguing climb it is had a grand view of the sandy desert, the green green plain stretching to Cairo & the City itself. Yesterday we nearly brought a babe back to the carriage. I saw it in the crowded Bazaar a dear little fat tiny thing & asked its age. 21 days a man seized & hoisted it into the carriage nearly naked and all the people laughed—The runners before the swells carriages is such a pretty sight, several men in white with gold and coloured waistcoats running so beautifully with bare feet—All English Ministers have them and the Kedive has mounted ones as well. We called on Miss Whately and found

she was up the Nile. She lives close to her school Jews Copts Egyptians We heard several read the English Testament so strange—They learn Arabic English & French we heard them read lovely French Then the little girls 150 uncovered some pretty & Egyptian, some blacks, they were embroidering in gold & colors & sung us two songs in Arabic Such a picture the little babies riding on their Mothers shoulders—little fat legs hanging down the head sometimes laid on hers—ladies ride like men on their donkeys clothes tight to them all round.''

Hotell Belle Vue, Beyrout   May 1st 87
Darling Mother.

We are going off to service at an English clergyman's house as otherwise there is only American Presbyterian which does not suit Samuel—Yesterday a bachelor who has a house here but lunches at the Hotel & has been 20 years in Beyrout offered to get us reliable horses and take us a nice round so we started at 4 o' I on a perfectly delicious grey Arab It went just like a race horse. simply flying over sandyish hills thro two tracts of mulberry trees for the silkworms Pomegranates in flower (a deep red waxy bell) on to a strand with foamy waves and on round thro' a huge pine forest—great avenues thro' it where we tore like the wind—it was splended and not like cantering at all but like the Roodees little nag as quiet as a lamb all the time—Two hours and a half brought us home. 6.30 The views were most lovely The sea is at both sides of Beyrout—they say it was an island once & we were on the neck yesterday weather enchanting—not the least hot but sunny & fresh We have the waves rolling on the rocks under our windows I am altogether enamoured of a charming little Armenian girl of five years who sits on my knee at dinner & talks French to me Armenian to her mother & German to a gentleman opposite and knows Arabic too—She stays & paints in my room as much as she is let and is the handsomest child I ever saw How easily they learn languages at that age Such a pity Fan's chicks are not getting on that way We are sending off a box with silk curtains please put in dry place We have heavy rain this evening which I hope will keep the sea down We get to Cyprus on Tuesday and anchor there some hours so shall land there then 36 hours to Rhodes where we stay some time too Write to Hotel Imperiale Vienna

Grande Hotel d'Angleterre
Athène—Gréce May 14
Dearest Nell,[2]

I wish I could make you feel the delights of this place, it is such a paradise—We have been nearly a week but must tear ourselves away. The weather is perfect the air so light & delicious but getting hot—Roses & flowers of all kinds grow like weeds The Palace gardens close by are a wonder of beauty—the trees and flowers so mixed for they grow under the trees liking shade. a perfect chorus of nightingales about 5 or 6 o'clock the Queen is fond of them King & Queen are travelling in the Morea so we have not seen

302

them. He is anxious to abdicate in favour of his son who is 18 Greek born & belongs like his mother to the Greek Church. We had a pleasant long talk with Doctor Shliemann yesterday His house is beautiful modern classic decorated in Pomperan style & he has quite a museum & shewed us many queer things and is a very dear old man We sail tonight to Constantinople and get there on Monday—we may stay a fortnight then by Bucharest & Vienna home hope to reach London 20th June We saw the sunset on the Acropolis last night & I have never seen anything finer! I have a photo of Mars Hill. a stony little hill just under the Acropolis & the market Paul spoke in just below We have been in such wild country for so long it seems odd to see everyone in European clothes—such a pity they adopt them! so unpicturesque & dirty.

Grand Hotel l'Angleterre
Athènes Gréce
My dear Emily,

I have a strange desire to send you a few lines from here perhaps for the sake of old Winnington days. Think of Cathie Christian being here (Mrs Robinson) a widow with her aunt another widow—the latter is a dear & full of knowledge about all the buildings and everything; sister of Mrs Chesham I am sure—This place is miles beyond anything I had imagined in situation grandeur & interest I enclose some flowers I picked on Mars Hill (The Areopagus) for St Paul's sake It is a queer little stony hill just under the Acropolis with steps up in the rock The market place St Paul spoke to the people just below The market is beside the very perfect Temple of Thesoras. Another hill close by (The Pryx) is where all the great orators spoke; steps in the rock & the platform all there—the sea behind the Acropolis above & the city stretched out below Oh! such a grand spot! This morning we started driving at 7.30 with four very nice men two of them parsons to a lovely spot on the sea where ruined temples, Island of Salamis in front, making the sea locked in like a lake about 5 hours there and back, for lunch at one, so jolly! Now Sam is off to the Pireus a long drive to the sea port where we landed to see two of our friends off meanwhile I set off to do frivolities and see the shops having got some money from the landlord with two nice girls and their Mother Mrs Penrose who have asked us to tea tomorrow where they live at the foot of Mt Lykalocttus They are the family of an antiquarian here & the girl a splendid guide She took us over the Museum such a treat & is a cousin of one of our parsons—Our steamboat trip here was the greatest fun such nice people on board 5 nights at sea Mrs Cubett & I and some men rowed on shore at Rhodes (S too lazy) wakened at 4.30 Captain said at our own risk as we only stopped an hour or hour and a half but we took but 11 minutes to row on shore & had an interesting walk up the street where the Knights Templars lived before they were turned out and went to live in Malta; numbers of their coats of arms large on the outsides of the houses quite perfect We found a baker's shop open and seized a large round bun and off to the boat to find our man had run off with our three shawls but we sent after him and got them back! Many on board were vexed they had not ventured—We had some hours on shore at Cyprus too which was amusing and I bought a dug up ancient little glass dish there very pretty with colours—and a wild pair of socks of the country—One night we went to a large party up to the Acropolis to see it by moonlight driving there the town looked like a sea of glowworms at our feet it is very quiet and solemn and grand among the pillars and ruins and they look so gigantic by moonlight—You cant think how funny it is to get here and be able to walk about the streets alone It is months since I could do that and you cant think how we enjoy a band here and even a barrel organ not having heard anything but the Eastern Tum tum for ages We have strawberries here twice a day and this is a thoroughly comfortable Hotel the best I think since we were in Seville.

King & Queen are away travelling in the Morea We have taken our berths We go to Constantinople direct in two nights—We enjoy this place tremendously We got a Times of 6th great treat as the Hotel in Syria take no English papers We hear the shops are bewitching at Constantinople more than anywhere else but alas no money.

Notes

1. Edward Augustus Ould, Flo Holmes's brother.
2. Ellen Scott.

45 / 1887—Two Letters From Tom Lyle in the U.S.A. To His Uncles, Edward Lyle and James Lyle (Copies from Ellen Scott's diary)

Chicastria Ranch
Norwich
Kansas
May 13 1887

My dear Uncle Ned
    I know you would like to know what kind of country this is & the work that is required in Stock Ranching I cant say much for the scenery for there is none the only thing to admire is the sunsets or when we have a large fire close by All the old grass is burnt generally twice a year sometimes the fire takes its own course especially if there is a high wind and burns everything it comes across and you can see it disappearing in the horizon The grass is not by any means high the usual height is 2 ft but as you go west it is longer. It is an awfully flat country & a very sandy soil We have one side of the

ranch a long stretch of sand supposed to be pasture for cattle but there's scarcely a blade of grass and ends up in sandhills with few small bushes scattered here andthere. The advantage of the place is that it abounds in water. There are wells or rather springs everywhere, besides a good sized river within ½ mile of the ranch with small streams running into it. I believe the Indian territory is very pretty as it is very woody and theres splendid shooting. I will enter an expedition down there as soon as I have a horse of my own. The account of the numbers of stock which I was told before coming out must have been very much exaggerated. There are two or three men of a very low extract who have shares in the stock and land so that when Turnly plows and prepares the land for sowing, they buy the seed and sow it and each takes an equal share of the profit. They sow principally Indian corn with which they feed the horses and hogs. It is a very fattening food but not at all strengthening. Also they sow a little oats and plenty of millet which they feed the cattle on in the wintertime. All kinds of vegetables are very difficult to get—some potatoes and they are wretched. The only meat we have to eat is corned beef as tough as leather. They kill a cow about every three months. They killed one the other day in the afternoon, had it all chopped up, and we had some for supper that evening. The stock consists of little over 200 head of cattle, not counting this year's calves, five milk cows, 100 hogs and about ten horses. I can't say how much the land is but I think it must be about 1600 acres, most of it in pasture. I have the care of the hogs at present and it is anything but agreeable or clean work. The Miss Turnlys are jolly goodnatured girls. The American women here consider themselves on the same footing as any lady and the servants especially they call you by your Christian name without even a Mr.

Your affectionate nephew
T.L.

Chicastria Ranch
Norwich
May 30 1887

My dear U.J. I like this place very much as yet. The climate is so very healthy tho' for the last few days it has been unbearably hot All the land here is being bought up. I wd hardly call it rich land it is so awfully sandy, a very flat country with here and there a sandhill—there's more land in grazing than cultivated Most of these fellows here have invested 2 or 300£ in land as it is always increasing in value—this land was bought for 3 dollars & now sells for 10—as the country is getting peopled and towns springing up everywhere, now if I made choice of a good piece of land of about 80 acres that is 100£ worth I could always sell it if I wanted and it would give me a kind of a claim to stop in the country I want 18£ to buy a horse I cannot herd cattle without it and it is the chief thing some fellows have invested in horses—going shares and buying a bunch—I know of a good horse. well recommended I owed $12 when I arrived but sold a pair of Hugh's boots and paid it off.

Nothing more about Tom Lyle's experiences in the United States is recorded in this collection of letters and diaries, nor is there anything to indicate whether the Turnlys mentioned in his letters were members of the Turnly family of Drumachose Carnlough Co. Antrim. Tom Lyle was back at Knocktarna at the turn of the century, but whether he made money in the United States, or returned because of failure there, or for health reasons is unknown.

1887—Two letters from Mrs. Wilson Cochrane in the Red River settlement in Canada (copies from Ellen Scott's diary).

You will not be astonished to hear that I am real delighted with this country. We had a pleasant trip over the sea, only one Sabbath evening the ship was tossed by a heavy sea but it did not inconvenience us much. I never was sick, only a headache now and then from the noise of so many people gabbing all round. I kept on deck the greater part of the time and enjoyed the fresh sea air. I renewed my health and strength and the children often say "Mama you look ten years younger". We were on the train for four days but could have come along in about three only waiting here at depots. Sister Mary Jane stood the trip well and is well pleased with our change. When we arrived brother David was waiting for us and I knew him at once but he did not recognise me until I got my arms around him. He says I have got so old looking. He has a splendid farm 935 acres of the best land ever the sun shone on. There is quite nice people around and every day since I came we have people coming to see the "new friends" and such fine horses. Everyone here drives two in hand and a four wheeled buggy. We would think them mad in the old country. David has 13 splendid horses, two mares and a foal and two mules, besides a pony. He has a splendid stock of cows too. Best of all he has four fine boys growing up to be men. David and Glyn look well and both are quite healthy. They have a nice new house with every convenience. I am here now and wish all my dear friends were around. We have a Presbyterian house of worship and Methodist both near at hand. Our children feel just at home. I had the pleasure of seeing Mrs Charles Canning. She is a fine woman, and also Mrs James Canning, she is a fine woman too.

From the same.

There is every chance for a man or a woman here to get along well and I think it was a step in the right direction when I plucked up courage to come along. I have bought a farm of 100 acres with land along the red river. It cost 2,000 dollars, about 400£ English. It is well timbered and our house will be ready in November. Our farm is about 12 miles from there but they think nothing of that distance in this country. They always drive two horses in their buggies and the horses are superior as a rule. My brother David sows

50 acres of oats for his own horses. The timber abounds with fruit of all kinds, plums, grapes, rasberries, gooseberries, and currants and the hops grow wild on the trees. I shall be about 2½ miles from church and railway. Charles Canning is a prosperous man and is worth more than 20,000 dollars. He has married an excellent wife and his two children are healthy and are thriving. Mary Canning has married James Cramie and he is well to do, has a beautiful place along the river. She has 400 chickens and their stock of horses and cows are worth seeing. The country is not much different in regard to heat from Ireland, but the air is pure and dry. but they have hotter summers.

The Red River Settlement, near the city of Winnipeg, was originally a Scottish colony. It was founded in 1811 by the Scottish Lord Selkirk, who at that time controlled the Hudson Bay Company. Later, quarrels arose between the Hudson Bay Company and the North West Fur Company. This led to violence, during which Governor Semple of the Hudson Bay Company and twenty of his twenty-seven attendants were killed. In 1869, the territorial rights of the Hudson Bay Company in the Red River Settlement were bought by the Dominion of Canada.

No more is heard of Mrs. Wilson Cochrane in this book.

46 / 1887–1888—Ellen Scott's Diary Records a Health Quest

In 1887, some anxiety was felt by his parents about George Scott's health. On November 3, Ellen Scott took him to Dr. Gordon in Dublin:

. . . . had been with Dr. Gordon in morning on 4 a.m. He thought for a little, took a book about climates, found Montreux would not do, mentioned Davos, but said its melancholy surroundings were against it. Said Cairo was the climate. He had been there in the spring and was charmed. Said George had a little wheeze which shewed the lungs wanted expansion, were as it were locked up and required dry air. Said his heart was improved and chest better developed was glad to see him looking so well, hoped a winter in Egypt would make him quite strong, said Lord Brabazon had got quite well from two winters at Davos. After George went out I said, "Is there really no place in England you could recommend." "None". I mentioned Montreux, Nice—No—so we felt it was to be done. While he was examining George I lifted up my heart in prayer that he might be guided to give us the right counsel, so I have felt more resigned than I otherwise would be. We crossed by Holyhead and N. Wales, lovely passage, sun 9.30 hot, arrived at Chester 5.30 and found S. Holme and Flo most hospitable and delightful She shewed us many curiosities, a relic of each place she had visited, envied us going to a sunny clime . . . visited the Holmes new house prettily situated, will be nice. Edward[1] architect . . . . found that the 9th was Lord Mayor's day so had to avoid the city. It was a wet dirty day, wretched for the show The Lord Mayor this year is ?? R.C. but "no way bigotty" Trafalgar Square full of police. The radicals had determined to have a monster meeting on Sunday to protest against the imprisonment of Mr O'Brien and it was proclaimed so Sir Charles Warren[2] head of the police took strong measures and was successful, only some wounds. The Guards were paraded and cheered—special constables are being enrolled. . . . Then to Wotton Rectory where we staid until Monday. Arthur and Alfred, who is gazetted to the 23rd . . . Had much talk with Mr. E[3] about Ireland—such a pity he has written letters lately greatly disgusting his Deptford constituents—offering them Mr Blunt, now a notorious nationalist . . . . The journey before us has been a weight and anxiety . . . We started yesterday, Liverpool Street Station 11 o'cl for Tilbury, paid 3/6 each there for tender . . . Our cabin very comfortable . . . Fresh nice day and sat out George having bought me a chair for 5/- I have so often wished for some bright friend to make it more cheerful to B.and G. Hope however they enjoy it. Am wroth with Flo not telling one to bring some tea, bootlaces, a candle, a general map, labels.

Nov.26th Friday The roll of the Bay began yesterday evening and I left the dinner table having taken soup and fish and had duck and green peas on my plate. There were many vacant chairs. Tuesday Nov.29th . . . . . Gib. much prettier than we expected—really beautiful. The great height and the range of peaked mountains and the glorious sun painting so many obelisks stuck here and there against the rock. . . . An orange seller, such a regular character in Spanish costume, offered us 100 for 2/- . . . Wednesday Nov.30th. . . . Had a long talk with old Mrs Talglour, who is going out to her son now at a station, S.W. Australia, Bombera George Sound. Her son at 17 was so delicate he could not go upstairs without being bathed in perspiration. He went out to a station and has got quite strong, taken a station himself and married. He had been jilted by a lady who would have been quite unsuited to the life and his present wife can do everything. Dec.1st. . . . wish poor Charlie Lyle was in this clime. . . . . Saw oil sketch yesterday of Maharanee done by a lady. . . . Dec.2nd. . . . All here full of expectation to hear if Egypt has dispensed with quarantine. A boat with a flag came out and announced that it had, so all were free to land. Then the babel began. 50 odd boats with screeching gabbering boatmen came rushing in and out. Some people came on board and we resolved to see what was to be seen so we reached a boat. . . . While we were on shore the Duke of Edinboro' came on board to pay his respects to the Maharanee and invited her to go to an opera got up specially for her as they have none usually on Fridays. So the Chief Officer took her off at 5 o'c. and a great many of our ships party have stayed on shore for it. . . . Mrs Willisma, a young wife going out to India with her two babies, talked to me of the much better custom in India where the wife shares the innocent amusements of her husband, joining him at his Club, even taking the children sometimes and waiting while the father smokes his pipe, comparing it with England where the wife is excluded and so for want of this—brandy is introduced.

The Scotts' journey continued, with Mrs. Scott recording the daily events of the voyage, where they stayed on shore, much history, and the sights they saw. Also, she recorded all details of her son's health. After stopping at many places, including Gibraltar, Malta, Cairo, Alexandria, Port Said, Jaffa, Jerusalem, Corfu, etc., Easter eve, March 31, 1888 found them at Beyrout, where Ellen Scott writes with thankfulness that Dr. Grant has pronounced George's lungs as sound; with only a rheumatic tendency remaining.

On April 8, George caught a bronchial cold. Two doctors were consulted on this occasion, Ellen Scott being very anxious. Both agreed it was only a cold, which would pass off in a few days. All April, George had variations from day to day in temperature, cough, and general condition.

On May 14, 1888, they landed at Tilbury, their journey at an end. There they saw Dr. Maine, who had been recommended to them. Ellen Scott notes in her diary, "Saw from his manner that he did not think well of G."

On May 17, George had a haemorrhage. "Dr White explained to George a small vein had ruptured and the heart action being hurried would remove the clot which should be left to settle and heal the place."

By July 7, the Scotts had returned home. Ellen Scott's diary records the daily variation in George's health, the improvements and setbacks, the temperatures, sometimes normal and sometimes high, the cough greatly improved, only to return, all the agonizing suspense and the cruel torture of raised hopes and renewed fears.

On July 22, while out in the garden with his mother, George said, "I think God must feel to repent when he looks at those who are fading away under his trials." To this, Ellen Scott replied, "He looks at things in the light of eternity." Later that evening, George said, "I don't think anything dreadful in dying. I wonder people make such work about it—if one is any way good."

Ellen Scott's diary continues:

Speaking of M not seeming happy I said "I think it is because she is not satisfied with God's will" He said "Oh that is a miserable thing. It keeps one fretting and discontented" Oh the mercy to find he is satisfied with God's Will. It has comforted me.

July 27 . . When he was suffering his indigest pain the other Night I sat by him he held my hand saying "Oh what it is to have a Mother. You don't mind so much when you have a Mother''

Aug 4th . . . Yesterday G. sat with me at the study fire, said he did not fear death if only he was better prepared. He wished his father would prepare him.

August 5th . . . One time I said Congreve cures cases worse than yours who recovered He said ''Oh yes, but I know I am getting worse, each day cough is worse''.

August 7 . . . Last Sunday out in the garden he said ''God is very good in gradually taking away one's care for things When you feel each day not able to do what you used to, you cease to care for it so a long illness is a good thing. Suddenly to leave all you liked would be worse''. After much pain and stuping for 2 hours he said ''If it was not God's will it could not be borne''.

Aug.11th . . . . He said to me ''I wish father would not break down so much, I want him to prepare me but he said when I talked to him about giving to Ada sone of what he intended for me—it is too sad don't talk that way, Father seems as if I were bad and not going to Heaven''. When going to bed he said ''I used to think death dreadful but now I don't feel like that I don't know why it is''. . . . He said ''I can't bear to think that when I go you & father will get so low and sink

Aug.12. . . . He asked Nurse if he would get much pain when it got near the end. She said difficulty in breathing would be all she thought. He will not entertain the thought of recovery.

Aug 21st . . . A few nights ago as I sat by his bed he said ''No one need feel badly off when they have a Mother like you''.

Sept. 6, 1888 We heard on Sunday of C. Lyle's death and I did not tell him till Monday. He said ''Why did you not at once tell me. I ought to have known at once''.

Before the end of 1688, George Scott, like Charlie Lyle, also died of consumption.

In the last paragraph of this diary, Ellen Scott included a sentence that will have brought comfort to her and her husband in their profound grief. ''I had a talk with George the other day which I cannot put down, my memory is so bad now but it shewed me how God was carrying on His work in his soul.''

Notes

1. Flo Holmes's brother.
2. Sir Charles Warren was still the police commissioner for London the following year, 1888, when the terrible murders of Jack the Ripper horrified the public. The failure of the police, in spite of intensive efforts to identify and arrest the murderer, led to Sir Charles's resignation.
3. Mr. Evelyn.

47 / 1889—Old Matty's Account of a Visit to Banagher Church by the Choir (of Ballyrashane Church) and Mrs. Cunningham's Household

I was going up the church walk just as usual and the key in my han'—well I saw movements of horses "In the name of goodness says I is a funeral coming to me?" I stud to see what was what The party cam out and I couldn't see clear I went on with my key The whole set were at the fut of the steps So the cook, she was in black! says she I'm coming to see the Church *I* thought the three in Black were young ladies They came forhead. I saw a young man, says I "This is Johnnie McAteer" says I "What are ye all and where did ye come from?" Says I to the cook Your a very nice party comin to see my Church Then the big man cam forhead a big dacent man. of some party from above He favored James Faith—large and goodlooking—Your very gran says he and everything very nice—you're the prettiest place ever I saw says he Christy made them welcome to the stable and Mrs Smith got them all sorts They had fine things they brought with them a salmon at the top and Mrs Smith gave them tablecloth and all in style So they passed on says I "You must see another scenery—The Lignum Paste" The big man put down the name—and says he Oh is there a waterfall We'll have to see that Willie says to them he would put them up as far as Katies but Willie never cam back till he saw them in the van I didn't hear if they had saw the old Church—They were just as dacent and modest a set as ever cam into the place. . . . .

This account was among Ellen Scott's diaries.

"The Lignum Paste" remains a mystery unless any reader can explain what and where it may be.

48 / 1889–1891—Annie F.E. Scott, Abroad and at Home

Tuesday May 28th 1889

Here we are once again at the Hotel du Nord Cologne It is now five years since we were abroad before and as the diary I wrote then was very interesting to myself I must try & keep one again of this our second tour on the Continent. We arrived at the Grosvenor Hotel last Thursday morning, had a lovely crossing & met Major & Mrs Little & Mr Edge on board the boat It was delightful being in London again the crowds in the park were most wonderful and the fashions marvellous especially in the way of hats, they are simply masses of flowers. Then steels have quite gone out & pads are rapidly following suit. . . . On Sunday the first wet day . . . went to the Abbey in the afternoon where Archdeacon Farrar preached on the Forgiveness of the Prodigal parts were beautiful but he was too strong upon his own theories. . . . The Warburtons were also at the Hotel certainly we met a lot of friends and it was very pleasant. . . . Yesterday we had lunch at the Campbells packed & started from Victoria at 8.30 We had a very calm passage & arrived here at 2 o'clock without any fusses. This Hotel is as charming as ever with garden & balcony where you can have your meals . . . . . then back in time for Table d'Hote Rather dull affair no one talked to any but their own party but afterwards Mrs & Miss Persse talked to us they live at Cape Town and knew J. Torrens there how small the world is!

Friday June 1st

On Wednesday morning we made our way once more to the Cathedral . . . . From this we made our way to St Ursula the church was being repaired but we were shewn the bones of the virgins a most wonderful & grewsom sight The walls were all lined with them & rows & rows of skulls circled the room. We saw the bone from Ursula's right arm & foot. A thorn from our Saviour's Crown. A pitcher from Canaan of Gal. etc. I need hardly say we did not believe all this information. The coffers containing the remains of St. U. & her bethrothed were very handsome gold enamelled & inlaid with precious stones At 12 o'cl. we left Hotel du Nord & drove to the station bound for Heidelberg . . . We took places in the train & then went to the Buffet to try & get some lemonade after some difficulty we got a bottle but they would not put it into our straw covered flask so I had to carry it back down the long platform under my dust cloak as it did not look well Papa carrying a bottle & me one too half way there pop goes the cork under my arm—K & several people turned to see what had happened but I walked on as cool as you please secretly trembling lest it would all pour out however it didn't & I got to the carriage in safety At Mayence we had to change & here we counted on 30 minutes wait but we were bundled into another train & off again in 4 much to Papa's disgust who declared we were going all wrong however two people in the carriage were going to Heidelberg so we knew we would reach it . . . at 7 o'cl. we reached Heidelberg but to our horror K's little handbag was nowhere to be found & it contained all our keys, this was a great misfortune as we had to break open our box much to the amusement of the good natured chambermaid who brought us a nail & hammer to assist us . . . K & I slept soundly but Papa was not so fortunate his bed collapsed & he had to ring the servants up at midnight. It must have been a horrid bore but also rather comic Papa in desabile making signs & pointing to the prostrate bed & the astonished Boots looking on . . . Next morning nothing having been heard of the keys we started at 10:30 for Neuhausen Papa got in rather a fuss as the tickets were for a different route to what we had intended so to prevent starvation we laid in a plentiful supply of eatables & started. The heat was terrible every time the train stopped we

312

felt as if we would suffocate. We soon discovered we had made a lucky hit & were going through one of the best parts of Black Forest At first we came to a valley with mountains each side—every now & then passed charming quaint villages nestling in under the hills the valley became narrower & narrower & the scenery wilder until we began to ascend & then we passed through a lovely bit higher & higher we went zigzagging up steep ascents until we got to a giddy height now we did not go round but up through mountains one after another & each moment the views got grander. . . . At Schaffhausen our luggage was searched or rather we were asked if we had anything to declare & having nothing we came on here to Neuhausen Hotel Schweigerhof just in time for 7 o'cl. Table d'Hote.

Saturday

There are nice people in the Hotel. Mr Gould & his sister sat next to us he has passed most of his life at the Cape & is fond of Flowers. . . . I struck up an acquaintance with a queer gray haired lady with a curled fringe who is rather a good artist she invited me to join her on the Terrace I discovered she is sister to Rev. Nottinge a fishing friend of Uncle C's it is so funny the way you meet people There are other people Johnstones a mother & daughter & niece they looked very nice but are slightly disappointing The daughter knew Eddie Bowen

Wednesday

On Monday soon after breakfast we started for the Falls. . . We soon reached Schloss Leufen and after paying 1 franc each we descended by steps to view the Falls Louder & louder sounded the roar of rushing water & coming to an opening cut for the purpose we found ourselves just overhanging the Falls It was a grand sight the lovely green light in the water & the white foam which rose in colums above it Through an arch in the rock we once again saw it but it gave one such a queer helpless feeling that we did not stay long. . . . At Table d'Hote we were much exercised in our minds about two bottles which were placed opposite two vacant chairs one Appolonaris Water the other a big bottle of whiskey we made various jokes about this when imagine our surprise when we saw the General as large as life & his wife taking the places. It was most amusing we have had a good deal of talk together & it is very pleasant having met. . . . . . We came upon a most amusing description of Uncle C. as one of the Commissioners in the Samoa Conference:Calignanis Messenger June 3rd 1889:

"Hon. Edward Scott! the second English Commission, was for a long time the First Secretary of the British Legation, & is well liked at court & in society, He is now Minister to Switzerland. He has a thorough knowledge of German diplomacy, & knows a great deal about Samoa. He is a young man, slightly above medium height somewhat inclined to embonpoint & wears a short full beard. He has *exquisite* manners''.

How we did laugh over this especially the embonpoint & exquisite manners. I wonder if he or Aunt Tina have seen it.

313

Grindelwald The G Bear

. . . . In the hall of this Hotel we were greeted by Mr Crommelin & Capt. Leslie Lowry whose wife & 2 daughters are staying here. At Table d'Hote. . . to our astonishment at a neighbouring table we spied Rev. G. Adams. . . . Next morning after much consultation we made up a party viz Capt Lowry & two daughters C. Crommelin & ourselves to go to the Weilspitz half way up the Faulhorn 2 hours climb We had two horses between us. . . . I mounted first but when I thought I had my share I got down & joined the walkers . . . . I walked 3 quarters of the way up & all the way down so feel rather proud of myself. . . . The view from here of the glaciers were beautiful with the tall dark pines for a foreground. At length we reached the Alpenrose Hotel & had a very merry picnic lunch which we had brought with us & were assisted by our guide, a goat, a dog & a cat Capt. L. was great fun not knowing a word of German he conversed in all sorts of languages with our hostess. . . . We became quite wild over the flowers. . . . We got some roots & sent them to Aunt Hatty It was so steep that we all decided to do it on foot as riding down seemed too dreadful. We got back to the Hotel about 5 o'cl. & it looked so settled we telegraphed to Uncle C. telling them to come. Alas next morning it clouded over & simply poured all day. We were in hopes they had not started but at 5.30 they drove up in a shut carriage having seen nothing of the beauties of the scenery.

Sunday June 30th

My birthday. K. gave me a quaint old Swiss bracelet Papa a pretty oil picture of the Jungfrau. I feel rather sad at growing so old 26, it seems a most venerable age. . . . .

Monday July 1st

This morning . . . we started K on a horse Papa & myself with a Guide to the Burez. It was rather a stiff climb the horse could only go halfway & is rather a mistake if you can walk at all. Towards the top the path overhung a steep precipice overlooking the glacier several hundred feet below. . . . We rested for a few minutes at the Chalet & then descended by two long ladders very horrid to the Glacier it was covered by a lot of stones & gravel so at first did not seem like Ice but it was delicious to walk in the cool bracing air. We walked as far as the centre of the glacier & looking up you saw this great stream of ice stretching right up the mountain on all sides—it appeared like a great torrent suddenly frozen in its mad career. I am so glad we did this as it gave me a far better idea of what a glacier really is.

Tuesday

. . . . We started at 10 o'cl. for the Little Scheideck. . . . Another party started from the Hotel about the same time & we soon joined forces. . . . Sir George Cornwall an elderly gentleman great botanist who told us the names of all the flowers, his son a nice youth at Cambridge shy & quiet but by degrees he became more conversational a Mr & Mrs Danniell very nice couple who live next to Col. Bruce in London who had told them all about Uncle C, they know Fred Heygate quite well. I got on wonderfully doing a good deal more than half It was too bad before the halfway house I was far ahead of the gentlemen & was very proud of myself when to my horror I saw young Mr C. stalking up a steep short cut & he got first it was awfully mean of them but I believe they could not stand the disgrace of being beaten by me so sent him on . . . . . There was very little view but we got occasional glimpses of the dazzling white Jungfrau. . . . . . .

On Monday July 8th . . . . we started for a long & happy day at St. Beatenberg first we trained it as far as Thun then got on board a steamer & after some little time reached St. B. where we got into a train a la pilatus only on the rope principle & in fear & trepidation in 15 m we got to the top it was a lovely bright day & the views were lovely dark pine against the brilliant blue green lake in the foreground & for a background lovely blue mountains every shade & every now & then the beautiful snow peaks of Jungfrau Eiger etc. appeared out of the clouds. . . . We got back to Berne at 10.30 after a delightful day though Uncle C. had been very naughty in the morning about starting. Next day we two & Miss McKnight went to Gossets in broiling sun for tea & tennis . . . Mr G. is a great man on glaciers and has taken up photography . . .

Thursday we went to the Gossets again for a big lunch in honour of Sir F. Adams such a spread as it was rather amusing. . . . We visited the studio again saw more photos Mr G. is really quite cracky he came on Wed & insisted on taking us out in the roasting sun to fish in what Uncle C. calls a ditch of course we caught nothing & nearly got sunstrokes. Friday Sir F. Adams Mr Cunningham & Leveson-Gore dined very dull watched an eclipse of the moon from the balcony Saturday went to the Circus very good & amusing . . . no cabs are to be had in Berne after dark unless specially ordered.

Friday Riffel Alp Hotel
. . . . Great excietment in the morning 2 parties were seen going up the Matterhorn they got safely passed the snow but at 12 clouds came down & they have not been seen since now it is raining & blowing I am afraid they are having a bad time of it.

Our visit at the Riffel Alp is now a thing of the past as we are once more at Berne & tomorrow we start for home via Paris I feel very sad as we have had a most delightful time especially the last part but I must write down a little of what we did To outsiders our visit to the Riffel must have seemed rather a disappointment as we had very bad weather it got colder & colder on Friday a grey mist all round & nothing whatever to be seen outside we tried to keep warm but failed . . . After luncheon we found ourselves on the verandah talking to Mr Webb about a white lily that has been found. After a little while it cleared & a walk was prepared We donned our short skirts & waterproofs & in the hall were joined by the others Mrs Thompson Mr Webb Rev H. Percy Thompson (brother in law) we all sallied forth together braving the snow which kept coming down in showers I walked with Mrs T. she was nice but a little hard to get on with K & Mr W drifted off together & papa & Mr T brought up the rear We scrambled on for about an hour then it got so wet as the path disappeared we turned & some way I & the clergyman got together I liked him very much we had a great political discussion but I was not sure that I did not talk a good deal of nonsense & he was laughing at me, he seemed full of fun When we got back to the Hotel we had tea with the Trondvilles in company with Mr Sandilands & the gentleman who had been up the Matterhorn Sunday we had breakfast next the Thompsons snow on the ground & very cold After Church & lunch Mr W proposed to take us to find Edelweiss we agreed To my surprise & pleasure when we came down Rev. Thompson came with us as well as Mr Webb we met Miss Trondville & Clifford outside so had to ask them to join us I am afraid I was naughty & kept the clergyman all to myself He talked *so* nicely about Church matters. I told him about my class which seemed to interest him & he advised me strongly to write to William McConnell & not lose sight of him. . . . I had a delightful walk back & a lighter conversation this time I tried to bring in the other girls every now & then so did not feel so selfish . . . After dinner Mrs Thompson came & sat beside me & we had a long talk her husband talked to Papa. She told me all about her brother-in-law such a sad story He was very clever had done well at school & promised great things at College when suddenly he nearly lost his eyesight & had to give up all reading the Drs gave him *no* hope nothing but blindness seemed before him, he cheerily set to work to learn the blind alphabet; A German doctor was next consulted & he did him a lot of good & saved one eye, now he once more thought he might try for ordination A sister read Greek & Latin *to* him He passed the exam quite easily & for a year worked at Wells taking *no* salary Then he travelled came back much better was introduced to the Rev Erskine Clarke who made him 2nd Curate at Battersea St Lukes & now he is in sole charge of doing a great work. When I heard all this my breath seemed taken away it so astonished me, he is so bright and merry you would never guess he had any great sorrow & his eyes look all right only a little near sighted to my mind he is little short of a hero I felt quite shy of him after this but he appeared in a few minutes as jolly & natural as possible. He talked to K & I & to Mr W They were all leaving next day as we were so we parted expecting to meet at St. Nicholas. So we did next day they reached the Hotel just as we drove up. . . . Next morning we started for our L2 mile walk Mrs T rode K & Mr Webb got together very quickly but I fell to Mr Thompson Sen. he was very nice but I did long for Papa to give up his companion & I was not disappointed shortly afterwards I heard a well known voice at my elbow asking a question & we sorted ourselves. Such a nice walk as that was, we talked of everything under the sun he told me about his eyes his work I told him of my life he said some such nice good things We were very serious then we got very merry & never once did he say a single word to make me uncomfortable. We reached Stolden far too soon & here we rested for a little while then on we went again & still there was no lack of con-

316

versation. I asked him to come to Willlsboro if he ever came to Ireland he said he would but I wonder if we will ever meet again. We had no real parting as they got into the same train at Visp but alas they went 2nd class so we only had a hurried Good Bye from the carriage window Mr Webb turned up on Thursday & on Friday we two & Papa took him to the Bears & Clock & brought him back for lunch Uncle C did not think him polished but he is very nice with a good honest face he has a big tea plantation in Ceylon & is home for a year & brought us Mrs Arthur Thompsons card she wants us to write to her when we pass through London as she will come up & see us I wonder who or what they are evidently they are very well off & certainly judging from appearances & manner they are very nice My friend especially so I wonder if in all his hard work he has ever thought of this day week or of a little maiden he walked with even if I don't ever see him again I am glad to have met such a brave good man. . . . . Looking back it seems so queer the way we rushed into friendship we who are generally so stand off It must be something in the mountains but it was not us who made the advance.

We left Berne on Monday August 5th it was horrid saying Goodbye Aunt Tina was quite sad & so were all the dear children certainly we had a most happy time with them. . . . . Uncle Charlie had left for Vevey the Fete de Vigerous on Sunday so only Aunt Tina & the three little children with Babette came to see us off by the 7 o'cl. train for Paris. . . We travelled all night & reached Paris at 7 o'cl. in the morning *not* very tired we had got pillows in the train which made it more resting. . . . We spent two days & one evening at the Exhibition it is a most marvellous place such a size & so beautifully done Glasgow was nothing compared to it. The street of Cairo & the street of Habitation were most interesting At first the Eiffel Tower was disappointing as one fails to realise the immense height of it but when we went up in the lift to the first etage that was quite enough for us, it was really too horrible coming down you felt suspended in the air in a most rickety fashion it is 300 metres high all made of iron at night when lighted up it looks most imposing. . . The crowds were perfectly astonishing and all the people walking about in their various national costumes made it all seem like fairyland We spent one whole day at Versailles . . . It seems quite sad that there should be no King or Court to enjoy all the splendours of the place but Republicans don't agree with this sentiment

Monday morning we left Paris & crossing by Calais we reached London at about 9 o'cl. . . . We called on the Daniells but they were out of town Alas we saw nothing of our Riffel Alp friends it now seems most improbable our ever meeting again. . . . On Thursday morning once more set foot on the shores of "Auld Oirland".

The extract from the *Galignanis Messenger* referred to Charles Stewart Scott, who, in 1883, had been transferred from a minor post in Coburg to be H.M.'s Secretary of Embassy in Berlin. During his five years in

Berlin, he had been engaged in most interesting and responsible work under Lord Ampthill and, after his death, under Sir E. Malet.

Samoa, an archipelago of fourteen islands in the Pacific Ocean, was of importance because of its geographical position. In 1879, the United States, Germany, and Great Britain agreed that no single power should possess the islands. In 1887 and 1888, there was a civil war in Samoa over the succession of a native king. Germany favored one candidate, while Great Britain and the United States supported another. This led to a conference of the three powers in Berlin. Charles Stewart Scott was one of the commissioners. The conference resulted in a treaty in 1889 under which America, and Great Britain ceded their interest in Samoa to Germany in return for Germany's refusal to join an anti-British coalition.

In 1888, Charles Stewart Scott was appointed envoy to Switzerland. It was his first independent mission, and he remained there for five years.

When Annie mentions that she and the Rev. Percy Thompson had "a great political discussion," it is a pity she did not mention their views. Undoubtedly, they would have discussed "Home Rule for Ireland," one of the most controversial political topics at that time.

Ever since the Act of Union, there had been Irishmen, overlooking the circumstances that led to the Union, who struggled, agitated, and resorted to violence in their efforts to secure its repeal. A number of Irish Parliamentary representatives at Westminster, led for a time by Parnell, also worked hard toward the same end. On those occasions, when the Irish members held the balance of power at Westminster, their votes became of great importance.

Gladstone, leader of the Whigs, supported home rule, while Lord Salisbury, the Conservative leader, opposed it.

The Westminster election of 1866 had been fought on the sole issue of home rule for Ireland. The election resulted in a decisive vote against home rule, the Conservatives being supported by antihome rule liberals.

Lord Salisbury did not believe that home rule would solve the Irish problem. He regarded Ireland as the home of two different races, with antagonistic traditions, bitterly opposed to each other. It was his view that Ulster would refuse to accept the inevitable domination by the Southern majority, which home rule would bring, and that they would resist to the point of civil war.

Salisbury also believed that home rule would endanger England by making Ireland the haunt of England's enemies, as so often in the past. Years later, these forecasts of Lord Salisbury proved correct. In the twentieth century, when, after a reign of terror, the republic of ireland won independence, Ulster, by making it clear that sooner than be forced under a Dublin Parliament, they would fight, won its struggle to remain

318

in the United Kingdom. In the Second World War, the ports of Southern Ireland were closed to British ships carrying vital supplies to Great Britain, while the German, Italian, and Japanese legations remained open in Dublin throughout the war, conveniently situated for gathering information helpful to Germany.

Only the open ports of Ulster saved Great Britain from the very serious threat of starvation.

It is not in connection with Ireland only that Lord Salisbury showed remarkable insight, amounting in many cases to prevision.

1890/92 Annie Scott's Diary

October 11th 1890

I seem to have quite given up my old habit of keeping even an occasional Diary which seems a pity. so tonight having nothing particular to do I will try & make a slight sketch of the year which is now over since I last wrote in this book. It was dreadfully hard settling down again after our delightful time abroad, everything seemed dull & uninteresting & it was a weary work picking up the dropped threads of our occupations. We went to Portrush Hotel for a week & then to Knocktarna after which the house was ready for us once more & we started off with a new young butler instead of poor old Pat who had been pensioned off . . . We had a dance at Drenagh about this time 26 of us all staying in the house, it ought to have been great fun but someway though we enjoyed it very much and danced everything it was slightly uninteresting the greatest fun was looking after Flo Lyle[1] who came to it under our wing & who got on capitally We had a great return Rounder Match here Derry v. Limavady, the latter won much to our delight. . . . . . John Torrens, Robt. O'Neill & Capt. Clarke all came for the Synod & we had a nice time John making himself very pleasant, then later on we two went to Somerset where we had a most jolly shooting party in fact we all went quite wild one night dancing etc. The house party was Hon. C & Mrs Alexander, a pretty Canadian who flirted tremendously with John. Robt. O'Neill. Mr Crabbe S. Grey Capt C. McClintock. such a nice man & Rev. J.A. Armstrong. We had one dinner party & of course lots of music. . . There was a horrid Bazaar in Derry for the Deanery Schools in the New Guild Hall which was just finished. it was very dull, cold & stupid, we were by way of selling but I fear did little in that line as we had nothing but rubbish given to us at the best Stall. Bazaars are vile institutions at least I think so at my time of life It used to be fun . . . In June we paid Uncle H. & Aunt Hatty a short visit at Portrush where we made acquaintance with Capt. Tipping & Capt. Knox of Clonleigh the latter was extremely nice. they dined one day & it was extremely jolly, they were cruising in a zutch The Mischief inspecting Life Boats. . . . Summer was very wet but we managed to have a good lot of fun Charley spent his holidays here & was most amusing it was something quite new having a small boy in the house.

319

December 5th 1890 was the date of the Ball at Baronscourt given in honour of the coming of age of the Marquis of Hamilton. It was a great affair one of the grandest I ever was at. Weeks before we were all in a state of excitement over it & wrote for smart new dresses for it from Miss Wilson. they turned out most satisfactory Mine was a lovely shade of green which looked so soft & pretty at night all silk quite plain in the skirt with a short train & round the front about 12 inches from the bottom Embroidered white Chiffon festooned & caught up with Rosettes of green silk the bodies cut round covered with the Chiffon dear little puffed sleeves of silk & round basque a soft fold of silk ending at the back in two rossettes from under which came the train I wore pearls round my neck & hair twisted in coils with pearls & small aigrettes The whole dress was completed by a lovely big chiffon fan to match a present from Papa. Katie was exactly the same only in pink which suited her remarkably well.

We all left Derry by the 4.40 train which was crowded with people going but nearly all got out at Strabane but we had settled to go with the Smylys at Castlederg further on, but the Dean said only an hours drive alas this proved a delusion & we would have been much better off if we too had gone to Strabane Unluckily for us the train was nearly an hour late so we had great hurry when we got to Castlederg Dora & we two hardly took any dinner & fled up to unpack & don our finery with all our hurry we did not get off until ¼ to 9 o'clock and then began our penance because instead of one hour it was quite two hours before we reached Baronscourt It was terrible I could have cried with disappointment when at length we reached the Avenue not a carriage was to be seen & we found we were quite the last to arrive it was too bad as this lost us all chance of getting partners McCullagh & our own butler Campbell greeted us with anxious faces & said it was a pity we were so late. We then went down a corridor to a Cloak Room where 6 very smart maids unrobed us & shaking out our finery we proceeded down a long corridor & were ushered in to a large vaulted room where the Duke & Duchess of Abercorn shook hands with us. She was so nice & had a bright word & smile for every one She was in a rich white brocade and a lot of Diamonds there is something most fascinating about her, I could not help constantly watching her Diamonds just suited her she seemed to sparkle all over & so very gracious to all The Duchess of Buccleuch was in black with row upon row of Diamonds & a Coronet in her hair Duchess of Montrose was very handsome in white & gold net all over the train & panels of handsome gold embroidery Lady Zetland & the Lord Lieutenant of course added greatly to the attractions & according to command in his honour all the officers came in Uniform, this made it all very bright & festive looking. At first one felt dazzled & bewildered by such brightness but by degrees got accustomed to it & could take more in. A dance had just stopped & we saw couple after couple trooping out of the dancing room Derry people seemed very prominent & we saw many well known faces we wandered into another room & soon saw W Lindsey's goodnatured face beaming on us he took me to get some tea which I was much in need of as I felt dead beat refreshed we came out again & I was taken to see the presents given to the Marquis all very handsome arranged on a table in the drawingroom an immense long room with pillars almost dividing it into several separate rooms. palms every here and there & comfortable chair settees in all sorts of corners also card tables for gamblers but there were none Cabinets of lovely china & curiosities against the wall a table of lovely silver ornaments It was a sumptuous room. Abraham Stewart soon found me out & carried me off for a dance the Dancing room was rather too crowded not being large enough for the numbers & the floor not very good, watching was more enjoyable & we had plenty of amusement doing this Capt. Pilkington was in full force dancing with all the swells but all the same he did not quite forget his old flame Sydney McClintock Nell Alexander in a peculiar coloured pink silk with embroidery seemed to be having a very good time joining in all the Lancers Reels etc I got back to a round room & with the Lowry girls who looked so very nice in white silk dresses, trains & front of Chiffon, had a good chat on a most comfortable ottoman The chief occupation was wandering through the different rooms with various people admiring everything & looking at all the people and their smart frocks nearly everyone had long trains I mean of the married ladies & the best dressed girls wore silks with short trains just on the ground. I don't think there were many prettier dresses than our own at least neither of us had any wish to change with anyone & certainly ours were the only chiffon fans. The dining room was another immense room you passed out of the dancing room which I believe is a Hall into a wide corridor with a handsome staircase at one side palms down each side of the centre making cosy sitting out places, at the end of which was the dining room where Supper was spread out on a buffet all round the Room. I feel rather hazy about the geography of the house but there seemed endless amount of room & comfort reigned supreme. I was rather disappointed at not meeting nicer men but except for the house party & some of the Rifle Officers the men were very much the same as those we meet at a Derry Ball & of course no one introduced. I had lots of people to talk to & enjoyed it more than I expected The Lancers they danced they call Kitchen L. rather pretty & more amusing than ordinary ones They had one reel which was fun watching a very smart Highlander played the bagpipes.

Time had flown once more & now it is in July 1891. Our winter on the whole very nice one we got a house in Dublin at least Katie did she & Papa went up together to look for one & after much difficulty got 24 Burlington Road a nice little house prettily furnished & a smart appearance but alas it was only an appearance Everything being patched mended broken etc. notwithstanding we had a very happy time only darkened by household troubles. Kathleen paid us a six weeks visit which was simply charming, so happy were we that the time simply flew. Papa who seemed a different man so much brighter & better & at heaps of meetings & dinners both of which he enjoyed. J. Torrens sent us tickets for Punchestown. . . . Cattle & Dog Show was nice Duke King went with us to it We had a good deal of outing among our friends & saw a good deal of Mr Phillips & like him better Played tennis 2 or 3 times with Louisa & did gooseberry with Mr McGusty the result is they are engaged We left Dublin May 15th. . . . I did a good deal about Gardening Society & got it fairly started held one Committee Meeting & told everyone what they were to do The Dublin Tennis Tournament was our next dissipation We two went to the Ingrams for it Mr P took us & the Adairs to the Review in the Park on the Queen's birthday he asked K to go to the Tennis Dance but she refused. . . . The final Champion Match. We just saw this finish then got dinner & off to the North Wall Boat where we met Papa. . . and reached London 7.30. Had breakfast at the Euston & reached Fleet at about 11 o'cl. where Cousin Horatio met us. . . . We also saw Eversleigh Church and Rectory Kingsleys home, which was interesting but the nicest of all was Winchester Cathedral & College which we went to one day, it was all charming so old & so very interesting especially the College such a jolly porter shewed us all over, he knew H. Lyle quite well & shewed us where his rooms were. . . . The influenza was still so bad in London we were afraid of staying there any length of time so just stopped one night at the Grosvenor.

Katie Scott, Annie's sister, who refused Mr. Phillip's invitation to the Tennis Dance, later married him and went to live in Dublin.

H. Lyle, who was at Winchester College, was probably Henry Lyle, son of James and Emily Lyle of Glandore. He was a first cousin of Kathleen Anette Lyle, their fathers being brothers.

Annie Scott never again met the young clergyman who made such an impression on her when they met in Switzerland. As often happens, her destiny differed from her dreams. Sometime after the end of this, her second diary, Willie Scott was driving into Derry. His daughter Annie, riding, accompanied him, often going on ahead. Suddenly, a riderless horse appeared, cantering toward the carriage. "That's Miss Annie's horse," exclaimed the coachman, increasing the carriage's speed. They found Annie lying on the road—dead. In her fall, its cause unknown, she had broken her neck.

Notes

1. Kathleen Annette, Lyle's sister.

Round rubber stamp with Institute Evangelico de Teologio around
it. And, on a scroll in the middle in smaller letters, Ora et Labora. Written
below the scroll is the date—Jan 1, 92.

My dear Mr & Mrs Scott.

I have had a strong desire for some time to write to you, and believing
that you will be glad to hear from me I am happy in taking the privilege on
this my first New Year's Day in this land of my adoption. Although I have
been hearing of your welfare from my mother & from Mr Glendinning, my
thoughts have been very much centred on you latterly. I trust you continue
in the enjoyment of good health, and experience much blessing in your
pastoral privileges and duties I heartily wish you much happiness during the
year on which we have just entered, and many happy returns of the Season.
I pray that your labours for the Master may be crowned with much success,
in the corner of the vineyard in which your lot is cast during the year 1892
I don't forget Mrs Scott's earnest exhortations & warnings to us when I had
the privilege of attending her class in Balteagh Sabbath School, although I
was then for the most part careless, and without a saving interest in the
Saviour But during the five years that have intervened since the Light Divine
dawned upon me, I have often thought of her faithful "pleadings and warnings" Dear Mrs Scott, I tell you this for your encouragement for "*The Word*
is still the Power of God unto Salvation" notwithstanding appearances to the
contrary Many an anxious seeking heart is hidden beneath an apparent outward
indifference, and a word in Season to such might be, in the hands of the
Spirit, of Eternal importance. Hence the necessity to be "instant in Season
& out of Season" When the Great Day of Account comes & each of us is
called upon to "restore the talents received", may we come each one with
joy, bearing many precious Sheaves, and receive the "Well done" of our
Blessed Master.

Since I came to this country I have seen many strange sights & many
strange people; much that is interesting & much that is very saddening I don't
know whether you are much acquainted with the Spanish character & Spanish
customs, but I expect you are, so I will not wait to give you any minute
descriptions of either. The Spanish character is, if really Spanish, not by any
means exemplary. This you will already have expected to hear, considering
the degrading and demoralizing influence of Rome, so long having full sway
over what would otherwise be a noble witty people, I believe. As it is,
untruthfulness, immorality, superstition & cowardice reign supreme. They
are not however so entirely under the power of the priests in some respects
as Roman Catholics in Ireland are. Indeed many of the people have simply

323

no religion & do not hesitate to express detestation of the priests. Many are quite willing to listen to the Gospel & are ready to express themselves in favour of Protestant belief, but lack of moral courage & fears for their future livelihood seems to prevent many from identifying themselves with us. Still we should praise God for the Grace which has enabled so many to come boldly out & declare themselves on the side of Christ & his Gospel. In many instances the children who attended the day & Sab. Schools & "heard the Word" have become real little missionaries in their homes, and not a few have thus been brought to the knowledge of The Truth as it is in Jesus. At the day Schools in Puerto we have a daily attendance of nearly 70 children, and about 80 on the Rolls. On Sat. 26th Decr. we had a Festival for the Scholars of Sab. & day schools and we had 83 present. This is a promising part of the work. By Spanish laws there is Religious freedom to everyone, but very often it is unknown in practice. The laws are scarcely ever carried out except in an instance when it is more *profitable* to do it than let it alone, and to a large extent, therefore, everyone is a law unto himself. The religious freedom enjoyed by Protestants, or the wrongs which they have to suffer in any particular town, depends largely or indeed entirely, on the character of the mayor of that town. If he is a Roman Catholic saint so-called, of course there is no toleration, or at least as little as possible; & if he has no great quantity of Romish fanaticism about him, he doesn't trouble himself so much with those who go about quietly & preach to & teach the people.

The climate of this part of the country seems very healthy. Just now the cold is pretty trying considering that we never have any fires, & of course the houses were built more for the heat of Summer than for the cold of Winter. While it is pretty cold morning & evening, yet when the sun at midday shines upon us, it is difficult for one who comes from Ulster to realise the fact that Christmas has already come & gone. I think it is very hot during midsummer, but I have not yet had the experience of it. I have enjoyed very good health since I came for which I thank the Giver of every perfect Gift. No doubt you would like to know something about my present sphere of work. This College has been established for the purpose of training native pastors & teachers. Last year some who entered upon the work (a pastor & teacher now at Cordova) were the first fruits of it. The Rev. W. Moore is the principal of it. Three ministers, who live respectively at Cadiz, San Fernando & Jerez come on their turn to teach from 11 to 3 o'clock each day. Of these three the former was educated in Switzerland & is in connexion with the Scotch Mission; the 2nd is a converted priest, (whose history is like a novel) & is in connexion with the Irish Pres. Church; while the third is of Jewish descent, & was educated in England & I think born in Constantinople. Mr Moore takes charge of the Theological part of the teaching, including Latin, Greek & Hebrew I am in charge of the students except when they are receiving lessons from these teachers; that is, when studying walking etc. I can also correct their English exercises. During six hours each day when they are studying I can also study. After some time I hope to be able to assist in teaching elementary Latin & Greek & take charge of some meetings for Mr

Moore. He is at present in very delicate health I am sorry to say. I hope to be of some use very shortly in the Sab. School. I like the Spanish language very much. It very much resembles French or Latin, but the pronunciation is so much easier than that of French. I can now converse a little. I am not yet three months here, so I cannot expect to know very much. It is not a pleasant experience to be thus cut off from *direct* work but it is certainly very necessary at times I have at times felt sad at the thought of being so very far from dear friends, as is natural, but I have never experienced more of the presence & power of Him whose command is "Go" his "lo I am with you alway" is my confidence, & He Himself is my portion.

I am entering on the New Year with prospects widely different from any I ever before had. Looking back over the past years of my life I thank God for the wonderful way in which He has led me. I have had many a turn & experience, but the Lord has been my Helper & the promise in Isaiah 42.16 is one over which I might write truly the words "tried & proved" (Deut. 1.31 & 1 Sam.7.12) My Guide of the past years will not forsake me for the future. Isaiah 42.6 & 1.13 are now very precious promises to me.

Now I must conclude this long letter and not weary you with it. I will be exceedingly glad to hear from you if you can write to me.

When you see *my mother* will you kindly let her know I have written you.

Again with good wishes for the New Year
I am
Dear Mr & Mrs Scott,
Yours Very Sincerely
William Scott
Rev. J.B. & Mrs. Scott
Banagher Rectory.

62 Palacios
Puerto St. Maria
Andalucia
May 24th 92

My Dear Mr Scott,
Your very kind & highly interesting letter of 27th ult. gladly received by me. Although I had been hearing from my mother constantly about your state of health & your gradual improvement still I was very glad to have the assurance from yourself that you were fully restored. The trying Winter that you experienced in Ireland, together with the terrible Influenza epidemic which prevailed, has left many sorrowful homes. I was very sorry indeed to hear about the death of Mrs. Stevenson. I am sure it was a trying time for you when so many in your Parish were suffering. Of course the climate of the South of Spain, as you remark, is much more genial, and to one coming from Ulster it seems as if he had missed a Winter altogether. Still, the past Winter in this country was very trying & stormy, so far as rain & winds were concerned. The floods were very destructive, and labour & traffic were for

some time entirely upset. Now we have a temperature of about 90 degrees, so that we have almost forgotten what the storms were like. Like too many at home the poor of this country never think of saving for a rainy day, and when a week of rain comes they are in utter starvation. It seems as if they consider it a part of their creed, in the strictest sense, to let every day provide for the wants of itself. As I get to see more of the people & of the language I think I am getting to like them better. Of course they are not any worse, nor so bad as our forefathers were, and yet see what has been the effect of the power of the Gospel in our country. This is certainly encouragement to those who long for the Salvation of Spain from ignorance & vice. Still there is another side to look at, which if true is very sad. No country in the world can furnish such a record of noble martyrs for the Faith of Christ; In no country in the World did the Gospel spread faster than it once did in Spain. But the powers of darkness rose up in all their fury to extinguish the Light which was so fast spreading. The history of the terrible Inquisition shows us, and, the after history of the country shows us how successful was the bloody work. The question sometimes arises to me ''Is it not possible that God may now 'mock at their Calamity', they having, it may be, sinned away their day of Grace''. However I trust that the past ages of being left to themselves may suffice for the ''Blood of the Saints'' and many things point in that direction. Some workers in the field for years are full of hope for the near future. With regard to Sr. Cabrera I have to say that I am not acquainted with him at all, but I have heard somewhat of his history before and after leaving the Presby. body. I am sending you herewith a (review) copy of the correspondence which Mr Moore had with the Archbishop of Dublin, about the time of his (Cabrero's) trying to be ordained Bishop in Spain. I leave you to judge of the man & of the circumstances from this pamphlet; & lest you might think me prejudiced against him I will make few remarks about him. From what I know about Mr Moore's desires in the matter, I am quite certain that he would rejoice to see the Episcopal Church forces & successes increased a hundredfold. The country is large enough for all, and how could any one having a spark of the love of Christ in his heart, quarrel with an Evangelical Church about doctrines, (however important they be) while so many millions are dying without the knowledge of the Truth. It is not, & it ought not to be, a matter of making Presbyterians or Episcopalians, but Christians. Besides what is mentioned in these letters of Mr Moore's, I think there were some matters which had reference to the character of some of his (Cabrero's) relations for which he was not altogether irresponsible, and which Mr M thought wd. not tend to bring respect for the system of which Cabrero would be head. However I believe C. is a clever man. With regard to the advantages which you say an Episcopal Mission would have, and which the Presbt. Church does not claim, I have very little to add except that I would not think I was saying much in favour of any Church if I said that in joining it the Spaniards would ''not have so much to give up'' as in joining any other Evangelical body. The question is ''is it an advantage to have little to give up?'' The work of all our Evangelical Churches in Spain is almost entirely

326

amongst the very poorest of the people. To those at home this may seem no disadvantage, but it is a very great one. The rich have the poor at their feet, so that if the upper classes could be reached, with them we wd. have the poor, whereas the poor are not at liberty, generally speaking, to follow the dictates of conscience, I think the Bible Society is breaking new ground in this respect.

Next Sabbath Day (29th) there is to be a bull fight in Puerto Sta Maria. Sixteen horses were killed at the last in Cadiz about two weeks ago. It is a wonder how man can find pleasure in such cruel sport. What a contrast from the pleasures of those who find their chiefest joy in Christ!

Now that you and Mrs Scott are again restored to the guidance & work of the Sabbath School, I trust you may have very much blessing in it. We have about 80 children in attendance at Sab. School & the same at the Day Schl. Mr Moore will be going home about the 20th June to remain away during the three months of holidays. I will be here in charge of some 4 or 5 students in the College, & a general oversight of all till his return. The summer months are very trying I believe when the temperature ranges from 95☆ to 110☆. I am now quite strong, thanks to the Great Giver of every good. I am gradually gaining some confidence in conversing in Spanish, and I hope that when I have completed a year, I will be able to be more useful in the work & I long for that.

Please convey my kind remembrances to Mrs Scott. I thank her very much for her nice letter which I should have answered, but I was waiting to hear from you. I trust you are both remaining quite well. I have not heard from Mr Glendinning for a long time. I conclude with best wishes & kind regards

I am dear Mr Scott
Yours Very Sincerely
Willie Scott

Rev. J.B. Scott,
Banagher Rectory,
Derrychrien.

P.S. I trust you will be preserved from Home Rule & Rome Rule in Ireland.

50 / 1898—James R. McClellan Writes to Ellen Scott From the U.S.A.

Highlands
35 Dorr St.
May 9/98

Dear Mrs Scott,

It gave me great pleasure to receive your kind letter of the 22nd April, and to hear that you were enjoying good health, for that is one of the greatest blessings that God can confer upon us in this world. I received the two sermons by the Rev. Canon Scott, preached on Palm & Easter Sundays of 1896, and I wish to return you my sincere thanks for your kindness in sending them to me, I read them with much pleasure and I trust some profit, and some friends to whom I lent them enjoyed them very much also; the Canon was a very kind friend of mine for whom I had a high respect and regard, I was much grieved, as well as shocked when I heard of his sudden death, coming so soon after having seen him in apparently good health, you and his whole family, as well as his many friends and parishioners among whom he labored so faithfully for many years have sustained a heavy loss by his being called away but it is a consolation to know that your loss is his gain. And that he has gone to receive the reward for faithful service in this world, from the hand of his Master in Heaven. As regards the War recently declared between this country and Spain, I cannot look upon it as being anything but unjust and uncalled for, and very many people here agree with me in this view; this Government declare that it is waged by it in the cause of humanity. And no doubt many good people here sincerely believe that view of it, having been misled by the outrageous exaggerations and misrepresentations published in our Newspapers, and I am sorry to say repeated by many of our Senators and public men about the wickedness barbarity and misgovernment of the Spaniards in Cuba and the treachery and wickedness of Spain as a Nation; Now without wishing to excuse in the least the faults of Spain, for no doubt she has many; and what Nation has not? I wish to bear my testimony, after having lived the greater part of fifteen years, among the Spaniards in Cuba, that I never saw any more proofs of oppression there than I did in any other Country in which I have lived, on the contrary I always considered Cuba one of the freest places I had ever seen, and all foreigners with whom I talked there on that subject agreed with me. And I have never lived among kinder or more refined people. And I can assert that in times of peace, No one ever suffered for want of food, nor was any one who wished to work without employment, And the wages paid were highter than in any other Country in which I have been, with these facts in view, And many more which I might adduce, it seems to me, the much talked of oppression in Cuba was more imaginary than real; and as regards the humanity on the part of this Country in this War, I must confess I cannot see where it comes in, is

328

it humane to deliberately sacrifice the valuable lives of thousands, and it may be hundreds of thousands before it is settled, for the pretended purpose of improving the Condition of a very few thousand rebels, who are principally composed of Negros and half breeds, and who are as a class ignorant & lazy, and are in no way Capable of governing themselves, neither could they have withstood the power of Spain for half this length of time had they not been assisted and encouraged by this Country, And assisted also by the climate of Cuba which has a deadly effect on foreigners in the rainy Season? And do you consider it is either Christian or humane for a great Nation of seventy five millions of inhabitants, and with boundless resources, to invade a poor weak Nation like Spain, with only seventeen millions of people, and wrest from her her remaining possessions? for I believe that will be the result, if the Great Powers of Europe do not interfere to prevent it, the Government declares that it has no intention of annexing Cuba, which my be quite true as far as it is concerned, but I know that a large majority of the Merchants & Capitalists here have been in favor of adding that Island to this Countrie's possessions, for many years past. I am sorry to see that Great Britain is giving all her sympathy & encouragement to this country in this business being the only Great Power which has done so; I think both countries have placed themselves in a very unenviable light, in the eyes of the rest of the World, but of course their Motives in so doing are too transparent to be hidden. Thanking you again for the Sermons, & for your kind letter, and wishing you many years of good health, and happiness, I am, with much respect, very sincerely yours.

James R. McClellan

Cuba, the largest of the islands of the West Indies, was discovered in 1482 by Christopher Columbus when he sailed west on his first journey of discovery. He believed Cuba to be part of a new continent.

Centuries passed, and the island remained in the possession of Spain. It became a center of the African slave trade and, later, the haunt of pirates and privateers, including French and English engaged in illegal trading activities.

In 1762, a dispute with England led to the siege of Havana, which was captured by a British force under the command of Adm. Sir George Pocock and the Earl of Albemarle. In the following year, in exchange for the Floridas,[1] Havana was returned to Spain.

The slave trade in Cuba became illegal as a result of treaties in 1817 and 1835 between England and Spain.

Outbreaks of insurrection occurred in Cuba at intervals during the nineteenth century.

America and England both maintained a continuing interest in Cuba. Both were suspected of an ambition to annex the island.

In 1895, there was another rebellious outbreak. President McKinley[2] of the United States made it clear that there was a possibility that America would intervene—to the fury of Spain.

In February 1898, the American battleship *Maine* was blown up in Havana harbor by an unknown perpetrator. In April 1898, America re-acted by demanding that all Spanish troops be withdrawn from Cuba. The result of this move was not withdrawal of troops but war.

The war, of which James McClellan so much disapproved, ended in December 1898 with the Treaty of Paris, under which Spain lost Cuba, and America took it over "in trust for its inhabitants." This was followed by American military rule from 1899 to 1902. A Cuban government then took over, with an agreement that the United States had the right to intervene "for the protection of Cuban independence, and the mainte-nance of Government adequate for the protection of life, property and individual liberty, and for discharging the obligation with respect to Cuba imposed by the Treaty of Paris on the United States, now to be assumed and undertaken by the Government of Cuba."

1900—Letter from Thomas McCully to Ellen Scott (Mrs. J.B. Scott). The envelope was registered on March 10, 1900, in Hendrum, and in the left-hand top corner of it is written, "If not called for in 10 days return to T. McCully Hendrum Minn U.S.America." The envelope is addressed "To Mrs J.B. Scott Bellevue Terrace Coleraine Ireland."

Hendrum March 10 1900

From Thomas McCully
To Mrs J.B. Scott
Dear Friend enclosed please find a draft or check for 1 Pound Sterling that I send to the Sustentation fund of the Protestant Church of Ireland I send it as a token that (without any disrespect to other denominations) I appreciate the Irish Pro Church In which you worship most of all I return you my sincere thanks for the 2 Sermons Preached by your Beloved Husband that you sent me It reminded me of old times the happy moments I spent in Bannagher Church listening with breathless attention With regard to my health I feel as well (thank God) as when I was 20 years of age Since I come to this I was never 2 days idle on account of bad health Till last winter The Door that leads to the cellar being open that I thought was closed I fell half way down the stairs without any serious injury but so sorely bruised that I had to leave off work for 2 months I felt worried for a week or two at first From which time I improved so fast that at the end of two months I was able to work as usual My Nephew Tommy expects soon to be Married and my Nephew William has rented his Farm to him for this season so that I expect to have

him and Mary Anne a little longer. I read your Letter very carefully and over again To see if I could get the least gleam of hope But I found that if you meant to give me such it was very very dim I found that you had consciencious scruples that I could not fathom and your Husband knew me so long that you were qualified to form a right opinion of me Bear with me when I give you another reason And that is when I saw you and your husband so diligent in the discharge of the duties of your high and holy calling And also working together as becomes man and wife I wished with all my heart that I had a wife to love me as you your husband and he you With regard to your con-scientious scruple Far be it from me to wish you to say or do anything for me that you might have just cause to regret My meaning is this that if you knew a young woman that you believed Equal Balance for me A young woman that (God so ordering it) Would be content to give birth to a Babe or Two You would open my case to her Parents or guardian and if granted a hearing you would let me know That we could correspond with each other as those believing that theyll have to give an account thereof at the great day of judgment

Pray see from the foregoing that I have opened my heart to you as I would do to very few Having done so I turn to rejoice with you on the Glorious victory achieved by that nobleminded Irishman Lord Roberts and also for the kind manner in which he received the surrender of Conje[3] a fallen but magnanimous foe

Lord Wellington at waterloo gained a victory that was a prelude of a long and glorious peace And I hope when peace is proclaimed it'll be on a firm and sure foundation that the iniqitous Bloodhounds of War may be restrained Please let me know is your nephew[4] thats travelling improving in health Goodbye from your friend and well-wisher Thomas McCully.

Ellen Scott's Diary:

Sunday 19th Feb.1905—Thomas Cully came in and for 1 ½ hours we had a conversation so sensible and pleasant. He took a year and has come 5000 miles to see his friends and I rather think to get a wife.
April 28, 1905—Got a card from Thomas McCully to say he had been ill.

Ellen Scott does not mention whether he got a wife.

Notes

1. The most southern of the United States, Florida, was the first discovered and colonized by Spain.
2. One of the many presidents of the United States of Ulster descent.
3. At Paardeberg in February 1900 (the Boer War).
4. Tom Lyle, who was suffering from consumption. He went to Switzerland but was not cured.

51 / 1903—The Wedding of Daisy Scott; Hatton O'Hara Writes to Elizabeth Lyle

Tuesday morning
British Embassy
Petersburg

Dearest Lizzie,

You will want to hear all about the wedding but the time will be short in the afternoon so I had better begin my letter now. We had a prosperous journey and though it was very long we were neither of us any the worse and arrived safely on Sunday morning. Found everyone looking well. Daisy a little white perhaps but that is only natural after all the excitement and fuss. Berty is very pleased with himself and Mrs Goff as fussy as usual I think her Husband's arrival yesterday evening quieted her. They have some very pretty presents but of course very few comparatively have come here. Daisy was delighted with your card case.

The Empress has given her a photo of herself in an enamelled frame and said she would certainly have come to the wedding only she has hooping cough.

The whole house is very grand I get quite lost in it, & we had a very smart dinner nearly 30 people last night, they were all English except one Swede who is married to an English woman, and a young Russian officer that speaks English quite well, it was rather curious about him Henry and I were out walking and were in rather a difficulty for we had lost our way and when we asked the driver of one of the little carriages to take us to the Embassy he shook his head and could not understand so H went to try and make a policeman understand and while talking a young Russian officer came up and asked him if he could help. So he put us into a carriage and told the coachman where to drive. He came here in the afternoon and told me that he had recognised Henry from the photos here and had been watching to see if he required help.

Petersburg is wonderful we went to see some of the principal Churches yesterday.

Now I must leave room for the afternoon news the wedding is to be at 10 minutes to 2 o'clock,—just got to my room after the festivities were over to write to you. Such a pretty sight as the wedding was. The Church has numbers of painted windows through which the sun was shining and was decorated with white flowers Lillies and Margareets, it gradually filled with ladies in wonderful dresses speaking many languages gentlemen in Court uniforms and Russian military uniforms and covered with decorations Japs in European dress, Chinese in their national dress etc. etc—The bride looked very pretty but very pale as she came up with her father the bridesmaids looked very well in soft white dressed with blue sashes and picture hats trimmed with blue and big Daisys. The bride had a very long train carried by a little boy in white Alice acted as best bridesmaid and fulfilled her duties well.

They had no less than 3 hymns and some of the responses sung. The Russians were delighted with the service said it was such a nice one. Copies of the service had been printed and left in the seats so that all could follow it.

After the service there was a great reception here and everyone was charmed at a telegram of congratulations coming from Our Queen. The Dowager Empress sent her lady in waiting who brought Daisy such a pretty broach from the Dowager Empress. Altogether we were very smart and Tina looked splendid and was much pleased with everything.

I have written to Annette and must write to Kate.

We hope to go back to Waterford about the 2nd of July. I have decided not to go with Henry to Cornwall, so if you could have me on the 14th or 15th I would go to you then we have promised to go to Belfast for the King's visit about the 25th and I could meet Henry there. I hope John is getting on well.

Your affectionate sister
Hatton J. O'Hara

Daisy Scott was one of the daughters of Sir Charles Scott, who had been appointed Ambassador to Russia in 1898. The bridegroom was Sir Herbert William Davis-Goff, who lived in Waterford in the South of Ireland.

Tina was the bride's mother, and Alice, the best bridesmaid, was her sister.

Hatton O'Hara, who wrote this letter was the wife of Henry O'Hara, Bishop of Waterford. She was stepsister to Sir Charles Scott, Elizabeth Lyle and Annette Scott being one of the children of Thomas Scott's third wife.

Our Queen was, of course, Queen Alexandra. The Empress of Russia had been Alix, Princess of Hesse, known in her own family as "Alicky" and, also, as the Empress Alexandra Feodorowna. The Empress was a grand-daughter of Queen Victoria, who had been bitterly opposed to her marriage to Czsar Nicholas II in 1894, partly because she wished her to marry one of her own grandsons but also because of her opinion of Russia. The mother of Emperor Nicholas II was a sister of Queen Alexandra. Queen Victoria's forebodings proved justified when, long after her own death in January 1901, the Empress was murdered with other members of the Russian Royal Family during the Russian Revolution.

Sir Charles Scott remained British Ambassador to Russia until his

The Right Honourable Sir Charles Stewart Scott GCB., GCMG. From 1898 to 1904 Sir Charles Scott was British Ambassador at St. Petersburg, Russia.

retirement in April 1904. By then he was the Right Hon. Sir Charles Stewart Scott, G.C.B.,G.C.M.G. He was a member of the Privy Council. He had also received the honorary degree of L.L.D. from Trinity College, Dublin.

52 / 1905—The Prince and Princess of Wales Visit India. Alice Lyle, Wife of Hugh Thomas Lyle, Writes to Her Mother-in-law, Elizabeth Lyle

Agra Dec.19th.
Dearest Mother,

The Royal Pair[1] leave Agra tonight—they have gone out in motors to Futtipore Sikri today—it is about 25 miles away & a great sight seeing place. Poor Hugh has been out of everything except the R.W.F.[2] lunch yesterday—for the day before the Royal party arrived his pony fell at polo & rolled on him breaking a rib or two—so he has to lie up ever since tho' he has had no pain at all. He is out walking in the garden now & presently he will come in & lie down again—he will be on the sick list for about 10 more days & he wont be able to play polo for another 3 weeks or so. On the Friday night the 15th (the day he broke his ribs) I dined out at the General's alone—on Sat. morning the 16th I drove Mrs. Lloyd to the Fort railway station to meet the Prince & Princess—I got a splendid seat in front on the platform & the train came in at 9.30 a.m. That afternoon there was a garden party at a place called Seccundra—I stayed at home with Hugh and we had young Mutting & another boy in to tea—that night I went to the dinner alone but the Prince & Princess were bored after the long afternoon out at Seccundra & the English mail letters had just come so they sent an excuse & didn't dine with us. On Sunday I drove Mrs. Lloyd to 11 a.m. service for which everybody had to have tickets—the Bishop of Lucknow gave us a very good sermon. Then Monday (yesterday) was our biggest day of all—& I am dead beat after it—we 23rd ladies were in the Mess all the morning arranging flowers on the lunch table—& driving backwards & forwards for vases etc. At 12.30 we had to be dressed in our best & seated out in the garden to know our places for the photograph which was taken after lunch. At 1. they arrived in motors & Hugh walked round the large ante room introducing us all separately to them both. Then we trooped into lunch. He sat between the Prince & Princess & I was on the Prince's right & Major Mantell (2nd in command) was on the Princess's left. Lord Crichton (a most awfully nice man) was on my right. The Prince I found quite delightful—he talked away & seemed absolutely content & happy. I asked him to order Hugh off to bed directly after lunch—which he did promptly. He had one of his favourite milky puddings

& he said he always makes his children eat them—but that they hated them. He told me it was painful to him unveiling monuments of the Queen & that he hoped this one in the Taj Park was a fairly decent one—for that the one of her he had to unveil at Amritza the other day was too appalling for words—that the figure was all bent & the wreath or crown on her head all on one side. I asked him what was the most tiring thing to him of all the functions he had to attend & he said meeting so many different people & all strangers—every day & having to make conversation for them all—I asked him if he minded making speeches & he said that he hated it & that it took so much out of him & when I asked him if the King couldn't get him out of so much speechifying—he spread out his hands in a foreign way & said 'no—it has to be done''. He gave me a splendid description of the Pindi Manoeuvres & he told me some touching things about His Highness Sir Pertab Sing who took me into dinner on Sat. night. He said the old man had the greatest respect & admiration for our late Queen—that when she was going to receive him he always took off his sword & laid it down in front of her & went down on his knees & put his forehead on her feet—& that the other day he was asked where he was going & he said ''I am going to my church'' & it was discovered afterwards that he had gone to the Queens Monument & knelt there for two hours—praying. Hugh got on very well with the Prince & Princess too & made them laugh—once the Princess dropt her handkerchief & Hugh couldn't stoop down to pick it up because of his broken ribs—so when I drew the Prince's attention to the fact—he said across to the Princess ''you mustn't let Col Lyle move'' & she waved his little speech off with her hand—as much as to say ''you needn't tell me that I hadn't the least intention of letting him'' After lunch the ladies sat in the ante room & we talked to the Princess & the men smoked & drank coffee outside in the veranda & Hugh talked to the Princess & then we all trooped out on to the lawn & had our photos taken & we will send you one. The Prince presented photos of himself & her to the Regt. for their Mess & then they drove away in their motors to the unveiling of the Monument. I drove Mrs. Mantell there & we had capital seats—the Prince read his speech out awfully nicely. When I got home I found Hugh & Mr. Nutting having tea in the tent & afterwards several others dropped in to tea. We had dinner at 8 sharp. Mr. Stockwell Mr. Nutting Hugh & I & at 8.30 Mr. Stockwell drove me to the Reception & Mr. Nutting spent the evening with Hugh playing the piano to him half the time. The Reception was in a huge enormous tent lighted by 3 enormous chandeliers. The Prince & Princess stood in front of two silver chairs on a magnificent raised gold embroidered carpet. All the ladies who were to be presented to the Princess were on her left (a little way off) & all the men to be presented to the Prince were on his right. The Princess wore the loveliest dress I have ever seen & her diamonds were gorgeous—the dress was old rose velvet with panels of pearl & gold embroidered lace—& she looked so Queenly. I borrowed a dress from Mrs. Stanwell for the occasion (as I had nothing good enough) it was pale green silk trimmed with green chiffon & the most lovely old Irish lace. Lucy & Henry are here in the Civil Lines with the Taylors & we saw them at the different functions & they came here to lunch the other day—we got young Bingham in to meet them—I did not care much for him. Henry & Lucy are both so cheery & look so well. We couldn't have them for Xmas because we have got a 23rd subaltern coming on Xmas eve for 2 or 3 days with his wife & baby—the latter have never been out here before & the baby is only a month or two old. We never dreamt that the Lyles would be here. However they may be able to come to us for a few days when the Vigorzans get into their own bungalow.

Dec.20th. Hugh is getting on capitally & all his brother officers come to see him—he has got a lady friend coming to see him this afternoon, & some of the men are coming for tennis

Ever your loving daughter
Alice

As Alice Lyle sat writing her letter from India, the last letter in this book, Queen Victoria's reign was already in the past, the British Empire had a new and very different ruler, Lord Salisbury, British Prime Minister for twelve years, was dead, and a new century had begun.

Few would then have forecast the great events and tremendous changes that the twentieth century would bring to the world, including India.

In Hitler's war, India loyally supported Great Britain, and famous Indian regiments fought side by side with those of Britain.

After the war, in 1947, the Labour government at Westminster accepted the disturbances and disorders that were making India increasingly difficult to govern, as the authentic voice of the Indian people desiring their freedom.

In August 1947, after negotiations with Indian leaders, Lord Mountbatten, the Viceroy of India, handed India over to Indian rule and, simultaneously, the British withdrew, leaving India newly divided into two states—India and Pakistan. A terrible blood bath immediately followed as Hindus slaughtered Moslems and Moslems massacred Hindus, but the complex problem of India in the twentieth century, before and after the British withdrew, cannot be dealt with in this book. At its closing dateline of 1905, India was, as depicted in Alice Lyle's letter to her mother-in-law, at peace.

Notes

1. The prince and princess of Wales, later, George V and Queen Mary.
2. Royal Welch Fusiliers.

337

In the preceding pages, the voices of many different people have spoken from the past—men, women, and children, the well known and the obscure, the rich and the poor.

In these unconscious revelations by people long dead, there is perhaps food for thought.

Were the Victorians really such hypocrites as many of us, living in the twentieth century, have been led to believe?

Has the average person today, even when interested, unbiased knowledge of human relations in the eighteenth and nineteenth centuries, for example, between men and women, parents and children, employers and employees, landlords and tenants?

Of course, the downtrodden governesses, the ill-paid, overworked domestic servants, women who were treated as inferior to men, and children deformed by long hours of work in factories all existed in Victorian times. It must be remembered, however, that in every century and in every country, many different types of people are to be found. This is a fact that must be recognized if a fair and balanced view of any particular era is to be formed. There must not be excessive concentration on the undesirable features to the exclusion of more admirable ones.

The people recorded in this book who pensioned off their old servant, treated their governess as a friend, reduced or remitted rents in times of disaster, were not exceptional in the nineteenth century. There were many, many of them in the period under review, and only a distorted picture will result if their existence is ignored.

Perhaps another question arises also:

Is it possible that the problems of Ireland are due more to the fact Ulster is inhabited by a racial stock very different from that which inhabits the rest of Ireland and also to the distortions and misunderstandings of Ireland's past history rather than to any of the causes most usually canvassed today?

But enough has been said. It is for the reader to decide.